William C. Weinrich, the editor of this *Festschrift*, is associate professor of early church history and patristic studies at Concordia Theological Seminary in Fort Wayne, Indiana.

THE
NEW TESTAMENT
AGE

Professor Bo Reicke

THE
NEW TESTAMENT
AGE

*Essays in Honor of
Bo Reicke*

Volume I

edited by
WILLIAM C. WEINRICH

MERCER

MUP

ISBN 0-86554-097-7

The New Testament Age
Essays in Honor of Bo Reicke
In two volumes
Copyright © 1984
Mercer University Press, Macon GA 31207
All rights reserved
Printed in the United States of America

All books published by Mercer University Press
are produced on acid-free paper
that exceeds the minimum standards set by the
National Historical Publications and Records Commission.

Library of Congress Cataloging in Publication Data

Main entry under title:
The New Testament Age

English, French, and German.
Bibliography: v. 2, p. 553.
1. Bible.   N.T.—Criticism, interpretation, etc.—
Addresses, essays, lectures.   2. Reicke, Bo Ivar,
1914–   . I. Reicke, Bo Ivar, 1914–   II. Weinrich,
William C.
BS2395.N495   1984   225.6   84-713
ISBN 0-86554-097-7

CONTENTS

EDITOR'S PREFACE

IT IS THE great merit of *Festschriften* that they allow the scholar to pay explicit tribute to a colleague. Despite the intense private effort expended in academic pursuits, the search for truth and understanding remains in large measure a communal endeavor. *Festschriften* are the thankful expressions of the community of scholarship to those who have generously and significantly contributed to the common endeavor. It is with that in mind that this *Festschrift* is gratefully proffered to Professor Bo Reicke.

Professor Bo Reicke exemplifies the scholarly excellence and Christian charity which coinhere in one who rightly claims the title of *doctor theologiae*. It was as his student that I became beneficiary of his broad learning and generous hospitality. As I am sure all of his students will agree, as a teacher Professor Reicke is superb. His gifts are not so much in the lecture hall with its impersonal atmosphere as rather in those private encounters with his students in which not only the substance of scholarship but also the spirit of scholarship are taught. Professor Reicke has always taken a personal interest in his students, and that no doubt explains the great respect and love which his students acquire for him who is, as it were, an icon of the high calling of *doctor theologiae* to which they, as his students, also aspire. It is not presumptuous, therefore, for me on behalf of all his students to extend to Professor Reicke heartiest best wishes and grateful thanks for his patient tutelage and steady guidance during our days of study.

This volume, however, is primarily an expression of the high honor in which Professor Reicke is held by his peers. Commensurate with Reicke's own work, the contributors represent the highest standards of theological scholarship. Their ready enthusiasm to participate in the *Festschrift* and the high quality of their contributions are testimony to the high regard in which Professor Reicke's own scholarship is held by all the scholarly community. The catholic character of the contributors reflects the wide recognition of Professor Reicke as a scholar and the breadth of his professional contacts, which transcend national and confessional boundaries. Through them the community of scholarship expresses its best wishes and congratulations.

Other than the broad scope of Professor Reicke's own professional work and interests, no thematic restrictions were placed upon the contributors. The authors were, therefore, quite free to choose their subjects. The results admirably coincide with the contours of Professor Reicke's own endeavors. Appropriately, studies on the New Testament predominate. The articles on the intertestamental period, Qumran, and the early history of the Church, however, testify to Reicke's own significant contributions in these areas of study.

The assumption of editorial responsibility for a *Festschrift* involves a serious commitment of time and energy. Without the assistance and encouragement of many this project would not have been possible. Especial thanks are to be extended to Professor Oscar Cullmann and to the late Professor W. C. van Unnik, whose advice and enthusiastic support in the early stages of the project were invaluable. The initial idea for a *Festschrift* in honor of Professor Reicke came from Mr. Dale Brownell of Basel, who rendered great assistance in the preparing of the manuscript. Also, the generous financial support of the Aid Association for Lutherans, which subsidized some of the editorial and publishing costs, is much appreciated. Finally, I thank Mercer University Press for its cooperation in making this volume a reality.

William C. Weinrich
3 August 1983

ZUM GELEIT

Oscar Cullmann

PROFESSOR BO REICKE hat oft selbst Festschriften für andere herausgegeben. So ist es denen, die am Zustandekommen der hier vorgelegten beteiligt sind, ein Bedürfnis, ihm eine solche anzubieten. Einleitend erlaube ich mir bei dieser Gelegenheit zunächst einige prinzipielle Bemerkungen über die manchmal umstrittene Sitte der Festschriften als Geburtstagsgabe, vor allem im christlichen Bereich.

Geburtstage zu feiern, galt in der alten Kirche als eine heidnische Sitte. In der Bibel, schreibt Origenes, sind es nur Heiden und Gottlose wie Pharao und Herodes, die ihre Geburtstage feiern. Das war auch wenigstens einer der Gründe, weshalb sogar die Frage nach dem Geburtstag Jesu im ältesten Christentum keinerlei Interesse weckte, während schon früh seiner Taufe in einem besonderen Fest gedacht wurde und weshalb erst mit der christologischen Konzentration auf die Inkarnation, also verhältnismäßig spät, die Weihnachtsfeier erscheint. Aber das Geburtsdatum verehrter Christen, der Apostel und Märtyrer, fand auch im Verlauf der Kirchengeschichte keine Beachtung. So wurde als der eigentliche "Geburtstag" der Märtyrer ihr Todestag angesehen.

Der heutige Gebrauch, die Zählung der Lebensjahre zum Anlaß eines Gedenktages zu nehmen, soll deshalb nicht als unchristlich abgetan werden. Denn Rückschau, Selbstprüfung, Dank, verpflichtende Ausschau auf die kommenden Jahre, sind gewiß eine mit der Bibel im Einklang stehende Pflicht. Sie sind es für den, dessen Geburtstag gefeiert wird, selbst, aber auch für die andern, die sich auf dem Wege mit ihm befinden, und wenn es sich um einen Gelehrten handelt, so gilt dies besonders für seine Schüler und Kollegen.

Allzuoft sind wir in unserem Gelehrtenbetrieb versucht, Lehre und Forschung der andern in *erster* Linie zu kritisieren und erst nachträglich (in Rezensionen etwa in dem bekannten "tröstlichen" kurzen Schlußsatz) positiv zu würdigen, während gerade umgekehrt die *erste*

Frage lauten sollte: Was habe ich von ihm gelernt, was habe ich ihm zu verdanken?

Darum ist ein Geschenk gerade an einem Tag, der einen Einschnitt im Leben eines Gelehrten und Forschers bedeutet, sinnvoll, und hier liegt die Berechtigung der Sitte der "Festschriften". Wo ein Dank in Form einer gelehrten Arbeit ausgedrückt wird, versuchen die Spender ihr Bestes zu geben, und zwar im Zusammenhang mit dem, was sie von dem Jubilar empfangen haben. Ein ganzes von einem einzelnen Autor verfasstes Buch einem geschätzten Freund zu widmen, das hat es schon in ältester Zeit gegeben (Lukas). Aber ein Kollektivwerk wie eine "Festschrift" zeigt die auf der Ausstrahlung des Lehrers beruhende *Verbindung* der Schüler untereinander und die *Solidarität* derer auf, die ihr Leben der gleichen Aufgabe widmen.

Die große Zahl der Mitarbeiter an dem vorliegenden Sammelband legt im Falle des hier Geehrten ein eindrückliches Zeugnis ab. Schüler und Kollegen aus aller Welt sind hier vereint. Der Tradition seiner skandinavischen Heimat getreu, hat Professor Bo Reicke von jeher das Bestreben, seine gelehrten Beziehungen nicht auf ein Land oder einen Sprachbereich zu beschränken.

Anderseits weist die reichhaltige Zusammensetzung des Werkes auf die große Spannweite der von ihm bearbeiteten verschiedenen Gebiete der neutestamentlichen Wissenschaft hin und bietet auch in dieser Hinsicht ein Spiegelbild der Gelehrtenpersönlichkeit des auf diese Weise Beschenkten. Innerhalb der Vielfalt seiner Interessen sind die von ihm mit besonderer Aufmerksamkeit behandelten Probleme der sogenannten intertestamentarischen Periode auch berücksichtigt.

Lehre und Forschung sind bei Professor Bo Reicke eng verbunden. Darum werden seine Kolloquien im kleinen Kreise von den Schülern besonders geschätzt. Wie sein verehrter Lehrer Anton Fridrichsen weiß er von jeher viele Doktoranden um sich zu scharen und ihre Dissertationen in ständiger Beratung zu fördern. So ist es erfreulich, viele von ihnen—die meisten sind inzwischen Kollegen geworden—in dieser Festschrift vertreten zu sehen.

Die ansehnliche Zahl der andern Neutestamentler, die sich in diesem Band zusammenfinden, haben die mannigfaltigen wissenschaftlichen Kontakte mit dem Jubilar miteinander gemeinsam: Benützung seiner Bücher und Artikel, Teilnahme an den von ihm so gern und fleißig besuchten Tagungen, Anhören seiner Gastvorlesungen, nicht zuletzt Mitarbeit an von ihm herausgegebenen Veröffentlichungen wie enzyklopädischen Sammelwerken und früher während langer Jahre der *Theologischen Zeitschrift*. Die durch den gebotenen Umfang der Festschrift auferlegte Begrenzung ist der Hauptgrund dafür, daß nicht noch weitere Namen hier erscheinen.

Die genannten Beziehungen zu Bo Reicke sind dadurch besonders geprägt, daß wissenschaftliche Zusammenarbeit mit persönlicher Freundschaft Hand in Hand geht. Viele Autoren, die hier mit Aufsätzen vertreten sind, haben den herzlichen Empfang durch ihn und seine ihm in allen Bereichen zur Seite stehende Gattin in seinem gastfreien Haus in Basel und seinem Sommersitz in Salvan erfahren dürfen. Als seinem länjährigen Fachkollegen innerhalb der gleichen Fakultät sei es mir erlaubt, auch unsere engen und nie getrübten theologischen und freundschaftlichen Bande zu erwähnen. Wenn auch jeder unabhängig, seinen Gaben und Interessen entsprechend, gearbeitet hat, bewahrte uns die gemeinsame glaubensmäßige, theologische und menschliche Grundlage vor jeglichen Spannungen, wie sie so oft das Verhältnis zwischen Fachkollegen bedrohen. Im Vorwort zu einer Festschrift, in der als solcher der Bezug auf den Jubilar als einigendes Band nicht aus dem Auge verloren wird, durfte neben dem Gelehrten auch der Mensch nicht vergessen werden.

So sind wir auch überzeugt, daß der mit diesem Buch Beschenkte sich gewiß zunächst über den gewichtigen Inhalt der Artikel freuen wird, aber gleichzeitig über seine Freundschaft mit den Spendern und ihre in dieser Gabe ausgedrückte Dankbarkeit. Dieser zweifache Wert, den die Festschrift mit jedem Geschenk gemeinsam hat, betrifft alle Arbeit, die mit großer Hingabe für ihr Zustandekommen geleistet worden ist: in der ersten Phase hauptsächlich von Herrn und Frau Dale und Judy Brownell, später von dem früheren Doktoranden und jetzigen Kollegen, Professor Dr. William C. Weinrich, der auch zusammen mit dem Ehepaar Brownell Initiant und Mitarbeiter des Unternehmens von Anfang an war. Bedauerliche Umstände haben die Veröffentlichung verzögert. Um so größer ist unser Dank außer Professor Weinrich unserem Kollegen Professor William Farmer und dem amerikanischem Verlag Mercer University Press gegenüber, die das schöne Werk herausgebracht haben, ein weiteres Zeichen für die Achtung, die Professor Bo Reicke in der ganzen Gelehrtenwelt genießt.

VERSUCH EINER ANALYSE
DES DIAKONIA—BEGRIFFES
IM NEUEN TESTAMENT

Sverre Aalen

PROFESSOR BO REICKE hat in einer Monographie aus dem Jahre 1951 die Diakonie des Urchristentums und der alten Kirche behandelt.[1] Er zeigt hier, daß die diakonale Hilfe ihren Quellort im Kultus hat und besonders dann in dem altchristlichen Gemeindemahl. Ich halte dies für einen berechtigten und fruchtbaren Gesichtspunkt.

In diesem Artikel möchte ich versuchen, die Diakonie im Neuen Testament mehr als Begriff und Begriffskomplex zu analysieren. Schlägt man in den theologischen Wörterbüchern zum Neuen Testament nach, so findet man, daß das Wort oft als ein Synonym zu dem Begriff Nächstenliebe aufgefaßt wird.[2] Der Unterschied gegenüber dem Begriff der Liebe liegt nach gewöhnlicher Auffassung höchstens darin, daß die Diakonie mehr die Nächstenliebe in ihrer praktischen Betätigung bezeichnet, also Liebestätigkeit. Auch das deutsche Wort "dienen, Dienst" erweckt wohl im allgemeinen, jedenfalls im christlichen und theologischen Sprachgebrauch, diese Assoziation. Dasselbe gilt für die entsprechenden Wörter in den nordischen Sprachen. Ist diese Auffassung des neutestamentlichen Begriffes richtig, dann gehört die Diakonie in das Ethos des Christentums.

Ich möchte hier diese weit verbreitete Auffassung mit einem Fragezeichen versehen. Zum ersten ist mir aufgefallen, daß die Wörter

---

[1]Bo Reicke, *Diakonie, Festfreude und Zelos, in Verbindung mit der altchristlichen Agapenfeier* (Uppsala Universitets Arsskrift 1951:5; Uppsala: Lundequistska Bokhandeln, 1951).

[2]Zum Beispiel Hermann Wolfgang Beyer, s.v. "διακονέω", *TWNT* 2 (1935) 81, 85; Klaus Heß, s.v. "Dienen", *Theologisches Begriffslexikon zum Neuen Testament*, ed. Lothar Coenen, Erich Beyreuther, Hans Bietenhard (Wuppertal: Theologischer Verlag Rolf Brockhaus, 1967), 1:187.

διακονία, διακονέω, διάκονος überall im Neuen Testament Funktionen und Tätigkeiten innerhalb der Kirche oder der Gemeinde bezeichnen, was ja nicht für die Liebe zutrifft. Die einzige Ausnahme befindet sich in Röm 13,4, wo die Obrigkeit als Gottes διάκονος bezeichnet wird. Diese Ausnahme steht jedoch dermaßen vereinzelt und am Rande, da sie unsere These einer Begrenzung der Diakonie auf Tätigkeiten im Rahmen der Kirche nicht gefährden kann.

Eine wirkliche Ausnahme bildet allerdings nach verbreiteter Auffassung Matt 25,44, wo im Endgericht die auf der linken Seite Stehenden fragen, wann sie Jesus in Bedrängnis gesehen und ihm nicht "gedient" haben. Das haben die zur Rechten getan, und ihre Hilfe ist also eine διακονία. Die Frage, die sich hier erhebt, ist inwiefern die Reihe von Notsituationen, in denen sich Jesus in beiden Fällen befunden hat, von einem sozialen Kontext geholt ist, wie man wohl im allgemeinen meint, oder vom Leben der Kirche. Eine genauere Untersuchung zeigt doch, daß diese Reihe nicht für die sozialen Bedrängnisse typisch ist, die in den "sozialen Reihen", die man aus verschiedenen Texten der Umwelt heranzieht, vorkommen. Vor allem fehlen in Matt 25,35-36 die Armen, Waisen, Witwen, alte Leute, Unterdrückte, alles Kategorien, die in die sozialen Reihen gehören (z.B. Hiob 22,6-9; 31,19; Jes 58,6-7; Sir 4,1-10; 34(31),21-22; 35(32),12-15; *2 Henoch* 10,5; 42,7-9).

Das Hungern, Durstigsein und Nacktsein findet man allerdings in solchen sozialen Reihen (vgl. auch Ezech 18,7), ebenfalls die Obdachlosen (Jes 58,7; vgl. CD 14,14-15; Ps.-Phokylides 24). Aber diese Kategorien lassen sich auch aus Situationen der urchristlichen Gemeinde belegen. Und das gilt überhaupt für die Situationen, die in Matt 25,35-36 genannt sind. Hunger, Durst und Blöße gehören zu den Nöten, die Paulus als Missionar erleiden mußte (2 Kor 11,27). In Jak 2,15 handelt es sich um einen Bruder, bzw. eine Schwester, also Mitglieder der Gemeinde, die ähnliche Bedürfnisse haben. Nach Röm 8,35 gehören Hunger und Blöße zu den Nöten der christlichen Märtyrer. Der Kontext ist an diesen Stellen nicht sozial, sondern vielmehr die christliche Existenz im Leben der Gemeinde.

Ähnliches gilt für die Kranken, die besucht werden. Im Judentum gehörte Besuch von Kranken zu den guten Werken.[3] In den sozialen

---

[3]Str-B, 4:573-78; vgl. auch *T. Benj.* 4,4.

Reihen, die gewöhnlich herangezogen werden, findet man Besuch von Kranken nicht. Die Sitte gehörte in die private Sphäre. Allerdings hören wir im Urchristentum nichts Explizites von dieser Sitte (vgl. jedoch Jak 5,14). Doch muß man hier nicht die Berichte übersehen, nach denen Jesus selbst vor einem Krankenbett steht (z.B. Matt 8,14-15 par.; 9,25 par.). Daß die ersten Christen sich ihrer Kranken besonders angenommen haben, ist im Blick auf die vielen Heilungen durch die Apostel sehr wahrscheinlich.

Wie oben erwähnt können Obdachlosen, die man in sein Haus empfangen soll, als eine Kategorie der sozialen Notleidenden genannt werden. Das ist aber etwas anderes als der Fremde, der nach Matt 25,35 "aufgenommen" wird. Das Wort συνηγάγετε darf nicht mit "beherbergen" wiedergegeben werden, falls man damit an eine dauernde Beherbergung denkt. Das Wort συνάγω entspricht dem hebräischen אָסַף (Richt. 19,18) und dem aramäischen כְּנַס (*Tg. Yer.* Gen 18,3; vgl. das hebräische הַכְנָסַת אוֹרְחִים [= Bewirtung der Gäste, eigentl. Hereinführen der Reisenden]). Diese semitischen Wörter bedeuten, wie συνάγω, "sammeln", "einführen", "empfangen" (bewirten), mit Hinblick auf Reisende und Gäste.

Das Wort ξένος umfaßt an sich einen ziemlich weiten Bedeutungskreis. Es kann den Fremdling im Sinne von Nichtbürger bezeichnen, und dieser war bei den Juden gewöhnlich ein Ausländer (= Nicht-Jude; Matt 27,7; Heb 11,13).[4] An unserer Stelle ist aber diese Bedeutung schon nach der obigen Analyse von συνάγω nicht am Platze. Das Wort ξένος ist im talmudischen Hebräisch als Fremdwort gebraucht (= אכסנאי) und bezeichnet hier den reisenden Fremden.[5] Wir haben es hier mit der Gastfreundschaft im Rahmen der Religionsgemeinschaft zu tun. Eine nahe Parallele ist die Gastfreundschaft der Essener. In jeder Stadt hatte bei diesen ein bestimmtes Mitglied der Sekte die Aufgabe, sich der reisenden Fremden (ξένοι) anzunehmen und sie mit Kleidern und dem sonst Notwendigen zu versorgen (Josephus, *Bell.* 2,125; vgl. *T. Hiob* 10,1.3). Die nächste Parallele zum Wort

---

[4]Vgl. Walter Bauer, s.v. "ξένος", *Griechisch-deutsches Wörterbuch zu den Schriften des Neuen Testaments und der übrigen urchristlichen Literatur*, 4th ed. (Berlin: Alfred Töpelmann, 1952) 994; LSJ, s.v. "ξένος", 1189.

[5]Samuel Krauss, *Talmudische Archäologie*, 3 vols. (Leipzig: Gustav Fock, 1910-12; repr. Hildesheim: G. Olms, 1966), 2:328; 3:25.

ξένος im Neuen Testament selbst finden wir in 3 Joh 5-6, wo die Leser gelobt werden, weil sie reisende Brüder, und zwar fremde, empfangen. In die Richtung von Gastfreundschaft im Rahmen der kirchlichen Gemeinschaft weisen auch die wiederholten Vermahnungen zur Gastfreundschaft in den Briefen des Neuen Testaments hin, wobei Vokabeln angewendet werden, die das Wort ξένος als Bestandteil haben (1 Tim 5,10; Heb 13,2; 1 Pet 4,9). Für die Missionare der urchristlichen Zeit war es wichtig, daß sie bei einem Glaubensbruder einkehren konnten (z.B. Röm 16,23; Apg 10,6.32; 21,16 [an den Stellen der Apostelgeschichte steckt das Wort ξένος im Verb ξενίζομαι]). In Röm 16,23 bezeichnet ξένος den Wirt, was auf eine gegenseitige Verpflichtung zur Gastfreundschaft hinweist.[6]

Von den in Matt 25,35-36 erwähnten Situationen ist noch das Gefangensein kurz zu behandeln. Auch diese Bedrängnis gehört in den Rahmen des Lebens in der Kirche, wie aus Heb 10,34; 13,3 (vgl. 11,36) zu ersehen ist. Der Besuch von den Gefangenen ist hier vorausgesetzt. Auch die Qumran-Gemeinde kümmerte sich um diejenigen Mitglieder der Gemeinde, die gefangen waren (CD 14,15).

Zusammenfassend können wir feststellen, daß es sich in Matt 25,35-36.42-43 nicht um die allgemeine Nächstenliebe handelt, sondern um eine innerkirchliche Hilfe, die im Zeichen der Glaubensgemeinschaft steht. Das ergibt sich ja auch von dem Ausdruck "diese meine geringsten Brüder" (25,40.45). Denn die Brüder Jesu sind die Mitglieder seiner Jüngerschar. Jesus hat ja ausdrücklich seine Jünger eine Gemeinschaft von Brüdern und Schwestern genannt (Matt 12,46-50 par.; vgl. 23,8). In diesem Zusammenhang gehört auch die Wendung "diese geringsten". Nach Matt 10,42 bezeichnet Jesus seine Jünger als "diese Geringen" (vgl. 18,6 par.; 18,10.14). Und im selben Zusammenhang sagt er, daß "wer euch aufnimmt, nimmt mich auf" (10,40). Auch nach dieser Stelle identifiziert sich Jesus in mystischer Weise mit seinen geringen Jüngern, genau so wie in 25,40.45. Wie das zu verstehen ist, ist eine Frage, die außerhalb der in diesem Artikel zu behandelnden Frage liegt. Nur so viel soll gesagt werden, daß auch dieser Zug auf die innere Gemeinschaft der Kirche hinweist. Dasselbe ist der Fall, was die Bezeichnung die Kleinen, die Geringsten betrifft. Ich möchte hier die Vermutung aussprechen, daß die Wurzel dieser

---

[6]Eine Bestätigung findet die obige Auslegung von ξένος in Matt 25,35 bei Justin, *1 Apol.* 67,6.

Bezeichnung im Wort צְעָרִים (= μικρούς [LXX]) in Sach 13,7 zu suchen ist. Allerdings ist dieser Vers bei Sacharia ein Gerichtswort, das gegen das Volk als Herde gerichtet ist. Aber nach Matt 26,31 par. hat Jesus es auf seine Jüngerschar angewendet.

Die Untersuchung von Matt 25,35-45 hatte den Zweck, zur Klärung der Frage beizutragen, inwiefern sich die Diakonie im Neuen Testament auf eine Tätigkeit innerhalb der Kirche begrenzt. Die Antwort ist ein positives Ja. Das für die übrigen Diakonie-Kontexte des Neuen Testaments nachzuweisen ist keine schwierige Aufgabe. Wichtig ist dabei das Wort Jesu vom Dienen in Matt 20,25-28 (= Markus 10,42-45; Lukas 22,25-27), das sicher den Ausgangspunkt der ganzen Diakonie-Vorstellung bildet: "Ihr wißt, daß die Fürsten der Völker über sie herrschen und die Großen über sie Amtsgewalt ausüben". Man braucht mit den gebrauchten Verben nicht etwas Negatives zu verbinden.[7] Es handelt sich einfach um eine objektive Feststellung.[8] Dementsprechend fährt die Aussage in Präsens fort: "So ist es nicht unter euch. Sondern wer unter euch groß sein will, sei euer Diener, und wer unter euch der Erste sein will, sei euer Knecht, wie der Menschensohn nicht gekommen ist, damit ihm gedient werde, sondern damit er diene und sein Leben gebe als Lösegeld für viele" (vgl. auch Markus 9,35 und Matt 23,11).

An diesen Stellen wird es mit allem Nachdruck gesagt, daß die Regel, die im Jüngerkreis und damit auch in der Gemeinde Jesu gilt und gelten soll, eine andere ist als in der weltlichen, d.h. der sozialen Gesellschaft, nämlich das Dienen, das Dienersein. Die Erhebung dieser Regel zu einem Grundsatz war in der Umwelt des Neuen Testaments ohne Entsprechung. Bei den Griechen war das Dienen eines freien Mannes unwürdig. Im Alten Testament finden wir noch keine Betonung des Dienens als einer allgemeinen Regel für das Verhalten zwischen Menschen. Nur Gott dient man, und außerdem seinem Herrn (hebr. עבד und שרת; aram. שמש und פלח). Ähnlich liegen die

---

[7]Wie Bauer, s.v. "κατακυριεύω", *Griechisch-deutsches Wörterbuch*, 747-48; s.v. "κατεξουσιάζω", *Griechisch-deutsches Wörterbuch*, 764: "mißbrauchen", "gewalttätig".

[8]Siehe besonders den Text bei Lukas 22,25: καὶ οἱ ἐξουσιάζοντες αὐτῶν εὐεργέται καλοῦνται. Vgl. LSJ, s.v. "κατεξουσιάζω", 924; ferner die Übersetzung von Matt 20,25 bei KJV: "Ye know that the princes of the Gentiles exercise dominion over them, and they that are great exercise authority upon them".

Dinge im rabbinischen Judentum, wo das Wort שָׁמֵּשׁ (aram. שַׁמֵּשׁ [Subst. שִׁמּוּשָׁא und שִׁמּוּשׁ]) die sprachliche Entsprechung von δια-κονέω, διακονία ist.[9]

Jesu Wort vom Dienen, anstatt zu herrschen und Einfluß auf äußere Macht zu bauen, war also tatsächlich nur in der Gemeinde Jesu wirksam. Wenn es sich dabei um einen ethischen Grundsatz gehandelt hätte, dann wäre wohl zu erwarten, daß sich dieser als eine universell geltende Maxime entfalten und als eine solche verstanden würde. Dies ist im Urchristentum nicht geschehen. Man darf nicht übersehen, daß Jesus in der grundlegenden Formulierung betont, daß die Regel des Dienens gerade in seiner Jüngerschar Gültigkeit haben wird und soll, zum Unterschied von der weltlichen Gesellschaft. Das stimmt zu der folgenden Entwicklung im Urchristentum. Die Kollekte des Paulus (2. Korintherbrief 8-9; vgl. Röm 15,25-28; 1 Kor 16,1-2; Gal 2,10) und die Hilfe, die die Gemeinde von Antiochien für die Bedürftigen der Jerusalemgemeinde besorgte (Apg 11,29; 12,25), waren offensichtlich für Glieder der Gemeinde bestimmt. Dasselbe gilt für die Gütergemeinschaft der Urgemeinde in Jerusalem wie auch für die diakonale Hilfe für die Bedürftigen dort (Apg 2,44-45; 4,32-37; 6,1-2).

Ist aber wirklich das Dienen nach dem Neuen Testament nicht ein allgemeines ethisches Prinzip? Ungefähr wie die Nächstenliebe? Es muß jedoch eine Erklärung der Tatsache gefunden werden, daß die Diakonie im Neuen Testament nur innerhalb des Rahmens der Kirche fungiert und daß diese Grenze nicht überschritten wird. Hier tritt uns die Möglichkeit entgegen, daß die Diakonie eine ekklesiologische Erscheinung ist eher als eine ethische und daß dies für Bestimmung des Begriffes seine Konsequenz haben muß. Zu dieser Konklusion bin ich tatsächlich gekommen. Die Diakonie steht in einem engen Zusammenhang mit der inneren Gemeinschaft der Gemeinde. Bei Paulus können wir beobachten, daß die beiden Begriffe διακονία und κοινωνία direkt als Synonyme auftreten können.[10] Nach Röm 15,25-26 Paulus fährt nach Jerusalem, um den Armen der dortigen Gemeinde Diakonie zu leisten (διακονῶν τοῖς ἁγίοις, 15,25). Er soll die κοινωνία überbrin-

---

[9]Str-B (1:920-21; 2:257-58) bringt einen Beleg aus der rabbinischen Literatur, der eine Parallele zu dem Worte Jesu bildet. Es handelt sich jedoch um einen Ausnahmefall, nicht um einen Grundsatz. Und nach Str-B (1:920) rief die berichtete Episode "mehr Staunen als Anerkennung vor".

[10]Vgl. Reicke, *Diakonie, Festfreude und Zelos*, 25-33.

gen, die die Gemeinden von Mazedonien und Achaja veranstaltet haben. Die Gabe der Kollekte ist also ein Ausdruck oder ein Zeichen der Gemeinschaft und zwar der christlichen Gemeinschaft, die sie mit der Gemeinde von Jerusalem haben.[11] Auch nach 2 Kor 9,13 ist die gleiche Spende, die als διακονία bezeichnet wird, ein Ausdruck der κοινωνία. Ähnlich verhält es sich in 2 Kor 8,4. Diese Gemeinschaft ist dabei kein subjektives Gefühl. Sie hat ihren Grund im Bekenntnis zum Evangelium, wie aus 2 Kor 9,13b zu ersehen ist. In Apg 2,42 ist dementsprechend die κοινωνία von der Lehre der Apostel und dem Gottesdienst umklammert. Nach Heb 13,16 folgt die praktisch ausgerichtete κοινωνία auf Abendmahl und Bekenntnis.

Überall im Neuen Testament findet also die Diakonie im Rahmen der Kirche statt (vgl. auch Röm 12,13). Wie Gottesdienst und Bekenntnis konstituierende Faktoren des inneren Lebens der Kirche und der Gemeinde sind, so auch die Diakonie. Diese Faktoren sind nach innen gewendet, nicht nach außen. Hier liegt ein Unterschied im Vergleich zur Nächstenliebe und der Barmherzigkeit vor, denn diese Lebensäusserungen des Glaubens strecken sich über die Grenze der Kirche hinaus. Die Diakonie ist eine innerkirchliche Erscheinung. Will man hier von Liebe reden, so muß man an die Bruderliebe denken, nicht an die Nächstenliebe. Auch Paulus kennt die Bruderliebe, die gegenseitige Liebe unter den Gläubigen (1 Thess 4,9; Röm 12,10; Kol 1,4; Phlm 5). Die Bruderliebe hat er wahrscheinlich in 2 Kor 8,7-8 im Auge (vgl. den Kontext und die Lesart in V 7: τῇ ἐξ ὑμῶν ἐν ἡμῖν ἀγάπῃ).

Läßt es sich aber tun, die Diakonie in dieser Weise von der grenzenüberschreitenden Nächstenliebe zu trennen? Hier ist es notwendig, daß man sich aufs neue darauf besinnt, was die eigentliche Grundbedeutung der Wortgruppe διακονία, διακονέω, διάκονος ist. Es kann wohl kein Zweifel darüber sein, daß die Grundbedeutung darin liegt, daß jemand Diener ist, der die Aufgabe eines Dieners besorgt. Wenn διακονία dasselbe wie Liebe wäre, dann wäre es unverständlich, daß sich Petrus bei der Fußwaschung zuerst heftig geweigert hat, Jesus seine Füße waschen zu lassen (Joh 13,8). Einen Erweis der Liebe lehnt man nicht ab, sondern nimmt ihn dankbar an. Das worauf Petrus reagierte, war, daß Jesus hier in der Rolle eines Dieners, ja, eines Sklaven auftritt. Der Unterschied zwischen einem διάκονος und einem

---

[11]Siehe Bauer, s.v. "κοινωνία", *Griechisch-deutsches Wörterbuch*, 795-96, bes. §3.

δοῦλος ist in diesem Zusammenhang nicht so groß, obwohl der διά-κονος anders als der δοῦλος ein freier Mann ist. Die Nähe der beiden Wörter zu einander ist an Stellen des Neuen Testaments ersichtlich (Matt 20,26-27 par.; Kol 4,7). Im Judentum kann das Wort עבד für beide Kategorien stehen, also auch den שַׁמָּשׁ (= διάκονος) umfassen.[12]

Auf jeden Fall ist der διάκονος ein Diener, und diese Bedeutung sollte den Ausgangspunkt für die Beinhaltung des ganzen Begriffes bilden. Der König hat seine Diener (Matt 22,13; Esther 1,10; 2,2; 6,3). In einem Hause sind Diener tätig (Joh 2,5; hebr. שַׁמָּשׁ; aram. שַׁמָּשָׁא).[13] Als Aufgabe der Diener wird besonders das Aufwarten am Tische erwähnt. Dies wird in den Evangelien gewöhnlich durch das Verbum ausgedrückt (Lukas 22,26-27; 17,8; 10,40; 12,37; Joh 12,2). Es liegt jedoch kein Grund vor, diese Beschäftigung als die ursprüngliche Bedeutung des Wortes zu betrachten. Das würde zu einer unnötigen Einengung des Begriffes führen. Die Aufgabe des Dieners umfaßte auch andere Pflichten. Josua war der Diener des Moses (Exod 33,11 [Targ. שַׁמָּשָׁא, LXX θεράπων, MT נַעַר]). Die Rabbiner wurden von ihren Schülern bedient.[14] Einige von den Begleitern des Paulus hatten die Aufgabe,seine Diener zu sein (Apg 19,22; 2 Tim 4,11; Phlm 13; vgl. auch Apg 13,5; 15,37.40; 16,1-3; 17,14-15). Paulus und seine Mitar-beiter sind Diener Gottes (2 Kor 6,4). Nach jüdischer Anschauung sind die Engel Diener Gottes (*b. Ros. Has.* 24b; *Tg. Ps.* 137,6; vgl. Heb 1,14).

Es dürfte über jeden Zweifel erhoben sein, daß die *amtlichen* Diakonen des Neuen Testaments (Phil 1,1; 1 Tim 3,8.12; Röm 16,1) diesen Titel erhielten, weil sie als Assistenten in der Gemeinde und für den Bischof tätig waren.[15] Auch in der Synagoge hatte man einen שַׁמָּשָׁא, einen Diener.[16]

[12]Krauss, *Talmudische Archäologie*, 2:101.

[13]Krauss, *Talmudische Archäologie*, 2:101. Jacob Levy, s.v. "שַׁמָּשָׁא", *Chal-däisches Wörterbuch über die Targumim und einen grossen Theil des rabbinischen Schriftthums*, 3rd ed. (Leipzig: G. Engel, 1866; repr. Darmstadt: Joseph Melzer, 1966), 2:497.

[14]Str-B, 1:527, 920.

[15]Siehe Beyer, s.v. "διάκονος", *TWNT* 2 (1935) 90-91; August Hermann Cremer, s.v. "διάκονος", *Biblisch-theologisches Wörterbuch der Neutestamentlichen Gräcität*, 7th ed. (Gotha: Friedrich Andreas Perthes, 1893) 264. Die Übersetzung Luthers mit "Diener" war korrekt.

[16]Siehe Jacob Levy, s.v. "שַׁמָּשׁ", *Neuhebräisches und chaldäisches Wörterbuch*

Der Diener ist eine Person (Mann oder Frau), der man Aufgaben und Pflichten gibt oder auferlegt. Der Diener bekommt auf diese Weise ein mehr oder weniger festgelegtes Geschäft. Dadurch erhält das Wort διακονία die Bedeutung "Amt". Diese Bezeichnung sollte man nicht für den neutestamentlichen Diakon reservieren.[17] Auch nicht darf die Bedeutung "Amt" als Dienstleistung m.E. theologisch im Sinne von dienender Liebe gedeutet werden.[18] Überhaupt halte ich es für zweifelhaft, ob das Wort διακονέω in seiner Grundbedeutung "die ganz persönlich einem anderen erwiesene Dienstleistung bezeichnet",[19] oder daß "bei διάκονος [liegt] der Nachdruck auf dem objektiven Gewinn, den sein Dienst für den mit sich bringt, dem er ihn zuwendet".[20] Ich würde eher vermuten, daß die Bedeutung "Geschäft", "Amt", "Auftrag", der einem auferlegt ist, von Anfang an, d.i. unabhängig von jeder Theologisierung des Begriffes, mit dem Worte verbunden war.[21]

Das Wort διακονέω kommt in der LXX überhaupt nicht vor, und διακονία und διάκονος nur einige Male in der Bedeutung Dienerschaft".[22] Es handelt sich von einem der wenigen theologischen Wörter des Neuen Testaments, die unabhängig vom Alten Testament ausgebildet worden sind. Das Wort muß seinen sprachlichen Inhalt vom jüdischen Sprachgebrauch übernommen haben. Das sprachliche Gegenstück ist dabei das Wort שמש (als Verb und Substantiv). Dieses Verb ist (als pi.) aus dem Aramäischen (vgl. Dan 7,10) in das Neuhebräische übernommen (vgl. Talmud).[23] Wie διακονέω so heißt auch שמש bedienen beim Essen. Ein interessantes Beispiel ist die Geschichte, die von Strack-Billerbeck als Parallele zu Jesu Aussagen

---

über die Talmudim und Midraschim, 4 vols. (Leipzig: F. A. Brockhaus, 1876-89), 4:582; Marcus Jastrow, s.v. "שמש", *A Dictionary of the Targumim, the Talmud Babli and Yerushalmi, and the Midrashic Literature,* 2 vols. (New York: Judaica, 1975), 2:1602. Str-B (1:290) erwähnt einen שמש, der Gerichtsdiener ist; vgl. K. H. Rengstorf, s.v. "ὑπηρέτης", *TWNT* 8 (1969) 539 Anm. 75.

[17]Gegen Heß, s.v. "Dienen", *Begriffslexikon,* 1:188.

[18]Gegen Beyer, s.v. "διακονία", *TWNT* 2 (1935) 87.

[19]Beyer, s.v. "διακονέω", *TWNT* 2 (1935) 81.

[20]Rengstorf, s.v. "ὑπηρέτης", *TWNT* 8 (1969) 533.

[21]Vgl. Heß, s.v. "Dienen", *Begriffslexikon,* 1:185.

[22]Hinzukommt 1 Makk 11,58.

[23]Rudolf Meyer, s.v. "λειτουργέω", *TWNT* 4 (1942) 229.

über Dienen angeführt wird,[24] und wo auf Abraham hingewiesen wird, der nach Gen 18,8 vor den Engeln "stand" und sie während des Essens bediente. *Tg. Onq.* Gen 18,8 übersetzt "stand vor ihnen" mit שַׁמֵּשׁ (pa.), das also "bedienen" bedeutet. In dem hebräischen Text des Berichtes hat die hebräischen Form (עָמַד pi.) die gleiche Bedeutung, "bei Tische bedienen".[25] In der selben Bedeutung kommt auch das Substantiv שִׁימוּשׁ vor (*Gen. Rab.* 87,10).[26] Die Übereinstimmung mit διακονέω ist, was diese Bedeutung betrifft, auffallend.

Die Übereinstimmung ist aber nicht nur für die Bedeutung "bei Tisch bedienen" zu beobachten. Die Schüler der Rabbiner mußten wie gesagt ihre Lehrer bedienen. Das wurde שִׁמּוּשׁ חֲכָמִים genannt, Bedienung der Weisen (*m. 'Abot* 6,6).[27] Als Elisa den Propheten Elia bediente (2 Kön 3,11), war das eine שִׁמּוּשָׁהּ שֶׁל תּוֹרָה, "ein Dienst im Sinne der Tora" (*b. ber.* 7b).[28] Dieser Ausdruck bildet sprachlich die nächste Parallele zur Formulierung ἡ διακονία τοῦ λόγου in Apg 6,4.[29]

Nun können wir ferner beobachten, daß das Wort שִׁמּוּשָׁא auch die Bedeutung "Geschäft", "Amt" haben kann. So steht das Wort in *Tg. Onq.* Gen 40,13; 41,13 für כֵּן, wofür Luther und die Züricher-Bibel beide "Amt" haben. In *Tg. Jes.* 22,19 steht שִׁמּוּשָׁא für מַעֲמָד,[30] was Luther mit "Amt" wiedergibt. Die prophangriechischen Lexika führen auch für διακονία die Bedeutung "Geschäft" auf. Das Wort kann parallel zu ἐπιμέλεια ("Beschäftigung") stehen (Aeschin. 3,13) oder zu ἔργον (Plato, *Rep.* 371c).[31] Luther hatte in seiner Übersetzung des Neuen Testaments mehrmals das Wort "Amt" für διακονία (z.B. Apg 1,17; 6,4; 20,24; 21,19; Röm 11,13; 1 Kor 12,5; 2 Kor 3,7.8.9; 4,1; 5,18; 6,3; Eph 4,12; Kol 4,17; 1 Tim 1,12; 2 Tim 4,5). Die

---

[24]Str-B, 1:838, 920; 2:257-58. Vgl. *b. Qidd.* 32b; *Mek. Exod.* 18,12; *Sipre Deut.* 11,10 38; zu der letztgenannten Stelle, vgl. die Übersetzung mit Noten von Gerhard Kittel (*Sifre zu Deuteronomium* [Stuttgart: W. Kohlhammer, 1922] 77).

[25]Vgl. Jastrow, s.v. ''שָׁמַשׁ'', *Dictionary*, 2:1602, bes. §2.

[26]Siehe Jastrow, s.v. ''שִׁימוּשׁ'', *Dictionary*, 2:1563.

[27]Str-B (1:527) hat *Aboth* 6,5.

[28]Str-B, 1:527; Levy, s.v. ''שִׁמּוּשָׁא'', *Chaldäisches Wörterbuch*, 2:497.

[29]Str-B, 2:647.

[30]Die Stellen des Targums bei Levy, s.v. ''שִׁמּוּשָׁא'', *Chaldäisches Wörterbuch*, 2:497.

[31]Siehe LSJ, s.v. ''διακονία'', 398.

nordischen Bibelübersetzungen folgten ihm hierin. Im Laufe der Jahr-
hunderte ist aber das Wort "Amt" von "Dienst" Verdrängt worden,
und entsprechend in den skandinavischen Sprachen. Wir wollen hier
nicht die umfassende Frage aufgreifen, inwiefern diese Entwicklung
eine glückliche war. Wir müssen uns auf die Beobachtung beschränken, das die Preisgabe des Wortes "Amt" wohl mit einer Verschie-
bung in der Bestimmung der Grundbedeutung des Wortes διακονία
(bzw. διακονέω) zussammenhängt. Wenn man die Hauptsache dieses
Wortes darin findet, daß es ein Synonym des Begriffes Nächstenliebe
(bzw. Liebesbetätigung) sei, oder darin, daß die διακονία als Begriff
auf die persönliche Hilfe für den anderen Menschen abziele, oder,
wenn man meint, der Nachdruck liege im Worte auf dem Gewinn des
anderen, dann muß notwendigerweise die Übersetzung "Amt" verblassen und schließlich ihre Berechtigung verlieren.

Wenn man aber daran festhält, daß die Grundbedeutung von
διακονία darin liegt, daß jemand ein Diener ist, dann liegt es sehr nahe,
sich vorzustellen, daß dieser Diener eine bestimmte Aufgabe, ein
Geschäft hat, also ein Amt. Daß das Dienen in diesem Sinne und die
Bedeutung Geschäft im selben Wort zusammenlaufen, sieht man auch
in anderen Sprachen. So bedeutet im Alten Testament עֲבוֹדָה
"Dienen", "Bedienung", aber zugleich "Arbeit", "Geschäft". Das
gleiche gilt für den aramäisch-hebräischen Stamm שמש, ferner für das
lateinische *ministerium*, für das englische "ministry" und für das
deutsche Wort "Dienst".

Wenn man auf diese Weise versucht, die verschiedenen
Abstufungen des Diakonia-Begriffes im Neuen Testament auf eine
Grundvorstellung zurückzuführen, dann erhebt sich allerdings an-
schließend die Frage, ob sich auch die Diakonia als Armenunterstützung
hier einfügen läßt. Zunächst muß dann hervorgehoben werden, daß
sowohl Amt wie Armenfürsorge im Urchristentum im Rahmen der
Kirche fungieren, eine Begrenzung, die für die Liebe nicht gelten kann.
Amt und Gemeindediakonie gehören beide in die Ekklesiologie, nicht
in das allgemeine christliche Ethos. Zweitens ist darauf hinzuweisen,
daß die Armenpflege historisch ihren Hintergrund in der Aufgabe des
Dieners hat. Der Diener ist nämlich derjenige, der ganz natürlich für
den Unterhalt der Familie sorgt, insofern er das Essen auf den Tisch
bringt, nachdem er es auf dem Markt eingekauft hat. Als eine Bedeutung von διακονέω führt Beyer auch "für den Lebensunterhalt sorgen"

an.[32] Für διακονία hat Bauer auch die Bedeutung "Unterstützung", und er fügt hinzu: "bes. durch Almosen u. Hilfeleistungen".[33] Als Beleg hätte er auch auf Testament Hiob hinweisen können, wo berichtet wird, daß Hiob täglich einen Tisch für die Armen anrichtete (10,7), unter denen besonders die Witwen hervorgehoben werden (13,4; 14,2). Das Wort διακονία ist dabei Bezeichnung für das Vornehmen auf diese Weise für die Armen zu sorgen (11,1-3), und das Verb διακονέω bezeichnet die Ausübung dieser Tätigkeit (12,1; 15,4). Die Arbeit wurde von den Sklaven Hiobs ausgeführt. Seine Söhne dagegen lehnen es in ihrem Hochmut ab, daran teilzunehmen, und sie fragen: "Warum sollen wir bedienen?" (διὰ τί δὲ καὶ διακονοῦμεν; 15,8). Wir sehen also, daß die Armenpflege als Sache der Diener angesehen wurde. Nach *Act. Thom.* 59 sendet der Apostel Thomas den Witwen Kleidung und Essen durch seine Diener (διάκονοι, was hier kaum Diakon bedeutet; so dagegen *Act. Thom.* 169).

Es scheint sich also so zu verhalten, daß die verschiedenen Seiten des Diakonie-Begriffes, die im Neuen Testament vorliegen, sich am besten ordnen und zusammenfassen lassen, wenn man als Grundbedeutung für den Begriff das Dienersein annimmt, und dabei nicht im Sinne der christlichen Liebe, sondern einfach von der alltäglichen Bedeutung des Wortes her. Der Diener ist ein Assistent. Dienen heißt Assistentsein. Dies scheint das Leitmotiv des Begriffes zu sein. Ferner scheint es eine Tatsache zu sein, daß Diakonie im Neuen Testament auf das innere Leben der Kirche begrenzt ist.

Einige werden wohl fragen, ob nicht der Begriff der Diakonie auf diese Weise den schönen und auch den weiten Inhalt verliert, den man heute sich gewöhnt hat, mit ihm zu verbinden.

Darauf kann geantwortet werden, daß es auch ein Gewinn für die Kirche sein muß, sich auf sein genuin inneres Leben zu besinnen. Wenn man Diakonie mit der allgemeinen christlichen Liebe identifiziert, besteht die Gefahr, daß die Diakonie sich in die allgemeine soziale Fürsorge und ihre Normen verliert.

Abschließend läßt sich fragen, ob nicht die Bereitschaft zum Dienen (im obigen Sinne) eine Voraussetzung für die Realisierung der christlichen Liebe ist. Nur wer gewillt ist, in die Rolle des Dieners

---

[32]Beyer, s.v. "διακονέω", *TWNT* 2 (1935) 81.

[33]Bauer, s.v. "διακονία", *Griechisch-deutsches Wörterbuch*, 334, bes. §4.

einzugehen, kann sich herabbeugen und demütigen, so wie die Liebe es in einer Welt voller unbeschreiblicher und für Menschen manchmal unwürdiger Notzustände fordert.[34]

---

[34]Es ist mir eine Freude, darauf hinzuweisen, daß die kleinen Artikel von Johannes Müller-Bardorff (s.v. "Diakon", *BHH*, ed. Bo Reicke and Leonhard Rost, 1:338-39; s.v. "Diakonisse", *BHH*, 1:339; s.v. "Dienen", *BHH*, 1:344) und Bo Reicke (s.v. "Diener", *BHH*, 1:344) in aller Kürze einer Anschauung Ausdruck geben, mit deren Tendenz ich mich in Übereinstimmung befinde.

Fig. 1. The 'Cross' of Herculaneum and the Cupboard underneath shortly after excavation.

THE "CROSS OF HERCULANEUM" RECONSIDERED

Leslie W. Barnard

THE CROSS OF HERCULANEUM was found in 1938 during the excavations of the Bicentenary House (Casa del Bicentenario), which proved to be the largest house in the Forum district of the buried city.[1] This dwelling is notable for the regularity of its plan and the austere, patriarchal appearance of its atrium, which was of normal Pompeian type. Maiuri, who excavated the house, held that ca. A.D. 50 a second storey was added or readapted as living quarters for two separate families. The larger of these apartments was over the front part of the house facing on the street, while the second, which contained the room with the cross, was approached by a separate stairway and spanned the west and south sides of the peristyle. Maiuri thought these alterations and improvements were made under the impulse of the growing commercial life of the Forum. More recently Maiuri has argued, with plausibility, that the modest upper apartments were let to a family of craftsmen or merchants who worked nearby.[2]

The family presumably would have belonged to the *plebs*, or the lowest class of freeborn, urban citizens. While in antiquity the plebs enjoyed a social advantage over slaves, freedmen and foreigners, they were often at a disadvantage in economic matters. Though immersed in urban civilization, they were not allowed the benefits and privileges which urban society had been designed to promote. Dio Chrysostom states tersely, "Of necessity they stand aloof in sentiment from the common interest, reviled as they are and viewed as outsiders" (*Orat.* 34.22). As second-class citizens they lacked capital to compete with foreign traders. The religion of the plebs, i.e., urban, lower-class

---

[1]Amedeo Maiuri, "La Croce di Ercolano," *Rendiconti, Atti della Pontificia Accademia Romana di Archeologia* 15 (1939) 193-218.

[2]Amedeo Maiuri, *Herculaneum and the Villa of the Papyri: Archaeological Guide of the Town* (Novaro: Instituto geografico De Agostini, 1962) 25.

religion, has been studied by Weber,[3] among others. Weber argued that the plebs could recognize the benefits of the higher social and economic status which they could rarely attain. This resulted in alienation from the existing social order and, in certain cases, an openness to new religious movements. In Rome we know that the lower classes were attracted to foreign cults. The possibility that the occupier(s) of the modest upper-floor rooms in the Casa del·Bicentenario at Herculaneum would be open to such a new religious movement as Christianity therefore cannot be ruled out.

On the wall of one of the smaller upper rooms measuring 3.00 x 2.70 meters, a cross marking was found engraved, at head height, in the recess of a stucco surface measuring 65 x 82 centimeters (fig. 1—seen by the writer in September 1977). The stucco is opposite a doorway which lighted the room from a window in the outside corridor. Nail markings are to be seen in and around the cross. Under the stucco surface a piece of furniture was found resembling a small cabinet, with a flat top surface and containing two rough clay lamps, a dice box and a die. Leaning against the front of the cabinet was a small wooden stool. It is altogether likely that this was the original position of the cross marking, as Herculaneum was engulfed by an immense muddy torrent in A.D. 79, which submerged the whole town. The houses, with their upper storeys, remained unchanged in form inside a sheath of hardened mud, unlike those in Pompeii, which were flattened by a rain of *lapilli* and hot cinders carried by the wind. As will be seen from the illustration, the measurements of the horizontal arms of the cross marking are slightly unequal, and the top piece is not quite aligned to the base, which suggests that it was not an accurately made liturgical object of a formal kind. The nail marks however suggest that the cross was originally of wood and that it had been removed before the eruption of A.D. 79. Maiuri thought that the nail marks around the stucco indicated that a movable panel had once covered the cross.

Maiuri, following the excavation, interpreted the discovery as that of the earliest Christian cross and linked it to Paul's preaching of the cross.[4] According to Acts 28:13-14 Paul arrived at Puteoli and was

---

[3]Max Weber, *The Sociology of Religion* (Boston: Beacon, 1963) 80-117.

[4]Maiuri, "Croce," 216. For a critique of Maiuri, see G. de Jerphanion, "La Croix d'Herculaneum?" *Orientalia Christiana Periodica* 7 (1941) 5-35, and Erich Dinkler, "Zur Geschichte des Kreuzsymbols," *ZTK* 48 (1951) 148-72, esp. 158-59 (repr. in

there met by Christian brethren. One inference was that from Puteoli, Christianity had spread to Herculaneum, some 25-30 km away. Maiuri later pointed out that Herculaneum was a small quiet town of some 5,000 inhabitants with commercial life confined to fishing, industry and coastal trade with Naples, Puteoli, Pompeii and Stabiae.[5] However, in scholarly circles reaction to Maiuri's interpretation soon set in, and since de Bruyne's investigation[6] the Cross of Herculaneum has been widely regarded not as a *Christian* cross but as a miscellaneous wall marking, perhaps caused by the imprint of a bracket once fitted to the wall. If it were a wall bracket it would be odd for it to have a vertical extension above the crossbar and for the "shelf" of the bracket to be smaller than the support underneath.[7]

1.

The case against the Cross of Herculaneum being Christian was originally conducted from a consideration of the place of the cross in the Christian cult. It is of course true that this cross is not a liturgical object and is unlikely to have been used as the focus of a liturgical cult. We would hardly expect this if the apartment was rented to a humble, lower class artisan. Certainly whoever placed the cross there was no artist. Moreover, the dice box found in the wooden cabinet under the stucco suggests that it was not a τράπεζα and so not a type of early Christian "sanctuary" or "oratory," unless the dice were placed there by a later occupant. Certainly the room at one stage was used for nonreligious purposes. However these observations do not prove that the cross is not Christian. It is a fallacy to read conditions of later centuries back into the period before A.D. 79. Christians in the first century kept to themselves and met in each other's houses. There were no specific Christian monuments or no Church buildings nor any liturgical cult until the third century. Justin Martyr, writing in the

---

Dinkler, *Signum Crucis: Aufsätze zum Neuen Testament und zur Christlichen Archäologie* [Tübingen: J. C. B. Mohr, 1967] 1-25). Margherita Guarducci ("Osservazioni sulla croce di Ercolano," *Mitteilungen des deutschen archaeologischen Instituts, Römische Abteilung* 60-61 [München: Römische Zweiganstalt, 1953-1954] 224-33) however argues in support of Maiuri's general contention.

[5]Maiuri, *Herculaneum*, 4.

[6]L. de Bruyne, "La 'crux interpretum' di Ercolano," *Rivista di Archeologia Christiana* 21 (1945) 281-309.

[7]Donald Atkinson, "The Origin and Date of the 'Sator' Word-Square," *JEH* 2 (1951) 17.

mid-second century, knows nothing of a *fixed* liturgy.[8] Lietzmann, as is well known, in his search for the origins of the liturgy found it impossible to recede further into the period before the beginning of the third century and was forced to rely on inference and conjecture when interpreting the scattered liturgical material from that early period.[9] Is it not possible that the cross was placed at head height in the stucco by a humble Christian as a sacred symbol and as a witness to his or her personal faith in a room used then (or later) for nonreligious purposes? Christianity, during the reign of Vespasian (A.D. 69-79) was largely tolerated and unmolested by the Romans—most probably Christians were regarded as adherents to Judaism and so shared the privileges of the Jews. It is unlikely that a cross on a wall of a modest upstairs room would cause any comment or attract attention.

These are however small points. The main burden of the case against the Cross of Herculaneum being Christian is succinctly stated by Dinkler: "Wir haben kein anderes Denkmal des 1. oder 2. Jh.s, das eindeutig von Christen gefertig worden ist und uns eventuell vorkommende Kreuz-Zeichen somit als christliche zu interpretieren erlaubt."[10] Dinkler denies also that cross markings on the ossuaries at Talpioth near Jerusalem are Christian. Rather they are akin to scribbles, although Dinkler concedes that the cross was known in Judaism, where in its standing or reclining form it represented the sign of the last letter of the Hebrew alphabet, tau. It was apparently used to indicate that a person was Yahweh's property and used also as an eschatological protective sign. Could the Cross of Herculaneum then be Jewish?

The position of the Jews in the reign of Vespasian is relevant in this connection. Vespasian celebrated Titus' capture of Jerusalem and the destruction of the Temple in A.D. 70 with a magnificent, triumphal procession through Rome, which was later recorded on the Arch of Titus. However the privileges which the Jewish population enjoyed in Rome and throughout the Empire, originally granted by Julius Caesar, were not diminished by the loss of national status. The diaspora Jews

---

[8]L. W. Barnard, *Justin Martyr: His Life and Thought* (Cambridge: Cambridge University, 1967) 145-47.

[9]Hans Lietzmann, *Messe und Herrenmahl: Eine Studie zur Geschichte der Liturgie* (Arbeiten zur Kirchengeschichte 8; Bonn: A. Markus und E. Weber, 1926).

[10]Dinkler, "Kreuzsymbol," 159.

had no quarrel with Rome and did not wish to jeopardize their favorable position—indeed we have no indication that the destruction of the Jerusalem Temple materially affected their position. The only significant change was the transfer of the Temple tax into a poll tax called *fiscus Iudaicus*. The end of the Jewish war, however, probably caused an increase in the Jewish population in Rome and other Italian cities. Puteoli had a Jewish colony, and the Sodom and Gomorrha graffito (to be mentioned later) appears to indicate the presence of Jews in Pompeii. There is no certain evidence however that there were any Jews in Herculaneum (although the argument from silence may be somewhat precarious in view of the lack of inscriptions from the city; della Corte[11] thought he could read the name "David" on a graffito in a nearby house in the Insula V region).

Even if there were Jews in Herculaneum, the argument that the cross is Jewish cannot be sustained. Jewish crosses from the first century A.D. are found only on ossuaries or on the walls of tombs—never on the walls of rooms.[12] The standing or reclining crosses found on Jewish tombs and slabstones invariably have equilateral arms, unlike the Cross of Herculaneum, which does not fit into the category of Jewish cross markings. If then the Cross of Herculaneum was not Christian, what was it? This question Dinkler never satisfactorily faces.

It is true that the Christian cross is usually found in the second and third centuries under the form of an anchor, trident or ship with rigging, or under forms employed by older cults, such as the cross *potencée* and the gammate cross. Aland has shown that a contracted form of σταυροῦν and σταυρός in the period ca. A.D. 200 is attested by the papyri of the *Bibliotheca Bodmeriana*.[13] He shows that in the transmission of biblical texts the New Testament papyri p[66] and p[75] use the

---

[11]Matteo della Corte, "Le iscrizioni scoperte nel quinquennio 1951-1956," *Notizio degli scavi di antichità* (Atti della Accademia Nazionale dei Lincei ser. 8 vol. 12 [=83]/ 10 [1958] 77-184) 180 no. 645.

[12]Dinkler, "Kreuzsymbol," 157-62. Duncan Fishwick ("The Talpioth Ossuaries Again," *NTS* 10[1963-1964] 49-61) argues that the ossuaries reflect Christian influence within Jewish syncretistic magic. On the possibility that the Talpioth ossuaries are Christian, see Bo Reicke, "De judekristna benskrinen från Jerusalems södra förort Talpijjot," *Svenska Jerusalems-Föreningens Tidskrift* 48 (1949) 2-14.

[13]Kurt Aland, "Neue Neutestamentliche Papyri II," *NTS* 10 (1963-1964) 62-79 and 11 (1964-1965) 1-2; further bibliography in Dinkler, *Signum Crucis*, 177-78.

contraction ⳨, formed from τ and ρ (for ταυρ in σταυρός), to form
σ⳨ος. He argues that the staurogram is in fact older than the *Christian*
use of the christogram ☧. Thus by ca. A.D. 200 Christians designated
the cross by the sign ⳨.[14] This papyrological evidence coheres with
other evidence from the second and third centuries that the sign
was in fact not used by Christians, but that the event of the crucifixion
was alluded to under a variety of other forms. The Christian cross
alone in its Latin form can be demonstrated archaeologically only
from the time of Constantine, when it began to appear on coinage. It
has been usual to connect this with the legend of the finding of the relic
of the cross by the Empress Helena. From then on the supremacy of the
† was absolute, and eventually it appeared on the imperial diadem
and elsewhere (on funerary inscriptions, altars, reliquaries, lamps,
jewels, even on the facades of houses, and on the tops of basilicas,
where it took the place of the imperial monogram). Before long it
became the ground plan of churches and other religious buildings.
However, these developments are all post-Constantinian.

Those scholars who assert so emphatically that a Christian cross in
the form † is an anachronism as early as the first century A.D.
overlook, however, one important consideration, namely, that the
circumstances of Christians in the first century differed markedly from
those which obtained in the second and third centuries. We can illus-
trate this from a scurrilous drawing found scratched on the wall of a
house on the Palatine Hill in Rome, which shows a man worshiping a
crucified human figure, which has the head of an ass with the words
"Alexamenos worships his God"[15] scrawled beneath. This parody of
the cross, which probably dates from the early third century, shows
how easily the crucifixion could be misrepresented in pagan slander.
The political factor may also have exercised an influence, for Jesus had
historically stood trial on political charges and had been executed as a
Roman prisoner on a charge of sedition. This was a useful symbol as

---

[14]It should however be noted that ⳨ was also used by pagans as a kind of
trademark to identify the contents of an amphora as χρηστός (CIL 4 Supp. 3, 9812; cf.
2777). Its Christian use must therefore be determined from its context, as is certain
from the papyri in this case.

[15]Henri Leclercq, *La vie chrétienne primitive* (Paris: Rieder, 1928) 85; S. G. F.
Brandon, "Christ in Verbal and Depicted Imagery: A Problem of Early Christian
Iconography," *Christianity, Judaism and Other Graeco-Roman Cults* (SJLA 12/2;
Leiden: E. J. Brill, 1975) 168.

long as Christianity was a small sect composed mainly of urban lower-class people. Jesus' death on the cross, then, identified him with the poor, outcast and alienated people of the world. However, as the Church, from the second century onwards, came into contact with Graeco-Roman society and had to define its attitude to contemporary culture, it would have been unwise to have provided a pictorial reminder of the potential political danger of Christianity to the State, exemplified in the crucifixion of its founder on a cross on political charges. The Church seems to have tacitly dropped the execution symbol and concentrated on the theme of life and deliverance, such as in the picture of the healing of the paralytic found at Dura-Europos or in the pictures of the healing of the woman with the issue of blood and the raising of Lazarus.[16] There is only one possible reference to the passion of Christ in early catacomb iconography—the scene in the catacomb of Praetextatus, dated by some scholars to the first half of the third century, which may show the crowning with thorns.[17] The figure of Christ, however, is not that of a tortured victim but of a serene figure wearing a laurel of leaves and acclaimed by bystanders holding palm branches, a symbol of victory. This is a transformation of the scene recorded in the Gospels and emphasizes the theme of deliverance and victory, rather than the sufferings of the Crucified. This is remarkable in view of the space accorded to the passion and crucifixion in the Gospel narratives (one quarter of Mark's Gospel alone) and the great emphasis on the cross in later western church doctrine and practice. I do not believe that this transformation was due simply to an inability on the part of the early Christians to grasp that Christ had died a real death—symbolized so vividly in the later pietas, such as that by Michaelangelo in the Cathedral at Florence.

I now wish to suggest that a study of early Christian apologetic literature throws fresh light on the question why no Christian crosses are found from the second century until the time of Constantine and why no portraits of a human Jesus or a dead Christ on the cross are found before the late fourth century. It is significant that none of the following second-century Christian writers mention the earthly life or death of Jesus: Athenagoras, Tatian, Theophilus, the compiler of the

---

[16]Pierre du Bourguet, *Early Christian Painting* (London: Viking, 1965) ill. 45, 99, 117, 129.

[17]du Bourguet, *Painting,* ill. 53; Brandon, "Imagery," 169.

Sentences of Sextus and Minucius Felix. However, we know that in approaching certain non-Christians this neglect of Jesus was a strength and not a weakness. This can be illustrated from the attitude of Galen, the celebrated physician, to Christianity. Galen's opinion of Christians was unbiased, sympathetic and nonpolemical, and he was particularly impressed by the high standard of morality found among Christians. He was impressed also by the attempt Christians were making to educate the multitude, which attempt he could fit into the categories provided by the Academic tradition. In the judgment of Walzer,[18] Galen was the first pagan author who implicitly placed Greek philosophy and the Christian religion on the same footing. Yet throughout his life Galen held that an uncritical faith in a particular founder of a school (whether Christian or pagan) was hostile to genuine knowledge and truth. He explicitly compared the followers of Moses and Christ to the degenerate philosophical and medical schools of the second century, which put loyalty to the founder and the school before loyalty to the truth. This pagan criticism of founders of schools, in which Christians were included, may be the reason why such writers as Athenagoras were careful to present Christianity as the "truth" rather than as a body of teaching laid down by Jesus.[19] Origen likewise was aware of pagan criticisms. He states that sometimes in conversing with pagan friends, he found them so hostile to Christianity and the name of Christ that he would conceal that his teaching was Christian until a point had been reached when the person approved of his teaching. Only then would he disclose that the teaching was that of the Christians (*Hom. in Jer.* 20.5).

Much early Christian art falls into the category of indirect apologetic, and this, I suggest, is one of the reasons for the neglect of the symbol of the cross, of the human portrait of Christ and of the crucifixion scene before the fourth century. The fact that so many pagan symbols were used in early Christian art was, I suggest, due not only to the artists' background and training but to conscious choice. They were conscious that the audience for their work was not only Christian but included pagans as well, and they were intent on appeal-

---

[18]Richard R. Walzer, *Galen on Jews and Christians* (Oxford Classical and Philosophical Monographs; London: Oxford University, Geoffrey Cumberlege, 1949) 43.

[19]L. W. Barnard, *Athenagoras: A Study in Second Century Christian Apologetic* (Théologie historique 18; Paris: Beauchesne, 1972) 56.

ing obliquely to non-Christians through their art. The pagan symbols
which they so readily used provided a bridge over which the pagan
could pass. The themes of the Good Shepherd, the Philosopher and the
Orans would have had no particular significance at first for these
pagans beyond what was already familiar to them. However, with a
deepening interest in and understanding of Christianity, they would
have taken on a new significance and predisposed the viewer towards
an understanding of Jesus. Daniélou has emphasized the missionary
intention of the early Christian apologetic literature, i.e., it represented
a genuine presentation of the Gospel to the pagan world, using categories and philosophical thought forms of the day.[20] Much earlier Christian art, I would claim, had this missionary intent and, like the
apologetic literature, provided stepping stones from paganism to
Christianity. It presents Christianity as a new life, which delivers men
from the power of sin and death, rather than as a body of teaching laid
down by Jesus, who had been crucified on a cross. The apologetic
writings show that there was a widespread interest in Christianity from
the second century onwards, and early Christian art, in one sense, was
not so much the art of an inner group as an attempt to demonstrate the
continuity between pagan culture and Christianity through the use of
familiar symbols, such as the Good Shepherd and the Philosopher. In
our view much early Christian art of the second and third centuries,
with its neglect of the cross, belongs to the category of indirect apologetic and was a conscious attempt to do this.

However this indirect apologetic did not exist in the first century
A.D. The Christians were still a small group who kept to themselves.
The attempt to build a bridge to the cultural world of paganism
belonged as yet to the future. There was in the first century, unlike the
second and third centuries, no reason for not using the symbol of the
Christian cross—no reason for underplaying the meaning of the cross.
The lack of Christian crosses from the first century A.D. may be due to
the vagaries of survival. Little else has come down from this early
period, but the picture might look very different if more towns like
Pompeii and Herculaneum had survived *in toto*. The fact that the

---

[20]Jean Daniélou, *A History of Early Christian Doctrine before the Council of Nicaea,* vol. 2: *Gospel Message and Hellenistic Culture* (London: Darton, Longman & Todd; Philadelphia: Westminster, 1973) 7-15.

archaeological and artistic evidence for early Christianity *in extenso* exists only from the late-second century does not prove that none exists from the first century.[21] I can see no good reason for the assertion, so confidently made by scholars, that the Cross of Herculaneum cannot be Christian. We should beware of the circular argument: the sign of the Christian cross is found in significant quantity only *after* the conversion of Constantine; therefore any cross found in the first century cannot be Christian. We know from I Clement that the Church in Rome survived the Neronian persecution, and we know that Christians existed by ca. A.D. 61 in Puteoli. It is possible, indeed likely, that Christians would also have existed at an early date in Ostia, Herculaneum and Pompeii.

2

It remains to discuss briefly indications that Christianity existed in Pompeii before its destruction in A.D. 79 and that the sign of the cross was also used there. Dinkler has dealt exhaustively with this question in his book *Signum Crucis*.[22] He comes to a negative conclusion, arguing that the so-called "Christian" graffiti are not Christian after all. It is true that the scratching, "Sodom and Gomorrha," in a house in Pompeii is unlikely to be Christian (cf. Rom 9:29; Matt 10:15; Mark 6:11 [Textus Receptus]). It is more likely to have been the work of a Jewish hand rather than of a pagan, as favored by Dinkler. Similarly the interpretation of the graffito is fraught with uncertainty, in spite of Guarducci's new rendering:

Bovios audi(t) Christianos
sevos o(s)ores[23]

"Bovos listens to the Christians, the cruel haters," i.e., a pagan is

---

[21] Dinkler (*Signum Crucis*, 175-76) points out that *Christian* monuments in the first and second centuries A.D. may have been indistinguishable from contemporary pagan examples; e.g., the origin of Christian cemeteries lay in private burials which were similar to those of pagans.

[22] Dinkler, *Signum Crucis*, 136-45, with full bibliography. In spite of disagreements with Dinkler, I am heavily indebted to his profound and detailed studies in the field of early Christian archaeology and inscriptions.

[23] Margherita Guarducci, "La piú antica iscrizione col nome dei Cristiani," *RQ* 57 (1962) 116-25.

making a mockery of a fellow citizen who had been listening to Christian propaganda. In 1871 Zangemeister[24] read PG. VIG SAVDI CIIRISTIRΛII, and as the graffito is now lost Guarducci's reconstruction cannot be put to the test. The precise rendering and meaning of the graffito therefore remains uncertain.

Again the monogram ☧, found in the excavations between 1951-56,[25] is not with certainty Christian. The Christian use of the monogram is, as is well known, well attested from Constantine's time, the earliest certain use being on a fragmentary inscription, dated A.D. 323, found beneath Saint Lorenzo's in Rome.[26] In Pompeii and elsewhere the monogram appears repeatedly on amphorae, some of which are certainly pagan. Examples of the chi-rho stamped on non-Christian coins are also known. The use of the monogram is not therefore proof of its use by Christians unless the context makes this unambiguously clear. This is not the case at Pompeii where the monogram is apparently used as an owner's, manufacturer's or examiner's mark.

The same caution is needed in interpreting the inscription found in 1954 at Pompeii: $\begin{smallmatrix} \text{Rex es} \\ \text{Xi do} \end{smallmatrix}$.[27] We know that many Jews in Rome were Latin speaking, and we cannot therefore exclude this possibility for Christians. However, we cannot be certain that the second line is an abbreviation for "Christus Jesus Dominus"; equally it might abbreviate a mocking gibe: X Id(us) O(ctobres).[28]

More to the point for our purposes is a scratched figure found in a house on Insula XIII in Region I of Pompeii in 1955:

The excavator of Pompeii, della Corte, took this as proof of the existence of Christians in Pompeii by reading: "viv(at) crux V(ivat),"

[24]Karl Zangemeister, ed., *Inscriptiones Parietariae Pompeianae Herculanenses Stabianae* (CIL 4; Berolini: Apud Georgium Reimerum, 1871).

[25]della Corte, "Iscrizione," 180 no. 645.

[26]E. Diehl, *Inscriptiones Latinae Christianae Veteres* (Berlin: Weidmanns, 1961), 2:3257.

[27]della Corte, "Iscrizione," 136, 183 pl. 5 no. 310.

[28]Dinkler, *Signum Crucis*, 145.

which he thought was an acclamation of the cross.[29] Dinkler disputes this interpretation on the grounds that such a development of Pauline and Johannine theology would have been highly improbable at such an early period.[30] However Dinkler does not explain the undisputed existence in this graffito of the *sign* of the cross. It is very unlikely that this is Jewish († or x), and we have no pagan parallels to ⊬ as is the case with ⸶ and ⸷. If it is not Christian, what is it? I can see no good reason for denying that the figure of the *Vivat Crux* refers simply to Christ's death and resurrection. The early kerygma, which can be reconstructed behind the New Testament documents, undoubtedly referred to this. We do not need to find in this figure an elaborate cult of the cross, or a development of Pauline or Johannine theology. What we have is a simple acclamation of faith that Jesus, who died on the cross, is alive. The reason that no figure of Jesus appears on the cross is due to the fact that the early Christians had no knowledge of his physical appearance, beyond a few details about his clothes, and they were loath to portray him. While it would be unscientific to bring in the Cross of Herculaneum to support a Christian interpretation of the "vivat crux" graffito at Pompeii, a view of both crosses independently does not rule out the possibility that they may be Christian and therefore the earliest archaeological witnesses to the Christian religion in the Roman Empire. Perhaps we should mention here also the similar cross at Pompeii made known long ago by Mazois but now lost.[31]

3

Our purpose in this paper has been to show that it is no longer possible to hold the dogma that the symbol of the Christian cross first appeared in the time of Constantine. Our contention is that it was used by humble Christians before the year A.D. 79, but that its use was dropped when Christians came into wider contact with the pagan world and had to face pagan attacks and slanders. It then became

---

[29]della Corte, "Iscrizione," 113, 183 pl. 5 no. 181; see also Agnello Baldi, *La Pompei Giudaico-Cristiana* (Di Mauro Editore, 1964) 67.

[30]Dinkler, *Signum Crucis*, 144-45.

[31]François Mazois, *Les Ruines de Pompei*, 4 vols. (Paris: Firmin Didot, 1824-1838), 2:84. If the 'Sator square' is Christian and dates from before A.D. 79, as I think it does, then we have a further witness to the use of the cross sign in the first century.

impolitic to refer to the crucifixion except under pagan guises and as the anchor, trident, ship of ⚓.[32] Instead the Christians concentrated on the themes of life and deliverance and tended to stress the continuity between paganism and Christianity. This can be illustrated, in literary form, from the apologists of the second century, some of whom even dropped all reference to Jesus' earthly life and death. This, strange though it is to our eyes, was a strength, not a weakness, in the second century. However this was not the case in the first century. When the wooden cross existed on the stucco wall of the upper room at Herculaneum and the cross mark was scratched in the house at Pompeii, only Mark's Gospel, with its strong emphasis on the passion, death and resurrection of Jesus, had yet been written. Christians kept to themselves and met in small groups. There were, as yet, no Christian monuments or buildings per se. In such a milieu as this, tolerated as they appear to have been by their pagan neighbors, they were perhaps not afraid to confess their faith by the use of a simple cross.

---

[32]It is interesting that the Jewish-Christian tract known as the *Epistle of Barnabas* (ca. A.D. 120-130) refers to the cross under the Jewish tau symbol: τὸ δεκαοκτὼ ί δέκα, ή ὀκτώ· ἔχεις 'Ιησοῦν. ὅτι δὲ ὁ σταυρὸς ἐν τῷ ταῦ ἤμελλεν ἔχειν τὴν χάριν, λέγει καὶ τοὺς τριακοσίους. δηλοῖ οὖν τὸν μὲν 'Ιησοῦν ἐν τοῖς δυσὶν γράμμασιν, καὶ ἐν τῷ ἑνὶ τὸν σταυρόν (9:8).

APOLLOS
AND THE TWELVE DISCIPLES
OF EPHESUS*

C. K. Barrett

THE PROBLEMS created by Acts 18:24-28 and 19:1-7 are too familiar to call for detailed exposition in this short essay. Apollos is introduced in terms that must suggest to the cursory reader that he, Apollos, is a Christian. His Alexandrian[1] origin and learning (or eloquence) indeed do not imply this, though they are not incompatible with it. That he was a powerful expositor of Scripture, when taken in the context of Acts, may hint at what is stated explicitly in 18:28—the power to prove that the Christ is Jesus. More significant is the fact that he was κατηχημένος τὴν ὁδὸν τοῦ κυρίου. The word "Way"[2] is used several times in Acts to describe the Christians, their company, and their manner of life (9:2; 19:9,23; 22:4; 24:14,22; cf. 2:28; 13:10; 14:16; 16:17), and κύριος, though it sometimes refers to the Lord of the Old Testament, naturally suggests the Lord Jesus. This apparently Christian reference seems to be confirmed by the next words, ζέων τῷ πνεύματι, which have a precise parallel in Rom 12:11, where Christians are urged

---

*This article was completed in April, 1978.

[1]According to D, Apollos received Christian instruction in Alexandria. The reading however is probably secondary. Arnold Ehrhardt (*The Acts of the Apostles: ten lectures* [Manchester: Manchester University, 1969] 101, 102) does not note this variant, though it might lend support to his view that Alexandria is represented here as heterodox: "Alexandria had rejected the Jerusalem influence, which the Church at Antioch had accepted." The twelve disciples of 19:1-7 were, according to Ehrhardt, Alexandrian Christians, not disciples of John the Baptist.

[2]There is no need here to discuss the origin of the Christian use of ὁδός, though if it refers primarily to instruction, as it appears to do in this passage, this would be consistent with some connection with the Qumran use of דרך. See Christoph Burchard (*Der dreizehnte Zeuge: Traditions- und kompositionsgeschichtliche Untersuchungen zu Lukas' Darstellung der Frühzeit des Paulus* [FRLANT 103; Göttingen: Vandenhoeck & Ruprecht, 1970] 43 n. 10) and the references there given.

to be τῷ πνεύματι ζέοντες. Apollos, one might conclude, was an inspired Christian and spoke under the influence of the Spirit (which would lead him to use the word κύριος of Jesus [cf. 1 Cor 12:3]). In his inspired speaking he taught accurately τὰ περὶ τοῦ 'Ιησοῦ, just as Paul does in the closing words of the book (28:31), which, coming from Luke's pen, can mean nothing at all if they do not mean that Paul preached the Christian Gospel as it ought to be preached. So then did Apollos too; whatever ambiguity there may be in the earlier phrases and in παρρησιάζεσθαι[3] which follows, there is none here. Yet this earnest, inspired and well instructed preacher of the Gospel knew only the baptism of John and was instructed further by Priscilla and Aquila in the way of God. Was Apollos, at the beginning of the story, a Christian or not? In the second paragraph the problem focuses on the word μαθητής. Luke normally uses the word to mean "Christian disciple" (so, for example, in the immediately preceding narrative [18:23]). But can these disciples, who had received John's baptism but not Christian baptism and had not heard whether there was a Holy Spirit,[4] have been Christians? If they were, why were they baptized? And since in fact they were baptized, why was Apollos not baptized, if he like them was a disciple of John the Baptist and not already a baptized Christian?

In face of such problems it is not surprising that some violent solutions have been adopted. It may be that in the end such solutions will prove necessary, but they should be accepted only when less violent measures have failed. Words should be given their plain sense, unless this becomes absolutely impossible. Thus "the baptism of John" (18:25) should be understood to refer to the "baptism that John proclaimed" (10:37; cf. 1:22) rather than to the baptism of Jesus by John, which, if it had been in mind, would hardly have been described

---

[3]According to Acts 18:26, Apollos began (ἤρξατο) to speak boldly in the synagogue. On the question whether ἤρξατο simply represents the Aramaic שׁרא, see Max Wilcox, *The Semitisms of Acts* (Oxford: Clarendon, 1965) 125-27. That seems very improbable. If ἤρξατο is not a mere auxiliary, the reference is probably to Apollos's first preaching in the synagogue at *Ephesus*, not to a totally new activity on his part. It comes at the wrong point in the narrative to be the result of a conversion.

[4]So, among others, Ernst Haenchen, *The Acts of the Apostles: A Commentary* (Philadelphia: Westminster; Oxford: Basil Blackwell, 1971) 553. But there are difficulties. No one can have read the Old Testament without becoming aware of the existence of the Holy Spirit. See n. 19 below.

simply as τὸ βάπτισμα 'Ιωάννου.[5] Again, we should not read out of
19:5 that those who were baptized by John were baptized by him into
the name of the Lord Jesus.[6] It is true that the plurals ἀκούσαντες
ἐβαπτίσθησαν could not unreasonably be read out of λαός (19:4) as a
noun of multitude, but αὐτοῖς in 19:6 must refer to the same persons,
and these were the twelve Ephesian disciples, baptized at Paul's orders.
Less violent are the suggestions that Luke inserted into a source either
18:25ab (οὗτος ἦν . . . 'Ιησοῦ), so as to make a Baptist Apollos into a
Christian, or 18:25c,26 (ἐπιστάμενος . . . θεοῦ), so as to make a
Christian Apollos into a not-yet-Christian follower of John, since it
must be supposed that Luke prepared for publication, that is, edited,
whatever source material he had, and that the editorial process may
have included supplementation. Yet if these accounts of Luke's editing
are accepted in anything like the form in which I have stated them, they
make Luke an incompetent editor who has produced a self-
contradictory text. If he had an axe to grind with regard to Apollos he
might have written *either*:

> This man was instructed in the way of the Lord Jesus, and in speech inspired
> by the Holy Spirit taught accurately the things concerning Jesus. Priscilla
> and Aquila, hearing this Spirit-filled preaching in the synagogue, were glad
> to recognize a Christian colleague.

or:

> This man was a Jew, familiar with the Old Testament Scriptures and a fine
> synagogue preacher, who continued the work of John, by whom he had been
> baptized. When Priscilla and Aquila heard him preach in the synagogue, they
> perceived his potential value as a colleague, taught him the way of Jesus,
> made a convert of him, and baptized him.

It is, however, possible that Luke may have used words in an unusual
way, and many writers have been known to mix up their pronouns. He
may have been a timid editor, ready to introduce a few words but

---

[5]Kirsopp Lake and H. J. Cadbury, *The Beginnings of Christianity*, Part 1: *The Acts of the Apostles*, vol. 4: *English Translation and Commentary* (London: Macmillan, 1933), 1/4:232.

[6]Karl Barth, *Church Dogmatics*, vol. 4: *The Doctrine of Reconciliation*, part 4: *The Christian Life (Fragment): Baptism as the Foundation of the Christian Life* (Edinburgh: T. & T. Clark, 1969), 4/4:62, 75. The suggestion goes back to Markus Barth, *Die Taufe - Ein Sakrament?: Ein exegetischer Beitrag zum Gespräch über die kirchliche Taufe* (Zollikon-Zürich: Evangelischer Verlag, 1951) 166-68. On this see G. R. Beasley-Murray, *Baptism in the New Testament* (Exeter: Paternoster, 1972) 111.

unwilling to leave any out. It may be necessary in the end to accept one or more of these expedients.

The two most notable attempts to make sense of these two difficult paragraphs are those of Käsemann[7] and Schweizer.[8] It will be well first to refer briefly to these[9] before attempting an independent assessment of the problem.

Käsemann's treatment of the question is so carefully and tightly worked out that it is very difficult to summarize. He first analyses the paragraph 19:1-7 in such a way as to bring out the problems inherent in the narrative as it stands. He also gives a critical account of earlier attempts to solve the problems and objects that earlier writers have not raised sharply enough the question of historicity, but have offered historical reconstructions that lacked adequate foundation. In particular he objects that "Luke himself does not depict either Apollos or the disciples in Ephesus as representatives of primitive Christian freedom but of an immature form of Christianity."[10] "The living context of the passage is the reception of ecclesiastical outsiders into the *Una sancta catholica*."[11] Only when this has been recognized is a true understanding of the passage possible. Historically, one must begin with the hypothesis that the μαθηταί of 19:1-2 had been baptized with John's baptism; they were disciples of John the Baptist. They need therefore to be taught that John had been not an independent figure but the forerunner of Jesus, and they need to be given Christian baptism which incorporates them into the church and imparts to them the Spirit. Such are the facts, as Käsemann conceives them. But Luke could not allow this view of John, which contradicted his and the church's understand-

---

[7]Ernst Käsemann, "The Disciples of John the Baptist in Ephesus," *Essays on New Testament Themes* (SBT 41; Naperville, Illinois: Alec R. Allenson; London: SCM, 1964) 136-48 (German original: "Die Johannesjünger in Ephesus," *Exegetische Versuche und Besinnungen I* [Göttingen: Vandenhoeck & Ruprecht, 1960] 158-68).

[8]Eduard Schweizer, "Die Bekehrung des Apollos, Apg 18,24-26," *Beiträge zur Theologie des Neuen Testaments: Neutestamentliche Aufsätze (1955-1970)* (Zürich: Zwingli, 1970) 71-79.

[9]See also the notes in the commentaries by Haenchen (*Acts*, 549-57) and Hans Conzelmann (*Die Apostelgeschichte* [HNT 7; Tübingen: J. C. B. Mohr, 1963] 109-10).

[10]Käsemann, "Disciples," 141 (German, 162). Käsemann is reacting to an article by Herbert Preisker ("Apollos und die Johannesjünger in Act 18:24-19:6," *ZNW* 30 [1931] 301-304).

[11]Käsemann, "Disciples," 141 (German, 162).

ing of him, to remain. He makes John (as the synoptic tradition did) into the herald of Jesus, and the disciples into "an odd species of Christian."[12] It is at this point that the equally problematical story of Apollos may be invoked. Apollos is described as a Christian, but one who knows nothing of Christian baptism—a pure contradiction. It follows that 18:25c must be regarded as a Lucan fabrication. Why did Luke introduce it? The question may be answered by reference to 8:14-17 and 10:44-48. "The Church of a later day could not admit the existence in the sacred past of primitive Christian free-lances and communities resting on any other than apostolic authority: because otherwise it would have granted letters patent to the gnostics and other heretics by whom it was being menaced."[13] In chapter 8 Philip's baptism must be represented as defective. In chapter 10 the spontaneous gift of the Spirit to Cornelius and his friends proves that the Gentile mission is the will of God, but it must immediately be followed by the incorporation of the converts into the apostolic church by baptism.

Käsemann sums up with four conclusions. (1) It is impossible to deduce from the Lucan writings a period when there was a disjunction between baptism and the gift of the Spirit. Acts must be understood not as a narrative based on sources but as the author's composition.[14] (2) The narrative about Apollos can now be explained. It was necessary to integrate him into the apostolic fellowship. It was impossible to describe the baptism of one known to be inspired, but he must at least receive supplementary instruction. The disciples at Ephesus supplied a useful hint, which Luke employed in fabricating 18:25c.[15] (3) There was also movement in the reverse direction (a *communicatio idiomatum* between the two narratives, Käsemann says): the disciples of John (perhaps transported to Ephesus from Palestine or Syria for the purpose) became immature Christians.[16] (4) The whole narrative shows that Luke must be understood and interpreted first as a theologian, and only then as a historian. His theology "reads back into the past as

---

[12]Käsemann, "Disciples," 143 (German, 163).

[13]Käsemann, "Disciples," 145 (German, 165).

[14]Käsemann, "Disciples," 146-47 (German, 166).

[15]Käsemann, "Disciples," 147 (German, 166). That Apollos was known to be inspired seems to undermine some of Käsemann's presuppositions.

[16]Käsemann, "Disciples," 147-48 (German, 167).

an historical reality the postulate of an *Una sancta* grounded on the apostolic fellowship and then, conversely, uses this postulate to validate the claims of the orthodox Church of his own times."[17]

Schweizer partly builds upon, partly disagrees with, Käsemann's essay. He recognizes the problems that the two narratives, taken as they stand, present. He questions however Käsemann's use of Acts 8:14-17 as an analogy. Was it a chief motivation of Luke's editing to show that the church of the first generation manifested an ideal and unbroken unity? If so, he would hardly have allowed 15:39 and 21:20,21 to stand, nor would he have omitted (save for 24:17) all reference to Paul's collection for the Jerusalem church. The narrative of chapter 8 is due to the combination of two sources, and Luke's main concern is not to show the *local* unity of the church in all places, but the *temporal* unity of its connection at all times with the original church in Jerusalem. "Lukas ist innerhalb des NT *der* Theologe der Heilsgeschichte."[18] So in 19:1-7 Luke is not concerned to show the adoption into the church of ecclesiastical outsiders. The pericope itself betrays a primary interest in the Spirit and in the displacement of water baptism by Spirit baptism, which rests upon a saying attributed to Jesus (1:5; 11:16).

The story of Apollos remains unexplained, but the point cannot be the incorporation of an independent preacher into the *una sancta*. If this were Luke's thought, why was baptism not employed (as in 19:1-7)? And why was not Paul, rather than Priscilla and Aquila, the agent of incorporation? In fact, Apollos should be thought of as the Jew Luke says he was (18:24). The "way of the Lord" (18:25) should be thought of in Old Testament terms as the way of life God requires (cf. 13:10). Ζέων τῷ πνεύματι referred originally to Apollos's glowing eloquence. The narrative tells the story of the conversion of a Jew. Luke has created problems because he misunderstood the "way of the Lord" as the "things concerning Jesus" (18:25) and took πνεύματι to refer to the Holy Spirit. Since Apollos had already received the Holy Spirit, and since nothing was said about his baptism, Luke did not introduce it; Apollos was not in the same case as the disciples of 19:1-7. From this conclusion a different view of Luke's historical and theological purpose results.

---

[17]Käsemann, "Disciples," 148 (German, 168).

[18]Schweizer, "Bekehrung," 74.

Is either of these very acute discussions of a very difficult problem entirely satisfactory? It is certain that both cannot be correct, and it is at least possible that neither is wholly right. We may take up Schweizer's criticism of Käsemann's use of the Samaritan episode of Acts 8. I have discussed this passage in detail elsewhere.[19] Schweizer may well be right in seeing here a combination of sources (though it was probably Simon who located the incident in Samaria) and in thinking that Luke wished to show a *heilsgeschichtlich* connection between new developments in the growth of the church and in the spread of the Gospel and their origin in Jerusalem, but the main drift of the passage is that the activity of the Spirit is not under human control, whether financial (Simon cannot buy the right to confer the Spirit) or liturgical and cultic (even baptism by an outstanding Christian such as Philip does not necessarily result in the gift of the Spirit).[20] That is, whatever Acts 8 may in the end contribute to the understanding of chapters 18 and 19, it is not a piece of *Frühkatholizismus* (at least, as that term is commonly understood). Indeed, Käsemann's assumption that Acts manifests a *frühkatholisch* tendency is one that can be challenged point after point.[21] Thus when using Acts 20:17-35 he says, "the Apostle can be reported as referring to the dangers and difficulties of his own time and contrasting with them the ideal of the *Una sancta*, the integrity of which is guaranteed by the teaching office of the Church resting upon the apostolic succession."[22] But what Paul says is that though he has suffered persecution it is in the later period[23] that the unity of the church will be threatened, and the whole notion of apostolic succession

---

[19]See C. K. Barrett, "Light on the Holy Spirit from Simon Magus (Acts 8,4-25)," *Les Actes des Apôtres: Traditions, rédaction, théologie*, ed. J. Kremer (BETL 48; Gembloux: Duculot; Leuven: Leuven University, 1979) 281-95.

[20]See Schweizer, "Bekehrung," 78 n. 23. I would go further than Schweizer does. There is, for example, no reference to baptism in the whole of the "first missionary journey" (Acts 13-14).

[21]Ernst Haenchen, *Die Apostelgeschichte*, 16th ed. (MeyerK; Göttingen: Vandenhoeck & Ruprecht, 1977) 62-62 n. 21: "Von 'Frühkatholizismus' sollte man besser hier noch nicht sprechen. . . . An die Stelle der Naherwartung des Endes ist die Aufgabe der Weltmission getreten."

[22]Käsemann, "Disciples," 145 (German, 165).

[23]Whatever ἄφιξις means (20:29)! It is clear that both internal rupture, in heresy and schism, and external attack, whether from persecutors or those who introduce error, are in mind.

is glaringly absent from the speech. Not a word is said about any provision for successors to the elders,[24] no doubt because as the Holy Spirit appointed them (20:28) he could be depended on to appoint more when more were needed.

If the theory of Lucan *Frühkatholizismus* is challenged, as I believe it must be, a very notable support of Käsemann's reconstruction and explanation of 18:24-19:7 is removed. This is not to say that the whole structure will collapse. Schweizer has not succeeded in making it seem improbable that Luke is concerned to show the unity of the church in a local sense. The separation between Paul and Barnabas was a historical fact (Gal 2:13). Luke provides it with a different basis of a kind that he can understand—he is much better with people than with theology—and allows it to stand in his text, partly perhaps for the simple reason that it was a fact, partly also because he has described one missionary journey in which Paul was accompanied by Barnabas and was now about to describe another in which Paul was known to have had other travelling companions. Luke probably did not take 21:20,21 to be inconsistent with his theme. The Jewish Christians had (he supposed) been misinformed; steps were taken to see that they understood Paul's true position; out of these steps the rest of his story developed. It is therefore quite reasonable to maintain that one of Luke's interests in the passages before us was to add to his picture of a united apostolic church—united not in formal structure[25] (a theme in which Luke shows no interest whatever) but in harmony, and in theology and proclamation.

If we now take a fresh look at the two paragraphs, it will appear that they are united by two themes: the work of John the Baptist, and the Holy Spirit.[26] Apollos knew only the baptism of John (18:25); the

---

[24]Contrast the concern for a continuation of ministry in the Pastorals and in 1 Clement. Timothy must commit Paul's preaching to faithful men who will be able to teach others (2 Tim 2:2—a *teaching* succession). The text of *1 Clem.* 44:2 is uncertain, but some sort of continuity (διαδέξωνται) is implied.

[25]Stephen G. Wilson, *The Gentiles and the Gentile Mission in Luke-Acts* (SNTSMS 23; Cambridge: Cambridge University, 1973) 240: "Luke himself has left hints which show that Jerusalem did not enjoy such a ubiquitous role as overseer of all missionary development as his overall scheme implies."

[26]I agree with Käsemann ("Disciples," 143) rather than with Schweizer ("Bekehrung," 76-77) on the interpretation of ζέων τῷ πνεύματι. For a conspectus of opinions, see Haenchen, *Acts*, 550.

twelve disciples had been baptized "into" John's baptism (19:3).[27] There is good, though hardly overwhelming, reason[28] to think that groups of John's disciples did persist after their master's death, and even after the death and resurrection of Jesus. The Lucan infancy narratives are probably to be taken as substantial evidence of this, though the anti-John polemic that has been found in the Fourth Gospel is not proved, and probably has been much exaggerated.[29] It is clear that the existence of such groups must have presented the early church with a difficult problem. You could not treat the disciples of that John who had baptized Jesus (and probably some of his first followers too) as if they were the enemy; yet they were not in any full sense Christians. If they decided to become Christians, what was to be done with them? It is interesting to recall (though of course there is no historical connection) the controversy that arose two centuries later over schismatical baptism. Did the baptism of returning schismatics count, or did baptism within the church have to be administered to them? More than one view was current, and was vehemently supported.[30] So it probably was in the different but analogous circumstances of the first century. Some would say: These men have received all the baptism that Jesus himself had; if they now accept him as Lord what else is needed? Others would say: The distinctive thing in Christianity is that one is admitted to it by a baptism in the name of Jesus that conveys the gift of the Spirit; this is the only way into the church, and disciples of John must receive it as anyone else would. It seems that such a divergence in practice would account for (as it is itself suggested by) the difference between 18:24-28 and 19:1-7. It was in the Ephesian

---

[27]Εἰς τὸ 'Ιωάννου βάπτισμα is an unusual and awkward expression, but I see no reason why it should not be regarded as an abbreviation (notwithstanding Käsemann's objection ["Disciples," 137 n. 2]). The baptism they had received was John's baptism. Εἰς was a preposition familiar to Christians in relation to baptism (extended to Moses at 1 Cor 10:2). Εἰς τί; was a not unnatural question and "into John's baptism" an almost inevitable answer. Of course, it might have been clearer to write: ποῖον βάπτισμα ἐλάβετε; τὸ βάπτισμα ὃ ἐκήρυξεν ὁ 'Ιωάννης.

[28]See J. H. Hughes, "Disciples of John the Baptist: an examination of the evidence of their existence, and an estimate of their significance for the study of the Fourth Gospel" (diss., Durham University, 1969).

[29]See C. K. Barrett, "The Prologue of St John's Gospel," *New Testament Essays* (London: SPCK, 1972) 39-45.

[30]The primary source is Cyprian (*Eps.* 69-75). In *Ep.* 73.24.3 and *Ep.* 75.8.1, 2 (by Firmilian) there are references to Acts 19:1-7.

period that different Christian and near-Christian groups began to meet and to be assimilated (and, we may add, on the basis of the epistles, not of Acts, to clash). Luke insists that Paul's version of the faith was both normative and victorious.[31]

This period of confrontation could well have ended (or its first phase could have ended) before Luke wrote Acts. This is suggested by the fact that the Fourth Gospel shows relics but not the present reality of controversy with John the Baptist's followers. It does not seem that Luke understood that he was simply dealing with diverse reactions to disciples of John. In this way his handling of the material can be accounted for. Why (he must have asked himself) was Apollos not baptized when the twelve in Ephesus were? The question will not have troubled him greatly,[32] but so far as it needed an answer he would give it by making Apollos more and the twelve disciples less Christian. Apollos not only has John's baptism, he is well instructed, ζέων τῷ πνεύματι, and teaches about Jesus. The twelve have John's baptism, but they have not even heard that the Holy Spirit exists (an incredible position if John had encouraged his people to read the Old Testament).[33] All possible steps have to be taken to remedy a defect that Apollos did not have.

Like many of the problems in Acts this one is too obscure, and too ill provided with clear-cut facts, for the student to feel confident that he has arrived at a final solution. The solution propounded here, however, has a good deal to commend it, and there is little to be said against it once the notion is given up that Luke was essentially *frühkatholisch* in his outlook, committed to a rigid sacramental scheme operated by an officially recognized ministry standing in ordered succession. Luke is depicting the glories of the primitive age of Christianity, which is to serve as an example to his contemporaries, and, as an admirer of Paul, he desires to show (before the conclusion of Paul's public work in chapter 20) that Paul was not only a great evangelist but also the great

---

[31]Apollos was instructed not by Paul himself but by his colleagues Priscilla and Aquila. If Luke had been freely inventing the incident, the teaching would surely have been given by Paul. It follows that he was using tradition, however much he may have modified it.

[32]See n. 19 above.

[33]See n. 4 above.

unifying agent in the church.[34] He is not however so "ecclesiastical" a Paulinist that he is unprepared to allow Paul to be represented by his colleagues, Priscilla and Aquila. He has at his disposal traditions that belong to an earlier stage of Christian development and are already in his time at least old enough to be no longer fully understood.

---

[34]Haenchen, *Acts*, 556-57: Luke "wanted in Chapter 19 to give a total picture of the successful work of Paul. To it this narrative contributes an important feature: Paul wins over the sects."

COLOSSIENS 2:2-3*

Pierre Benoit

CETTE MODESTE contribution veut être un hommage au Professeur Bo Reicke, dont les recherches, étendues à des domaines étonnamment variés, et menées avec une érudition et une rigueur scientifique remarquables, ont apporté bien des lumières originales sur de nombreux problèmes du Nouveau Testament, du christianisme primitif, et de leur milieu.

On a pu écrire que Col 2:2 offre une "difficulté textuelle de première grandeur."[1] Les manuscrits grecs, les versions et les Pères présentent tout un arc-en-ciel de variantes, dont voici la liste, accompagnée d'une mention sommaire des principaux témoins:[2] εἰς ἐπίγνωσιν τοῦ μυστηρίου

1. τοῦ Θεοῦ D² H P 424** 436 1912 quelques mss sahidiques
2. τοῦ Χριστοῦ 81 1241 1462
3. Χριστοῦ 1739
4. τοῦ Θεοῦ Χριστοῦ P⁴⁶ B Hilaire
5. τοῦ Θεοῦ ὅ ἐστιν Χριστός D* d e Pélage Augustin Vigile de Thapse
6. τοῦ Θεοῦ (τοῦ) ἐν Χριστῷ 33 (add. τοῦ) Clem. Alex. Ambrosiaster
7. τοῦ Θεοῦ καὶ Χριστοῦ Cyrille d'Alexandrie
8. τοῦ Θεοῦ πατρὸς τοῦ Χριστοῦ S* 048 (omettent le 2ᵉ τοῦ) A C Vgʷʷ Sah Boh

---

*This manuscript was submitted on 29 March 1978.

[1]Francis W. Beare, *The Epistle to the Colossians* (*IB* 11; New York/Nashville: Abingdon, 1955) 185: "a textual difficulty of the first magnitude."

[2]Pour une énumération plus complète des témoins, voir les apparats des éditions critiques. Comparer aussi des listes commodes de Bruce M. Metzger (*The Text of the New Testament: Its Transmission, Corruption, and Restoration* [New York/London: Oxford University, 1964] 236-38) et de Eduard Lohse (*Die Briefe an die Kolosser und an Philemon*, 14th ed. [MeyerK 9/2; Göttingen: Vandenhoeck & Ruprecht, 1968] 129).

9. τοῦ Θεοῦ καὶ πατρὸς τοῦ Χριστοῦ S³ Ψ qq minuscules grecs syrhcl

10. τοῦ Θεοῦ πατρὸς καὶ τοῦ Χριστοῦ 0208 441 1908 syrpes Vg^cl Chrys. Theod. Mops

11. τοῦ Θεοῦ καὶ πατρὸς καὶ τοῦ Χριστοῦ D³ K L masse des minusc. Txt receptus.

Un premier coup d'oeil fait sentir aisément les efforts variés et croissants d'expliquer un texte original jugé obscur ou trop simple. Pour la plupart des exégètes le texte original dont tous les autres dérivent doit être le n°4. Lightfoot, par exemple, explique toutes les autres leçons par mode d'omission (1 à 3), d'interprétation (5 à 6), d'amplification (7 à 11).[3] Metzger qui tient aussi la leçon 4 pour primitive, voit dans toutes les autres leçons des essais de clarifier, ou d'éliminer, la difficile relation des deux génitifs juxtaposés θεοῦ et Χριστοῦ.[4] Leur connexion est, en effet, malaisée à entendre: (a) le Dieu (qui est) Christ? (b) le Dieu du Christ? (c) le mystère de Dieu (qui est) Christ? Un moyen simple d'éluder la difficulté aura été de supprimer l'un ou l'autre des génitifs embarrassants (leçons 1 à 3). Une autre solution fut d'expliciter leur relation dans le sens de (c) en précisant ὅ ἐστιν Χριστός, à la manière de 1:27 (leçon 5), ou encore en adoptant la fréquente formule paulinienne ἐν Χριστῷ (leçon 6). Le plus radical était de séparer nettement Χριστοῦ de θεοῦ en intercalant entre eux καί (leçon 7) ou πατρός (leçon 8), ce qui par combinaisons variées de ces deux additions a entraîné des leçons de plus en plus chargées (leçons 9 à 11).

Sans entrer si avant dans l'analyse de l'évolution du texte, la plupart des commentateurs font le même choix de τοῦ θεοῦ Χριστοῦ comme leçon originale. Ainsi Klöpper (Berlin 1882), Ewald (Leipzig 1910), Knabenbauer (Paris 1912), Masson (Neuchâtel 1950), Dibelius-Greeven (Tübingen 1953), Moule (Cambridge 1957), Bruce (Grand Rapids 1957), Mussner (Paderborn 1965), Ernst (Regensburg 1974), Conzelmann (Göttingen 1976).[5] La critique textuelle semble d'ailleurs

---

[3]J. B. Lightfoot, *Saint Paul's Epistle to the Colossians and to Philemon* (London: Macmillan, 1904) 250-51.

[4]Metzger, *Text of the New Testament*, 237.

[5]Jacques Dupont (*Gnosis: la connaissance religeuse dans les épîtres de Saint Paul* [Louvain: Nauwelaerts; Paris: J. Gabalda, 1949] 16) adopte la leçon 4 en remarquant que "les leçons ne portant qu'un seul des deux termes, 'Dieu' ou 'Christ', manquent d'autorité dans la tradition manuscrite." Cet argument de critique externe est exact,

recommander ce choix. La leçon τοῦ θεοῦ Χριστοῦ peut, en effet, se réclamer de témoins peu nombreux mais vénérables: le codex Vaticanus et Hilaire de Poitiers, du ivᵉ siècle, auxquels le papyrus Beatty P⁴⁶ vient d'ajouter son suffrage. Aussi, à part Hetzenauer et von Soden qui préfèrent la leçon 8, τοῦ θεοῦ πατρὸς τοῦ Χριστοῦ et Vogels qui adopte la leçon 11, τοῦ θεοῦ καὶ πατρὸς καὶ τοῦ Χριστοῦ, la plupart des éditions critiques modernes acceptent la leçon 4, τοῦ θεοῦ Χριστοῦ: ainsi Tischendorf, Westcott-Hort, Nestle, Souter, Merk, Bover, le Greek NT de la Bible Society.

Pourtant, s'il est un cas où la critique externe doit laisser parler la critique interne, c'est bien celui-ci. La dispersion des témoins, souvent excellents, ne permet pas dans notre cas de faire un choix fondé sur leur antiquité et leur autorité. L' "éclectisme intégral" est ici recommandé.⁶ Nous avons vu d'ailleurs Lightfoot et Metzger justifier leur choix par un examen de critique interne.

Or on peut apprécier d'autre manière l'évolution du texte. Il n'est certes pas question de vouloir réhabiliter les leçons longues, dont le caractère d'amplification est manifeste. La leçon 11, par exemple, la plus confluente de toutes, ne saurait être sauvée par la grande masse de tradition qui l'appuie: onciaux de la Koinè antiochienne, nombreux minuscules, enfin Textus receptus. L'addition facilitante de καί et de πατρός condamne les leçons 7 à 10. On ne peut davantage préconiser les leçons interprétatives 5 et 6. Si la leçon 5 était primitive, on ne voit pas comment on l'aurait abandonnée pour lui substituer une des leçons 1 à 4. Le choix à faire est certainement entre ces quatre leçons "breviores." Laquelle est plus vraisemblable et explique mieux toutes les autres? Metzger prétend que la leçon 4 est la leçon originale, parce que toutes dérivent d'elle tandis qu'elle ne peut dériver d'aucune autre. Ceci n'est pas certain et je pense qu'on peut invoquer de bons arguments en faveur de la leçon 1.

---

mais il ne saurait être dirimant. André Feuillet (*Le Christ, Sagesse de Dieu, d'après les épîtres pauliniennes* [EBib; Paris: J. Gabalda, 1966] 302) adopte aussi, "avec une certaine hésitation," la leçon 4. J'ai moi-même évolué sur ce point. Après avoir relevé avec intérêt la leçon 4 dans le Papyrus Beatty 46 ("Le codex paulinien Chester Beatty," *RB* 46 [1937] 76), je l'ai adoptée dans la première édition du fascicule de la Bible de Jérusalem consacré aux Épîtres de la captivité (1949). Mais à partir de la deuxième édition (1953), dans le fascicule et dans la Bible en un volume, je lui ai préféré la leçon 1 que je défends ici.

⁶J. K. Elliott, "Plaidoyer pour un éclectisme intégral appliqué à la critique textuelle du Nouveau Testament," *RB* 84 (1977) 5-25.

Plusieurs commentateurs l'ont déjà fait et je voudrais appuyer leur choix. Chez Oltramare (Paris 1891) ce choix est clair et décidé. Il reconnaît que la leçon τοῦ θεοῦ est "faiblement documentée"; mais, observant qu'ici "aucune leçon n'est bien documentée tant est grand le désaccord des mss., et que, par un phénomène singulier, les leçons qui le sont le mieux ne sauraient être admises," il estime qu'"on n'a pas le droit d'être exigeant sur la partie diplomatique." Abbot (Edinburgh 1897) est hésitant et reconnaît que la leçon τοῦ θεοῦ supprime toute difficulté et représente bien un premier état d'où seraient dérivés tous les autres; mais il se sent retenu de l'adopter par la date tardive de son attestation. Haupt (Göttingen 1902) est, lui aussi, embarrassé. Après avoir adopté et commenté la leçon communément reçue, avec Χριστοῦ, il reconnaît en terminant qu'elle est d'une lourdeur obscure ("etwas Schwerfälliges und Undurchsichtiges") et que tout irait mieux si l'on acceptait de considérer Χριστοῦ comme une glose marginale, inspirée par 1:27 et introduite après coup dans le texte, en surcharge à μυστηρίου τοῦ θεοῦ qui serait la leçon originale. Cette suggestion a été soutenue fortement par Lohmeyer (Göttingen 1929). Certains considérants apportés par ce dernier sont, à vrai dire, discutables: la leçon simple μυστηρίου τοῦ θεοῦ lui paraît mieux convenir à un arrangement ternaire des vv2b-3 (trois stiques de trois membres chacun), qui est selon moi fort douteux; et il admet d'autre part que les témoins qui contiennent cette bonne leçon ne le font pas par transmission directe du texte original, mais par une nouvelle et heureuse correction ("wiederum Korrektur") de la leçon déjà corrigée μυστηρίου τοῦ θεοῦ Χριστοῦ, dont elle aura retiré la glose Χριστοῦ. Quoi qu'il en soit de ces considérants discutables, Lohmeyer apporte en faveur du rejet de Χριστοῦ comme glose marginale des arguments excellents que je reprendrai plus loin. Plusieurs exégètes (Ewald, Masson, Beare, Lohse) ont refusé explicitement cette hypothèse d'une glose insérée après coup dans le texte. Je la tiens cependant pour excellente et très digne d'intérêt.[7]

Avant de justifier davantage cette option, je veux encore mentionner les critiques qui essaient de retrouver un texte original aujourd'hui

---

[7]D'après Bruce, *Colossians* (Grand Rapids, 1957), 222 n. 1 cette interprétation de Χριστοῦ comme glose fut déjà proposée par John Nelson Darby(*The New Testament: A New Translation* [London: Morrish, 1871]) et par William Kelly (*Lectures on the Epistle of Paul to the Colossians* [London: Morrish, 1869] 40).

perdu, ou qui désespèrent de pouvoir le faire. Je pense à Hort et à Beare.

Hort, dans le volume d'Introduction qui accompagne l'édition critique du Nouveau Testament publiée par lui et Westcott, postule un texte original μυστηρίου τοῦ ἐν Χριστῷ qui sera devenu μυστηρίου τοῦ θεοῦ Χριστοῦ par mauvaise lecture de ɛΝχω͞ comme θΥχΥ.[8] La leçon postulée expliquerait également la leçon 6 de notre liste μυστηρίου τοῦ θεοῦ ἐν Χριστῷ soit par addition de θεοῦ sous l'influence de la leçon 4, soit par redoublement fautif de του en θῦ. Cette conjecture ingénieuse, trop ingénieuse, suppose des confusions de lecture fort peu vraisemblables et n'a été retenue par personne.

Beare admet avec Lightfoot que la leçon 4 explique toutes les autres, mais il reconnaît la difficulté que pose la relation des deux génitifs θεοῦ et Χριστοῦ. Comme il répugne par ailleurs à ne voir qu'une glose dans la mention du Christ, qui lui paraît bien convenir à la pensée maîtresse de Colossiens, il se résigne à admettre que le texte, tel qu'il nous a été transmis, est corrompu et que nous sommes incapables de recouvrer sa teneur originale. C'est par référence explicite à ce scepticisme de Beare que Metzger formule avec prudence sa conclusion que θεοῦ Χριστοῦ "is the earliest attainable form of text preserved among the extant witnesses."[9]

Il me semble pourtant qu'on peut être moins pessimiste. C'est ce que je voudrais développer maintenant, 1) en insistant sur les difficultés qui dissuadent d'accepter la leçon 4 comme originale, 2) en montrant que l'originalité de la leçon 1 μυστηρίου τοῦ θεοῦ et l'elimination de Χριστοῦ comme glose représentent l'explication du texte qui a les meilleures chances.

1) Les exégètes discutent à l'envi sur la façon d'entendre τοῦ θεοῦ Χριστοῦ. Trois constructions sont possibles:

a) Χριστοῦ apposition à θεοῦ: le Dieu Christ. C'est ainsi que semble l'avoir entendu Hilaire de Poitiers. Il cite ainsi le texte: *in agnitionem sacramenti Dei Christi, in quo sunt*, qu'il commente: *Deus Christus sacramentum est* (*De Trin.* 9.62 [PL 10.331]). Comme le remarque Beare, une telle exégèse peut s'entendre chez un théologien qui a traversé la crise arienne; elle est impensable au premier siècle.

---

[8]Westcott and Hort, *The New Testament in the Original Greek* (London: Macmillan, 1907) 125-26 de l'Appendix, sous la signature de Hort [H.] contre Westcott [W.].

[9]Metzger, *Text of the New Testament*, 238.

"Dieu Christ" est une expression qui n'a pas de parallèle chez Paul, quoi qu'il en soit des passages discutés Rom 9:5 et Tit 2:13.

b) Χριστοῦ dépendant de θεοῦ comme un génitif d'appartenance: le Dieu du Christ (Klöpper, von Soden). La pensée n'est pas impossible. Le Christ a Dieu pour Père et pour Dieu (2 Cor 1:3; Rom 15:6; Col 1:3; Eph 1:17). Il le possède en tant qu'il le révèle, bien mieux que les Puissances célestes vers lesquelles se tournent les docteurs colossiens (Klöpper). Une telle pensée et son expression inaccoutumée seraient cependant bien obscures; on attendrait au moins τοῦ θεοῦ τοῦ Χριστοῦ.

c) Χριστοῦ apposition à μυστηρίου: le mystère de Dieu, (à savoir) le Christ. Cette construction, grammaticalement possible, serait à coup sûr la moins mauvaise. Elle a inspiré l'explicitation des variantes 5 à 6, et c'est à elle que se rallient la plupart des exégètes. Elle ne va cependant pas elle-même sans difficulté.

D'abord elle suppose entre θεοῦ et Χριστοῦ une virgule qu'introduisent les éditeurs et commentateurs modernes, mais qui n'était nullement spontanée pour le lecteur ancien. Pour faire entendre ce sens, il aurait mieux valu écrire ὅ ἐστιν Χριστός, comme l'a fait la leçon 5. Mais cette variante est évidemment une interprétation clarifiante. Si elle était primitive, on l'aurait gardée sans essayer tant d'autres lectures du texte.

Ensuite, et plus profondément, cette identification pure et simple du "mystère" avec le Christ n'est pas vraiment paulinienne. Pour Paul, le mystère tel que l'exposent les épîtres aux Colossiens et aux Ephésiens, c'est "le Christ parmi vous," c'est-à-dire le salut du Christ accordé au monde païen (Col 1:26-27; Eph 3:3-6). C'est parce qu'il prêche ce mystère, en tant qu'apôtre des païens, que Paul est enchaîné (Col. 4:3; Eph 6:19-20; cf. Col. 2:1; Act 21:27-29 l'arrestation et la captivité qui s'ensuit).

La construction de ἐν ᾧ εἰσιν πάντες soulève une autre difficulté. Certains exégètes rattachent ce relatif à Χριστοῦ (Lightfoot, Ewald, Knabenbauer): c'est dans le Christ que se trouveraient tous les trésors de la sagesse et de la connaissance, cachés. D'autres exégètes, plus nombreux, rapportent le relatif à μυστηρίου; il convient mieux assurement de trouver dans le mystère ces trésors à l'état caché. C'est là un thème connu de l'apocalyptique. Mais, outre que cette construction grammaticalement possible n'est pas la plus spontanée, le fait qu'on a identifié le mystère au Christ ramène à entendre que c'est dans le Christ, en tant que mystère, que les trésors de la sagesse et de la connaissance se trouvent cachés. La plupart des exégètes sont d'accord pour donner à εἰσιν la force d'un "verbum existentiae" et pour regarder ἀπόκρυφοι comme une détermination secondaire qui qualifie le mode d'existence: les trésors se trouvent en lui (le Christ ou le mystère), et ils y sont à l'état caché. Mais cela n'enlève rien à la difficulté, cela l'accentue au contraire, car ἀπόκρυφοι ainsi détaché n'en reçoit que plus de poids.

Est-il légitime de faire dire à Paul que les trésors de la sagesse et de la connaissance se trouvent dans le Christ-mystère à l'état caché? Ne répète-t-il pas au contraire que le plan divin de salut jadis caché dans le mystère est maintenant révélé dans le Christ (Rom 15:16; Col 1:26; Eph 3:5; cf. Rom 1:17)? L'observation très juste, faite par beaucoup, que ἀπόκρυφοι n'est pas ἀποκεκρυμμένοι ne change rien à l'affaire. On maintient malgré tout dans le Christ un trait caractéristique du mystère avant sa révélation, et c'est cela qui est étrange.[10]

On le sent, à lire les explications embarrassées que tentent les exégètes. Bien que révélés dans le Christ pour ceux qui croient, les trésors du mystère restent cachés pour ceux qui ne croient pas (Klöpper, Haupt, Masson, Mussner, Beare, Lohmeyer). Ou bien, même pour ceux qui croient et ont donc reçu la révélation dans le Christ, ils restent cachés dans la mesure où ils exigent une recherche assidue de la foi pour être pénétrés toujours davantage (Klöpper, Ewald, Knabenbauer, Huby).[11] Ou encore, on peut dire qu'ils restent cachés parce que l'eschatologie est seulement commencée (Bornkamm, *TWNT,* IV, 828). L'embarras est si manifeste que certains commentateurs ne craignent pas de paraphraser le texte en disant que les trésors du mystère sont maintenant révélés dans le Christ,[12] ce qui est vrai, mais va manifestement contre le sens de ἀπόκρυφοι.

---

[10]Cf. Beare, *Colossians*, 186: "We are bound to ask why this emphasis is laid on the 'hidden' nature of these stores of truth, when we should expect rather the affirmation that in Christ these things are *revealed*."

[11]Cette exégèse n'est fausse. Elle est la meilleure pour qui se croit obligé de maintenir Χριστοῦ dans le texte. Elle trouve un appui dans des passages tels que Eph 3:18.19.

[12]Haupt, *Gefangenschaftsbriefe*, 68: Christus "ist der Gegenstand und zugleich die Enthüllung dieses Geheimnisses"; Bruce, *Colossians*, 224: "Christ Himself is the mystery of God revealed. . . . It is in Christ that all the treasures of divine wisdom and knowledge have been stored up—stored up in hiding formerly, but now displayed to

Voir une allusion aux adversaires "gnostiques" de Colosses, qui se réclament d'une doctrine secrète qu'ils cherchent en dehors du Christ, auxquels Paul (ou l'auteur de Colossiens) répondrait que les trésors de sagesse du plan divin sont bel et bien dans le Christ d'une façon également secrète mais plénière (Lightfoot, Abbott, Moule, Beare, Bruce, Conzelmann) est une exégèse ingénieuse, qui ne s'impose d'ailleurs pas, mais qui ne résout toujours pas la difficulté. *Tous* les trésors sont dans le Christ, soit, mais ils y sont *cachés*!

Dupont,[13] qui adopte la leçon 4, explique les trésors de sagesse et de connaissance cachés dans le Christ par le thème qu'il dit paulinien du Christ substitué à la Loi. Car c'est dans la Loi que pour les Juifs se trouvent ces trésors. Il cite à juste titre Isa 33:5-6 (LXX); Bar 3:14-15 et 3:37-4:1; Sir 24:23-25; 2 *Apoc. Bar.* 44:14; 54:13-14. Mais ces trésors sont-ils "cachés" dans la Loi? Oui, peut-être, au sens qu'ils requièrent intelligence et ouverture de coeur pour être scrutés toujours plus profondément. Non, au sens où les "mystères" du plan divin ont été longtemps voilés, pour n'être révélés que dans l'ère eschatologique. La Loi a été révélée au Sinaï. Les thèmes de la Loi et du Mystère empruntent tous deux le même vocabulaire de sagesse. Cela n'autorise pas à les confondre.[14] On peut dire que le Christ se substitue à la Loi comme moyen de salut; on ne peut pas dire qu'il se substitue au Mystère. Il en est l'objet et il le fait disparaître en le révélant.

On ne saurait non plus invoquer Col 3:4 qui suppose implicitement le Christ "caché" parce que, assis à la droite de Dieu, il attend sa manifestation finale. Car cet éloignement céleste temporaire ne vient pas de ce que son mystère est encore caché. Il ne s'agit que de l'ultime expectation eschatologique (Phil 3:20; Act 3:21). Le plan de salut qu'il a réalisé, et qui est l'objet de la connaissance de sagesse dont traite Col

---

those who have come to know Christ"; Lohse, *Kolosserbrief*, 130: "Unter dem verhüllenden Schleier des Geheimnisses liegt die Gabe, die Gott durch Offenbarung den Erwählten hat zuteil werden lassen", citant *1 Hénoch* 46:3 qui va dans le même sens: "Celui-ci est le Fils de l'Homme, qui a la justice, avec qui demeure la justice, et qui révèle tous les trésors de ce qui est caché"; Ernst, *Kolosserbrief*, 190: "Christus ist der Träger aller Weisheit und Erkenntnis und der 'Ort', an dem alle Schätze des göttlichen Geheimnisses '*geborgen*', *d.h. für den Lebenden enthüllt sind*" (C'est moi qui souligne).

[13]Dupont, *Gnosis*, 16.

[14]De même la "volonté" salvifique de Dieu, objet du mystère en Eph 1:9, n'est pas à confondre avec la "volonté" divine à accomplir par une sainte conduite morale (Col 1:9). Un même terme est utilisé sur deux plans différents, apocalyptique et éthique.

2:2-3 n'a plus, lui, à être manifesté. Il l'a été par la révélation faite aux "saints" (Col 1:26), aux "apôtres et prophètes" (Eph 3:5) et il est proclamé par leur prédication.

Un recours à 1QH 5:25-26; 8:10-11 est également déconseillé.[15] Le thème du mystère caché dans le Maître de Justice méconnu et souffrant a un meilleur parallèle en 1 Cor 2:8. Paul peut dire là que le mystère de la sagesse divine était encore caché dans le Christ aux Princes de ce monde quand ils l'ont crucifié sans reconnaître en lui le Seigneur de la gloire. Il ne saurait dire cela dans le contexte de Col 2:2, où il s'agit du salut désormais accordé aux païens, mystère désormais révélé et proclamé, même aux Puissances célestes (Eph 3:10).

La solution obvie n'est-elle pas dès lors de supprimer le mot Χριστοῦ qui cause tout l'embarras et de songer seulement au "mystère de Dieu" comme tel, dans son caractère propre de secret qui demande révélation? On retrouve ainsi, en effet, la définition classique du "mystère" de l'apocalyptique: secret du plan divin qui a recélé durant de longs siècles des trésors[16] de sagesse et de connaissance et qui requiert le "plein épanouissement de l'intelligence" (πληροφορία τῆς συνέσεως) pour être maintenant pénétré dans le νῦν eschatologique, à la lumière du Christ. Eschatologie seulement commencée (Bornkamm), soit, mais par une manifestation de ce qui demeura longtemps caché et qui, aux yeux de Paul, est désormais révélé de façon décisive.

Bref, le texte s'entend mieux, il ne s'entend vraiment bien que, si l'on supprime le mot Χριστοῦ et ne retient comme objet de ce passage que le "mystère de Dieu."

---

[15]1QH 5:25-26: "Et le Mystère que tu as celé en moi, ils l'allaient calomniant près des fils des malheurs; mais c'est afin que fût exal[tée] ma [vo]ie, et à cause de leur faute, que tu as caché la source d'intelligence et le secret de vérité"; 1QH 8:10-11: "Et celui qui fait pousser le Rejeton de sa[in]teté pour la plantation de vérité est resté caché sans qu'on pense à lui, et, sans qu'il soit connu, son Mystère a été scellé." (Traduction par André Dupont-Sommer, *Les écrits esséniens découverts près de la mer Morte* [Paris: Payot, 1960] 231, 241).

[16]L'expression "trésors cachés" n'est pas spécifique de ce thème apocalyptique. Elle relève d'une image spontanée, aux applications multiples. On la trouve dans des textes bibliques qui n'ont rien d'apocalyptique (Isa 45:3; 1 Macc 1:23). Il ne s'impose donc pas de reconnaître en Col 2:3 une réminiscence de ces textes, comme le voudraient certains commentateurs. On n'a pas davantage de raisons d'y pressentir un écho d'expressions employées par les docteurs de Colosses. L'expression évoque plutôt tout simplement le vocabulaire de sagesse, repris à Qumrân (voir infra), si manifeste en ce passage; voir en particulier Prov 2:4-7. L'image de "trésor" appliquée à la "sagesse" se rencontre chez Platon, *Philèbe* 15e; Xénophon, *Mem.* 4.2.9.

2) Or Paul a fort bien pu n'écrire que μυστηρίου τοῦ θεοῦ. On en a des parallèles. A vrai dire, cette expression n'a en Col 4:3 qu'un appui très faible dans le tradition manuscrite, B L quelques minuscules, et l'on doit préférer là, avec toutes les éditions critiques et les commentaires, la leçon μυστηρίου τοῦ Χριστοῦ. Remarquons que cette leçon est très naturelle et ne saurait être invoquée en faveur de Χριστοῦ en 2:2, car la formulation et le contexte sont différents: il n'est pas dit en 4:3 que le mystère est identique au Christ mais qu'il concerne le Christ, et d'autre part il n'est pas présenté comme caché dans le Christ, bien au contraire Paul doit l'annoncer. Il en va de même pour Eph 3:5, où il est dit que ce mystère du Christ, jadis caché, vient d'être maintenant manifesté.

En revanche, la formule μυστηρίου τοῦ θεοῦ peut se recommander de 1 Cor 4:1 (οἰκονόμοι μυστηρίων θεοῦ), et surtout de 1 Cor 2:1 où la leçon μυστήριον paraît préférable à μαρτύριον. Ici la tradition manuscrite se partage d'une façon qui rend le choix difficile. Les éditions critiques, à l'exception de celle de la Bible Society (avec hésitation), adoptent μαρτύριον. Cependent la construction avec καταγγέλλειν et le contexte (v 7) recommandent de préférer μυστήριον; ainsi les commentaires de Weiss et de Lietzmann,[17] ainsi que les remarques de Strathmann et de Bornkamm.[18]

Au reste l'expression "mystère de Dieu"est tout à fait normale dans l'apocalypse juive, et bien attestée à Qumrân. Elle se rencontre là à plusieurs reprises soit sous la forme רָזֵי אֵל "les mystères de Dieu" (1QpHab 7:8; 1QS 3:23; 1QM 3:9; 16:11.16), soit sous les formes équivalentes "ses mystères" (1QM 17:9) ou "tes mystères" (1QS 11:19; 1QH 12:20; 13:2; 1Q36 9:2; 16:2; 1Q40 1:2). On sait que les doctrines que Paul affronte à Colosses ont des affinités avec celles des Esséniens et que les épîtres aux Colossiens et aux Ephésiens présentent plus d'un contact doctrinal et littéraire avec les écrits de Qumrân. Ici même on trouve comme là, en relation avec "mystère" les termes ἐπίγνωσις (השׂכיל: cf. 1QS 9:18; 11:18; 1QH 7:26.27; 11:10; 12:20; 13:13); σοφία (חכמה: cf. 1QS 4:18; 1QH 9:23); γνῶσις (דעת, דעה: cf.

---

[17]Johannes Weiss, *Der erste Korintherbrief*, 9th ed. (MeyerK 5; Göttingen: Vandenhoeck & Ruprecht, 1910) 45-46; Hans Lietzmann-W. G. Kümmel, *An die Korinther I-II*, 4th ed. (HNT 9; Tübingen: J. C. B. Mohr, 1949) 10-11.

[18]Hermann Strathmann, s.v. "μαρτύριον," *TWNT* 4 (1942) 510 n. 78; Bornkamm, s.v. "μυστήριον," *TWNT* 4 (1942) 825 n. 141.

1QS 4:6; 9:18; 11:3.6.18; 1QH 2:13; 12:13; 1QM 17:8); ἀπόκρυφος (סתר, חבה: cf. 1QS 4:6; 11:5.6; 1QH 5:25.26; 8:6.10; 9:24).

Quand on voit Χριστός s'ajouter maladroitement à ce vocabulaire essénien, on peut juger avec Kosmala qu'il est une "christianisation pas très heureuse d'une pensée qui relève primitivement d'un pur essénisme."[19]

Plutôt que d'attribuer cette christianisation maladroite à Paul lui-même, ou à son disciple-secrétaire, on songera, comme l'ont fait déjà plusieurs critiques, à la glose d'un copiste ou d'un lecteur qui, se rappelant 1:27, a cru bon de préciser que ce mystère dont parle Paul se réalise dans le Christ. Le génitif Χριστοῦ pensé comme apposition à μυστηρίου était sommaire comme toute glose, mais cela pouvait passer tant que cela restait en marge. Le malheur est que cette glose est ensuite entrée dans le texte,[20] causant tout le désarroi des manuscrits et des exégètes modernes. La solution la meilleure est assurément de la supprimer, sinon en invoquant les quelques témoins où son omission n'est peut-être que l'effet d'une correction heureuse, du moins pour les raisons de critique interne que nous avons exposées.

Je reconnais n'avoir guère apporté d'élément nouveau à une discussion déjà vieille. J'ai tâché du moins de plaider en faveur d'une solution trop généralement écartée qui, en rétablissant comme texte primitif μυστηρίου τοῦ θεοῦ, ἐν ᾧ, fait disparaître une crux exégétique gênante et inutile.

---

[19]Hans Kosmala, *Hebräer-Essener-Christen: Studien zur Vorgeschichte der frühchristlichen Verkündigung* (SPB 1; Leiden: E. J. Brill, 1959) 274: "eine nicht ganz geglückte Christianisierung eines ursprünglich rein essenischen Gedankens."

[20]Il faut admettre que cette glose et son insertion dans le texte sont très anciennes, puisqu'elles figurent déjà en p⁴⁶.

TWO UNUSUAL NOMINA DEI
IN THE SECOND VISION OF ENOCH

Matthew Black

NO SINGLE TERM for deity in the intertestamental literature is as well-known as the Ethiopic title "Lord of spirits" from the so-called *Book of the Parables of Enoch*, a section of 1 Enoch described by the author himself as "the second vision which [Enoch] saw" (*1 Enoch* 37:1).[1] At the same time, there can be no other single title for deity in Jewish tradition whose origin and significance has received so little attention from biblical scholars. It is an absolutely unique term in the literature of Judaism, found only in this part of Enoch, where it occurs no fewer than 104 times in thirty-four chapters. Moreover, it is found in all parts of the book, including those sections generally regarded as "interpolations". It was clearly the preferred and favorite divine name of the final redactor of the Second Vision.[2]

The biblical parallel usually adduced as the possible origin of the expression is Num 16:22; 27:16. In the second passage Moses appeals to "the Lord, the God of the spirits of all mankind" (NEB; יהוה אלהי הרוחות לכל בשר) to appoint his successor. This particular epithet of deity is peculiar to these two passages in the Old Testament. It is usually attributed to the advanced ideas of the priestly redactor; while Jahweh was indeed the God of Israel, He was also the God of all mankind on whom all "flesh", i.e. all human beings, depend (cf. Ps 104:29). The Hebrew expression here could certainly, formally at least—if there is no better explanation—be a biblical source of the

---

[1]See Józef Tadeusz Milik, ed., *The Books of Enoch: Aramaic Fragments of Qumran Cave 4*, with collaboration by Matthew Black (Oxford: Clarendon, 1976) 89. I find it, nevertheless, convenient still to refer to this part of Enoch as "(the Book of) the Parables."

[2]For other names of God found only in the Parables and not discussed in this article, see R. H. Charles, *The Book of Enoch: translated anew from the Editor's Text, with Introduction, Commentary, Critical Notes, and Appendices* (Oxford: Clarendon, 1912) 66.

Ethiopic title.[3] The Targums reproduce the Hebrew literally, with the exception of Neofiti which paraphrases "the God who rules over (שליט) the souls of all flesh."

The closest parallel hitherto cited occurs at 2 Macc 3:24, using an expression similar to that of Neofiti. The Seleucid tyrant Antiochus Epiphanes had dispatched his grand-vizier Heliodorus to Jerusalem to ransack the Temple treasury: "But at that very moment when he arrived with his bodyguard at the treasury, the Ruler of spirits and of all powers (ὁ τῶν πνευμάτων καὶ πάσης ἐξουσίας δυνάστης) produced a mighty apparition, so that all . . . were . . . stricken with panic at the power of God" (2 Macc 3:24, NEB). There then appeared an angelic warrior, clad in golden armor and of terrible aspect, accompanied by two young men "of surpassing strength" who struck down Heliodorus on the spot (2 Macc 3:25-27). The blows were not fatal for he appears later offering sacrifice and making lavish vows to the Lord (2 Macc 3:35).

The NEB appears to take ἐξουσίας as an abstract for something concrete, giving the word the sense of the "principalities and powers" of the New Testament. This may be arguable, but there is no doubt that we are here in the realm of supernatural powers or celestial spirits of which the mighty apparition was a visible demonstration. The divine title is here designedly selected to match the context of the story—it is the Ruler of celestial spirits and angelic agencies who was responsible for this miraculous deliverance.

The expression "Father of spirits" at Heb 12:9 is also frequently quoted in this connection. The writer of Hebrews is using the analogy of respect for earthly fathers as a reason for submitting "even more readily to our spiritual Father" (NEB; τῷ πατρὶ τῶν πνευμάτων). The context justifies the rendering of the NEB by "our spiritual Father." There do not seem to be any grounds for understanding the expression here as meaning "Father of celestial spirits,"[4] as at 2 Macc 3:24. The meaning of "spirits" in this context is much the same as at Num 16:22, 27:16, i.e., all men as "spiritual beings." It seems unlikely that the expression in Hebrews has anything to do with the origin of the "Lord of spirits."

---

[3]See Félix Marie Abel, *Les Livres des Maccabées* (EBib; Paris: Gabalda, 1949) 324.

[4]Abel, *Maccabées*, 324: "esprits célestes."

In the Qumran scrolls רוח 'spirit' is used of disembodied spirits, angels, and at 1QH 10:8 God is said to be "Lord of every spirit" (אדון לכול רוח). In discussing this usage, with particular reference to the angelology of the War Scroll, Yadin adds: "A title of God, frequently found in the Apocrypha and Pseudepigrapha, is 'Lord of spirits'."[5] As we have noted, the title is, in fact, confined to the Parables of Enoch, unless we include 2 Macc 3:24 as an example. But the implied suggestion of Yadin that 'spirits' in this title in the Parables is a term for disembodied spirits, angelic beings, points the way to the probable origin of this enigmatic title for deity. It should be pointed out, however, that the idea that 'spirits' in this title referred to angels is not new; it was made by August Dillmann more than a hundred years ago.[6]

It seems on the whole very unlikely that the Ethiopic translator of the Parables would invent for himself an entirely new name for God, especially since everyone agrees he is translating traditional Jewish (or Jewish-Christian) sources. Moreover, when we find again in the scrolls references to the "hosts of His spirits" (צבא רוחין) parallel to "hosts of angels" (צבא מלאכים; 1QM 12:8-9), the possibility emerges that "Lord of Spirits" is, in fact, something like an "interpretative transformation" (in a phrase of Streeter)[7] of the traditional, and indeed probably the most popular, title in the Old Testament, "Lord of hosts." This hypothesis becomes increasingly attractive, and indeed receives virtual confirmation when we find the *trisagion* from Isa 6:3 quoted at *1 Enoch* 39:12 in the following form:

> The vigilant ones [i.e., the Watchers] bless Thee,
> They stand before thy Glory, saying:
> Holy, Holy, Holy, is the Lord of spirits:
> He filleth the earth with spirits.

The motivation for this interpreted version of the traditional title "Lord of hosts" is evident from the last sentence. The world of the author of the Parables, like that of the Qumran Essenes, was one full of

---

[5]Yigael Yadin, *The Scroll of the War of the Sons of Light against the Sons of Darkness: Edited with Commentary and Introduction* (Oxford: Blackwell, 1962) 231.

[6]August Dillmann, *Lexicon Linguae Aethiopicae cum Indice Latino* (Lipsiae: T. O. Weigel, 1865) 709.

[7]B. H. Streeter, *The Four Gospels: A Study of Origins* (London: Macmillan, 1951) 372.

angelic beings and disembodied spirits. This permutation on the traditional title has been dictated by the theology of the circles from which
this book ultimately came. The primary purpose of the Parables is to
speak to the circumstances and condition of people living, often suffering and dying, in a world whose evil human environment—Gentile
oppressors, rich exploiters, the wicked and the hostile—were parts and
expressions only of that larger cosmic environment filled, at times
infested, but certainly dominated by celestial as well as terrestrial (and
sub-terrestrial) "spirits." Thus at *1 Enoch* 41:8 we are told that the Lord
who has divided the light from the darkness has also divided the spirits
of man, establishing the spirits of the righteous. These words might
have been written by the author of the doctrine of the two spirits at 1QS
3:13-26.

The interpretation was certainly one which could readily be made,
in view of the cosmic use of the title "Lord of hosts" in the Hebrew
prophets, and the identification of the "hosts of heaven" not only with
the heavenly bodies, stars, planets and constellations (cf. 1 Kgs 22:19),
but also with angelic beings (themselves identified with stellar phenomena; cf. Ps 103:21, Luke 2:13).[8] Probably the earliest example of this
translation by interpretation is the LXX's κύριος τῶν δυνάμεων 'the
Lord of (celestial) powers' (e.g. 3 Kgdms 17:1; 18:15, Ps 42:12; elsewhere LXX transcribes σαβ(β)αώθ or translates by κύριος παντο-
κράτωρ). The LXX is followed by the Peshitta and the Ethiopic: (e.g.
ܡܳܪܶܐ ܚܰܝܠܳܐ [Jer 25:28,32, 26:18]; *'egzī'a hayālān* [Jer 11:17,
16:9]). The meaning is unquestionably angelic powers and agencies or,
again, abstract for concrete, the angelic beings themselves.

Was this interpreted version of the traditional "Lord of hosts" the
creation of the Ethiopic translator of the Parables or was it already
present, in some form, in his *Vorlage*? It may be felt that, since there
does not appear to be any trace elsewhere of 'spirit' (רוח, πνεῦμα) in
this name, its appearance in the Parables is simply a singularity of the
Ethiopic translator. What original expression he was thus interpreting

[8]For modern views of the origin and meaning of the name, see Otto Eissfeldt,
"Jahweh Zebaoth," *Miscellanea academica berolinensia. Gesammelte Abhandlungen
zur Feier des 250 jährigen Bestehens der deutschen Akademie der Wissenschaften zu
Berlin*, 2 vols. (Berlin: Akademie, 1950), 2:128-50; Gerhard von Rad, *Old Testament
Theology*, vol. 1: *The Theology of Israel's Historical Traditions* (New York: Harper &
Row, 1962) 18-19.

will depend on the view taken of the original language of the *Vorlage* or *Grundschrift*.[9] If the original was in Hebrew and read simply the traditional title, יהוה צבאות, the Ge'ez version being interpretation, should we not then render by "Lord of hosts" and explain in a note the unusual and singular "Lord of spirits"? Or did a Hebrew *Grundschrift* actually read אדון (ל) רוחות, not unparalleled in view of 1 QH 10:8? A corresponding Aramaic would be מדה חילותא / רוחות, and could have been transmitted to the Ethiopic translator—the usual explanation of his tertiary version—by way of a Greek κύριος τῶν δυνάμεων or κύριος τῶν πνευμάτων.[10] 2 Macc 3:24 may be held to support this last alternative, for the expression there, ὁ τῶν πνευμάτων καὶ πάσης ἐξουσίας δυνάστης, has all the appearance of being a similar interpretative paraphrase *in Greek* of the traditional יהוה צבאות, a cultic term no doubt familiar to Greek as well as to Hebrew ears. It also has precisely the same meaning as the Ethiopic title.

In view of the fact that the title "Lord of spirits" is so central to the main theological orientation of the Parables, I would suggest that ultimately in the original Hebrew *Grundschrift* it was the classical Hebrew expression which was employed, but that the Ethiopic *nomen dei* comes from a Greek κύριος τῶν πνευμάτων.

The second epithet occurs in the first Son of Man apocalypse, in a passage which reads almost like a midrash on Dan 7:13:

> "And there I saw *One who had a head of days*,
> And His head was white like wool" (*1 Enoch* 46:1).

It is generally agreed that the Ethiopic expression re'ĕsa mawā'el corresponds to Daniel's 'Ancient of Days' (Dan 7:9 עתיק יומין), but different explanations have been offered of its origin and meaning. Dillmann took the first noun in the expression at 46:1 in its literal sense

---

[9]See Matthew Black, "The Composition, Character and Date of the 'Second Vision of Enoch,' " *Text-Wort-Glaube: Studien zur Ueberlieferung, Interpretation und Autorisierung biblischer Texte, Kurt Aland gewidmet*, ed. Martin Brecht (Arbeiten zur Kirchengeschichte 50; Berlin: Walter de Gruyter, 1980) 19-30.

[10]Constantine Tischendorf (*Novum Testamentum Graece*, 2 vols. [Lipsiae: Giesecke & Devrient, 1872; repr. Graz: Akademische, 1965], 2:583) cites Tertullian for reading at 2 Cor 3:18 *tanquam a domino inquit, spiritum* for καθάπερ ἀπὸ κυρίου πνεύματος. Hermann Freiherr von Soden (*Die Schriften des Neuen Testaments in ihrer ältesten erreichbaren Textgestalt hergestellt auf Grund ihrer Textgeschichte*, vol. 2: *Text und Apparat* [Göttingen: Vandenhoeck & Ruprecht, 1913] 732) attributes the reading to Marcion.

of "head" and paraphrased "betagtes Haupt," which is, for this reason, then described as "white like wool."[11] The expression then becomes a *nomen dei* and appears as such at 47:3; 48:2; 55:1; 60:2; 71:10,12,13. Charles took the whole expression to mean "the sum of days" but always translated "Head of Days."[12]

At 46:2; 47:3 Ethiopic scribes altered the first noun to "ancient" (beluya) and read as in the Ethiopic version of Dan 7:9, "Ancient of Days" (beluya mawā'el); 46:2 Eth^ry12, 47:3 Eth^ull).[13] All this in fact means is that these scribes correctly recognized the title as equivalent to the Danielic "Ancient of Days" and not that the original reading has been preserved in these two manuscripts of the traditional text (Eth^ry12 corrects to the familiar re'ĕsa mawā'el).

The title in Dan 7:9 is rendered in both LXX and Theodotion by the literal equivalent παλαιὸς ἡμερῶν 'old of days', but this is not the only possible rendering. As Montgomery pointed out, the expression appears fairly often in Syriac literature, meaning simply "old man," e.g., Wisdom 2:10 (LXX πρεσβύτης). The regular Greek equivalent of ܣܒ is ἀρχαῖος, so that an alternative rendering of עתיק יומין would be ὁ ἀρχαῖος ἡμερῶν. This seems to supply the most likely translational basis for the Ethiopic expression, where, however, an original ὁ ἀρχαῖος has been altered to ἡ ἀρχή under the influence of biblical passages such as Isa 41:4; Rev 21:6; 22:13 (ἐγώ εἰμι ... ἡ ἀρχὴ καὶ τὸ τέλος). In this case we almost certainly have to do with a translational coinage which has been arrived at by way of interpretation of a Greek or Hebrew/Aramaic original.

As Dillmann noted, the title occurs only in the second part of the Parables (from 46:1-60:2) and in the concluding chapter (71:10,12,13). It is relatively infrequent, compared with the more regular 'Lord of Spirits' and appropriately appears in visions inspired by Daniel 7. There is no known Hebrew equivalent of the title so that we have to consider the possibility that the *Grundschrift* for these later passages in the Parables was composed in Aramaic.

---

[11]August Dillmann, *Das Buch Henoch* (Leipzig: F. C. W. Vogel, 1853) 156.

[12]Charles, *Enoch*, 85.

[13]See Michael A. Knibb, *The Ethiopic Book of Enoch: A New Edition in the Light of the Aramaic Dead Sea Fragments*, I: *Text and Apparatus* (Oxford: Clarendon, 1978), 1:128-32.

In some of the passages where the title is used, just as at *1 Enoch* 46:1, the emphasis is on the thought of the One who is ancient, primordial, at the beginning of all time, eternal:

> "And at that hour that Son of Man was appointed in
>   the presence of the Lord of Spirits,
> And his name announced before the Head of Days,
> Even before the sun and signs were created,
> Before the stars of heaven were made" (*1 Enoch* 48:2-3).

In other passages the accent is on His majesty as the Chief, the First of Days:

> "And in those days I saw the Head of Days seated
>   on His glorious Throne,
> And the Books of the living were opened before Him,
> And His heavenly host above, around Him, were standing
>   before Him" (*1 Enoch* 47:3; cf. 60:2).

Dillmann, again, rightly calls attention to the consistent way in which the author, all through this section of the book, as in the rest of *1 Enoch*, employs the divine names in the closest connection with their context.[14]

---

[14]Dillmann, *Das Buch Henoch*, 156.

"CALLED TO FREEDOM":
A STUDY IN GALATIANS

F. F. Bruce

"YOU WERE CALLED to freedom, brethren," says Paul to the Christians of Galatia (5:13); he expresses his earnest desire that they should enjoy this freedom and not give it up for a legalistic way of faith and life, and, on the other hand, that they should not abuse this freedom and let it degenerate into libertinism.

1. Freedom from Law

Paul knew that his converts were called to freedom, because he had experienced the same call to freedom himself on the Damascus road. The gospel meant for him liberation. He rejoiced in his liberation; there never lived a more completely liberated Christian than Paul. Had he been asked from what he had been liberated, he probably would have said, "From law." He might have added "From sin, and death"—but liberation from sin and death was a corollary of liberation from law. This was what he experienced in the call to freedom and what he apprehended in it, when Torah was displaced from the central position which it had occupied in his being and thinking up to that moment, to be replaced immediately by the risen and glorified Christ.

Yet, until that moment he probably had no sense of bondage. Life under the law was congenial; in fact, the law was his life. If he spoke of the "yoke" of the law, it was a yoke which he wore gladly and proudly, not one under which he groaned and from which he longed to be released.

It is well known that pious Jews in general did not consider the yoke of the law to be a burden. Peter indeed is recorded as referring at the Council of Jerusalem to "a yoke which neither our fathers nor we have been able to bear" (Acts 15:10). But Peter, for all his early scruples about eating "unclean" food or entering a Gentile house, was essentially one of the (עם הארץ) " people of the land. " He could recognize forbidden flesh when he was invited to eat it, and for him it went without saying that a Jew should not accept hospitality from a Gentile.

However, a Galilean fisherman had little time or, possibly, inclination to master the finer points of the oral law, so by Hillel's definition he could not be really pious.[1] But we have ample evidence of those who did master the finer points and found the business of observing them no unwelcome task but an exhilarating delight.

The dicta usually adduced to establish this come from later generations than Paul. Nehunya ben Qanah, for example, a contemporary of Aqiba, said, "He who takes on himself the yoke of the law will be relieved of the yoke of the kingdom and the yoke of worldly care"[2]— which is as much as to say that the theological student is relieved of the responsibilities of public administration and commercial activity. Those who wish to follow these ways of life are welcome to do so, provided the student can devote himself to what is nearest to his heart; and what is nearest to his heart is not felt to be a burden. Similarly Joshua ben Levi, a century and a half later, can say, "You will find no free man but the one who occupies himself with the study of the law."[3] This is another way of saying, with Philo, that "every good man is free"; in fact, it perpetuates the tradition of the *hasidh* to whom we owe Psalm 119. He finds nothing burdensome in the law to which he yields such complete heart-devotion; if it is his "meditation all the day" (v 97), that is because he loves it so. Not only is it a lamp to his feet and a light to his path, it is a source of inexhaustible enjoyment (v 103): "How sweet are thy words to my taste, sweeter than honey to my mouth!" Freedom, not bondage, is what it brings to him (v 45): "And I shall walk at liberty for I have sought thy precepts." And far from finding that the commandment which promised life proved to be death to him, he found its promise abundantly fulfilled (v 93): "I will never forget thy precepts; for by them thou hast given me life."

So long as Paul lived under the law, those sentiments were his. It was in the light of his Damascus-road experience that he made the negative assessment of the law which finds repeated expression in his writings. While he lived under it, he recognized in it the way to life; he acknowledged it as holy and just and good. After his conversion, he continued to acknowledge it as "holy and just and good" (Rom 7:12). How could he do otherwise? It was God's law. He continued similarly

---

[1] *Pirqe 'Abot* 2:6.

[2] *Pirqe 'Abot* 3:6.

[3] *Pirqe 'Abot* 6:2.

to recognize in it "the very commandment which promised life"(Rom 7:10). Again, how could he do otherwise? In his eyes it was still the word of God which said, "You shall . . . keep my statutes and my ordinances, by doing which a man shall live" (Lev 18:5).

Yet Paul the Christian found that this holy law which promised life to the one who kept it had turned out in practice to be a "law of sin and death" (Rom 8:2). It was, he conceded, through no defect of its own that it did not fulfill the promise of life which it held out. If it was unable to impart life, that was because of the unsatisfactory human material with which it had to operate; it was "weakened by the flesh" (Rom 8:3). The law which promised life proved to be the law of death, because it pronounced a sentence of death upon the lawbreaker. Worse than that, the holy law proved to be a law of sin, because it stimulated the very thing it forbade. Paul illustrated this principle by describing how the commandment, "Thou shalt not covet," produces "all kinds of covetousness" when sin misuses the commandment to establish a beachhead in human life (Rom 7:7-8). "Through the law," he says, "comes knowledge of sin" (Rom 3:20)—not merely in the sense that it teaches us objectively what sin is but in the sense that it imparts personal consciousness of sin. Worst of all, in Paul's own experience it actively incited him to sin. It was his devotion to the law that made him such a zealous persecutor of the followers of Christ. True, his Damascus-road confrontation with the risen Christ revealed to him how exceedingly sinful this persecuting course of his had been. Yet the law did nothing to guard him against this sin of sins or to show him its real character. On the contrary, it was the law that incited him to engage in it.

It was his conversion, then, that opened his eyes to the inadequacy of the law; it was his experience of the liberating power of Christ that opened his eyes to the bondage of the law. Henceforth, as Paul looked back on his earlier life, he viewed it not only as life under law but as life under the power of sin, life after the "flesh"—the "flesh" being, in Paul's distinctive usage, the old unregenerate, unliberated self. The antithesis to that life was the life which he subsequently lived—life in Christ, life in the Spirit, a life of liberty, a life of holiness, in which it was possible to do the will of God spontaneously from the heart, not by painstaking conformity to an external law-code.

But in the days when Paul lived under the law, would he not have claimed that he was doing the will of God spontaneously and joyfully?

Probably he would. It was in the light of the difference that Christ had made in his heart that he looked back on life under the law as a life of bondage.

His Gentile converts had not lived under the Jewish law, except insofar as some of them had tried to regulate their lives by it as Godfearers. They had lived under another form of bondage, enslaved to pagan superstitions and pagan vices. But the gospel which liberated Paul from his form of bondage liberated them from theirs. They had seen Jesus "publicly portrayed as crucified" (Gal 3:1) in the preaching of the gospel; they had been justified by faith in him, and through that same faith they had received the Spirit.

Now news is suddenly brought to Paul that his converts in the churches of Galatia are being urged to add some elements of legal obligation to their faith in Christ, and he reacts violently. This so-called adding of legal obligations to the gospel which they had accepted is no mere "adding"; it is a subversion of that gospel, a different message altogether, one which offers them bondage in exchange for their surrender of the freedom to which Christ had liberated them.

It may be (though this is very doubtful) that Paul had been brought up in a school of thought which expected the age of law to be set aside when the Messiah inaugurated his new age. "If the 'Days of the Messiah' have commenced, those of the Torah came to their close. On the other hand, if the Law, the Torah, still retained its validity, it was proclaimed thereby that the Messiah has not yet appeared."[4] On this showing, if the agitators in the churches of Galatia were declaring or implying that the Torah retained its validity, it followed that the Messiah had not come and that Jesus therefore was not the Messiah. No wonder, then, that Paul anathematized the preachers of such a message! But it is not necessary to suppose that Paul had believed before his conversion that the age of the Messiah would put an end to the reign of Law. The logic of his conversion experience taught him that Christ was "the end of the law, [so] that every one who has faith may be justified" (Rom 10:4). Such propaganda as was being intro-duced among the Galatian believers therefore denied the work of Christ and in effect cast doubt on Jesus' claim to be the Messiah. Whoever might spread such propaganda, says Paul, ἀνάθεμα ἔστω.

---

[4]Leo Baeck, "The Faith of Paul," *JJS* 3 (1952) 93-110, esp. 106.

2. Freedom from the Στοιχεῖα

Paul's experience of the law was exceptional. This helps to explain the difficulty that many Jewish expositors have had in coming to terms with him. Even among fellow disciples of Jesus there were probably few of Jewish birth who appreciated a sense of liberation from legal bondage in quite the way that Paul did. Still less could his converts from paganism enter into his experience. The gospel had certainly brought them liberation from many things, but not liberation from the Jewish law. Yet Paul writes to his Galatian converts as though the legal obligations which they were being encouraged to assume belonged to the same order as their former way of life. Since Christ had set them free, they should not "submit *again* to a yoke of slavery" (Gal 5:1). Indeed, this need not imply that the new yoke was identical with the yoke which they had formerly worn; but something like that is what Paul does imply when he chides them for being disposed to "turn *back* again to the weak and beggarly στοιχεῖα, whose slaves you want to be *once more*" (Gal 4:9). Whatever those στοιχεῖα were, they were forces which operated both through the Jewish law and through pagan religion.[5]

Paul appears to associate himself with the Galatian Christians when he says, "when we were children [before we came of age through the gospel], we were slaves to the στοιχεῖα of the universe" (Gal 4:3). The "we" seems to be inclusive. But what features could Jewish monotheism and pagan polytheism have in common? For those Galatians had been polytheists: "when you did not know God, you were in bondage to [those] beings that by nature are no gods" (Gal 4:8). And in placing themselves under the yoke of the στοιχεῖα, they would in effect be reverting to the service of "beings that by nature are no gods."

The aspect of the new bondage to the στοιχεῖα that Paul goes on to mention immediately (4:10) is the observance of a sacred calendar: "You observe days, and months, and seasons, and years!" So serious a matter in his eyes was this observance that he remarks, "I am afraid I have laboured over you in vain" (Gal 4:11). It is a later and more mature Paul who makes allowances for differences of conviction and

---

[5]According to Bo Reicke ("The Law and the World according to Paul: Some thoughts concerning Gal. 4:1-11," *JBL* 70 [1951] 259-76, esp. 261-63) the ardent observance of the law made the Galatians slaves to the στοιχεῖα τοῦ κόσμου.

practice in the matter of observing special days: "Let every one be fully convinced in his own mind" (Rom 14:5). He uses no such language to the Galatians. But perhaps he made allowances for Christians who had been brought up as Jews and were not disposed to abandon their sacred calendar. He himself frequently regulated his apostolic schedule by the Jewish festivals and fasts, but he did so voluntarily, not as a matter of religious obligation. It was a different situation when Gentile Christians, who had not been brought up to observe the Jewish calendar, were now beginning to regard its observance as a religious duty.

In what respect, however, was their observance of the Jewish calendar a reversion to the service of the στοιχεῖα? Paul's language about the calendar is reminiscent of Gen 1:14, where the heavenly luminaries are created to be "for signs and for seasons and for days and years." The "days, and months, and seasons, and years" which the Galatians were observing were regulated by the heavenly luminaries. But pagan cults also had their sacred calendars, which were similarly regulated by the heavenly luminaries. The new sacred calendar which the Galatians were accepting was not the same as what they had previously followed, but the principle behind all sacred calendars was the same. For a former Pharisee, to whom the Jewish calendar commemorated the epochs in God's dealings with his people Israel, this was a radical reappraisal indeed.

A less remote antecedent for the association of the luminaries with the sacred calendar is provided in the book of Daniel. "Some of the host of the stars," the little horn of Dan 8:10 "cast down to the ground, and trampled on them." This language, which may reproduce ancient imagery, expresses what is said more prosaically of the little horn of Dan 7:25, who planned "to change the times and the law." The reference is to Antiochus Epiphanes's interference with the religious law of Israel, of which the sacred calendar was an integral part.

Are the στοιχεῖα of Gal 4:3,9, then, the heavenly luminaries in a semipersonified aspect? Are they the angels through whom, according to Gal 3:19 (cf. Acts 7:53; Heb 2:2), the law was promulgated? Little can be built on this passing reference to angels, and it would be precarious to identify them either with the στοιχεῖα or with the heavenly luminaries. One might make this identification more confidently when dealing with the στοιχεῖα of Col 2:8,20; but the treatment of the στοιχεῖα in Colossians is a development from that in Galatians and should not be incautiously used in the interpretation of the earlier epistle. It is perhaps best to say that Paul designed the phrase τὰ στοιχεῖα τοῦ κοσμοῦ (4:3) to denote those forces which kept the souls of men and women in bondage, whether they used the Jewish law or pagan convention as their instruments in doing so.[6] So long as men and women submitted to them, they were powerful; in relation to those who had been liberated by Christ they were "weak and beggarly"(4:9). They could exercise no power over his people unless they deliberately and foolishly accepted their yoke all over again.

A certain validity appears to be conceded to the στοιχεῖα at one stage in the spiritual growth of mankind, at least where they exercised their domination by means of the Jewish law. As children must be under guardians or tutors until they come of age, so the people of God had to be kept in the leading strings of the law until they attained spiritual maturity. Spiritual maturity, however, came through faith-union with Christ. Until then the law served as a παιδαγωγός, 'slave-attendant' (3:24), but its tutelage was no longer required with the coming of new life in Christ. Like children who have reached their majority, the people of Christ have received their freedom and must learn to use their freedom responsibly. The responsible freedom is received and enjoyed through the indwelling Spirit, who enables them to realize their status as full-fledged sons and daughters of God. No one was ever more truly free than Jesus, the archetypal Son of God. That the Spirit imparted to his people is the Spirit who rested on him is shown clearly when they address God with the same invocation "Abba" as he used (Gal 4:6; Rom 8:15-16; cf. Mark 14:36).

3. Freedom from Apostolic Dictation?

Contrary to popular opinion, Paul did not impose a new law on his converts in the form of his own apostolic authority. He appeals to his authority much more readily in warning interlopers off the mission field which has been allotted to him by the Lord than in teaching his converts the way of Christ more perfectly. Just as his example was to be followed insofar as he followed Christ, so the authority with which he teaches does not belong to him personally; his authority is the authority of the Lord who has commissioned him. If ever he should prove

[6]Cf. Reicke, "Law," 261-63.

untrue to that commission, he would lose the authority forthwith.

Thus, when he invokes an anathema on anyone who brings a different gospel from that which the Galatian churches first received, he envisages (theoretically, at least) the possibility that he himself might be the preacher of that new message. No matter, should such a thing happen, his friends must not reckon Paul's second thoughts to be wiser. They must not argue, "Paul is our apostle; if he has changed his mind, let us change ours accordingly." Far from it, "even if we, or an angel from heaven, should preach to you a gospel contrary to that which we preached to you, let him be accursed" (Gal 1:8). It is the true message that is supremely authoritative; the messenger is vested with authority only so long as he remains faithful to the message. The gospel is not to be accepted as true because Paul proclaims it. Paul is to be accepted as the messenger of Christ so long as he proclaims Christ's gospel.[7]

What applies to the gospel as they first received it applies to the implications of the gospel in their continuing church life. Paul has no thought of imposing his own judgments on them as a new kind of law. It would defeat his central purpose if they got the idea that they should accept a set of Pauline commandments in preference to the Mosaic commandments. Even with the Corinthians, whose besetting tendency led much more in the direction of libertinism than of legalism, he did not wish to take this line. At times it may appear that he was doing so, but it is plain that he invited them to agree that the way he recommended was the right way: "I speak as to sensible men; judge for yourselves what I say" (1 Cor 10:15; cf. 11:13).

But what if, in following Paul's earnest warning not to lapse into legalism, his converts erred in the opposite direction? If the temptation to let liberty degenerate into license was not to be curbed by law, how could it be curbed? Paul was well aware that this temptation posed a threat, and he puts the Galatian Christians on their guard against it. "You were called to freedom, brethren; only do not use your freedom as an opportunity for the flesh" (Gal 5:13)—that is, do not use it to gratify the propensities of unregenerate human nature. But if such a

---

[7]Cf. Hans von Campenhausen, *Ecclesiastical Authority and Spiritual Power in the Church of the First Three Centuries* (London: Adam and Charles Black, 1969) 43-54; R. P. C. Hanson, *Groundwork for Unity* (London: SPCK, 1971) 23-24.

temptation is not to be curbed by law, what will hold it in check? This, says Paul, "walk by the Spirit, and do not gratify the desires of the flesh" (Gal 5:16).

It appears that the particular manifestation of the "flesh" against which the Galatians needed to be warned at this time was internal animosity, an animosity, perhaps, arising from the assertion of conflicting dogmatisms. "If you bite and devour one another take heed that you are not consumed by one another" (Gal 5:15). But the fruit of the Spirit is, in the first instance, love (Gal 5:22); therefore, "do not use your freedom as an opportunity for the flesh, but through love be servants [sc. slaves] of one another," δουλεύετε ἀλλήλοις (Gal 5:13). So, there is at least one form of δουλεία that is not incompatible with Christian freedom. As Paul himself is the δοῦλος of Christ (Gal 1:10), so his converts should be δοῦλοι of one another. But this is a completely different form of slavery from that against which he otherwise warns them. It is as though he said, "If you must live in slavery, here is a form of slavery in which you may safely indulge—the slavery of practical love one to another." We could similarly imagine him as saying, "If you must live under law, live under the law of love—that is to say, the law of Christ." One example of this law is commanded in Gal 6:2, "Bear one another's burdens, and so fulfil the law of Christ." To bear burdens *for another* was a common form of slavery or forced labor, like the instance to which reference is made in the Sermon on the Mount (Matt 5:41); but to bear burdens *for one another* is a different matter entirely. It falls under the comprehensive commandment of Lev 19:18 which Paul, following Jesus' precedent (Mark 12:31), quotes as fulfilling the whole law in one word, "You shall love your neighbour as yourself" (Gal 5:14; cf. Rom 13:9).

This commandment is cast in the same form as the other ordinances (דְּבָרִים) of the Pentateuchal law, but in content it belongs to a different class. Love is not the kind of activity that can be externally constrained; it is generated from within by the Spirit. "If you are led by the Spirit you are not under the law" (Gal 5:18). Life in the Spirit is the counteractive power both to life under law and to life after the flesh. But Christ's law of love has nothing to do with either of these forms of existence. (In Paul's experience, they were together one form of existence.) On the contrary, to practice the law of love is the outward and visible sign of the indwelling Spirit; it is the very expression of Christian liberty.

4. Freedom from Discrimination

Freedom from law carried with it freedom from various forms of discrimination which were bound up with the law. The law of Moses naturally discriminated between those who were under it (the people of Israel) and those who were not (the Gentiles). According to Paul, in the gospel this discrimination was abolished. Twice in the Epistle to the Romans he emphasizes that "there is no distinction" between Jew and Gentile—once in respect to humankind's universal sinfulness (3:22-23) and once in respect to God's universal grace (10:12).

It is not easy to determine how early is the order of Jewish morning prayer which includes the three benedictions: "Blessed be thou, O LORD our God, King of the universe, who hast not made me a Gentile. Blessed be thou, O LORD our God, king of the universe, who hast not made me a slave. Blessed be thou, O LORD our God, who hast not made me a woman."[8] Certainly one could well believe that Paul was familiar with these benedictions from the particularity with which he affirms that in the gospel these three areas of religious privilege, *in that order*, have been superseded: "There is neither Jew nor Greek, there is neither slave nor free, there is neither male and female; for you are all one in Christ Jesus" (Gal 3:28).[9] Under the law, as Paul knew it, it was a positive advantage, and something for which to thank God, to be a Jew and not a Gentile, a free man and not a slave, a man and not a woman. (One incidental objection to retaining circumcision as a religious obligation could have been that it implied a distinction between male and female in their status before God.) But in the new law-free order inaugurated by Christ these distinctions, so important in the old order, were irrelevant to one's relationship with God. They were caught up into the all-embracing unity "in Christ Jesus."

The call to freedom, then, is a call to oneness in Christ and a call to loving service within the Christian community. The liberty of the gospel is not to be exercised in isolated independence. The Christian

---

[8]The earliest rabbinical attestation of this threefold benediction is in *t. Ber.* 7.18, where it is commended and expounded by Judah ben El'ai (c. A.D. 150).

[9]This passage, according to R. Scroggs (*IDB Sup*, 966), "is almost surely a fragment of an early baptismal formula."

does not emulate the self-sufficiency of the Stoic *in se ipso totus teres atque rotundus* (Horace, *Sat*. 2.7.86). His sufficiency is in Christ, and he is involved in the interdependent fellowship of the people of Christ.

It is a pleasure to pay this tribute to Professor Bo Reicke, whom I have known and esteemed for over thirty years as a friend and colleague. He has exemplified, in this interdependent fellowship, "the glorious liberty of the children of God." May he long continue to do so, to the increasing enrichment of many!

SON BY APPOINTMENT

G. B. Caird

TWENTY-FIVE years ago Professor Bo Reicke contributed one of the seven essays in *The Root of the Vine*,[1] for which Hebert claimed in the introduction that they exemplified a new style of typological exegesis. "The effort of the exegete is to avoid the ever-present danger of reading meanings of his own into the text, and to gain insight and understanding to discern aright the meanings which the Biblical writers put there."[2] This principle seems to me to have been characteristic of Professor Reicke's work both before and since the publication of that book, for he has consistently demonstrated the first rule of scholarship: to start from the ascertainable and to allow that to determine the exegesis of the problematical. In tribute and emulation I propose to offer a brief study of Christology in the Epistle to the Hebrews. When theologians are fighting again the Christological battles which led to the uneasy truce of Chalcedon,[3] it is time for New Testament scholars to ask themselves whether they have yet done enough to ensure that Scripture is allowed to speak with its own voice, whether they have not too lightly permitted or even encouraged the contestants on both sides of the debate to impose their preconceptions upon the texts which they profess to expound.

---

[1]Bo Reicke, "A Synopsis of Early Christian Preaching," *The Root of the Vine: Essays in Biblical Theology*, ed. Anton Johnson Fridrichsen and other members of the Uppsala University. Introduction by A. G. Hebert (Westminster, London: Dacre; New York: Philosophical Library, 1953) 128-60.

[2]A. G. Hebert, "Introduction," *The Root of the Vine: Essays in Biblical Theology* (Westminster, London: Dacre, 1953) vi.

[3]See, for example, Hans Küng, *Um Nichts als die Wahrheit: Deutsche Bischofs-konferenz contra Hans Küng, eine Dokumentation*, ed. W. Jens (München: Piper, 1978); Walter Kasper, *Jesus the Christ* (New York: Paulist; London: Burns & Oates, 1976); John Hick, ed., *The Myth of God Incarnate* (London: SCM; Philadelphia: Westminster, 1977); and Michael Green, ed., *The Truth of God Incarnate* (London: Hodder & Stoughton; Grand Rapids, Michigan: Wm. B. Eerdmans, 1977).

One of the unquestioned assumptions of Christological debate is that certain New Testament writers (Paul, the author of Hebrews and the Fourth Evangelist at least) came, whether by the development of ideas inherent in the primitive tradition or by the accretion of ideas alien to it, to believe in the "preexistence" of Christ; and the vast majority of those who use this term further assume that it is self-explanatory. The literature contains many discussions of the origin of the concept, very few analyses of its meaning. Yet what do we suppose we mean when we speak of Christ as preexistent, and in what sense may we justifiably attribute such notions to the biblical writers?[4]

The case for a belief in the preexistence of Christ in Hebrews rests mainly on the opening sentence, with some support from the catena of quotations which immediately follows. It runs somewhat like this: the epistle opens with a reference to the eternal Son of God, to his place in God's eternal plan, to his activity in creation, revelation and providence; then and only then comes a brief mention of his earthly life, leading to his consequent exaltation to heavenly dignity; and the impression made by this first sentence is confirmed when we find transferred to Christ a psalm originally addressed to God the Creator.

My contention is that this traditional interpretation starts with the problematical instead of with the ascertainable. There are several difficulties about it, the first and most important being that it does not exactly represent what the author has said. The epistle does not begin with a reference to the eternal Son. It begins with a contrast between what God has said in the past through the prophets and what he has now, in these last days, said through Jesus. Here, as in the Fourth Gospel, "the Son" is always a title for the man Jesus. He it is whom God appointed heir to the universe and who has now by his heavenly exaltation entered upon that inheritance. Moreover, in one passage after another where the title is used, the idea of appointment is present in the context. In contrast to Moses who was faithful in God's house-

---

[4]The problem is recognized by Robert G. Hamerton-Kelly (*Pre-existence, Wisdom and Son of Man: A Study of the Idea of Pre-existence in the New Testament* [SNTSMS 21; Cambridge/New York: Cambridge University, 1973]) and further illuminated by C. F. D. Moule (*The Origins of Christology* [Cambridge/New York: Cambridge University, 1977]). See also George B. Caird, "The Development of the Doctrine of Christ in the New Testament," *Christ For Us Today*: Papers read at the Conference of Modern Churchmen [50th], Somerville College, Oxford, July 1967, ed. William Norman Pittenger, with an appended essay by Edward Carpenter (London: SCM, 1968) 66-80.

hold as servitor, Jesus was faithful as son "to God who appointed him" (3:1-6). Admittedly we might here claim, as in 7:28 and 8:3, that Jesus was already God's son, and that the appointment mentioned was to the high priesthood. But that option is not open to us in the comparison between Aaron and Christ (5:4-6):

> And nobody arrogates the honour to himself: he is called by God as indeed Aaron was. So it is with Christ: he did not confer upon himself the glory of becoming high priest; it was granted by God, who said to him, "Thou art my Son; today I have begotten thee"; as also in another place he says, "Thou art a priest for ever, in the succession of Melchizedek" (NEB).

The author interprets the first of these quotations (Ps 2:7), just as a modern Old Testament scholar would do, as a formula of appointment to the royal status of "Son," and assumes in the light of the second quotation (Ps 110:1-4) that this appointment carries with it the further office of priest in perpetuity.

It is reasonable to infer that the citation from Ps 2:7 is intended to have exactly the same significance at 1:5 as we have seen it to have at 5:5. Christ ranks higher than the angels because, by God's decree, he holds a superior appointment; and this theme is sustained throughout the whole sequence of the seven quotations. But the workings of our author's mind in the construction of the sequence are not always obvious. The third quotation asserts that Christ's status as Son entitles him to the homage of angels, but it has a longer introductory formula than the others, and one which, though clear enough in meaning, is obscure in motive. The title "firstborn" poses no problem to those who know the psalter: "And I will appoint him my firstborn, highest among the kings of earth" (Ps 89:27).

But why does our author go out of his way to assert that God declared his firstborn entitled to angelic homage at the time when he brought him into the world? The angels he has in mind are all "ministrant spirits, sent out to serve, for the sake of those who are to inherit salvation" (1:14), but they undoubtedly include the mediators and guardians of the Torah (2:2), to whom God gave authority over the present age, though not over "the world to come" (2:5). During his earthly life Jesus was "lower than [sc. subject to] the angels" (2:9), and only through death was he exalted to the glory and honor of a higher status than theirs. We cannot escape from this dilemma by saying that the bringing of the firstborn into the world refers to the world to come, since this would destroy the important cross-reference to 10:5, to which we shall return later. Rather, it seems that what our author is saying is

this: Christ's appointment to sonship and thus to "the highest place
that heaven affords" rests on an eternal decree, reiterated (πάλιν) by
God when Christ appeared on earth, even though the full implications
of his status would be realized only when he had qualified for it by his
earthly career.

The problem of the sixth citation (Ps 102:25-27) is commonly
misstated. Most scholars have been content to remark that the author
of Hebrews applies to Christ a psalm originally addressed to God the
Creator, and to deduce from this that he regarded Christ as divine (and
preexistent). But this is imprecise. Like most of the other scriptural
passages he quotes, the author regards this one as a word spoken *by*
God, addressed by him to the Son, of whom he has just said in the
words of another psalm, "Your God has anointed you above your
fellows" (Ps 45:7). Difficult as the idea may be to us who have been
taught to think in very different terms, Christ is now said to be raised
above his fellows, and incidentally above the ministrant angels, by
being appointed to a cosmic role; he is the man in whom the divine
Wisdom has been appointed to dwell, so as to make him the bearer of
the whole purpose of creation.

Anyone who dislikes the direction in which this argument is tend-
ing may, of course, counter it with the assertion that the author of
Hebrews thought of Christ as from first to last a heavenly being and did
not draw any distinction between his eternal and his temporal
existence:

> His earthly life is described, . . . as nothing but an interlude in a larger,
> heavenly life. . . . an episode in a higher existence, which had suffered no real
> interruption. . . . The death in which it culminated was the sacrifice offered by
> the High Priest to secure His entrance into the holy place, and was not so
> much a break between two states of being as the link that united them with
> one another.[5]

Against all such crypto-docetism it cannot be too strongly affirmed
that for the author of Hebrews the earthly life of Jesus was paramount
and provided the indispensable foundation for any claims that might
be made on his behalf. The earthly Jesus does not come "trailing clouds
of glory" from his preincarnate status, nor is there a single one of his
dignities which he is said to hold in virtue of his heavenly origin. He
had to *become* superior to the angels and to *inherit* the loftier name

---

[5]E. F. Scott, *The Epistle to the Hebrews: Its Doctrine and Significance* (Edinburgh:
T. & T. Clark, 1922) 151-53.

(1:4). It was because of his death that he entered upon his heavenly glory, through suffering that he attained perfection as the pioneer of man's salvation (2:9-10); and that process of perfecting involved the learning of obedience (5:8-9). The theme of τελείωσις is one of the leitmotivs of the epistle. Our author certainly did not believe that Christ started from moral imperfection, but he did believe that his life was a growth in understanding and experience, as he explored to the uttermost what it means in the circumstances of this world for a man to be God's son.

It is characteristic of our author's style to make bold asseverations well in advance of the argument by which he explains or justifies them. Thus, for example, the designation of Christ as high priest in 2:17 and 3:1 is left hanging in the air for two whole chapters, to be picked up in 4:14-16, and to be expounded in full in 5:1-10 and 7:1-28. Similarly, when we start to read the epistle at the beginning, we have to wait until the quotation of Ps 8:4-6 in the second chapter to discover why he has devoted the first chapter to scriptural proofs of Christ's superiority to angels. Using the LXX ("You made him for a short while lower than the angels"), he takes it to mean that God has arranged for human history to take place in two stages: the present age is under the authority of angels (sc. of the Torah), but not the age to come; in the new age, when man is crowned with glory and honor, the whole universe is to be under his authority—but this is a state of affairs as yet unrealized, except in the representative person of Jesus. It follows from this that he must have understood the aorist verbs of the psalm quotation ("you made," "you crowned," "you subjected") as all referring to acts of God located in his eternal purpose; God may be said to have done all this, but only in the verbal acts of his eternal decree. Christ's earthly life, lived under angelic authority, and his subsequent promotion through suffering and death to the higher status so fully detailed in chapter one, are in keeping (ἔπρεπεν) with the purpose of God to bring all mankind ("many sons") to the glory for which he has destined them.

But the life and death of Christ and his exaltation over the universe are something more than a partial fulfillment of God's design for man. God intended from the beginning to put his plan into effect in precisely this way. Christ was "appointed heir to the whole universe" (1:2). Yet this rank is his, not in virtue of some precosmic divine existence, but as the pioneer of man's salvation, destined to lead God's many sons to glory. He has indeed his part in creation and providence, but as the goal to which the whole process is directed. It used to be thought that the world view of this epistle was Platonism, mediated by the hellenistic Judaism of Philo. If its author was under any philosophical influence whatever, which is exceedingly dubious, it might as well be argued that there is something distinctly Aristotelian about a theology in which the final cause operates as efficient cause also.

We have not yet, however, reached the heart of the author's Christology, which is emphatically Hebraic. It is not enough for him that Christ fulfilled God's eternal decree for man. What must be added is that Christ himself knew that decree and accepted the role which it laid upon him:

> That is why, at his coming into the world, he says:
> "Sacrifice and offering thou didst not desire,
> but thou hast prepared a body for me.
> Whole-offerings and sin-offerings thou didst not delight in.
> Then I said, 'Here am I: as it is written of me in the scroll,
> I have come, O God, to do thy will.' "
> . . .And it is by the will of God that we have been consecrated,
> through the offering of the body of Jesus Christ once and for all
> (10:5-10).

In passing let us observe that the LXX, differing as it does in the second line from the MT, provided an opportunity for a disquisition on incarnational theology which our author simply passes by; he picks up the term "body" only to assert that what Christ offered as sacrifice to God was that which God in his eternal wisdom had furnished.[6] The point which instead he chooses to develop is that man's salvation depends, as any reader of the Old Testament might have gathered, on the doing of God's will, not by the meticulous execution of the commands of the Torah with its endless levitical sacrifices, which the Old Testament itself constantly declares to be ineffective, but by Christ's obedience to a purpose of redemption in which he was cast in the central role—a purpose the Torah could only foreshadow (10:1; cf. 1:14). The purpose of salvation and Christ's obedience to it were both

---

[6]Equally there seems to be no attempt here to develop the distinction between the body and the blood of the sacrificial victim to which allusion is made at 13:11.

"written in the scroll," but the divine will had to be made actual in Christ's surrender to it.[7]

This proposition, however, has a converse which is equally important. Just because it took place "in that will," Christ's sacrificial death belongs to the eternal order. Levitical priests die and hand on their office to successors, and their sacrifices need to be repeated from day to day and from year to year. "But Christ offered for all time one sacrifice for sins" (10:12). How then did our author reach this staggering conviction that Christ's death was the sacrifice to end all sacrifice, efficacious in perpetuity? Perhaps, accustomed as we are to New Testament statements that the work of Christ is finished, and inured to the worldly evidence that it is not, we do not often enough pause to ask such a question. It is no answer to say that our author, like all his fellow Christians, believed that Christ was alive for evermore and therefore no longer subject to transience and death. For his sacrifice occurred precisely at the point where he was obviously still so subject. Moreover, the author knows that in other respects the work of Christ is unfinished. His pioneer work of bringing God's many sons to glory is unfinished, as long as "we do not yet see all things in subjection to man" (2:8). His kingly task is unfinished, since, enthroned though he is at God's right hand, "he waits henceforth until his enemies are made his footstool" (10:13).

How then does he come to be so confident that Christ's priestly task is complete? There can be no real doubt that the grounds for his confidence are scriptural. It is from scriptural passages, of which Ps 40:6-8 is but one example, that he draws his knowledge that "sins can never be removed by the blood of bulls and goats" (10:4), and in this he finds the explanation for Jeremiah's prediction of a new covenant, with its implication that the old one is "obsolete and growing old and is ready to vanish away" (8:13 [RSV], cf. 7:18). Similarly, it is from Ps 110:4 that he learns of Christ's appointment as "priest in perpetuity" (εἰς τὸ διηνεκές), and it is interesting to note that, whenever he speaks of Christ's death as "once for all," his mind at once turns to this psalm for scriptural warrant. "And it is by the will of God that we have been consecrated, through the offering of the body of Christ once for all [ἐφάπαξ] .... Christ offered for all time [εἰς τὸ διηνεκές] one sacrifice

---

[7]Cf. Rev 5:1-5, where God holds in his right hand the scroll of the world's destiny, but will not himself break its seals; that must be done by an agent worthy of the task.

for sins, and took his seat at the right hand of God, where he waits henceforth until his enemies are made his footstool" (10:10-13 [NEB]; cf. 7:27-28). The very psalm which points to the incompleteness of Christ's kingly work asserts the perpetuity of his priesthood and implies the perpetual efficacy of the sacrifice he offers. But for our author this means that the place of Christ's death in the eternal order was included in the terms of his appointment.

Any talk about eternity is of course notoriously liable to end in confusion. But at least we can endeavor not to impose our confusions on the epistle we are trying to understand. It is all too easy to assume that time is characteristic of earth and eternity of heaven, and that Christ's preexistence and postexistence belong to heaven—whatever may be thought of the "interlude" of his earthly life. But our author is not a naive prisoner of mental pictures inherited from the Old Testament. His theology begins and ends with God; heaven, eternity, life and holiness are to be found where God is and have no separate existence apart from him. Religion for him is the means of access to the presence of God. The weakness of levitical religion was that it symbolized access without genuinely providing it. It could not deal with man's dilemma; man is created for holiness, but is disqualified by sin from entering the divine presence where alone one can become holy. Christ is "the source of eternal salvation" (5:9), has "secured an eternal deliverance" (9:12), not only because his death itself stands in the eternal order, but because it is the means whereby "those whom God has called may receive the inheritance he has promised" (9:15). The fact that the inheritance is eternal does not place it in a world beyond death. Here and now "the blood of Jesus makes us free to enter boldly into the sanctuary by the new, living way he has opened" (10:19-20a). Christians are not in the position of the faithful saints of the old era, who waited expectantly for "the city with firm foundations, whose architect and builder is God" (11:10); for they already possess full access to Mount Zion and to the city of the living God (12:22). In the midst of a world of created things shaken by the earthquakes of the Lord's judgment, they have been given a kingdom which cannot be shaken (12:28).

We are now in a position better to appreciate what our author intends us to understand by τελείωσις. "The Law brought nothing to perfection; but a better hope is introduced, through which we draw near to God" (7:19). For the Christian τελείωσις is access to God, which carries with it all other benefits he can ask or think. For Christ it was the process by which, in obedient acceptance of the role laid upon him by God's redemptive purpose, he attained access, both for himself and for those whom as high priest he represented, to the true sanctuary of the eternal presence. It was clearly in keeping with God's purpose in creation that "in bringing many sons to glory, [he] should make the pioneer of their salvation perfect through suffering" (2:10 [RSV]). "Son though he was, he learned obedience in the school of suffering, and, once perfected, became the source of eternal salvation for all who obey him" (5:8-9 [NEB]). "The high priests made by the Law are men in all their frailty; but the priest appointed by the words of the oath which supercedes the Law is made perfect now for ever" (7:28).

Dom Gregory Dix warned us many years ago against supposing that, if we compare a Christology expressed in functional, Hebraic terms with one expressed in ontological, Greek terms, the first necessarily will be "lower" and the second "higher."[8] The author of Hebrews has no place in his thinking for preexistence as an ontological concept. His essentially human Jesus attains to perfection, to preeminence, and even to eternity. Yet his is a high Christology. He could have sung with Thomas Kelly:

> The highest place that heaven affords
> Is His, is His by right.[9]

But the right was guaranteed by the place he held in the eternal purpose of God.

---

[8]Gregory Dix, *Jew and Greek: A Study in the Primitive Church* (Westminster, London: Dacre; New York: Harper, 1953) 79.

[9]From the hymn by Thomas Kelly, "The head that once was crowned with thorns," *The English Hymn with Tunes* (London: Oxford University; A. R. Mowbray, 1906; repr. 1976) no. 147, v 2.

"AH! SI TU PEUX! . . .
TOUT EST POSSIBLE EN FAVEUR DE CELUI QUI CROIT"
(MARC 9:23)

Jean Carmignac

EN MARC 9:23, le père d'un épileptique, après avoir recouru en vain aux disciples de Jésus, s'adresse à Jésus lui-même: "Si tu peux, aide-nous, par pitié pour nous!"[1] Et Jésus lui répond: Τὸ εἰ δύνῃ, πάντα δυνατὰ τῷ πιστεύοντι.

Cette phrase soulève deux difficultés: quel est le sens de τό et quelle est la valeur du datif τῷ πιστεύοντι?

A la première difficulté les grammairiens répondent qu'en grec l'article peut être mis devant une phrase pour indiquer qu'elle constitue une citation.[2] Mais cette réponse ne satisfait pas pleinement: "Dans cette phrase τό indique une citation: cf. Mt xix,18. Cependant la phrase demeure obscure, et serait plus claire si l'on écrivait τί τὸ εἰ δύνῃ . . . *quid est si quid potes?* (Blass, 160). Il faut du moins supposer une interrogation. La difficulté du texte a amené de nombreux mss. à insérer πιστεῦσαι après δύνῃ."[3] C'est d'ailleurs à cause de cette difficulté que certains manuscrits omettent l'article τό, mais les éditions critiques le maintiennent à juste titre: "The extreme compression of the sentence has given trouble to copyists. Not seeing that in τὸ εἰ δύνῃ Jesus is repeating the words of the father in order to challenge them, a variety of witnesses have inserted πιστεῦσαι, which has the effect of changing the subject of the verb 'can' from Jesus to the father. As a

---

[1]En tout ce chapitre la numérotation de la Vulgate est en retard d'un verset sur le grec.

[2]Voir par exemple James Hope Moulton, *A Grammar of New Testament Greek*, vol. 3: *Syntax* by Nigel Turner (Edinburgh: T. & T. Clark, 1963) 182.

[3]Marie Joseph Lagrange, *Évangile selon Saint Marc*, 4th ed. (Etudes Bibliques; Paris: J. Gabalda, 1929) 241.

result the τό now seemed more awkward than ever, and many of these witnesses omit it."⁴

Or, l'interrogation (ou l'exclamation) que demande le contexte et qu'on ne voit pas en grec, apparaît, si l'on retraduit ce passage en hébreu, car on obtient presque à coup sûr תוכל, avec le ה interrogatif ou exclamatif devant la conjonction אם, comme en Nomb 17:28 et en Job 6:13. Mais ce ה risquait fort d'être considéré comme un article par le traducteur grec. Ainsi s'expliquerait le texte actuel, dont le sens primitif serait bien: "Ah! Si tu peux!"⁵

La seconde difficulté provient de ce que la plupart des traducteurs comprennent: "Tout est possible à celui qui croit." Mais alors la logique du récit est perturbée, car Jésus dirait en somme au père de l'épileptique: "Si tu as la foi, tout t'est possible. Donc à toi de le guérir et de faire toi-même le miracle que tu sollicites!"

En fait, la formule grecque admet une double interprétation, selon la valeur qu'on attribue au datif: ou bien "Il est possible pour celui qui croit de tout faire," ou bien "Tout peut être fait pour celui qui croit." Dans le premier cas c'est le croyant qui fait tout, dans le second c'est en faveur du croyant que tout est fait. Les deux sens sont en théorie également admissibles, puisque δυνατός contient les deux idées de "pouvoir" et de "faire" et que le datif peut se rapporter soit à l'idée de "pouvoir" (= première interprétation) soit à l'idée de "faire" (= seconde interprétation).

Quand on veut être tout à fait précis, on peut employer παρά ou ἐξ pour spécifier de qui provient le pouvoir le faire, comme on le constate en Marc 10:27: παρὰ ἀνθρώποις ἀδύνατον, ἀλλ' οὐ παρὰ θεῷ· πάντα γὰρ δυνατὰ παρὰ τῷ θεῷ ("de la part des hommes c'est impossible, mais non de la part de Dieu, car tout est possible de la part de Dieu"), dans le parallèle de Matt 19:26: παρὰ ἀνθρώποις τοῦτο ἀδύνατόν ἐστιν, παρὰ δὲ θεῷ πάντα δυνατά ("de la part des hommes c'est impossible, mais de la part de Dieu tout est possible") et dans le parallèle de Luc 18:27: τὰ ἀδύνατα παρὰ ἀνθρώποις δυνατὰ παρὰ τῷ θεῷ ἐστιν ("les choses

---

⁴Bruce M. Metzger, *A Textual Commentary on the Greek New Testament: A Companion Volume to the United Bible Societies' Greek New Testament*, 3rd ed. (New York/London: United Bible Societies, 1971) 100.

⁵Si l'on voulait supposer non pas un substrat hébreu, mais un substrat araméen, cette explication ne serait plus valable, car l'araméen, qui emploie le ה comme particule interrogative ou exclamative, ne l'emploie pas comme article, et donc la confusion n'y est plus possible.

impossibles de la part des hommes sont possibles de la part de Dieu"); de même en Rom 12:18: εἰ δυνατόν, τὸ ἐξ ὑμῶν ("s'il est possible, en ce qui vient de vous").

Si l'on recourait toujours à cette construction pour désigner l'auteur de l'action, alors la construction par le simple datif indiquerait clairement le destinataire en faveur de qui est réalisée l'action, comme c'est le cas ici. La même construction avec le simple datif se retrouve en Matt 17:20 (οὐδὲν ἀδυνατήσει ὑμῖν), où le sens est clairement "rien ne sera impossible en votre faveur," comme le confirme le parallèle de Luc 17:6: "[Dieu] vous exaucera." C'est ainsi qu'en Marc 11:23-24, à propos de la montagne à jeter dans la mer, on trouve ὃς ἄν... πιστεύῃ ὅτι ὃ λαλεῖ γίνεται, ἔσται αὐτῷ.... πιστεύετε ὅτι ἐλάβετε, καὶ ἔσται ὑμῖν ("celui qui croira que ce qu'il dit sera fait, [cela] se produira pour lui... croyez que vous recevrez et [cela] se produira pour vous").[6] En tous ces textes il est bien clair que le miracle n'est pas accompli par le croyant, mais par Dieu, qui le réalise en faveur de ceux qui ont la foi.

Certes, on peut aussi négliger ces précisions et employer le simple datif là où παρά serait préférable, comme en Marc 14:36: ὁ πατήρ, πάντα δυνατά σοι ("Père, tout t'est possible") c'est-à-dire "tout est possible de ta part" ou bien "tu peux tout faire." Mais ce texte fait figure d'exception et, dans les Evangiles, le datif indique plutôt "en faveur de qui" une chose est possible.

En définitive, le contexte et l'usage des Evangiles (à une exception près) s'accordent pour montrer que le sens réel n'est pas, comme on le suppose généralement, "tout est possible de la part de celui qui croit," mais bien "tout est possible en faveur de celui qui croit."

Une telle interprétation[7] a déjà été proposée[8] plus ou moins timide-

---

[6] Le parallèle de Matt 21:22 est encore plus clair: "Tout ce que vous demanderez dans la prière en ayant la foi, vous (le) recevrez." Là, le croyant est bien celui qui reçoit, non pas celui qui réalise!

[7] Une interprétation un peu différente a été proposée par August Klostermann (*Das Markusevangelium nach seinem Quellenwerthe für die evangelische Geschichte* [Göttingen: Vandenhoeck & Ruprecht, 1867] 192): "Nur dann ist ein richtiger Gedankenfortschritt da, wenn der Dativ die Beziehung des Urtheils ausdrückt: 'für den Glaubenden', d.i. 'nach seinem Urtheile ist Alles möglich', gerade wie wenn Paulus sagt (Tit 1,15) πάντα καθαρὰ καθαροῖς oder Plato τὰ ἀγαθὰ τοῖς ἀγαθοῖς ὄντως ἀγαθά, τοῖς δὲ κακοῖς κακά (gegen de Wette, Meyer, Bleek 2,71). Es ist also der Sinn der: wenn Du glaubtest, so könntest Du von einer bedingten Möglichkeit der Hülfe gar nicht reden; denn das Wesen des Glaubens besteht eben darin, dass der Mensch sich von dem Gedanken an die Bedingungen losgemacht hat."

[8] Cette interprétation m'a été suggérée par M. l'Abbé Joseph Leroy, prêtre du

ment par quelques exégètes, mais sans gagner beaucoup d'adhérents:
Bernhard Weiss et Johannes Weiss en 1892: "Alles ist möglich ..., scil.
zu erlangen, für den Glaubenden,"[9] puis la traduction de Moffatt:
"Anything can be done for one who believes,"[10] et enfin tout récem-
ment la Traduction Oecuménique française: "Tout est possible pour
celui qui croit."[11]

---

diocèse de Cambrai, auquel j'adresse toute ma reconnaissance.

[9]Bernhard Weiss und Johannes Weiss, *Die Evangelien des Markus und Lukas*, 8th
ed. (MeyerK; Göttingen: Vandenhoeck & Ruprecht, 1892) 157.

[10]C. E. B. Cranfield (*The Gospel According to Saint Mark: An Introduction and
Commentary*, 2d Impression with supplementary notes [Cambridge Greek Testament
Commentary; Cambridge: Cambridge University, 1963] 303) a pressenti cette solution,
mais finalement ne l'a pas adoptée: "Various interpretations are possible: 'There is
nothing which a man who has faith cannot do'; 'There is nothing which cannot be done
(*sc.* by Jesus or by God) for a man who has faith'; 'There is nothing which is impossible
for (i.e., in the view of) a man who has faith' (in other words, 'A man who has faith will
not set any limit to what I (Jesus)(or perhaps God?) can do'). Of these the last fits the
context best." Selon l'argumentation développée ci-dessus, ce serait au contraire la
seconde des interprétations mentionnées qui serait à retenir.

[11]*Traduction Oecuménique de la Bible: Nouveau Testament* (Paris: Cerf, 1972)
Marc 9:23. Avec en note: "Plutôt que *à celui qui croit*. Dieu peut tout *pour* lui."

ΕΚ ΠΙΣΤΕΩΣ
IN THE LETTERS OF PAUL

Bruno Corsani

THE PURPOSE OF this article is to investigate Paul's usage of the phrase ἐκ πίστεως and to see if this usage permits one to draw conclusions as to the meaning of these words in several difficult passages.[1]

1.

According to Morgenthaler's *Statistik* Paul uses πίστις eight times in 1 Thessalonians, seven times in 1 Corinthians, seven times in 2 Corinthians, five times in Philippians, twenty two times in Galatians, and forty times in Romans.[2] This is sufficient to show that Paul was more concerned with the topic πίστις at the time of the composition of Galatians and Romans than at any other time of his epistolary activity.[3]

A close scrutiny of the texts shows that ἐκ πίστεως is found only in Galatians (9 times) and in Romans (12 times). At the same time it may be recalled that in these two letters Paul employs the Habakkuk quotation "He who through faith [ἐκ πίστεως] is righteous shall live" (Hab 2:4; Rom 1:17; Gal 3:11). In the LXX there is only one occurrence of the words ἐκ πίστεως and that is precisely in Hab 2:4.

---

[1]Quotations of the New Testament are from the RSV unless otherwise stated.

[2]Robert Morgenthaler, *Statistik des neutestamentlichen Wortschatzes* (Zürich/Frankfurt: Gotthelf, 1958) 132.

[3]We assume that Galatians and Romans were composed within a very short interval of time. Cf. Udo Borse, *Der Standort des Galaterbriefes* (BBB 41; Köln: Hanstein, 1972) 135-39.

2.

'Εκ πίστεως may be appended to verbs to modify their meaning or to show the sphere of their application. Five times ἐκ πίστεως is joined to the verb δικαιόω 'justify'.[4] Twice it is used with δικαιόω in the active form: "foreseeing that God would justify the Gentiles *by faith*" (Gal 3:8), and "He will justify the circumcised *on the ground of their faith*" (Rom 3:30); three times ἐκ πίστεως is joined to δικαιόω in the passive form: "we have believed in Christ Jesus, in order to be justified *by faith* in Christ, and not by works of the law" (Gal 2:16); "the law was our custodian until Christ came, that we might be justified *by faith*" (Gal 3:24); "since we are justified *by faith*, we have peace with God" (Rom 5:1).

In addition, ἐκ πίστεως is found with the verbs δίδωμι ("But the scripture hath concluded all under sin, that the promise *by faith* of Jesus Christ might be given to them that believe" [Gal 3:22, KJV])[5]; ἀπεκδέχομαι ("For through the Spirit, *by faith*, we wait for the hope of righteousness" [Gal 5:5]); and ἀποκαλύπτω ("In it [in the Gospel] the righteousness of God is revealed *through faith* for faith" [Rom 1:17]). In two of these three passages it is "righteousness" that is revealed or expected.

---

[4]The translation suggested by Kendrick Grobel (in Rudolf Bultmann, *Theology of the New Testament,* vol. 1 [New York: Charles Scribner, 1951; London: SCM, 1952] 253 note) is "to rightwise."

[5]The KJV justifies the association of this passage with those in which ἐκ πίστεως depends upon a verb. It might be argued that ἐκ πίστεως could be related to ἐπαγγελία 'promise'. The RSV seems to have made that choice, hence the translation, "But the scripture consigned all things to sin, that what was promised to faith in Jesus Christ might be given to those who believe." Yet the majority of commentators do not support this interpretation. See Ernest de Witt Burton, *A Critical and Exegetical Commentary on the Epistle to the Galatians* (ICC; Edinburgh: T. & T. Clark, 1921) 196-97; Pierre Bonnard, *L'Épître de Saint Paul aux Galates,* 2nd ed. (CNT 9; Neuchâtel: Delachaux & Niestlé, 1972) 75; Heinrich Schlier, *Der Brief an die Galater,* 13th ed. (MeyerK; Göttingen: Vandenhoeck & Ruprecht, 1965) 165; José M. G. Ruiz, *Epistola de san Pablo a los Galatas: traducción y comentario* (Comentario al Nuevo Testamento 2; Madrid: Instituto Español de Estudios Eclesiasticos, 1964) ad loc.; John Bligh, *Galatians: A Discussion of St. Paul's Epistle* (Householder commentaries 1; London: St. Paul Publications, 1969) 313.

3.

Paul at times uses the phrase ἐκ πίστεως to describe the true nature of something of which he is speaking. Twice ἐκ πίστεως is appended to the word δικαιοσύνη 'righteousness': "that Gentiles who did not pursue righteousness have attained it, that is, righteousness *through faith*" (Rom 9:30); "but the righteousness *based on faith* says" (Rom 10:6). In the two quotations of Hab 2:4 the formula modifies the adjective δίκαιος 'righteous': "he who through faith is righteous shall live" (Rom 1:17; Gal 3:11).[6]

---

[6]Were one to accept the translation of the KJV, "the just shall live by faith," one would place Rom 1:17 alongside those passages in which ἐκ πίστεως is related to the verb. That is the interpretation of Theodor Zahn, *Der Brief des Paulus an die Römer*, 3rd ed. (Kommentar zum Neuen Testament 6; Leipzig: A. Deichert, 1925) 85; William Sanday and Arthur C. Headlam, *A Critical and Exegetical Commentary on the Epistle to the Romans*, 5th ed. (ICC; Edinburgh: T. & T. Clark, 1902) 28; Hugues Oltramare, *Commentaire sur l'Épître aux Romains*, 2 vols. (Genève: A. Cherbuliez; Paris: Fischbacher, 1881-1882), 1:277; Frédéric L. Godet, *Commentary on the Epistle to the Romans*, trans. A. Cusin, revised and ed. Talbot W. Chambers (New York: Funk & Wagnalls, 1883; repr. Grand Rapids, Michigan: Zondervan, 1956) 98 (= *Commentaire sur l'Épître aux Romains*, 2 vols. [Paris: Sandoz & Fischbacher, 1879-1880] 204-5); C. H. Dodd, *The Epistle of Paul to the Romans* (MNTC; New York: Harper, 1932) 14-16; Otto Michel, *Der Brief an die Römer*, 13th ed. (MeyerK; Göttingen: Vandenhoeck & Ruprecht, 1966) 55; Gottlob Schrenk, s.v. "δίκαιος," *TWNT* 2 (1935) 193; Franz J. Leenhardt, *The Epistle to the Romans: A Commentary* (London: Lutterworth, 1961) 58 (*L'Épître de Saint Paul aux Romains* [CNT 6; Neuchâtel: Delachaux & Niestlé, 1957] 57); Herman Ridderbos, *Aan de Romeinen* (Commentaar op het Nieuwe Testament; Kampen: J. H. Kok, 1959) 39-40; Heinrich Schlier, *Der Römerbrief* (HTKNT 6; Freiburg: Herder, 1977) 46. I prefer the interpretation in which ἐκ πίστεως is related to δίκαιος. So also Hans Lietzmann, *An die Römer*, 3rd ed. (HNT 8; Tübingen: J. C. B. Mohr, 1928) 31; Ernst Kühl, *Der Brief des Paulus an die Römer* (Leipzig: Quelle & Meyer, 1913) 40; Marie-Joseph Lagrange, *Saint Paul Épître aux Romains* (EBib; Paris: J. Gabalda, 1950) 20-21; C. K. Barrett, *A Commentary on the Epistle to the Romans* (HNTC; New York: Harper; Black's New Testament Commentaries; London: Adam & Charles Black, 1962) 31; Anders Nygren, *Commentary on Romans* (Philadelphia: Muhlenberg, 1949) 82-91; Otto Kuss, *Der Römerbrief* (Regensburg: Friedrich Pustet, 1957), 1:24-25; Hans Wilhelm Schmidt, *Der Brief des Paulus an die Römer* (THKNT 6; Berlin: Evangelische Verlagsanstalt, 1963) 28; C. E. B. Cranfield, *A Critical and Exegetical Commentary on the Epistle to the Romans*, vol. 1: *Introduction and Commentary on Romans I-VIII* (ICC; Edinburgh: T. & T. Clark, 1975) 101-2; Matthew Black, *Romans* (New Century Bible; London: Oliphants, 1973) 46-47; Ernst Käsemann, *An die Römer* (HNT 8a; Tübingen: J. C. B. Mohr, 1973) 28-29; Ulrich Wilckens, *Der Brief an die Römer* (EKKNT 6/1; Zürich/Köln: Benziger, 1978) 88-90. Cf. the translation of Rom 1:17 in NEB: "he shall gain life who is justified through faith"; Today's English Version: "he who is put right with God through faith shall live"; RSV: "he who through faith is righteous shall live."

In a few passages ἐκ πίστεως is used with the article and thereby is virtually turned into a noun: "so you see that it is men of faith [οἱ ἐκ πίστεως] who are the sons of Abraham" (Gal 3:7). After quoting Gen 12:3 (cf. Gen 18:18) in the following verse (Gal 3:8), Paul goes on to speak of the believers in parallel with Abraham himself: "so then, those who are men of faith [οἱ ἐκ πίστεως] are blessed with Abraham who had faith" (Gal 3:9). Rom 3:26 speaks of the man of faith who is justified by God: "he himself is righteous and ... he justifies him who has faith in Jesus" (τὸν ἐκ πίστεως).

4.

In some passages ἐκ πίστεως is used in contrast to something else. In this way Paul intends not only to mark the difference between the way of faith and other (false) ways of salvation but also to throw fuller light on the meaning and implications of the way of faith. Especially important are those passages in which Paul contrasts the way of faith with the way of the law or the works of the law: "we have believed in Christ Jesus, in order to be justified by faith in Christ, and not by works of the law, because by works of the law shall no one be justified" (Gal 2:16); "but the law does not rest on faith [the law rests on the doing of works], for 'He who does them shall live by them' " (Gal 3:12; cf. Gal 3:22). Here Gal 5:4-5 should also be quoted: "you are severed from Christ, you who would be justified by the law; you have fallen away from grace. For through the Spirit, by faith, we wait for the hope of righteousness." In Romans 4:16 "the adherents of the law" (ὁ ἐκ τοῦ νόμου) are contrasted to "those who share the faith of Abraham" (ὁ ἐκ πίστεως Ἀβρααμ). A similar antithetical parallelism occurs in Rom 10:5-6. This time "the righteousness which is based on the Law" (ἡ δικαιοσύνη ἡ ἐκ τοῦ νόμου) is opposed to "the righteousness based on faith" (δικαιοσύνη ἡ ἐκ πίστεως).

The simplest way of putting forth this contrast occurs in Rom 9:32, where Paul says with a powerful ellipsis: "because they did not pursue it [i.e., righteousness] through faith, but as if it were based on works" (ὅτι οὐκ ἐκ πίστεως ἀλλ' ὡς ἐξ ἔργων).

5.

To my knowledge there is but one passage where ἐκ πίστεως is explained by a parallelism with another formula of positive value and not by way of contrast. This passage is Rom 4:16: "that is why it depends on faith, in order that the promise may rest on grace" (διὰ τοῦτο ἐκ πίστεως, ἵνα κατὰ χάριν). It is interesting to observe that in 4:13-17 Paul begins with the contrast of "law" and "faith justice" (δικαιοσύνη πίστεως, 4:13). Here however the preposition used by Paul is διά (both for "law" and for "faith justice"). His beginning with the negative side ("did not come through the law") probably shows his polemical intention.

6.

It is now possible to draw some conclusions:

1) Paul's use of the formula ἐκ πίστεως is parallel to the frequency of his use of the word πίστις .

2) The frequent use of the formula ἐκ πίστεως in Galatians and Romans is parallel to the frequent use of the word πίστις to connote justifying faith. According to Bultmann, for Paul "faith" is not a gift of the Spirit, and he notes that it is not mentioned in the list of the gifts given by the Spirit to the congregation in 1 Cor 1:4-7.[7] But it is certainly mentioned in 1 Cor 12:9 ("to another, faith by the same Spirit"), and in 1 Cor 13:2 we find it along with "tongues" (13:1), "prophetic powers" (13:2) and "knowledge" (13:2). However, in Galatians and Romans it is much more frequently related to the saving acts of God in Jesus Christ and to justification.

3) The formula ἐκ πίστεως has more to do with the objective fact of Christ's coming, dying and rising from the dead than with the subjective attitude of man. Which is the "faith" that justifies? It is the faith in "God who justifies the ungodly" (Rom 4:5), and in Jesus our Lord "who was put to death for our trespasses and raised for our justification" (Rom 4:25).

4) The preeminence of the objective character of πίστις over its subjective aspect finds confirmation in the study of Kramer which

---

[7] Rudolf Bultmann, s.v. "πιστεύω," *TWNT* 6 (1959) 221, 221 n. 335.

demonstrated that among the christological titles πίστις (or πιστεύω)
is usually associated with "Christ" (two exceptions: Phlm 5 where we
find "Lord," and Gal 2:20 where we find "son of God"); and that
"Christ" is a key-word that points synthetically to the saving event of
the death and resurrection of Jesus.[8]

5) All this may have relevance for that puzzling passage, Rom 1:17:
"for in it the righteousness of God is revealed ἐκ πίστεως εἰς πίστιν ."
What does ἐκ πίστεως mean here? Some have seen in the two occur-
rences of "faith" two different kinds or levels of faith, e.g., from faith in
the Law to faith in Christ, or from germinal faith to fully grown faith.
Calvin says that Paul "points out the daily progress that is made by
every one of the faithful,"[9] and Luther interprets: *semper magis ac
magis credendo, ut 'qui iustus est, iustificetur adhuc', ne quis statim
arbitretur se apprehendisse et ita desinat proficere i.e. incipiat deficere*
(WA 56.173). Another line of interpretation takes a more positive view
of ἐκ πίστεως. Augustine sees in this passage the transition from the
faith of those who preach to the faith of those who obey (*de Spiritu et
Littera*, 11). Barth suggests that the righteousness of God is revealed
from the faithfulness of God to the faith of man.[10] Wilckens thinks that
the proclamation of the righteousness of God has its starting point in
the faith of the believers and aims at the faith of the nations.[11] A third
type of interpretation takes the phrase as a kind of endyadis, used by
Paul to emphasize the sphere of faith in which the revelation of the
power of God takes place.[12] If our points 3 and 4 above are correct, it is
probable that with ἐκ πίστεως Paul wanted to point to the justifying

---

[8]Werner Kramer, *Christos Kyrios Gottessohn: Untersuchungen zu Gebrauch und
Bedeutung der christologischen Bezeichnungen bei Paulus und den vorpaulinischen
Gemeinden* (ATANT 44; Zürich/Stuttgart: Zwingli, 1963) 15-40, 41-44 (=*Christ,
Lord, Son of God* [Studies in Biblical Theology 50; Naperville, Illinois: Alec R.
Allenson; London: SCM, 1966] 19-44, 45-48). Cf. Hans Conzelmann, "Was glaubte
die frühe Christenheit?," *Schweizerische Theologische Umschau* 25 (1955) 64; Dieter
Lührmann, *Glaube im frühen Christentum* (Gütersloh: G. Mohn, 1976) 48-49.

[9]John Calvin, *Commentaries on the Epistle of Paul the Apostle to the Romans*
(Grand Rapids, Michigan: Wm B. Eerdmans, 1955) 65.

[10]Karl Barth, *The Epistle to the Romans* (London: Oxford University, 1933; repr.
1968) 41 (= *Der Römerbrief*, 11th ed. [Zürich: Evangelischer Verlag, 1976] 17).

[11]Wilckens, *An die Römer*, 88.

[12]Cf. Barrett, *Romans*, 30-31: "on the basis of nothing but faith... faith from start
to finish"; Today's English Version: "it is through faith alone, from beginning to end."

acts of God in Jesus Christ. Εἰς πίστιν might then refer to the hearing and the accepting of the proclamation of that message.

6) Another interesting case is Rom 14:23. The NEB translates: "A man who has doubts is guilty if he eats, because his action does not arise *from his conviction*, and anything which does not arise *from conviction* is sin." The italics correspond to ἐκ πίστεως. A similar translation can be found in the French Bibles of Segond, Ostervald, TOB; in the German *Gute Nachricht* and in the Italian *Versione Riveduta*. This way of translating is not faithful to the objective character of πίστις in the passages where Paul uses the formula ἐκ πίστεως and reflects the subjective and sometimes emotional interpretation of "faith" common in Protestantism before Barth.

1 PETER 3:19 RECONSIDERED

William J. Dalton

IN THE INTRODUCTION to a work published in 1965 on the interpretation of 1 Pet 3:18-4:6,[1] I referred to Professor Bo Reicke's treatment of the same general topic as "the classical modern work on 1 Peter 3:19."[2] He took up the theme again in a more limited fashion in his commentary on 1 Peter.[3] In addition, since the publication of *Christ's Proclamation to the Spirits*, there have been quite a number of commentaries on 1 Peter and of treatments, more or less extensive, of 1 Pet 3:19.[4] Hence it would seem an appropriate moment to reconsider this famous text. After having noted the chief differences between Professor Reicke's view and my own, we shall see how the text has fared at the hands of scholars from 1965 onwards.[5] This discussion, in an area where Bo

---

[1]William J. Dalton, *Christ's Proclamation to the Spirits: A Study of 1 Peter 3:18-4:6* (AnBib 23; Rome: Pontifical Biblical Institute, 1965).

[2]Bo Reicke, *The Disobedient Spirits and Christian Baptism: A Study of 1 Pet. iii. 19 and its Context* (ASNU 13; Copenhagen: Ejnar Munksgaard, 1946).

[3]Bo Reicke, *The Epistles of James, Peter, and Jude: Introduction, Translation, and Notes* (AB; Garden City, New York: Doubleday, 1964).

[4]Cf. John H. Elliott, "The Rehabilitation of an Exegetical Step-child: 1 Peter in Recent Research," *JBL* 95 (1976) 243-54; Franz-Josef Schierse, "Ein Hirtenbrief und viele Bücher," *BK* 31 (1976) 86-88.

[5]José Salguero, "Primera Epístola de San Pedro," *Biblia Comentada: Texto de la Nácar-Colunga*, vol. 7: *Epístolas Católicas Apocalipsis* (BAC 249; Madrid: La Editorial Católica, 1965), 7:88-146; Herbert Vorgrimmler, "The Significance of Christ's Descent into Hell," *Concilium* 11 (1966) 147-59; Ceslaus Spicq, *Les Épîtres de Saint Pierre* (SB; Paris: J. Gabalda, 1966); Josef Kürzinger, "Höllenfahrt Christi," *Bibeltheologisches Wörterbuch*, 3rd ed., ed. Johannes Bauer, 2 vols. (Graz: Styria, 1967), 1:745-50; A. R. C. Leaney, *The Letters of Peter and Jude* (Cambridge Bible Commentary; Cambridge: Cambridge University, 1967); Rudolf Schnackenburg, "Konkrete Fragen an den Dogmatiker aus der heutigen exegetischen Diskussion," *Catholica* 21 (1967) 12-27; Joseph A. Fitzmyer, "The First Epistle of Peter," *JBC*, eds. Raymond E. Brown, Joseph A. Fitzmyer and Ronald E. Murphy (Englewood Cliffs, New Jersey: Prentice-Hall, 1968), 2:362-68; Johann Michl, *Die Katholischen Briefe*, 2nd ed. (RNT

Reicke has worked so fruitfully, is offered as a modest contribution to honor his eminent services to biblical scholarship.

1

The text of 1 Pet 3:18-20 runs as follows in the RSV:

For Christ also died [ἀπέθανεν][6] for sins once for all, the righteous for the unrighteous, that he might bring us to God, being put to death in the flesh but made alive in the spirit; in which he went and preached to the spirits in prison, who formerly did not obey, when God's patience waited in the days of Noah, during the building of the ark, in which a few, that is, eight persons, were saved through water.

And the Greek text of 3:19 runs: ἐν ᾧ καὶ τοῖς ἐν φυλακῇ πνεύμασιν πορευθεὶς ἐκήρυξεν.

The commentator, in offering an interpretation of 3:19,[7] must ask the following questions: What is the function of this text in the general context? What is the background of religious thought which gives an understanding of the text? How should ἐν ᾧ be translated? Who are "the spirits in prison"? Where did Christ go? What was the content of his proclamation?

8/2; Regensburg: F. Pustet, 1968); Charles Perrot, "La descente du Christ aux enfers dans le Nouveau Testament," *Lumière et Vie* 17/87 (1968) 5-29; J. N. D. Kelly, *The Epistles of Peter and Jude* (HNTC; New York: Harper & Row; Black's New Testament Commentaries; London: Adam & Charles Black, 1969); Francis W. Beare, *The First Epistle of Peter,* 3rd ed. (Oxford: Blackwell, 1970); K. H. Schelkle, *Die Petrusbriefe, der Judasbrief,* 3rd ed. (HTKNT 13/2; Freiburg: Herder, 1970); Francis C. Synge, "1 Peter 3:18-21," *Exp Tim* 82 (1970-1971) 311; D. H. Wheaton, "1 Peter," *The New Bible Commentary Revised,* 3rd ed., ed. Donald Guthrie and John Alexander (Grand Rapids, Michigan: Wm. B. Eerdmans; London: Inter-Varsity, 1970) 1236-58; Ernest Best, *1 Peter* (New Century Bible; London: Marshall, 1971); Heinrich Schlier, "Eine Adhortatio aus Rom: die Botschaft des ersten Petrusbriefes," *Exegetische Aufsätze und Vorträge,* vol. 3: *Das Ende der Zeit* (Freiburg: Herder, 1971), 3:271-96; Fausto Salvoni, "Cristo andò nello spirito a proclamare agli spiriti in carcere (1 Pet 3:18-20; 4:6)," *Ricerche Bibliche e Religiose* 6 (1971) 57-86; Horst Balz and Wolfgang Schrage, *Die Katholischen Briefe: die Briefe des Jakobus, Petrus, Johannes und Judas* (NTD 10; Göttingen: Vandenhoeck & Ruprecht, 1973); Heinz-Jürgen Vogels, *Christi Abstieg ins Totenreich und das Läuterungsgericht an den Toten: eine bibeltheologisch-dogmatische Untersuchung zum Glaubensartikel "descendit ad inferos"* (Freiburger Theologische Studien 102; Freiburg: Herder, 1976); Jean Cantinat, "La première épître de Pierre," *Introduction à la Bible, Nouveau Testament, tome III, Les Lettres Apostoliques* (Paris: Desclée, 1977), 3:259-73.

[6]Another well attested reading is ἔπαθεν 'suffered'.

[7]A full discussion of 3:19 would involve a study also of 4:6 and of the possible link between the two verses, but this is beyond the scope of this short article.

With regard to the first question, Reicke links 3:19 very closely with 3:13-16. In the latter text we have an "exhortation to patience and courage before the heathen."[8] This attitude finds its foundation in the attitude of Christ, who died for men (3:18) and who preached the gospel even to the most abandoned sinners (3:19). And so Reicke sums up: "And here, too, Christ is described as the great Pattern. Just as He announced the Gospel for the beings from the Flood, so should the Christians without fear or selfish reserve tell of the Gospel to the pagans in their environment."[9]

In my treatment of the context, I preferred to see in Christ's saving activity of 3:18-19 not a moral example set up for Christians to follow, but rather the objective ground for the Christians' confidence in persecution. Thus 2:20 does not provide a real parallel to 3:18 despite the verbal similarities. In addition, 3:13-16 does not so much stress the conversion of the pagans as the need for Christians to be strong and faithful in the stress of persecution. In the general context, while the pagans are on occasion considered as potential Christians, they are presented even more strongly as adversaries of the gospel (4:1-5,17-18). Thus it would seem more likely that in 3:19 we are dealing with Christ's victory over evil, which gives strength to the Christians to overcome the evil active in their pagan adversaries.[10]

I followed Reicke in his use of the intertestamental literature, especially 1 Enoch, in establishing the most useful religious background for our text. The story of Enoch's meeting with the fallen angels, the close relationship between their fall and the sin which preceded the flood, the influence of these angels on the sin of the pagan world, all point to a remarkable parallel between Enoch's announcement to the "watchers" and Christ's proclamation to the spirits.[11]

However, when we came to the discussion of ἐν ᾧ we parted company.[12] Reicke took the relative as a temporal conjunction referring back to the death of Christ mentioned in the main verb of 3:18. I

---

[8]Reicke, *Disobedient Spirits*, 128.

[9]Reicke, *Disobedient Spirits*, 131.

[10]Dalton, *Christ's Proclamation*, 106-12.

[11]Reicke, *Disobedient Spirits*, 93-103, 131-35; Dalton, *Christ's Proclamation*, 163-76.

[12]Reicke, *Disobedient Spirits*, 103-15; Dalton, *Christ's Proclamation*, 135-45.

took it as referring to the immediately preceding "spirit." One important reason for this difference of interpretation was to be found in the different ways in which we understood the "flesh-spirit" contrast of 3:18. Reicke took "flesh" and "spirit" to refer to the soul and body of Christ,[13] while I saw in the two terms not two parts of Christ, but two aspects of his being, that of mortal existence and that of the new spiritual life of the resurrection.[14]

About the identity of the "spirits" of 3:19 we were largely in agreement[15]: these are the fallen angels associated in Jewish traditions with the flood. Reicke regarded it as probable that the souls of the human sinners of the flood could also be included, a view which I was unable to accept.

Since Reicke saw in the death of Christ the occasion on which he made his proclamation to the spirits, he naturally favored the view that Christ's journey was actually his descent to the underworld.[16] On the other hand, I understood "made alive in the spirit" as a reference to the bodily resurrection of Christ and the following ἐν ᾧ as a reference to the new spiritual existence of the risen Lord. Thus the occasion of his journey was rather his ascension. The later Jewish tradition which presented the fallen angels as guarded in the heavens seemed to give further ground for this view.[17]

For Reicke the term ἐκήρυξεν retains its common meaning, that of preaching the gospel. Christ revealed himself as "the humbly suffering, and thereby victorious Messiah." The angels "surrendered in the presence of the Revealer of the Divine Glory." Nothing is said about their future fate.[18] For my part, I understood the same term in a neutral sense, "to make proclamation"; and, given the context, I preferred to see a proclamation similar in content to the announcement of Enoch to the fallen angels—the definitive subjection of the powers of evil, a subjection which at the same time indicated the liberation of men from their power.[19]

---

[13]Reicke, *Disobedient Spirits*, 105-7.

[14]Dalton, *Christ's Proclamation*, 124-34.

[15]Reicke, *Disobedient Spirits*, 52-92; Dalton, *Christ's Proclamation*, 143-50.

[16]Reicke, *Disobedient Spirits*, 115-18.

[17]Dalton, *Christ's Proclamation*, 177-85.

[18]Reicke, *Disobedient Spirits*, 118-25.

[19]Dalton, *Christ's Proclamation*, 150-57.

So far we have been considering Reicke's interpretation of 1 Pet 3:19 as found in his earlier work, *The Disobedient Spirits and Christian Baptism.* Eighteen years later he discussed the same verse in his commentary on 1 Peter. This treatment, given the nature of the commentary, was necessarily restricted, but the same line of interpretation was followed. One notes a small change in the explanation of ἐν ᾧ: he seemed to move away from his earlier suggestion that Christ's journey was associated with his descent to the abode of the dead in the *triduum mortis*, preferring to leave the occasion less determined—Christ's journey was on the occasion of his death and resurrection.[20] As I review my own work now, I think I would be happy to agree with Reicke about the meaning of the proclamation of Christ: it could be taken as the proclamation of the gospel. We must not forget that we are dealing with a myth, a story of angels who sinned with women, whose offspring were giants, who continued their rebellion by instigating the human sin which led to the flood. We are wasting our time in trying to work out what were their psychological reactions to Christ's message. The important thing is that through his proclamation the power of evil was definitely overcome.[21] The situation is just as vague as that of the subjection of the powers in 3:22. We are not told how the powers became subject. What we have in 1 Pet 3:19,22 is an anticipation of that final, universal peace in which God will be "everything to everyone"(1 Cor 15:28).

2

It would be impossible in this short study to give a detailed account of the literature which has appeared on 1 Pet 3:19 since 1965. It must suffice to give some indication of the direction which such literature has followed.

In Salguero's commentary in Spanish on 1 Peter (1965), we find a treatment of 3:19 which probably marks the end of an era. He follows the older Roman Catholic view which presents the soul of Christ descending in the *triduum mortis* to the abode of the dead and there

---

[20]Reicke, *Epistles*, 109, 138 n. 37.

[21]Reicke, *Epistles*, 111: "Ever since the spirits in prison listened to the preaching of Christ, the power of paganism has been broken."

preaching to the souls of the just. The sinners of the flood entered this category by repenting before death. He does not favor the view that these spirits are fallen angels.[22]

Among the other commentaries on 1 Peter which have appeared since 1965, the later editions of Schelkle's and Beare's works, both dated 1970, need no discussion, since the treatment of 3:19 has not been updated.

If we return to the questions of interpretation listed above and restrict ourselves to those which bear directly on the text of 1 Pet 3:19, we may be able to see the way in which interpretation generally has moved. Thus Spicq[23] and Michl[24] agree that ἐν ᾧ refers to the preceding "spirit," that the "spirits" are the souls of men, that Christ's "going" was a descent to the abode of the dead and that he proclaimed salvation. Best[25] differs from this view in understanding the spirits in prison as supernatural beings or angels; he also leaves the interpretation of ἐν ᾧ open. Leaney[26] and Schrage[27] also follow this line of interpretation, except that they would include among the spirits both angels and human souls. Kelly[28] and Fitzmyer[29] support the interpretation I had already proposed: they take ἐν ᾧ as a relative referring to "spirit"; they see in the term "spirits" a reference to fallen angels and in the "going" of Christ his ascension; they understand his proclamation as an announcement of victory.[30] Wheaton[31] agrees with this explanation, except that he takes "spirit" in 3:18 as the equivalent of "soul"; thus Christ's "going" was that of his soul to the underworld.

When we come to consider other expositions of our text outside the regular commentaries, we have a somewhat similar division of opin-

---

[22]José Salguero, *Primera Epístola de San Pedro*, 129: "Hay bastantes autores, sobre todo de tendencia racionalista, que ven en esos *espíritus* a los ángeles caídos."

[23]Spicq, *Épîtres*, 32-35.

[24]Michl, *Katholische Briefe*, 136-37.

[25]Best, *1 Peter*, 143.

[26]Leaney, *Letters*, 51.

[27]Schrage, *Katholische Briefe*, 102-3.

[28]Kelly, *Epistles*, 152-56.

[29]Fitzmyer, "First Epistle of Peter," 367.

[30]Kelly (*Epistles*, 152-56) has arrived at conclusions almost identical with those proposed in my *Christ's Proclamation*.

[31]Wheaton, "1 Peter," 1243-44.

ions. Schnackenburg,[32] Perrot[33] and Salvoni[34] agree with the interpretation of Kelly and Fitzmyer noted above. Whatever the original meaning of the text, Schlier[35] finds in its present context a reference to Christ's descent to the underworld to preach salvation to human sinners. Vorgrimmler's brief treatment[36] follows similar lines. Synge's note[37] suggests that the sinners of the flood had already been "baptized" in its waters; he connects Christ's preaching to them with this baptism—a new approach which needs much more evidence before it can be regarded as helpful. Kürzinger[38] leaves the more disputed points of interpretation open. Cantinat[39] sees in the text an announcement to the infernal powers that their sway over man is at an end.

An inspection of some of the more modern translations of the New Testament does not normally reveal what interpretation of 1 Pet 3:19 is understood, but at least one point is made clear, namely, the function of ἐν ᾧ. The NEB, *Good News for Modern Man*, The NAB all understand it as a relative referring to "spirit"; so does the new official Italian version.[40] On the other hand, the recent ecumenical French translation[41] prefers to take it as a temporal conjunction: "c'est alors"; and the new Spanish version of J. Mateos and L. Alonso Schökel[42] does the same.

This survey of scholarly opinion on 1 Pet 3:19 since the year 1965 hardly presents anything like a consensus. In any case, a counting of heads is hardly in itself an indication of exegetical values. However, it is clear that the majority of scholars still persist in taking ἐν ᾧ as a relative referring to the preceding "spirit." Another important point of

[32]Schnackenburg, "Konkrete Fragen," 24.

[33]Perrot, "Descente du Christ," 20-24.

[34]Salvoni, "Cristo andò nello spirito," 57-65.

[35]Schlier, "Adhortatio," 275-76.

[36]Vorgrimmler, "Christ's Descent," 152, 156.

[37]Synge, "1 Peter 3:18-21," 311.

[38]Kürzinger, "Höllenfahrt Christi," 748.

[39]Cantinat, "Première épître de Pierre," 267.

[40]*La Sacra Bibbia*, 2nd ed. (Roma: Unione Editori Cattolici Italiani, 1974).

[41]*Nouveau Testament*; Traduction oecuménique de la Bible (Paris: Cerf, 1972).

[42]Juan Mateos, trans., and Luis Alonso Schökel, collaborator, *Nuevo Testamento* (Madrid: Cristiandad, 1974).

interpretation has definitely become more common: the view, proposed by Professor Reicke, that we are dealing in the text with a
proclamation of Christ principally or solely to fallen angels. In addition, the majority of commentators, whether they agree with this last
view or not, prefer to see a proclamation of the gospel.

I have left to the end of our discussion a new and major work on the
subject which demands fuller treatment. It is that of H.-J. Vogels,[43]
who, in an extensive treatment of the creedal article of Christ's descent
to "hell," has given much attention to the interpretation of 1 Pet 3:19.[44]
This author maintains that, according to the text, the soul of Christ
descended to the world of the dead to proclaim pardon to the souls of
the human sinners of the flood. This interpretation is a vital part of his
total presentation of the descent of Christ.[45]

Let us take up again the six questions which one needs to ask about
the text and discuss the answers that Vogels proposes. According to
him,[46] the dominant theme in the context is the imitation of Christ,[47]
who is presented in 3:18-19 as the one who shows the way, in his
treatment of abandoned sinners, how Christians should act towards
their pagan adversaries. Vogels, to my mind, exaggerates the pastoral
drive of the Christians to convert their pagan persecutors to the faith.
Certainly this theme is not absent, especially in the fine injunction of
2:12. But in other examples it is at least muted—Christians are to put
senseless people to silence (2:15) and their revilers to shame (3:16). The
situation of a believing wife and her unbelieving husband (3:1) is not
that of persecution. But the emphasis throughout the letter and in this
context is rather on the endurance of Christians, on their being tested
by fire (1:7; 4:12) and on their not giving way to fear (3:14). After all,
they have to face a ravaging devil and stand firm (5:8); and presumably
the devil had something to do with persecution and persecutors.[48]

---

[43]Vogels, *Christi Abstieg* (see n. 5).

[44]Vogels, *Christi Abstieg*, 15-141.

[45]*Lumière et Vie* 17/87 (1968) is totally dedicated to various aspects of Christ's
descent into "hell." A very different view from that of Vogels is there presented, one
which personally I find more convincing. There is no reference to this volume in
Vogel's work.

[46]Vogels, *Christi Abstieg*, 31-44.

[47]Cf. particularly 1 Pet 2:19-24.

[48]Vogels (*Christi Abstieg*, 40-41) curtly dismisses the proposal that the context of

Throughout the letter, it is stated that Christ dies for "you" (2:21,24; 3:18); on the other hand, unbelievers are condemned (2:8; 4:5,17). Actually, if one simply looks at the persons involved in 3:18-4:5, one will find a constant contrast (implied or expressed) between "you" (3:18 [ὑμᾶς], 21 [ὑμᾶς]; 4:1,4) and "they" (3:19,20,22; 4:2-5). Obviously no drastic conclusions need be drawn about the final fate of the unbelievers; it is simply a question of where the writer puts his emphasis.

Vogels does not accept the view that the Enoch literature provides a helpful religious background for our text. In particular, he denies that there is a parallel between the meeting of Enoch with the "watchers" and the meeting of Christ with the "spirits."[49] He examines closely the texts normally cited from 1 Enoch and rightly points out a defect in the common argument which supposes that the "watchers" are in prison at the time of Enoch's announcement. Actually, in 1 Enoch 14:15 the "watchers" are condemned to future imprisonment. But, on the other hand, for the purposes of his argument, he tends to treat this work as a logically developed and unified whole, whereas in fact it is an inconsistent and loosely composed work.[50] Vogels, in addition, does not even mention other valuable sources in the same general tradition which clearly connect the sin of the angels and the flood. It is particularly regrettable that he neglects 2 Enoch, which, to my mind, is of primary importance for the study of 1 Pet 3:19.[51] It is in the gospels, above all, that he tries to find a helpful background to explain our text[52]; but his study of John 5:25-29 and of Luke 12:58-59 will hardly convince the reader that in these texts we have either a preaching of Jesus in the world of the dead or the existence of a "prison" in the afterlife.

As we have already seen, the interpretation of ἐν ᾧ is of great importance for the understanding of our text. Vogels sees in this phrase

---

3:19 is that of Christ's victory over evil and the Christians' share in that victory: "An einen Sieg über die Heiden, wie Dalton aus 3,16ff erhebt, konnten weder Christus noch die Christen interessiert sein."

[49] Vogels, *Christi Abstieg*, 74-86.

[50] Cf. Martin Rist, "Book of Enoch," *IDB*, 2:105: "It is quite obvious that Enoch is a complex book, lacking unity of treatment and of concepts. Consequently, it is exceedingly difficult, if not impossible, to state the actual views of the compiler."

[51] Cf. Dalton, *Christ's Proclamation*, 180-83.

[52] Vogels, *Christi Abstieg*, 51-71.

a temporal conjunction referring to the previous context, which is dominated by ἔπαθεν of 3:18: Christ's journey took place on the occasion of his "suffering" ("dying").[53] This interpretation seems to me too dubious to provide a foundation for the important consequences drawn from it. It is not clear how Vogels could conduct his argument if one were to assume that the activity of Christ were that of the risen Lord, a view which must retain some probability.

The author understands the "spirits" as the souls of the human sinners of the flood.[54] Since he already regards the explanation based on the Enoch literature as an "impossibility,"[55] it is not difficult to make out a case for this view. However, the argument based on the vocabulary of Gen 6:17; 7:15,22 is unconvincing.[56]

If we ask where Christ went on his journey, Vogels replies that he went as a dead person to the place of the dead.[57] He rules out any proclamation to the fallen angels in the heavens because their abode can only be in the abyss.[58] He is unaware of the Jewish tradition which situates them "guarded" in the heavens.[59]

The proclamation of Christ, according to the author, was a message of salvation. This brings him to the problem of conversion after death. He maintains that the preaching of Christ was not aimed at the conversion of these dead sinners (*Bekehrungspredigt*), but that it was an announcement of salvation (*Heilsankündigung*).[60] Their meeting with Christ was for them a purifying judgment (*Läuterungsgericht*). These souls apparently passed, without conversion, from a situation presented by the New Testament as complete alienation from God to that of salvation. I have to admit that I am puzzled by this explanation. While I must confess that I am generally in sympathy with Vogels' universalist outlook, I would find the argument far more convincing if he took the activity of Christ in "hell" (whether it is found in 1 Pet 3:19

---

[53]Vogels, *Christi Abstieg*, 88-97.

[54]Vogels, *Christi Abstieg*, 101-11.

[55]Vogels, *Christi Abstieg*, 103 n. 353.

[56]Vogels, *Christi Abstieg*, 104-8.

[57]Vogels, *Christi Abstieg*, 116-20.

[58]Vogels, *Christi Abstieg*, 118.

[59]Cf. *2 Enoch* 7:1-3; *T. Levi* 3:2.

[60]Vogels, *Christi Abstieg*, 121-22.

or not) as a mythical element in Christian tradition, as a way of saying that Christ calls all men, even those regarded as the most abandoned, to faith and salvation—but always, of course, in this present life.

Whatever the final verdict on Vogels' work, future students of 1 Pet 3:19 will be challenged by his forceful and highly original study. To do it justice, the book needs a discerning reader, ready to sift the value of the arguments, since the author tends to marshall every sort of argument, great and small, to support his thesis. And the whole study is constructed with a dangerous logic, with the conclusion of one section basing the argument of the next; whereas, with such a difficult text, the best we can hope for is a reasonable probability based on converging evidence. One thing is clear: the debate on this famous text, to which Bo Reicke has contributed with such distinction, is still alive.[61]

---

[61]Leonhard Goppelt's commentary on 1 Peter (*Der erste Petrusbrief*, 8th ed. [MeyerK 12/1; Göttingen: Vandenhoeck & Ruprecht, 1978]) came to my attention after the completion of this article. This is a completely new work, which gives an extensive treatment of 3:19 (pp. 246-54). Goppelt sees in ἐν ᾧ a conjunction referring to the preceding context as a whole, but he also understands the activity of Christ as that of one who had died and had risen (pp. 246-47). He does not accept the "spirits" as wicked angels because it is unthinkable that they could receive a proclamation of salvation, and also because the angels of Gen 6:1-4 "disobeyed" long before "the days of Noah." Thus he understands Christ's proclamation as the preaching of salvation to the human sinners of the flood. This should be understood as a mythical presentation of Christ's universal call to salvation, which is extended even to those who, in this life, had no opportunity of hearing the gospel (p. 250). The author does not discuss the apparent contradiction between the two ideas: the descent of the soul of Christ in the *triduum mortis* to the abode of the dead, and the visit of the risen Christ, presumably after the *triduum mortis*, to the sinners of the flood. Nor does he discuss the problem that the only "journey" of the risen Lord, otherwise known in the New Testament, is that of his ascension.

REFLECTIONS ON A PAULINE
ALLEGORY IN A FRENCH CONTEXT

W. D. Davies

IN A RECENT contribution[1] I ventured to make a suggestion as to the force of the allegory of the two olives in Rom 11:13-24. Paul used that allegory in addressing Gentile Christians who were falling into anti-Judaism.

The context demands that the olive in Rom 11:17 be a cultivated one, as over against a wild olive (ἀγριέλαιος) mentioned in 11:17. Certain (τίνες) of the branches of the tree of the people of Israel have been lopped off (11:17). The use of the term "certain" is noteworthy. Whereas the translation "certain" suggests a minority, Paul here intends that the majority in Israel be understood as unbelieving and that most or a considerable number of the branches have been cut off. The use of "certain" points to Paul's sensitivity in referring to the unbelief of his people and of their having been cut off as a result.[2]

From what have the unbelieving Jews been cut off? It cannot be that they have been cut off from the Jewish people considered as an ethnic entity. They are still Jews. The branches broken off (the use of the passive verb ἐξεκλάσθησαν indicates the action of God Himself), then, are those Jews who have refused to be part of Israel conceived as the Remnant that has believed in Christ. The cultivated olive in 11:17 stands for the community of Christian believers, the Church, at first composed of Jewish Christians of the root of Abraham. In cutting themselves off from these, or in refusing to believe, the Jews were cutting themselves off from the life of the root as Paul understood it, although they still remained Jews after the flesh. Paul expresses him-

---

[1]W. D. Davies, "Romans 11:13-24. A Suggestion." *Paganism. Judaïsme. Christianisme, Melanges Offert à Marcel Simon*, ed. M. Philonenko (Paris: E. de Boccard, with Univ. des Sciences Humaines de Strasbourg, 1978), 131-144.

[2]Johannes Munck, *Christ and Israel: An Interpretation of Romans 9-11* (Philadelphia: Fortress, 1967) 123-24.

self laconically and clumsily. As the text stands, the Gentiles (the wild olive) who believe are grafted by God into or among (ἐν αὐτοῖς [11:17])³ the branches lopped off so that they share in the cultivated olive. The horticultural process is unthinkable, and Paul himself admits that it is unnatural (11:24). But the Apostle's intent is clear. Through their acceptance of the Gospel the Gentiles have been ingrafted into the People of God, the olive tree. And this olive tree—by the very principle of solidarity to which Paul had appealed in 11:16—is continuous with the root of Abraham, so that through incorporation "in Christ" the Gentiles share in the root which is Abraham, as 11:18 indicates.

But Paul is anxious to insist that the priority always lies with Abraham and the Jewish people. Now that they were counted among the People of God, Gentile Christians were tempted to regard themselves as superior not only to the Jews, who had been lopped off, but also to Jewish-Christians, whom they already outnumbered (11:18). Paul confronts this emerging Gentile arrogance head on.

He refers deliberately to the Gentile Christians as a wild olive. The condition of the Gentiles is that of wildness: they are, for Paul, not "cultivated." Over against Israel, even Israel after the flesh, they have not undergone an equal divine discipline. In Rom 9:4 Paul enumerates the benefits of being a Jew simply by natural descent. To his mind the privileges of the Jews had been the means of producing the cultivated olive which could bear fruit. However, Gentiles constitute a "wild olive" which by nature, be it noted, never produces oil. The Gentiles in being engrafted into the Jewish root contribute nothing. Perhaps it is the necessity of bringing this out forcefully that explains Paul's use of the symbol of the olive rather than that of the more customary one of the vine. The wild vine does produce wild grapes; the wild olive produces nothing useful.⁴

---

³The Greek ἐν αὐτοῖς ("among them") must refer to the branches lopped off. As Ernst Käsemann rightly insists (*An die Römer* [HNT 8a; Tübingen: J. C. B. Mohr, 1973] 296) it cannot mean "instead of." Paul is not dealing with the processes of nature, but with the astonishing activity of Divine Grace. The attempts made to find horticultural parallels to the grafting here described do not convince! See Munck, *Christ and Israel*, 128-30 (Excursus 3: "The True Olive Tree and the Wild Olive Tree"). The most thorough discussion is still that of Myles M. Bourke (*A Study of the Metaphor of the Olive Tree in Romans XI* [Studies in Sacred Theology, 2nd series, no. 3; Washington, D. C.: The Catholic University of America, 1947] 65-111).

⁴As far as I am aware, the first to point out that the wild olive does not bear fruit was

The Gentiles through Christ have now, indeed, been made partakers of the People of God and share in the benefits that spring from its root, Abraham. But this does not eliminate the priority of the Jews in that root. Paul tells the Gentiles: "It is not you who bear the root, but the root bears you" (11:18). The Jewish root is a necessity to Gentile Christians; they cannot live without it. All Gentile boasting over Jews is ruled out.

In 11:19 Paul meets still another Gentile misconception. Some Gentile Christians had the idea that the branches which had been broken off, that is, the unbelieving Jews, had suffered this fate by divine purpose in order that the Gentiles might be engrafted into Israel. The implication is that God had, in fact, "favored" Gentiles over Jews, who were thereby regarded as inferior. Against this the Apostle insists that the responsibility for the unbelief of the Jews rests squarely on themselves, not on divine preference for Gentiles. It was not that God had rejected the Jews. Rather the Jews themselves had chosen not to believe. The Gentiles had not been grafted into the olive because of any superior virtue on their part. In fact, they had not produced spiritual fruits. They were a wild, fruitless olive. The sole reason for their engrafting was their belief (11:19-20). So too, just as with the Jews who had not believed and were lopped off, those Gentiles who were now engrafted through their belief could also lose that status through disbelief. Gentile Christians, therefore, have no ground for claiming any superiority over Jews whether believing or unbelieving. Gentile Christians no less than Jews cannot count on any privilege: God deals with Gentile and Jew alike. In fact, since Jews were by nature related to the root, while Gentiles are not, the probability that those Jews who had been "lopped off" could be re-engrafted into the olive was more likely than that Gentiles should have been grafted into it in the first place. The privileges of Jews are real privileges, although they cannot be the ground of their acceptance.

Outside the confines of the symbols of the olive and the wild olive, but not unrelated to them, Paul announces a special mystery which should rein the arrogance of Gentiles. The unbelief that has befallen Israel is temporary. When what Paul calls "the fullness of the Gentiles" has been brought into "Israel," then all Israel, that is, the totality of the

---

Gustav Dalman (*Arbeit und Sitte in Palästina*, 6 vols. [Gütersloh: C. Bertelsmann, 1928-39], 1: 680). See further Munck, *Christ and Israel*, 128-30.

Jewish people, will be saved (Rom 11:25-26). To justify this position
Paul appeals to God's irrevocable election of the Jews and to the merit
of their fathers (זְכוּת אָבוֹת).[5] In the end, both Gentiles and Jews are included in God's mercy which is as wide as the world.

The symbols of the cultivated olive and the wild olive are used by
Paul, then, in his efforts to formulate a philosophy of history, if we may
so put it, which would acknowledge the place of the Jewish people in
the Christian dispensation. At the very least we may claim that—
altogether apart from Christ—Paul regards Jews as spiritually "cultivated" and the Gentiles as "underprivileged." To be of the root of
Abraham physically was a privilege. The Jewish people were, in this
regard, more fortunate than Gentiles. In 9:1-5 Paul expresses both his
yearning for the salvation of his own people and his awareness of the
advantages of the Jewish people.

The question of the relative importance of Gentiles and Jews in
civilization, which, as we shall see, occupied Voltaire, Paul did not
directly discuss. He was not, as a Jew, narrowly opposed to Hellenistic
culture in all its forms—some of these he adopted as in 1 Cor 5:1,
11:13-14; he recognizes what is fitting for all men (Rom 1:28). His
habitat as an Apostle was mostly the Hellenistic world; he knew its
languages well.[6] He could be a Greek to the Greeks (1 Cor 9:19-23).
Such a person could not have had a "racist" view of the Greeks and
Romans as inferior. When he insisted that he was a Hebrew born of
Hebrews (Phil 3:5), he was not speaking antithetically to criticize or
reject Hellenism, but pointing to a tradition in which he was rooted and

---

[5]This probably is to be taken as a technical phrase. See Solomon Schechter, *Some
Aspects of Rabbinic Theology* (London: The Macmillan Company, 1909) 170-98;
Arthur Marmorstein, *The Doctrine of Merits in Old Rabbinic Literature* (Jews'
College London, Publication 7; London: Oxford University, 1920; New York: KTAV,
1968) 37-107. See W. D. Davies, *Paul and Rabbinic Judaism: Some Rabbinic Elements in Pauline Theology*, 3rd ed. (New York: Macmillan; London: SPCK, 1971)
268-73.

[6]A great classicist, Ulrich von Wilamowitz-Moellendorff, sees in Paul's writing "a
classic of Hellenism" *(Die Griechische und Lateinische Literatur und Sprache*, 3rd
ed. [Leipzig/Berlin: B. G. Teubner, 1912] 232 [= *Die Kultur der Gegenwart* 1/8, ed. P.
Hinneberg]). One of the most salutary changes in recent studies of the first century is
the recognition that there was no rigid separation between the Hellenistic and Jewish
worlds. See especially Martin Hengel, *Judaism and Hellenism: Studies in their
Encounter in Palestine during the Early Hellenistic Period*, 2 vols. (Philadelphia:
Fortress, 1974) and Davies, *Paul and Rabbinic Judaism*, 1-16.

of which he was proud, because to that tradition belonged the spiritual privileges to which we have already referred. As a Christian Paul did not think of Gentiles as inferior to Jews because of their race, but only because they were outside what he regarded as a superior religious tradition.[7]

It was the Jews' participation in that tradition that led Paul to ascribe to them a mysterious role in the history of mankind which enabled him to insist that Israel had a function even after Christ had appeared. In the *Festschrift* for Marcel Simon I suggested that Paul's allegory of the olive and the wild olive is doubly deliberate. It points not only to his high estimate of Israel but also to his low estimate of the spiritual attainments of the Gentiles. The true olive is a symbol of culture represented by Jewish tradition in its strictly Jewish and Christian expression.

While writing for the Simon *Festschrift*, my examination of the cultivated olive as a symbol for the Jews led me to ask how Paul's estimate of the Jewish people had fared in the thought of two French writers whose highly significant engagement with the Jews has much occupied me. In the thought of the first, Paul played a very important role; whereas in that of the other the Apostle was an object of contempt. I refer to Jacques Maritain and Voltaire.

1. Jacques Maritain and the Jews

For many reasons (for example, the influence of his wife Raïssa, a Jewess who became, like him, a convert to Catholicism) Jacques Maritain was agonizingly—an adverb used advisedly—concerned with the people of Israel. Writing at a time when anti-Semitism oversha-

---

[7]The question of the relation of Paul to culture is difficult. His main contacts were not with the higher intellectual currents of the Graeco-Roman world but more with the religious which, to judge from his epistles, took on a gnostic cast. See Hans von Campenhausen, "Faith and Culture in the New Testament," *Tradition and Life in the Church: Essays and Lectures in Church History* (Philadelphia: Fortress, 1968) 19-41; Hans von Campenhausen, "The Christian and Social Life according to the New Testament," *Tradition and Life*, 141-59; also W. C. van Unnik, "The Critique of Paganism in 1 Peter 1:18," *Neotestamentica et Semitica: Studies in honour of Matthew Black*, ed. E. Earle Ellis and Max Wilcox (Edinburgh: T. & T. Clark, 1969) 129-42. It is interesting to read Raïssa Maritain's description of the Sorbonne in the light of von Campenhausen; see Raïssa Maritain, *We Have Been Friends Together. Memoirs* (New York: Longmans, Green and Co., 1945), esp. 60-78.

dowed Western Europe, he found in Paul's Epistle to the Romans especially a scriptural ground on which he could stand to oppose the horror and from which he could expound what he conceived of as the "mystery" of the existence of the people of Israel. He refused the facile explanations of that existence in terms of race, nation or people, and preferred Paul's characterization of it as a "mystery." He did not enlarge upon the Apostle's precise use of that term but did give his full assent to Paul's recognition of Israel as irrevocably elect.[8]

To appreciate the thrust of Maritain's insistence on "The Mystery of Israel," certain attitudes towards the Jews among the French have to be borne in mind. Brought up in a distinguished Protestant family but converted to Catholicism, Maritain inevitably encountered in his life and in his studies an attitude towards Jews which had become largely endemic in Roman Catholicism and the main currents of Protestantism. The criticism of Judaism which had accompanied the birth of Christianity, at a later date feeding on certain cultural and economic factors, developed into the fear of and hatred towards Jews to which the medieval period in Europe witnesses. Medieval anti-Jewish attitudes had persisted both in Tridentine Catholicism and in Protestantism. The majority of the clergy before the French Revolution were purveyors of what might be termed medieval anti-Judaism.[9] These attitudes to which we refer were not seriously challenged until this century and especially Vatican II. Waiving the question of whether the term "anti-Semitism" with its racial connotations can legitimately be used of these attitudes, and granting the occasional presence of Christian clergy who sought to champion the Jews, it is impossible to deny that traditional Christian anti-Jewish attitudes in Europe did nothing to dispel the climate within which anti-Semitism, properly so-called, could and did develop. Maritain was sadly and acutely aware of this. He knew those traditional Christian prejudices which had thrust Jews outside the main stream of civilization because they were alleged to be a people who had deliberately placed themselves outside salvation. And yet it was not with this traditional anti-Judaism that Maritain was

---

[8]Jacques Maritain, "The Mystery of Israel," *Ransoming the Time* (New York: Charles Scribner's Sons, 1941) 147-49.

[9]See Arthur Hertzberg, "Churchmen and the Jews," *The French Enlightenment and the Jews* (New York: Columbia University; Philadelphia: The Jewish Publication Society of America, 1968) 248-67.

directly engaged.[10] Rather he was concerned with two positions, one political and the other religious.

Maritain wrote his work *Le Mystère d'Israël* in 1937, when it was still possible in a France nauseated by anti-Semitic trends, "to consider the Jewish problem in a purely philosophical, objective and dispassionate manner."[11] But even at that date, as Maritain points out, there was a political liberalism in which it was possible to conceive of a "decisive solution" to the Jewish question. He does not enlarge upon the phrase "decisive solution."[12] But it seems clear that he refers to that long standing "liberal" tradition which saw in the emancipation of Jewry and the increasing recognition of their rights a means towards their complete assimilation and silent disappearance as a distinct people. This liberal tradition insisted that the existing conditions and character of the Jews had been created by the persecutions from which they had suffered, that it was necessary to "enlighten" them, that this enlightenment would gradually lead to their assimilation. But by the time *Le Mystère d'Israël* had been translated into English in 1941, the situation had ominously changed: the thought of a new kind of solution had appeared. The precise date at which the doctrine of "the final solution" emerged in Germany and was deliberately pursued and implemented is not here important. By 1941, if not earlier, Maritain was aware of it. He writes of the "anti-Semitic nightmare spreading like a mental epidemic even among some groups of democratic people."[13] It is against both the liberal political quest for a "decisive solution" and the more barbaric Nazi threat of a "final solution" that Maritain responded:

> Israel is a mystery. . . . If Saint Paul is right, we shall have to call the *Jewish problem* a problem *without solution*—that is, until the great reintegration foreseen by the apostle, which will be like a "resurrection from the dead." To

---

[10]The main elements in the traditional anti-Judaism were 1) the crucifixion of Jesus by the Jews, 2) the dispersion as a proof of the merited punishment of Jews and of the divinity of Christ, 3) the continued existence and persistent misery of the Jews as a theological necessity. These emerge conveniently, for example, in Pascal (*Pensées. Édition nouvelle revue sur les manuscrits et les meilleurs textes avec une introduction, des notes et un index analytique par Victor Giraud* [Paris: C. Crès et Cie, 1924] nos. 571, 601, 619, 620, 638, 675, 640).

[11]Maritain, *Ransoming the Time*, 141.

[12]Maritain, *Ransoming the Time*, 149.

[13]Maritain, *Ransoming the Time*, 141.

wish to find, in the pure, simple, decisive sense of the word, a *solution* of the problem of Israel, is to attempt to stop the movement of history.[14]

On the purely human, political plane, Maritain—as Paul in Martain's view had insisted—urges that there is no "solution" to the Jewish problem.[15] The Jew is here to stay. We must not simply learn to "tolerate" him as a "squalid nuisance" (a horrible phrase used in this connection) but to co-exist with him in grateful appreciation.

Maritain points to what makes it impossible to ignore the presence of the Jew. There is above all his intensity. The presence of the Jew in any society ensures tension.

> The solution of a practical problem is the end of tension and conflict; the end of contradiction, peace itself. To assert that there is no solution—in an absolute sense—to the problem of Israel is to ensure the existence of struggle.[16]

Or again:

> Israel is here—Israel which is not of the world—at the deepest core of the world, to irritate it, to exasperate it, to *move* it. Like some foreign substance, like a living yeast mixed into the main body, it gives the world no quiet, it prevents the world from sleeping, it teaches the world to be dissatisfied and restless so long as it has not God, it stimulates the movement of history.[17]

Or again:

> Often despite itself, and at times manifesting in various ways a materialized Messianism, which is the darkened aspect of its vocation to the absolute, the Jewish people, ardently, intelligently, actively, give witness, at the very heart of man's history, to the supernatural. Whence the conflicts and tensions which, under all kinds of disguises, cannot help but exist between Israel and the nations.
>
> It is an illusion to believe that this tension can disappear (at least before the fulfillment of the prophecies). It is base—one of those specimens of baseness natural to man as an animal (be he an Arab, and himself of the lineage of Shem, or a Slav, or a Latin, or a German . . .) and a baseness of which Christianity alone can, to the degree that it is truly lived, free mankind—to wish to end the matter by anti-Semitic violence, whether it be of open persecution, or politically "mitigated." There is but one way, and that is to accept this state of tension, and to make the best of it in each particular

---

[14]Maritain, *Ransoming the Time*, 149.

[15]That Paul knew of the Jewish "problem" appears from Romans. See W. D. Davies, "Paul and the People of Israel," *NTS* 24 (1977-1978) 4-39.

[16]Maritain, *Ransoming the Time*, 149.

[17]Maritain, *Ransoming the Time*, 156,

case, not in hatred, but in that concrete intelligence which love requires of each of us, so that we may agree with our companion—with our "adversary" as the gospel says—quickly while we are with him on the way; and in the awareness that "all have sinned and have need of the glory of God"—*omnes quidem peccaverunt, et egent gloria Dei.* "The history of the Jews," says Leon Bloy, "dams the history of the human race as a dike dams a river, in order to raise its level."[18]

Or again:

I have already said that Israel's passion is not a co-redemptive passion, achieving for the eternal salvation of souls what is lacking (as concerns application, not merits) in the Saviour's suffering. It is suffered for the goading on of the world's temporal life. In itself, it is the passion of a being caught up in the temporal destiny of the world, which both irritates the world and seeks to emancipate it, and on which the world avenges itself for the pangs of its history.[19]

The price paid by Israel for its life as "a goad," or as Bloy's dike that raises the river in history has been high. The persecution of the Jews is the price of their peculiar contribution and status as elect. The matter is illuminatingly, though laconically stated by Maritain as follows:

It has been said that the tragedy of Israel is the tragedy of mankind; and that is why there is no solution to the Jewish problem. Let us state it more precisely: it is the tragedy of man in his struggle with the world and of the world in its struggle with God. Jacob, lame and dreaming, tireless irritant of the world and scapegoat of the world, indispensable to the world and intolerable to the world—so fares the wandering Jew. The persecution of Israel seems like the sign of the moments of crisis in this tragedy, when the play of human history almost stops at obstacles that the distress and moral weakness of nations cannot surmount, and when for a new start it demands some fresh horror.[20]

To the political liberals offering a decisive solution and to the National Socialists offering a final solution, Maritain opposes the Pauline doctrine: Israel is the chosen olive tree.[21]

But Maritain faced a less obvious religious criticism of his interpretation of Paul as justifying the continuance of Jewry. Most "enlight-

---

[18]Maritain, *Ransoming the Time*, 168.

[19]Maritain, *Ransoming the Time*, 177. Is there not here a strange "dualism" in Maritain's position?

[20]Maritain, *Ransoming the Time*, 151.

[21]Maritain, *Ransoming the Time*, 183.

ened" Christians had approached the Jewish question from the religious angle somewhat as follows. The emphasis of Judaism is on the One God. The service of Him just because God is One and there is no other, must within itself contain universality and should have led to the search for a universal community. But historically Judaism remained concentrated on Israel. The Gospel offered it a choice: was it prepared to become a truly universal religion? Judaism rejected that challenge and despite the large humanism of many of its sages, chose to become an essentially closed society. Fortunately Christianity has carried on the values of its Jewish heritage. It follows that there is no *raison d'être* for the continuance of Judaism. Christians could justifiably welcome the disappearance of Jewry on religious grounds. Christians who held such a view were far removed from the advocates of a "decisive solution" or a "final solution." But they usually did ignore the history of Jews since the first century and refused to take seriously the continuing presence and mystery of Israel in the world.[22]

Maritain opposes these liberal Christian views as he did the politically liberal and Nazi ones. Drawing upon Romans 9-11, he asserts that there is a continuing *necessity* for the existence of the Jewish people. Not only are they not to be subjected to a "final solution" by annihilation or to a "decisive solution" by assimilation, but to consider them as religiously irrelevant, as did liberal Christians, was a denial of the Christian scriptures themselves. What is now the cultivated olive, the community of believing Christians, is of the same root as the non-believing Jews. Like Paul, Maritain insists that without its Jewish root the Christian community itself cannot live. The covenant of the Jewish people with God is eternally valid; they still have a function even in the Christian dispensation (Rom 11:1,2).[23]

But, over against the interpretation of Paul advocated by Maritain, it has been urged that, in fact, there is implicit in Paul himself an attitude towards Jews which ultimately requires their absorption, both

---

[22]This position was probably most forcefully expressed by Arnold Joseph Toynbee, *The Study of History*, 12 vols. (London/New York/Toronto: Oxford University, 1954-61), 5:74-75; 8:580-83.

[23]See Jacques Maritain, *La Pensée de Saint Paul* (New York: Editions de la Maison Française; Longmans, Green & Co., 1944) 141: "A travers toutes les vicissitudes de son exil et de l'histoire du monde Israël reste toujours le peuple de Dieu—frappé mais toujours aimé à cause de ses pères."

by assimilation into the general society and by the Christian community itself. Does not Paul look forward to a time when all Jews will be saved and *ipso facto* lose their identity? Does he not too envisage at the End the cessation of Israel after the flesh? On the basis of Romans 9-11, on which Maritain rested his case, even Paul has been declared an "anti-Semite."[24] Such an astounding charge requires a careful examination and definition of terms.

In the nineteenth and twentieth century sense in which the term anti-Semitism has come to be used, as denoting an hatred towards Jews on the grounds of their racial inferiority, it cannot apply to Paul. The justification for rejecting any anti-Semitism in the strict sense in Paul is that Romans 9-11 makes clear that the root of the cultivated olive, the true Israel, is Abraham, the father of the Jewish people. If we should use racial terms at all, and this seems dubious, the descent of the Jews from Abraham immediately makes anti-Semitism in any racial sense impossible for Paul. Maritain expresses himself more convolutedly: "The ingenious anti-Semites who vituperate 'Jewish racism' forget that the first one responsible for the concept of an elect race, that concept being taken at its pure source, is the God of Abraham, of Isaac, of Jacob, the God of Israel—*your* God, dear Christians who turn yourselves against the chosen olive tree into which you were grafted."[25]

But what of the more subtle charge that the Pauline hope for the End demands the end of the Jews as Jews. Does he reveal what might be called an eschatological anti-Semitism? Simply to point to Paul's expressions of concern for his own people (9:1-5; 10:1) as making such a charge unthinkable is not enough. Maritain is aware of the need to

---

[24]So Rosemary Radford Ruether, *Faith and Fratricide: The Theological Roots of Anti-Semitism* (A Crossroad Book; New York: Seabury, 1974) 95-107, esp. 104: "Paul's position was unquestionably that of anti-Judaism"; p. 107: "he [Paul] enunciates a doctrine of the rejection of the Jews (rejection of Judaism as the proper religious community of God's people) in the most radical form, seeing it as rejected not only now, through the rejection of Christ, but from the beginning. The purpose of Paul's "mystery" is not to concede any ongoing validity to Judaism, but rather to assure the *ultimate vindication of the Church*. If the Church is the eschatological destiny of Israel, then this truth must finally win out by having the 'Jews' themselves testify to it. They must admit finally that it is not through Torah, but through faith in Jesus as the Christ, that they are intended to be saved" (her italics). Ruether does not sufficiently distinguish anti-Semitism and anti-Judaism. She uses both terms apparently interchangeably. See my "Paul and the People of Israel" (n. 15) for a critique of her position.

[25]Maritain, *Ransoming the Time*, 183.

face the charge squarely. What mainly concerns him is the continued
role of Jews in history. Like the cultivated olive, that is, the believing
Christian community, the Jewish people also, born of the same root,
remains to stir and to sustain mankind, although in a different way
from that of the Church, to the End. Moreover, Maritain insists that
the nature of the final salvation of all Jews, as Paul understands it,
safeguards their identity. One could have wished Maritain to have been
as explanatory at this very crucial point as he is emphatic. He writes:

> But when the Jewish people as such shall convert itself and pass under the
> Law of the new covenant, it will be within its own ancient privileges,
> extended to all the peoples in accordance with the very universality of the
> Church, and transfigured in accordance with the truth of the spirit, that, in
> joining itself to the Gentiles in one single field, *it will find itself received anew.*
> (our italics)[26]

Or again:

> And as for the extraordinary promise concerning the future conversion of
> Israel according to the flesh, does it not indicate for this people, as God's
> people, an astonishing and permanent prerogative?[27]

This is Maritain's understanding of Paul. No one has sought to do
greater justice to that Apostle's care for his own people. That he truly
interpreted that care we do not doubt. But that the final engrafting of
all Israel on to the cultivated olive, in the mind of Paul, would not be
the abandonment of its identity but its reinterpretation on a higher
level, requires a more detailed and subtle treatment of Rom 11:25ff., in
particular, than Maritain provides. He is, unfortunately, more
emphatic at this point than he is explanatory.

Throughout his treatment, Maritain makes abundantly clear his
Roman Catholic *point de départ.* His central emphasis in his understanding of the mystery of Israel is on its sacred, theological or supernatural character. The elect olive is what concerns him. It is very
significant that he nowhere refers to the symbol of the wild olive,
bearing no fruit, as denoting the Gentiles. "Israel" for him was and is
the astounding interweaving of the natural and the sacred, of the
supernatural and the temporal: its case was unique. But unique as
Israel is, Paul enabled the French scholar to appeal to the profound,

[26]Maritain, *Ransoming the Time*, 186.
[27]Maritain, *Ransoming the Time*, 187-88.

indeed essential, continuity of the Christian faith with Judaism and of the Church with the people of Israel. This meant that for Maritain Jews were not "outsiders" in the Christian dispensation who had to be assimilated or annihilated, but part of the very root and continuing life of Christendom. Israel had introduced into Western civilization a supernatural order, which gave it meaning. Salvation was and is from the Jews (compare John 4:22). Although Maritain does not dwell on the symbol of the wild olive for the Gentiles, the implication of his position is that that symbol is an appropriate one.

2. Voltaire and the Jews

The contrast with another tradition in France leaps to the eye. One might have expected Maritain, in insisting on the necessity for the full recognition of the people of Israel, while primarily resting on Scripture, to have appealed also to the tradition of the French Enlightenment. Would not its emphasis on tolerance and universalism have furthered that acceptance of Jews on their own terms that Maritain desiderated? The emancipation of the Jews in the French Revolution has generally been understood as the fruit of the enlightened *philosophes*. They insisted on a rationality and tolerance extending even to Jews. Their enlightened attitude was conveniently reinforced by the financial prudence which led eighteenth century France to recognize the benefits that Jewish capital would bring. In the Enlightenment a philosophic and an economic climate combined to make a more humane attitude to Jews acceptable and even necessary. And yet Maritain makes no appeal to this. The reason is not far to seek. The record of the Enlightenment on the Jewish question is not unambiguous.[28] That ambiguity surfaces most strikingly in its most luminous figure, Voltaire.

---

[28]See especially Hertzberg, *The French Enlightenment and the Jews*; Fadien Lovsky, "L'Antisémitisme Rationaliste," *Antisémitisme et Mystère d'Israel* (Paris: Albin Michel, 1955) 261-300. For a different view, see Pierre Aubery, "Voltaire et les Juifs: ironie et démystification," *Studies on Voltaire and the Eighteenth Century,* ed. Theodore Besterman (Genève: Institut et Musée Voltaire Les Delices, 1963), 24:67-79; Paul H. Meyer, "The Attitude of the Enlightenment towards the Jews," *Studies on Voltaire and the Eighteenth Century*, ed. Theodore Besterman (Genève: Institut et Musée Voltaire Les Delices, 1963), 26:1161-1206.

It is not for an outsider to Voltairean studies, even one intensely involved in the question concerned, to settle the problem of Voltaire's attitude to Jews. Aubery refuses to be intimidated by those who find it anti-Semitic. He admits that, as are all born into Christendom, Voltaire was inevitably touched by that disease even as he urged the brotherhood of man. Beginning with a quotation from Voltaire's own works, Aubery writes: " 'Oublions nos querelles,' 'le monde entier n'est qu'une famille, les hommes sont frères; les frères se querellent quelque fois; mais les bons coeurs reviennent aisément.' (M. XXIX. 582) Ces phrases de Voltaire . . . expriment une idée sur laquelle, à son habitude, il revient sans cesse."[29] Aubery insists that "En réalité ni antisémite ni philosémite Voltaire s'est toujours efforcé de juger les Juifs avec équité."[30] Voltaire, he suggests, treated Jews with irony and demystified them, but except insofar as he had inherited the endemic anti-Semitism of Christendom,[31] he cannot be charged with that prejudice. His virulent attacks on Jews are on those of the ancient world not on those of his own time; a rigid distinction must be made between these two categories. "Il prend bien soin de distinguer entre la grossièreté, la

---

[29]Aubery, "Voltaire et les Juifs," *Studies*, 24:73.

[30]Aubery, "Voltaire et les Juifs," *Studies*, 24:71.

[31]That the anti-Semitism of the Enlightenment is the residue of Christian influences has been used to explain the traces of it in Voltaire and others, who could not escape Christian contamination. Thereby the Enlightenment is exculpated. Related to this is the claim that Voltaire's attacks on the Old Testament and on Jews are motivated by his concern to attack Christianity, as was Hitler's "final solution." In the eighteenth century as in the twentieth, Christianity was too well established to be attacked directly. The wiser course was to attack it through its supposedly weaker progenitor, Judaism. This in turn points to a factor which must be fully recognized. Voltaire and other critics of the establishment were not facing paper tigers. When they attacked the established order in Church and State, they risked severe punishment and even death. See, for example, Hugh Trevor-Roper, "The Historical philosophy of the Enlightenment," *Studies on Voltaire and the Eighteenth Century*, ed. Theodore Besterman (Genève: Institut et Musee Voltaire Les Delices, 1963), 27:1667-87. It is not easy to condemn Voltaire for attacking Christianity through Judaism. But, even *if* he did so, his motives, though not justifiable, are not incomprehensible. His personal position was fraught with insecurity. See John McManners, *Reflections at the Deathbed of Voltaire: the Art of Dying in Eighteenth Century France*, an inaugural lecture delivered before the University of Oxford on 21 November 1974 (Oxford: Clarendon, 1975). Others have pointed to Voltaire's unfortunate personal experience with Jews as a source of his anti-Judaism. On exposing the anti-Christian origin and character of Hitler's anti-Semitism, see Maurice Samuel, *The Great Hatred* (New York: A. A. Knopf, 1940) and W. D. Davies, "Chosen People: The Approach to Antisemitism," *The Congregational Quarterly* 26 (1948) 327-41.

barbarie des anciens Hébreux et les moeurs de ses contemporains juifs."[32] But apart from the natural tendency of minds in the least inclined to anti-Semitism—and such minds do not lend themselves to refinements historical or otherwise; see Jean-Paul Sartre, *Anti-Semite and Jew* (New York: 1965) 17-54 (=*Réflexions sur la Question Juive* [Paris: 1946])—to ignore such a distinction deliberately, it would be difficult not to be influenced in the direction of anti-Semitism by such sentences as the following by Voltaire: "N'est-il pas clair (humainement parlant, et ne considérant que les causes secondes) que les Juifs, qui espéraient la conquête du monde, ont été presque toujours asservis, ce fut leur faute? Et si les Romains dominèrent, ne le méritèrent ils pas par leur courage et par leur prudence? *Je demande très humblement pardon aux Romains de les comparer un moment avec les Juifs*"[33] (our italics). The underlined words would jump across any chronological distinctions! Voltaire closes his article on "Juifs" in *Dictionnaire Philosophique* as follows: "Enfin vous ne trouverez en eux qu'un peuple ignorant et barbare, que joint depuis longtemps la plus sordide avarice à la plus détestable superstition, et à la plus invincible haine pour tous les peuples qui les tolèrent et qui les enrichissent. Il ne faut pourtant pas les brûler."[34] Such irony is always difficult to assess; it so easily passes over into cynical cruelty.

It is not surprising, then, that there are others who do not deal so gently with Voltaire. They find that his tolerance and generosity did not extend to the Jews. Anti-Semitism is one of the rare Christian errors he did not condemn.[35] That he was only thinking in negative terms of Jews in the distant past and not of his contemporaries seems to be contradicted by the ridicule with which he met the proposition made in Great Britain in 1753 that Jews should be given citizenship. Whether or not Voltaire himself should be regarded as an anti-Semite, his treatment of the Jews certainly could and did provide ammunition for anti-Semites in later years. In *Essai sur les Moeurs* Voltaire writes:

[32]Aubery, "Voltaire et les Juifs," *Studies*, 24:71.

[33]François Marie Arouet de Voltaire, "Questions sur les Conquêtes des Romains et leur décadence," *Essai sur les moeurs et l'esprit des nations et sur les principaux faits de l'histoire depuis Charlemagne jusquà Louis XIII*, ed. René Pomeau, 2 vols. (Classique Garnier; Paris: Garnier frères, 1963), 1:183.

[34]Voltaire, s.v. "Juifs," *Dictionnaire Philosophique, Oeuvres Complètes de Voltaire*, new edition (Paris: Garnier frères, 1879) 521.

[35]Lovsky, "L'Antisémitisme Rationaliste," 263.

> Vous êtes frappés de cette haine et de ce mépris que toutes les nations ont
> toujours eus contre les Juifs: c'est la suite inévitable de leur législation; il
> fallait, ou qu'ils subjuguassent tout, ou qu'ils fussent écrasés. Il leur fut
> ordonné d'avoir les nations en horreur (Deut. VII:16) . . . . Ils gardèrent tous
> leur usages, qui sont précisément le contraire des usages sociables; ils furent
> donc avec raison traités comme une nation opposée en tout aux autres; les
> servant par avarice, les détestant par fanatisme, se faisant de l'usure un devoir
> sacré. Et ce sont nos pères.[36]

The denigration of ancient Jews in the article "Juifs" (section IV:
"Résponse à quelques objections") in the *Dictionnaire Philosophique*
is clear: in number inferior; they massacred the inhabitants of Palestine
whose land they took; their law was cruel; their military prowess
dubious; Solomon had wealth and concubines but no timber or
workers for the Temple; Judah and Israel hated each other; they
borrowed an alphabet in Babylon; learnt little from the Babylonian
sages ("Il parâit que les Juifs apprirent peu de chose de la science des
mages: ils s'adonnèrent aux métiers de courtiers, de changeurs, et de
fripiers, par là ils se rendirent nécessaires, *comme ils le sont encore*, et
ils s'enrichirent" [our italics]); only the worst party returned to Israel
from Babylon; they had internal dissensions; the Jews loved money
more than the Temple ("L'esprit séditieux de ce peuple se porta à de
nouveaux excès: son caractère en tout temps était d'être cruel, et son
sort d'être puni"). Only their fecundity preserved them ("Les Juifs ont
regardé comme leurs deux grands devoirs: des infants et de l'argent").
Militarily they were ineffective; they had no navy; they had no industry; their government was as ineffective as their military discipline;
their philosophy was negligible ("Celui que aurait mangé du boudin ou
du lapin aurait été lapidé, et celui qui niait l'immortalité de l'âme
pouvait être grand-prêtre"); it was nothing noble like their horror of
idolatry that caused them to be hated but their cruelty to those whom
they conquered. "Les Hébreux ont presque toujours été ou errants, ou
brigands, ou esclaves, ou séditieux; *ils sont encore vagabonds aujour-
d'hui sur la terre, et en horreur aux hommes, assurant que le ciel et la
terre, et tous les hommes, ont été créés pour eux seuls*" (our italics).[37]

Small wonder in the light of such assertions that Labroue, an
anti-Semite during the occupation of France in the forties, wrote:
"Notre antijudaïsme d'État s'inspire si peu de prosélytisme confessio-

---

[36]Voltaire, *Essai sur les moeurs*, 2:64.

[37]Voltaire, s.v. "Juifs," *Dictionnaire Philosophique*, 512-20.

nel qu'il trouve sa référence la plus décisive dans la tradition Voltai-
rienne."[38] Hitler himself, through Frederick II, it has been asserted,
drank from Voltairean springs.[39] To understand how the Enlightenment could spawn or feed anti-Semitism, we should consider two
aspects of it present in Voltaire.

First, to the rationalist seeking for a universal, ordered society, the
very existence of the Jews, who challenged him with what seemed to be
irrational claims, was itself irrational. The *philosophes,* like some later
Christian liberals, found a scandal in the particularity of the Jews; they
refused to fit into a rational universe.[40] The attacks of Voltaire on
Christianity and on the Jews again and again emphasize the sheer
irrationality of the two faiths.[41] In the world of the Enlightenment a
chosen people was anathema.

But secondly, equally offensive to Voltaire would have been the
notion that the Gentiles were a wild olive as Paul had held. His attitude
to Jews is bound up with his understanding of Western civilization.
Mutatis mutandis, his attitude could be taken as the exact opposite to
that of Paul (Voltaire's treatment of whom is consistently more unfa-
vorable than his treatment of Jesus)[42] and to that of Maritain. For
Paul, as later for Maritain, the olive, "the Israel of God," ultimately
deriving from a Semitic root, provided for salvific agent in history,
whereas the wild olive, signifying the Gentile world, was spiritually
fruitless. For Voltaire on the other hand, the Semitic tradition was
despicable. To him the people of the Bible suffered from an unreasona-
ble and extreme pride: "C'était, il faut avouer, un chétif peuple arabe
sans art et sans science, caché dans un petit pays montueux et ignoré . . .

[38]Henri Labroue, *Voltaire antijuif* (Paris: Documents contemporains, 1942) 8
(quoted by Lovsky, "L'Antisémitisme Rationaliste," 267). Lovsky, however, recognizes Labroue's tendentiousness and the questionableness of some of his citations.
Aubery ("Voltaire et les Juifs," *Studies,* 24:70-71) dismisses Labroue.

[39]Lovsky, "L'Antisémitisme Rationaliste," 267.

[40]Aubery ("Voltaire et les Juifs," *Studies,* 24:68) quotes Voltaire's *Sermon des
Cinquantes,* 1762: "La Religion doit être conforme à la morale, et universelle comme
elle."

[41]See especially, Peter Gay, ed., "Introduction," *Voltaire's Philosophical Dictionary* (New York: Basic Books, 1962) 3-52, esp. 35-52.

[42]A. J. Bingham, "Voltaire and the New Testament," *Studies on Voltaire and the
Eighteenth Century,* ed. Theodore Besterman (Genève: Institut et Musée Voltaire Les
Delices, 19), 24:203.

il ne fut connu des Grecs que du temps d'Alexandre, devenu leur
dominateur, et ne fut-apperçu des Romains que pour être bientôt
écrasé par eux dans la foule."[43] Hertzberg describes Voltaire's outlook
as follows:

> At the very heart of the whole of Voltaire's outlook there was, as André
> Maurois has seen, a vision of universal history that was constructed in
> opposition to the orthodox one of Bossuet. Voltaire did not see the Jews and
> biblical history as central; he looked back to pagan, Greco-Roman antiquity
> as the golden age. Then there had been true philosophy and culture. This
> would have been ruined by the advent of Christianity. In his own mind
> Voltaire was a Cicero *redivivus* who had come to recreate that world. The
> glory of the new age of enlightenment would be that Europe would be
> restored to its true foundations.[44]

In short, the wild olive was the Jews, the cultivated olive the Greeks
and Romans.

> The nucleus of Voltaire's view of the Jews, however, amounts to this: there is
> a cultural, philosophical, and ethnic tradition of Europe which descended,
> through the human stock of that continent, from the intellectual values that
> were taught by the Greeks. Those were in turn carried to all the reaches of the
> European world by the Romans. This is the normative culture of which
> Voltaire approved. The Jews are a different family, and their religion is
> rooted in their character. Christianity is the Jewish religion superimposed on
> people of a different world, both ethnically and culturally. It is somewhat
> better than Judaism because it has been affected by the nature of those who
> have adopted it and by their earlier, healthier tradition. It is possible to
> redeem Europe by reviving its attachment to its own fundamental nature and
> tradition. European men can be freed effectively of Christianity because
> Christianity is here a longstanding infection; it is not one of the foundations
> of the European spirit, deriving from its character. The case of the Jews is
> radically different. Being born a Jew and the obnoxiousness of the Jewish
> outlook are indissoluble; it is most unlikely that "enlightened" Jews can
> escape their innate character. The Jews are subversive of the European
> tradition by their very presence, for they are radically other, the hopelessly
> alien. Cure them of their religion and their inborn character remains.[45]

The interpretation of the Enlightenment as a taproot of modern
anti-Semitism is beyond our competence adequately to assess. The
incalculable liberating influence of the Enlightenment is not in ques-

---

[43]Voltaire, *Chrétien-contre six Juifs* 1776, M. XXIX, p. 504.

[44]Hertzberg, *The French Enlightenment and the Jews*, 299. Compare Gay, ed.,
Voltaire's Philosophical Dictionary, 1:xii-xiii.

[45]Hertzberg, *The French Enlightenment and the Jews*, 306-7.

tion.[46] Maritain's own critical exegesis of Paul's epistle would hardly have been possible without it.[47] But at least an interrogatory conclusion does seem justified. In some of its expressions, did the Enlightenment fail in its treatment of the Jews as did the Christian tradition (both in its orthodox and liberal expressions) which it so critically dismissed? And did that unenlightened failure in the end have even more disastrous consequences than Christian anti-Judaism? Can it be that Voltaire was a link in Western intellectual history between the anti-Judaism of classical paganism and the anti-Semitism of our age?[48]

The aim of this brief and inadequate treatment has been to indicate that a thinker who took Paul seriously in Romans 9-11 found an antidote to an anti-Semitism, which, in the judgment of many, had been present in the most distinguished representative of the Enlightenment in France who had not found Paul congenial. Although not directly within his special field of interest, these comments, I trust, will not be unacceptable to a scholar whom it is a delight to honor and who in his own specialized work, especially on "Zeal," has revealed an unusual awareness of social and political realities such as we have touched upon here.[49]

---

[46]But see John Hallowell, ed., *From Enlightenment to Revolution/ Eric Voegelin* (Durham: Duke University, 1975).

[47]Meyer, who recognized anti-Semitism especially in the later Voltaire, quotes a Jewish writer, Isadore Cohen, commemorating the centenary of his death in 1878 ("The Attitude of the Enlightenment toward the Jew," *Studies*, 26:1177-78): "si Voltaire nous a été funeste, la voltairéianisme nous a été éminemment utile . . . le bien qu'il a fait—bien inestimable—en déracinant la tyrannie ecclésiastique, en minant les principes de l'Inquisition, en éteignant la flamme des bûchers, lui a survécu. C'est là le plus clair de son oeuvre, et les méprises ou les petitesses de ses appréciations sont effacées par la grandeur des résultats que lui doit la civilisation."

[48]Hertzberg, *The French Enlightenment and the Jews*, 10. He goes so far as to consider Voltaire a precursor of Hitler.

[49]Bo Reicke, *Diakonie, Festfreude und Zelos in Verbindung mit der altchristlichen Agapenfeier* (Uppsala: Lundequistska, 1951). Unfortunately the excellent chapter by Bernard E. Doering in his work *Jacques Maritain and the French Catholic Intellectuals* (Notre Dame/London: University of Notre Dame Press, 1983) 126-67, came too late for use in this chapter.

LA TUNIQUE "NON DIVISÉE" DE JÉSUS, SYMBOLE DE L'UNITÉ MESSIANIQUE

Ignace de la Potterie

LA BRÈVE péricope de Jean 19:23-24 sur le partage des vêtements de Jésus et la tunique sans couture avait une importance théologique considérable aux yeux des anciens.[1] On constate avec stupéfaction qu'aucune étude spéciale ne lui a été consacrée dans l'exégèse moderne.[2] Les commentateurs ne s'y attardent guère. Ce récit, dirait-on, ne leur pose aucun problème.

Une difficulté existe cependant: celle du bien-fondé de l'exégèse symbolique, courante chez les anciens et toujours défendue par un bon nombre de modernes. Mais pour la rendre convaincante, il ne suffit pas de se référer aux Pères. Il faut appuyer cette exégèse sur des données littéraires. Notre interprétation rejoindra celle des anciens, mais sous une forme nouvelle: Jean veut évoquer ici l'unité messianique du Peuple de Dieu.

C'est un réel plaisir pour nous de pouvoir offrir cette étude en hommage au Professeur Bo Reicke, en signe d'estime pour son oeuvre exégétique, mais aussi comme un témoignage de ce profond désir d'unité qui anime désormais toutes les confessions chrétiennes.

1. Analyse de Jean 19:23-24

1.1. *Place des deux versets dans la section du Calvaire (19:16b-37)*

La section du Calvaire, la quatrième des cinq sections du récit johannique de la passion, se compose d'une introduction (19,16b-18)

---

[1]Michel Aubineau, "La tunique sans couture du Christ. Exégèse patristique de Jn 19,23-24," *Kyriakon: Festschrift Johannes Quasten*, 2 vols. (Münster: Aschendorff, 1970), 1:100-27.

[2]Cf. cependant Aristide Serra, *Contributi dell'antica letteratura giudaica per l'esegesi di Giovanni 2,1-12 e 19,25-27* (Scripta Pontificiae Facultatis theologicae "Marianum" 31; Roma: Herder, 1977) 428-29; Damiano Marzotto, *L'unità degli uomini nel Vangelo di Giovanni* (Supplementi alla Rivista biblica 9; Brescia: Paideia, 1977) 201-19 (sur 19,23-42).

suivie de cinq tableaux:
1) 19:19-22: le titre de la croix;
2) 19:23-24: le partage des vêtements et la tunique sans couture;
3) 19:25-27: la Mère de Jésus et le Disciple bien-aimé;
4) 19:28-30: la mort de Jésus;
5) 19:31-37: le côté transpercé.

Avec Brown, nous admettons que les cinq tableaux sont disposés en forme de chiasme[3]; il serait facile de montrer que le premier et le cinquième, le deuxième et le quatrième, ont entre eux diverses correspondances. Au centre se trouve la scène de 19,25-27, qui décrit la constitution du nouveau peuple de Dieu en la personne de la Mère de Jésus et du Disciple bien-aimé.[4] Les deux versets que nous étudions servent d'introduction à cette scène centrale. Les deux péricopes sont fortement liées entre elles par les particules μέν . . . δέ, au point de jonction des deux épisodes. Pour expliquer la scène des vêtements, nous devrons donc également parler de la suivante; l'une et l'autre, comme nous le verrons, ont fondamentalement le même sens.

1.2. *Jean et les synoptiques*

Le fait que Jean consacre à l'épisode des vêtements une péricope spéciale et que celle-ci occupe une place organique dans la structure de la section, montre déjà l'importance que lui donne l'évangéliste. Cela apparaît plus nettement encore quand on compare son texte avec celui des synoptiques (Matt 27:35; Marc 15:24; Luc 23:34).

Le texte de Jean se distingue de ceux-ci par toute une série de traits:
1) Son récit est le seul qui constitue une unité littéraire.
2) Le nombre des mots chez Jean est de six à onze fois supérieur à celui qu'utilisent les trois synoptiques: 6 - 11 - 7 - *67 (69)*.[5]
3) Jean est le seul évangéliste qui parle explicitement de l'accomplissement de l'Écriture; et comme il ne le fait que rarement, cette idée d'accomplissement doit avoir ici une réelle importance.

---

[3]Cf. Raymond E. Brown, *The Gospel According to John (xiii-xxi): Introduction, Translation, and Notes* (AB 29A; Garden City, New York: Doubleday, 1970) 910-12.

[4]Cf. Ignace de la Potterie, "La maternità spirituale di Maria e la fondazione della Chiesa, Gv 19,25-27," *Gesù Verità: studi di cristologia giovannea* (Collana biblica; Torino: Marietti, 1973) 158-64.

[5]Pour Jean, nous indiquons deux chiffres (67 et 69), parce que l'authenticité de ἡ λέγουσα est incertaine.

4) Mais voici la différence majeure: Jean introduit ici une distinction très nette entre "les vêtements" de Jésus (τὰ ἱμάτια αὐτοῦ) et sa "tunique" (ὁ χιτών), le vêtement de dessous. Et il fait refluer cette même distinction dans la citation du psaume. Or, dans l'hébreu et dans les LXX, les deux termes sont synonymes: בֶּגֶד au pluriel = 'les habits'; לְבוּשׁ au sens collectif = 'les vêtements'; pareillement dans les LXX: τὰ ἱμάτια, 'les vêtements'; ὁ ἱματισμός aussi est collectif 'la garde-robe'. Jean au contraire restreint la portée de ce dernier terme et lui fait designer *une pièce* de vêtement: la tunique. L'idée de faire cette distinction lui est très probablement venue de la tradition, qui parlait de deux faits distincts dans le comportement des soldats. Jean reprend cette distinction: les soldats *divisent* les habits en quatre parts; et ils décident de *ne pas déchirer* la tunique mais de la tirer au sort.

5) A propos de cette tunique, sur laquelle il désire attirer l'attention, Jean donne plusieurs détails: elle était ἄραφος (ou ἄρραφος: de α et ῥάπτω, coudre), sans couture: ce mot, un *hapax* biblique, est aussi extrêmement rare dans la littérature profane (unique exemple connu: Galien, *De usu partium* 11,19; la référence à Fl. Josèphe, *Ant.* 3.7.4, dans Liddell-Scott, est erronée); la tunique était depuis le haut tout entière (δι' ὅλου) d'un seul tissu; contrairement à ce qu'ils firent pour les autres vêtements, les soldats tombèrent d'accord pour ne pas la "diviser" (μὴ σχίσωμεν). Par trois indications convergentes sur la tunique, Jean insiste donc sur l'idée d'unité.

1.3. Structure littéraire de la péricope

Notre passage est structuré de deux manières complémentaires: l'ensemble de la péricope suit une structure concentrique (A, B, C, B', A'); mais à l'intérieur de celle-ci, les éléments principaux B et B' sont disposés suivant une structure parallèle (*a, b, c - a', b', c'*). Pour plus de facilité, nous présentons la texte de la Vulgate, car, mieux que les versions modernes, elle suit exactment l'ordre des mots grecs selon le diagramme présenté ci-dessous (p. 130).

Cette construction très régulière appelle plusieurs remarques:
1) On constate immédiatement que A et A' forment inclusion.
2) Au centre de la structure (C) on trouve les mots "afin que l'Ecriture fût accomplie." Autour de ce pivot sont répartis tous les autres éléments du passage (A, B et B', A').
3) En B et B' (les deux parties principales de la péricope), les

A   MILITES   ergo, cum crucifixissent Iesum,

----

      acceperunt *vestimenta eius* (τὰ ἱμάτια αὐτοῦ)

  a   et *fecerunt* quattuor *partes* (ἐποίησαν --- μέρη),

      unicuique militi *partem* (μέρος),

      et *tunicam* (τὸν χιτῶνα). Erat autem

B   *b* *tunica* inconsutilis,

        desuper contexta per totum.

          Dixerunt ergo ad invicem:

         c Non scindamus eam (μὴ σχίσωμεν αὐτόν),

           sed *sortiamur* (λάχωμεν) de illa cuius sit;

           ut Scriptura

C

           impleretur (dicens):

     a' *Partiti* sunt (διεμερίσαντο)

    vestimenta mea (τα ἱμάτιά μου) sibi;

        et in

B'   *b'*

        vestem meam (τὸν ἱματισμόν μου)

           miserunt

        c'

           sortem (κλῆρον).

A'   Et MILITES   quidem haec *fecerunt* (ἐποίησαν).

matériaux s'échelonnent en trois mouvements *(a, b, c* et *a', b', c'),* qui se
correspondent exactement entre eux. Or, B' n'est rien d'autre que le
texte du Ps 22 (21):19; B, qui lui est parallèle, est la description de ce
que *firent* les soldats. L'intention de l'évangéliste est évidemment de
montrer que les deux manières d'agir différentes des soldats étaient
l'accomplissement précis de la prophétie.

    4) Mais entre B et B', il faut également noter des différences
significatives:

a) Les deux premiers membres (*a* et *a'*), certes, sont parallèles (*vestimenta eius/vestimenta mea; fecerunt* . . . *partes/partiti sunt*), mais avec un changement de verbe (ἐποίησαν. . . μέρη / διεμερίσαντο); on notera également le redoublement du mot *partes* (*-em*) dans la partie narrative.

b) Entre *b* et *b'* aussi il y a parallélisme; on constate néanmoins deux différences: le substantif de la partie narrative est différent de celui du psaume (*tunicam/vestem*); ce mot, ici encore, est répété une deuxième fois (*erat autem tunica*), et accompagné d'une description qui n'a rien d'équivalent dans le Ps 22 (21): Jean insiste sur le fait que la tunique était d'une seule pièce. Tout ce qui concerne la tunique est donc nouveau.

c) Le cas est semblable en *c* et *c'*: sans doute, d'après la Vulgate, le parallélisme semble exact (*sortiamur/miserunt sortem*); mais dans le grec, une fois de plus, nous trouvons deux mots différents (λάχωμεν / ἔβαλον κλῆρον). On dirait que, par ces modifications de vocabulaire, Jean veut laisser entendre que "l'accomplissement" (C) dont il parle n'est pas automatique: il ne peut se comprendre qu'à la lumière de l'évènement lui-même; celui-ci permet de lire d'une manière nouvelle le texte du psaume. De plus, Jean ajoute un membre de phrase (*non scindamus eam*) à quoi rien ne correspond dans le psaume. Cette formule "ne la *divisons* pas" est très caractéristique: Jean n'utilise pas le verbe "déchirer" (διαρρήσσειν), dont l'emploi, quand il s'agissait de vêtements ("déchirer ses vêtements"), était stéréotypé[6]; il écrit plutôt μὴ σχίσωμεν, "ne divisons pas." Ce verbe (fendre, diviser) est appliqué très rarement à des vêtements: dans la LXX, on ne trouve qu'un unique exemple, dans deux versets consécutifs d'Isaïe (36:22—37:1), et un seul dans le Nouveau Testament (Luc 5:36). Or, dans ce dernier passage—et peut-être même déjà dans le texte d'Isaïe[7]—σχίζειν a un sens métapho-

---

[6]Dans les LXX, on le trouve environ cinquante fois; cf. par exemple Gen 44:13 (διέρρηξαν τὰ ἱμάτια αὐτῶν); pour le Nouveau Testament, Matt 26:65 par; Act 14:14 (διαρρήξαντες τὰ ἱμάτια αὐτῶν). Le contraire de "coudre"(ῥάπτω, racine de α-ραφος) n'était pas "diviser," mais "déchirer" (Qoh 3:7).

[7]Il s'agit du siège de Jérusalem par Sennachérib: il menaçait de dévaster la Ville sainte et de déporter les Juifs en Assyrie. A cette nouvelle, les parlementaires d'Ezéchias et le roi lui-même déchirèrent leurs vêtements. Était-ce simplement "une manière bien orientale et biblique d'exprimer la douleur"(Dennefeld)? Dans ce cas, pourquoi le grec ne porte-t-il pas διαρρήσσειν comme partout ailleurs? Uniquement à cet endroit, on trouve le verbe "diviser": ἔσχισεν τά ἱμάτια (37:1). Nous suggérons une explication à partir du contexte: il ne s'agit pas ici d'un péril quelconque, mais de la *scission* du

rique: il ne faut pas, écrit Luc, "*déchirer* une pièce d'un *vêtement neuf* pour le rajouter à un *vieux vêtement*; autrement on aura *déchiré* le neuf." Dans cette version lucanienne de la parabole, le vieux vêtement et le vêtement neuf symbolisent les observances judaïques et l'Évangile qui doivent être *séparés*[8]; il s'agit donc, pour Luc, de la "division" désormais inévitable entre le judaïsme et le christianisme. Mais il faut surtout remarquer ceci : σχίζειν, dans le Nouveau Testament, est devenu un mot technique pour parler de la "scission" du peuple (Act 14:4; 23:7; allusion probable en Jean 21:11); et c'est toujours en ce sens que le dérivé σχίσμα est employé dans Jean (7:43; 9:16; 10:19), comme d'ailleurs aussi dans Paul (1 Cor 1:10; 11:18; 12:25).

Par l'analyse qui précède, nous avons réuni un certain nombre d'indices qui vont nous permettre de présenter maintenant l'exégèse du passage.

2. Interprétation de Jean 19:23-24

Tout ce que nous avons dit jusqu'à présent nous invite à penser que Jean, en insistant sur l'épisode de la tunique "non divisée," y a vu le symbole d'une vérité théologique. C'était l'opinion des Pères (avec pas mal de variations dans le détail du symbolisme), et elle est partagée par un nombre croissant d'exégètes contemporains. Nous voudrions montrer, dans cette deuxième partie, que l'exégèse symbolique nous est pour ainsi dire imposée par le vocabulaire et la structure du texte.

Certains exégètes ont voulu voir ici une allusion au sacerdoce du Christ, parce que la robe du grand prêtre, d'après Fl. Josèphe (*Ant.* 3.7.4 §161), était sans couture.[9] Comme nous l'avons déjà montré

---

peuple d'Israël, d'une atteinte à son *unité*; en effet, la masse des habitants risque de devoir partir en exil; mais "un reste" de la maison de Juda demeurera, les rescapés du mont Sion (37:4,31-32). Dans cette interprétation, la "division" des vêtements (plutôt que leur "déchirement") devient l'expression symbolique de la menace de *division* qui pèse sur Israël. Contre Christian Maurer, s.v. "σχίζω," *TWNT* 7 (1964) 960: "Ein Grund für das Ineinandergreifen von σχίζω und ῥήγνυμι wird nicht ersichtlich."

[8]Cf. Heinz Schürmann, *Das Lukasevangelium* (HTKNT 3/1; Freiburg: Herder, 1969) 298.

[9]D'après Bernhard Weiss (*Das Johannes-Evangelium*, 9th ed. [MeyerK; Göttingen: Vandenhoeck & Ruprecht, 1902] 652-53), cette exégèse fut déjà proposée par Theodor Keim (*Geschichte Jesu von Nazara*, 3 vols. [Zürich: Orell, Füssli, 1867-1872], 2:226 n. 3; 3:421 n. 1). Plus près de nous on la retrouve chez G. H. C. Macgregor, *The Gospel of John* (MNTC; New York/London: Harper, 1928) 346; Ceslas Spicq, *L'épître aux Hébreux*, 2 vols. (EBib; Paris: J. Gabalda, 1952-1953), 1:122; François Marie Braun, *Jean le Théologien*, 3 vols. (EBib; Paris: J. Gabalda, 1959-1972), 2:98-101;

ailleurs plus en détail n. 9, cette expliction est à écarter pour plusieurs raisons. Qu'il nous suffise ici de faire observer qu'elle repose sur une équivoque: le vêtement du grand prêtre fait d'une seule pièce était son *manteau de pourpre*, et non pas sa tunique, ce qui serait requis pour un éventuel rapprochement avec la *tunique* de Jésus.

En regroupant les diverses corrélations du texte qu'a mises en lumière l'étude de sa structure et de son vocabulaire, on arrive à la conviction que le symbolisme fondamental contenu dans le passage est celui de l'unité.[10] Mais il faut préciser: il ne s'agit pas encore de l'unité de l'Église, mais de l'unité messianique de Peuple de Dieu.

Joachim Gnilka, "Die Erwartung des Messianischen Hohenpriesters in den Schriften von Qumran und im Neuen Testament," *RQ* 2 (1959/1960) 423; Marie Émile Boismard, "La Royauté du Christ dans le quatrième évangile," *Lumière et Vie* 11 no. 57 (1962) 55; Benedikt Schwank, "Erklärung von Joh 13-21 in Einzelaufsätzen," *Sein und Sendung* 29 (1964) 295; voir également Walter Grundmann, *Zeugnis und Gestalt des Johannes-Evangeliums: Eine Studie zur denkerischen und gestalterischen Leistung des vierten Evangelisten* (Arbeiten zur Theologie 7; Stuttgart: Calwer, 1961) 87; André Feuillet, "L'heure de la femme (Jn 16,21) et l'heure de la Mère de Jésus (Jn 19,25-27)," *Bib* 47 (1966) 374 (mais la tunique non déchirée est aussi un symbole d'unité). Par contre "La tunique sans couture, symbole du Christ grand prêtre?," *Bib* 60 (1979) 225-69.

[10]On peut citer en faveur de cette exégèse D. F. Strauss, *Das Leben Jesu, kritisch bearbeitet*, 2 vols. (Tübingen: C. F. Osiander, 1936; repr. Darmstadt: Wissenschaftliche Buchgesellschaft, 1969) 2:541-44; Alfred Loisy, *Le quatrième Évangile*, 2nd ed. (Paris: E. Nourry, 1921) 485-86; Thomas Calmes, *Évangile selon Saint Jean*, 2nd ed. (EBib; Paris: Lecoffre, 1906) 439; Alfred Durand, *Évangile selon Saint Jean*. Traduit et commenté, 25th ed. (VS 4; Paris: G. Beauchesne, 1938) 490-91; Edwyn C. Hoskyns, *The Fourth Gospel*, ed. Francis N. Davey (London: Faber and Faber, 1947) 529; R. H. Lightfoot, *St. John's Gospel: A Commentary* (Oxford: Clarendon, 1956) 316; C. K. Barrett, *The Gospel According to St. John: an introduction with commentary and notes on the Greek text* (New York: Macmillan; London: SPCK, 1955) 457-58; Brown, *John*, 2:921-22 (hésitant); cf. en outre Albert Janssens, "La structure des scènes du récit de la passion en Joh. XVIII-XIX," *ETL* 38 (1962) 504-22 (cf. 514 n. 10); Édouard Cothenet, "Le quatrième évangile," *Introduction à la Bible*, 3/4: *La tradition johannique* (Paris: Desclée, 1977) 157: "La robe sans couture que les soldats ne déchirent pas représente symboliquement l'unité de l'Église qui doit être sauvegardée malgré la diversité de ses membres." Fait significatif: certains auteurs, qui avaient d'abord écarté cette exégèse, s'y sont ralliés dans la suite; ainsi Donatien Mollat qui change d'opinion de la 1e à la 3e éd. du fascicule de la *Bible de Jérusalem* (Paris: Cerf, 1955, 1973); Marie Émile Boismard ("La Royauté du Christ," 55) admettait le symbolisme sacerdotal, mais songe maintenant à l'unité de l'Église, cf. *Synopse des quatre évangiles*, vol. 3: *L'évangile de Jean* (Paris: Cerf, 1977) 442; Braun excluait tout symbolisme dans son commentaire (1934); dans *Jean le Théologien*, vol. 2: *Les grandes traditions d'Israël* (Paris: J. Gabalda, 1964) 98-101, il se montrait favorable aux deux formes de l'interprétation symbolique; dans *Jean le Théologien*, vol. 3/1: *sa théologie, le mystère de Jésus Christ* (Paris: J. Gabalda, 1966) 233, il ne parle plus que de l'unité de l'Église.

Dans le texte structuré donné ci-dessus, les éléments les plus impor-
tants sont *a* et *c*. Jean nous y dit ce que firent les soldats avec les
vêtements et avec la tunique.

1) Le psaume parlait du *partage des vêtements (a')*, mais Jean dit
que les soldats en firent *quatre parts (a)*. Le symbolisme n'est donc pas
celui du *déchirement* des habits (il n'en est pas question), mais plutôt,
semble-t-il, celui des morceaux en lesquels on réduit un vêtement pour
donner un signe. Un tel symbolisme est biblique: on songe immédiatement au cas du prophète Ahiyya, qui, devant Jéroboam, déchira son
manteau tout neuf en *douze morceaux* pour annoncer le *schisme des
douze tribus* d'Israël après le règne de Salomon (1 Rois 11:30-40). Les
quatre parts que firent les soldats avec les vêtements de Jésus semblent
donc devoir représenter la division qui régnait jusqu'ici. Mais de quelle
division s'agit-il?

On peut s'en rendre compte en rapprochant le verset avec deux
autres textes johanniques sur l'unité. Dans la parole de Caïphe rappor-
tée en Jean 11:50, Jean discerne une prophétie: Jésus allait mourir,
"afin de rassembler dans l'*unité* les enfants de Dieu *dispersés*" (11:52).
Ce passage évoque le grand thème biblique du rassemblement d'Israël
après la déportation.[11] Dans la pensée de Jean, Jésus, par sa mort,
constituait le nouveau peuple de Dieu: il rassemblait dans l'unité les
enfants de Dieu, Juifs et païens, qui étaient divisés. Ici pointe en outre
l'idée d'universalité. Il est donc possible que la mention des "quatre
parts" suggère elle aussi cette idée, le chiffre quatre, dans la Bible, étant
un symbole d'universalité.[12] Un autre texte sur l'unité, dans l'allégorie
du Bon Pasteur, va dans le même sens: Jésus doit encore mener
"d'autres brebis," qui sont en dehors (de cet enclos) du judaïsme, et qui
viennent du monde païen; c'est pour les réunir toutes en "un seul
troupeau" que le Pasteur donne sa vie (10:15-17).

Conformément à la conception structuraliste du symbolisme,[13] il

---

[11]Cf. Serra, *Contributi*, chap. 5 (pp. 303-429): "Il raduno dei dispersi figli di Dio
(Gv 11,52) e la maternità spirituale di Maria (Gv 19,25-27)."

[12]Les quatre coins de la terre, les quatre points cardinaux, les quatre vents indi-
quent toute l'étendue d'un territoire, et sont donc un signe d'universalité (cf. Horst
Balz, s.v. "τέσσαρες," *TWNT* 8 [1969] 127-34): le thème sert encore à illustrer l'étendue
de la *dispersion* (Jér 49,36: les Élamites), mais aussi celle du *rassemblement des
dispersés* "des quatre coins de la terre" (Is 11,12).

[13]Cf. Raymond Didier, *Les sacrements de la foi* (Le Centurion, 1975) 24-30 (avec
bibliographie): "Développement sur le symbole."

ne s'agit pas seulement, en 19:23-24, de la valeur représentative d'une ou de deux données (les vêtements, la tunique) prises isolément, mais de leur *rapport* à l'intérieur d'une structure: les textes cités (10:16; 11:52) parlent du passage de la dispersion à l'unité; en 19:23-24 également, Jean décrit le *rapport* antithétique (v. 23*d*: ἦν δέ) entre les quatre parts des vêtements et la non-division de la tunique. C'est à l'intérieur de cette *corrélation* que chacun des deux éléments se colore de symbolisme. Il est donc très probable que les quatre parts des vêtements évoquent la division générale qui régnait jusqu'ici.

2) Mais il reste que l'élément le plus important du passage est celui qui concerne la tunique (*c*, préparé par *b*). Jean présente ici le thème complémentaire du précédent: après l'allusion à la "dispersion" du peuple de Dieu, il évoque maintenant sa "non-division," c'est-à-dire "l'œuvre d'unité réalisée par Jésus dans sa mort même."[14] Tout le poide du récit tombe ici sur la formule négative "ne la *divisons pas*": la division qui existait entre les enfants de Dieu doit être supprimée; au moment de sa mort, Jésus va accomplir son œuvre messianique, en *réalisant* l'unité tant désirée du Peuple de Dieu.[15]

3) Car le thème de l'unité n'est pas seulement suggéré par le symbole de la tunique: il se prolonge dans l'épisode suivant (v. 25-27). Par le jeu des particules μέν . . . δέ, le groupe des quatre soldats trouve pour ainsi dire sa "contrepartie" dans celui des quatre femmes (dont une seule cependant va jouer un rôle: la Mère de Jésus).[16] L'explication la plus vraisemblable est la suivante: le thème de l'unité est d'abord annoncé sous forme symbolique; Jean en présente ensuite la réalisation concrète dans la scène de la Mère de Jésus et du Disciple bien-aimé, qui représentent tous deux la communauté messianique.

Pour Jean, en effet, cette scène est capitale. Non seulement il la place au centre de la section du Calvaire, mais il souligne encore son importance au v. 28: "*Après quoi*, sachant que *désormais* tout était

---

[14]Mollat.

[15]Severino Pancaro, " 'People of God' in St John's Gospel," *NTS* 16 (1969/1970) 114-29, esp. 129: "Christ dies to form the new people, which is to gather together into one the scattered children of God. His death makes children of men and it is because they are made children that they are united, but John wishes to insist more on the 'gathering into one' than on the act of becoming a child of God."

[16]Lightfoot, *John*, 316.

achevé pour que l'Écriture fût parfaitement accomplie."[17] Par le dernier épisode de sa vie terrestre (v. 25-27), Jésus accomplit en perfection son œuvre messianique tracée dans l'Écriture. Les dernières paroles de Jésus à sa Mère et au Disciple sont donc bien autre chose qu'une expression de piété filiale; c'est un acte messianique, par lequel Jésus, en mourant, indique le rôle que devront dorénavant jouer sa Mère et le Disciple dans le prolongement de son œuvre de salut.

Marie, comme à Cana (2:4), est interpellée comme "Femme"; Jésus déclare qu'elle sera désormais la "Mère" du disciple, et celui-ci deviendra "son fils." Ce sont là trois thèmes connus des textes prophétiques sur le rassemblement dans l'unité aux temps messianiques: Sion y est représentée comme la *mère* de tous les peuples; vers elle reviennent et en elle *se rassemblent ses enfants* dispersés—on notera des contacts précis de vocabulaire avec Jean 11:52; 19:26-27: μήτηρ Σιων (Ps 87 [86]: 5); ἰδὲ συνηγμένα τὰ τέκνα σου, ἰδοὺ ἥκασιν πάντες οἱ υἱοί σου μακρόθεν (Is 60:4); ἰδοὺ ἔρχονται οἱ υἱοί σου . . . συνηγμένοι ἀπ' ἀνατολῶν ἕως δυσμῶν (Bar 4:37); *Sion mater nostra* (4 Esdr. 10:7).

On saisit mieux maintenant la raison du rapport étroit entre les vv 23-24 et 25-27. L'épisode du partage des vêtements en "quatre parts" et, par contraste, celui de la tunique "non divisée" évoquent symboliquement les deux thèmes antithétiques de la division des enfants de Dieu et de leur rassemblement dans l'unité. Cette unité messianique se réalise immédiatement après: la Mère de Jésus est l'image concrète de la Sion messianique qui, telle une mère, voit se rassembler autour d'elle tous ses enfants; dans la personne du Disciple sont présents tous les croyants: ils sont désormais tous un, en devenant "fils" de leur "mère," le peuple de Dieu eschatologique que représente ici la "Femme," la Mère de Jésus.

3) L'exégèse présentée ci-dessus est à la fois semblable et différente de l'interprétation de la Tradition. Comme les anciens, nous avons découvert dans ce passage le thème de l'unité si cher à saint Jean. Les Pères toutefois songeaient directement à l'unité de l'*Église*, qui, malgré ses divisions internes, malgré les schismes et les hérésies, sauvegarde sa cohésion profonde. Mais si c'était là le sens immédiat des deux versets, Jean aurait parlé de l'avenir, ce qui est invraisemblable et n'est suggéré

---

[17]Cf. Ignace de la Potterie, "La sete di Gesù morente e l'interpretazione giovannea della sua morte in croce," *La sapienza della Croce oggi*, vol. 1: *La sapienza della Croce nella rivelazione e nell' ecumenismo* (Torino: Elle Di Ci, 1976) 33-49, esp. 42-44.

par rien dans le texte; d'autre part, l'allusion aux divisions postérieures de l'Église aurait ici quelque chose d'anachronique.

Le double épisode du Calvaire (v. 23-24 et 25-27) décrit plutôt l'unité comme *point d'aboutissement* de l'Ancien Testament: après les divisions du Peuple de Dieu, son unité *se réalise* finalement à la Croix. C'est ce qu'implique la coloration messianique du passage; et c'est ce que Jean indique formellement lui-même en 11:52: "Jésus allait mourir ... afin de rassembler dans l'unité les enfants de Dieu dispersés." Les quatre parts des vêtements de Jésus sont comme un rappel des divisions antérieures; mais dans la tunique non divisée, Jean voit un symbole de *l'unité messianique du peuple de Dieu*: elle va devenir une réalité à la mort de Jésus.

4) Mais la réalisation de l'unité demande aussi la participation des disciples. Comme toujours dans les réalités de l'Alliance, la communauté doit manifester sa disposition d'accueil, et exprimer sa foi. Après la parole de Jésus "Voici ta Mère," Jean conclut: "Dès cette heure-là, le Disciple *l'accueillit* dans ses biens."[18] On se souvient que λαμβάνειν, appliqué à des personnes, équivaut à "croire" dans Jean; dès lors, on ne peut que souscrire à ce commentaire de Mollat: "Docile à la parole de son Maître, *il l'accueille avec foi* comme sa mère. L'heure de Jésus devient l'heure de la naissance de l'Église."[19] Cette valeur d'eschatologie anticipée de la foi du Disciple est impliquée aussi dans le don de l'Esprit (cf. 19:30), que symbolise ensuite l'eau qui sort du côté transpercé (19:34), et elle ressort plus clairement encore de la phrase finale de l'épisode (19:37), où Jean décrit le regard du croyant vers le Christ élevé sur la Croix. L'œuvre de Jésus va se prolonger dans l'Église, par le don de l'Esprit et la foi des disciples. Il n'est pas indifférent que Jean décrive ici l'attitude du Disciple, non seulement comme un accueil du *Christ* dans la foi (1:12; 19:37), mais aussi comme l'accueil de la *Mère de Jésus* et de ce qu'elle représente: il l'accueille "dans ses biens," dans cet espace spirituel que constituait pour lui tout ce qu'il avait reçu de Jésus. En ce sens on peut dire que recevoir Jésus implique que l'on reçoive aussi de Jésus Marie pour Mère et que l'on deireme ses fils.[20]

---

[18]Ignace de la Potterie, "La parole de Jésus 'Voici ta Mère' et l'accueil du Disciple (Jn 19,27b)," *Marianum* 36 (1974) 1-39; " 'Et à partir de cette heure, le Disciple l'accueillit dans son intimité' (Jn 19,25b)," ibid. 42 (1980) 84-125.

[19]Mollat.

[20]Cf. le commentaire d,Origène, *In Joan.,* 1, 4, 23 (SC, 120, 70-72).

Qu'il nous soit permis, pour terminer, de souligner l'importance de notre passage pour la recherche oecuménique de l'unité. A l'époque de Jésus, les enfants de Dieu étaient divisés. Mais au moment de sa mort, Jésus accomplit son oeuvre en les "rassemblant dans l'unité"; il le fait en constituant le peuple de Dieu messianique, qui va devenir l'Église. Depuis lors, hélas, celle-ci a connu de nouvelles divisions. Mais aujourd'hui et demain, exactement comme hier, la réalisation de l'*unité* dépendra surtout de l'intensité de la foi de tous ceux qui sont devenus vraiment les disciples de Jésus, et qui le "regardent" élevé sur la croix (19:37).

LE DOUZIÈME APÔTRE (ACTES 1:15-26): À PROPOS D'UNE EXPLICATION RÈCENTE*

Jacques Dupont

LA PLACE accordée à l'épisode de l'élection de Matthias, entre l'Ascension et la Pentecôte, semble indiquer que Luc attache une importance particulière à la reconstitution du collège des Douze. Il faut avouer cependant que la raison de cette importance n'apparaît clairement ni dans le discours attribué à Pierre en cette occasion (Actes 1:16-22), ni dans la suite des Actes des Apôtres, où le nom de Matthias ne revient plus et où les Douze ne sont mentionnés qu'une seule fois (Actes 6:2).

On ne s'aventure guère en supposant que le nombre des Apôtres chez Luc doit être mis en relation avec le nombre des tribus d'Israël. Il reste que cette relation peut être envisagée de différentes manières. On peut la comprendre par rapport au peuple juif, et deux voies s'ouvrent alors, suivant qu'on adopte la perspective eschatologique de Matt 19:28 (Luc 22:30),[1] ou la perspective sotériologique de Menoud: les

---

*Cet article paraît simultanément dans la revue *Bibbia e Oriente* (Bornato, Brescia, Italia). Depuis qu'il a été rédigé, la méthode de Max Wilcox a fait l'objet d'une critique sévère de la part de Earl Richard ("The Old Testament in Acts: Wilcox's Semitisms in Retrospect," *CBQ* 42 [1980] 330-41). Son auteur y propose un nouvel examen de 24 passages des Actes étudiés par Wilcox dans son ouvrage *Semitisms of Acts* (Oxford: Clarendon, 1965); il ne mentionne pas l'article de 1973 et ne s'occupe pas du texte relatif au remplacement de Judas. Il n'y a pas d'allusion à l'hypothèse d'une dépendance d'Act 1:17 à l'égard du targum dans les commentaires récents de R. Fabris (*Atti degli apostoli* [Roma: 1977]) et de Jürgen Roloff (*Die Apostelgeschichte* [NTD 5; Göttingen: Vandenhoeck & Ruprecht, 1981]). Cette hypothèse est simplement mentionnée, mais sans retenir l'attention, dans l'article de A. Weiser, "Die Nachwahl des Matthias (Apg 1,15-26). Zur Rezeption und Deutung urchristlicher Geschichte durch Lukas," *Zur Geschichte des Urchristentums*, eds. G. Dautzenberg, H. Merklein, K. Müller (Freiburg: Herder, 1979) 97-110, 103 n. 22; Weiser, *Die Apostelgeschichte, Kap 1-12* (Oekumenische Taschenbuchkommentar zum Neuen Testament 5/1; Gütersloh/Würzburg: 1981) 67. Les explications de Wilcox et de Nellessen sont sommairement prises et considération et critiquée par G. Schneider, *Die Apostelgeschichte*, I (HTKNT 5/1; Freiburg: Herder, 1980) 215. Il semble donc qu'une discussion plus précise puisse encore rendre service.

[1]Il peut suffire ici de rappeler Jacques Dupont, "Le logion des douze trônes (Mt 19,28; Lc 22,28-30)," *Bib* 45 (1964) 355-92.

Douze demeurent à jamais pour l'Eglise le signe que le salut est destiné d'abord à Israël.[2] Mais il est également possible de se situer dans une perspective intra-ecclésiale, celle qui a été adoptée, en particulier, par le Professeur Bo Reicke, qui voit dans les Douze les représentants du nouvel Israël.[3]

La question de la signification du nombre des Douze peut encore être envisagée à différents niveaux: si la réponse qu'il convient de lui donner n'est pas entièrement claire au niveau de la rédaction du texte que nous avons sous les yeux, elle pourrait s'imposer avec beaucoup plus d'évidence au niveau des traditions sous-jacentes. C'est sur ce point précisément que deux études récentes nous offrent une lumière nouvelle. Nous espérons faire oeuvre utile en rappelant d'abord les explications qui sont proposées, en signalant ensuite les observations qu'elles nous suggèrent.

1

L'article publié en 1973 par Wilcox[4] s'attache à montrer que le discourse de Pierre sur la fin lamentable de Judas et sur la nécessité de lui donner un remplaçant repose sur un matériau traditionnel très ancien, dont il reste possible de reconnaître les traits caractéristiques dans le texte remanié par Luc. Au v 16, il retiendrait la mention de "l'Ecriture" et la précision "au sujet de Judas"; cette précision peut faire penser au passage de Gen 44:18-47:27, la section qui concerne Juda (le patriarche).[5] Wensinck avait déjà signalé un parallèle entre Actes 1:17a et un targum palestinien de Gen 44:18[6]; Wilcox montre que le parallèle

---

[2]Philippe Menoud, "Les additions au groupe des douze apôtres, d'après le livre des Actes," *RHPR* 37 (1957) 71-80, surtout 78-79 (= Menoud, *Jésus-Christ et la foi: recherches néotestamentaires*[Bibliothèque théologique; Neuchâtel/Paris: Delachaux et Niestlé, 1975] 91-100; [English] "Additions to the Group of the Twelve Disciples According to the Book of Acts," *Jesus Christ and the Faith: A Collection of Studies* [Pittsburgh Theological Monograph Series 18; Pittsburgh: Pickwick, 1978] 133-48).

[3]Bo Reicke, *Glaube und Leben der Urgemeinde: Bemerkungen zu Agp 1-7* (ATANT 32; Zürich: Zwingli, 1957) 22. Dans une perspective analogue voir Johannes Bihler, *Die Stephanusgeschichte im Zusammenhang der Apostelgeschichte* (Münchener theologische Studien 1/16; München: Hueber, 1963) 181-82.

[4]Max Wilcox, "The Judas-Tradition in Acts I.15-26," *NTS* 19 (1972/1973) 438-52.

[5]Wilcox, "Judas-Tradition," 450.

[6]Voir Wilcox, "Judas-Tradition," 447 n 2.

s'étend au v 17b.[7] Le v 18 et une partie du v 19 feraient l'application au cas de Judas grâce à un jeu de mots permettant de passer de חלק (κλῆρον) à חקל (χωρίον).

Pour se rendre compte de la portée de ces remarques, il faut savoir que les targums palestiniens contiennent en Gen 44:18 un long développement haggadique rapportant la réaction de Juda au moment où Joseph annonce son intention de garder Benjamin en otage. Juda se fâche et menace[8]:

> N'as-tu pas entendu parler de ce que firent Siméon et Lévi, mes deux frères, dans la place forte de Sichem? Ils y sont entrés et ont tué tous les mâles parce qu'ils avaient souillé Dinah notre soeur, qui ne fait pas partie des tribus et n'a ni part ni héritage dans le partage du pays. Combien plus à cause de Benjamin, notre frère, qui fait partie du nombre des tribus et qui a part et héritage dans le partage du pays!

Le text du Targum Neophyti se prolonge et reprend les paroles de Juda sous une forme un peu différente:

> . . . parce qu'ils avaient souillé Dinah, notre soeur, qui n'était pas comptée avec nous parmi les tribus et ne recevra pas d'héritage avec nous. Combien plus (fera-t-on) pour notre frère qui est compté avec nous parmi les tribus et recevra avec nous part et héritage dans le partage du pays.

Cette seconde forme, correspondant à celle du manuscrit de Cambridge publié par Kahle, est celle qui se rapproche le plus des termes employés dans Actes 1:17.

Les conséquences d'une dépendance des Actes a l'égard de cette tradition araméenne sont évidemment considérables, non seulement pour ce qui concerne la qualité des sources utilisées par Luc, mais aussi pour l'antiquité de la signification donnée au collège des Douze dans la communauté chrétienne.

---

[7] Wilcox, "Judas-Tradition," 447-50.

[8] Wilcox ("Judas-Tradition," 447) cite le targum du manuscrit D (Cambridge B 8), édité par Paul Kahle (*Masoreten des Westens*, vol. 2: *Das palästinische Pentateuchtargum. Die palästinische Punktuation. Der Bibeltext des Ben Naftali. Mit einem Beitrag von R. Edelman* [Texte und Untersuchungen zur vormasoretischen Grammatik des Hebräischen 4; Stuttgart: W. Kohlhammer, 1930; repr. Hildesheim: G. Olms, 1967] 21-22). Un manuscrit d'Oxford (2305) donne un texte un peu différent. Les deux versions sont juxtaposées dans le Codex Neophyti (Alejandro Díez Macho, *Neophyti 1: Targum palestinense. MS de la Biblioteca Vaticana*, vol. 1: *Genesis* [Textos y Estudios 7; Madrid/Barcelona: Consejo superior de investigaciones cientificas, 1968] 293-95). Nous citons les deux passages intéressants dans la traduction qu'en donne R. Le Déaut (*Neophyti 1*, 1:472-73).

Dans son ouvrage de 1976, Nellessen[9] revient à une manière de voir plus courante, qui croit pouvoir distinguer à la base de la péricope qui nous occupe, non pas une tradition seulement, mais deux traditions distinctes: l'une qui se rapportait à la mort de Judas et au "Champ du Sang," l'autre qui concernait le remplacement de Judas par Matthias. Mais il acquiesce entièrement[10] à ce que Wilcox dit de la dépendance d'Actes 1:17 par rapport aux targums palestiniens de Gen 44:18: cette dépendance concerne la tradition relative au remplacement de Judas. Il ajoute simplement que cette tradition a dû se présenter sous la forme d'une parole d'apôtre[11] (probablement de Pierre). Cette parole atteste que la communauté de langue araméenne avait déjà une théologie du ministère apostolique, rapprochant le rôle des Douze par rapport à l'Eglise au rôle qu'Israël reconnaissait aux patriarches. C'est dire qu'à ce stade déjà la signification des Douze était comprise dans une perspective ecclésiologique, et non plus proprement eschatologique.

L'énorme portée des conséquences d'une dépendance de Actes 1:17 par rapport aux targums oblige à s'interroger sur le point de savoir si cette dépendance est aussi assurée qu'on le dit.

2

2.1. Il peut sembler d'abord qu'il n'est pas prudent de parler du v 17 sans tenir compte de l'inclusion qui unit ce verset à la finale du récit. Il y a correspondance entre les termes du v 17b (καὶ ἔλαχεν τὸν κλῆρον τῆς διακονίας ταύτης) et ceux du v 25a (λαβεῖν τὸν τόπον[12] τῆς διακονίας ταύτης). Et il ne paraît pas contestable que v 17a (ὅτι κατηριθμημένος ἦν ἐν ἡμῖν) trouve son écho dans v 26b (καὶ συγκατεψηφίσθη μετὰ τῶν ἔνδεκα ἀποστόλων). Le verbe rare καταριθμέω,[13] celui qui a précisément attiré l'attention sur le targum de Gen

---

[9]Ernst Nellessen, *Zeugnis für Jesus und das Wort: Exegetische Untersuchungen zum lukanischen Zeugnisbegriff* (BBB 43; Köln/Bonn: P. Hanstein, 1976) 164-68.

[10]Y compris les coquilles typographiques: le *mem* est remplacé deux fois par un *teth*!

[11]"Il était compté parmi *nous*" (Actes 1:17).

[12]Au lieu de τόπον variante significative κλῆρον.

[13]Hapax dans le Nouveau Testament, il figure trois fois dans la LXX (Gen 50:3; Nom 14:29; 2 Chron 31:19).

44:18,[14] devrait trouver une explication qui n'ignore pas l'autre verbe rare, συγκαταψηφίζω.[15]

2.2. Avant de faire appel à un targum pour expliquer le participe κατηριθμημένος en Actes 1:17, il importe méthodologiquement de s'interroger par priorité sur la portée de la retouche rédactionnelle opérée par notre auteur en Luc 22:3.[16] Là où Marc 14:10 écrivait: "Judas, l'un des Douze s'en alla," Luc précise: "Satan entra dans Judas, qui était du nombre des Douze (ὄντα ἐκ τοῦ ἀριθμοῦ τῶν δώδεκα) et il s'en alla." En substituant à "l'un des Douze" la formule plus explicite "qui était du nombre des Douze," Luc veut simplement insister. Il le fait en employant le substantif ἀριθμός, qui caractérise son vocabulaire (Matthieu 0, Marc 0, Luc 1, Actes 5), et qui n'est pas sans relation avec le verbe qui en dérive dans Actes 1:17.

Puisque nous avons observé que ce verbe du v 17 trouve son parallèle dans le verbe συγκαταψηφίζω du v 26, il n'est pas sans intérêt de noter que, si ce composé est un hapax biblique, son emploi s'explique facilement à partir des verbes ψηφίζω de Luc 14:28 et συμψη-φίζω de Actes 19:19.

2.3. Le v 17b emploie le verbe rare ἔλαχεν, là où on aurait pu attend le verbe plus courant ἔλαβεν (cf. v 25 et Actes 26:18). Le parallèle de Actes 1:26 (ἔπεσεν ὁ κλῆρος ἐπὶ Μαθθίαν) fait penser que ce verbe a été choisi à bon escient, comme dans le cas de Luc 1:9: Zacharie "obtint" (par le sort) de faire brûler l'encens.[17]

2.4. Le substantif κλῆρος relève du même registre que le verbe λαγχάνω. Le v 17 l'emploie dans un sens métaphorique, tandis que le v 26 l'utilise deux fois au sens premier (tirage au sort). Le mot revient au sens propre dans le récit de la Passion (Matt 27:35; Marc 15:24; Luc 23:34; Jean 19:24). Au sens métaphorique, on le retrouve en Actes 8:21; 26:18 et Col 1:12 (Actes 20:32 lui substitue κληρονομία). On devine ici l'influence du vocabulaire de la Bible grecque.

2.5. La manière dont les vv 17 et 25 caractérisent l'apostolat comme une διακονία correspond évidemment au langage et au point de vue de

---

[14]Participe hithpa de מני (מתמני).

[15]Hapax biblique.

[16]Voir Ernst Haenchen, *Die Apostelgeschichte*, 7th ed. (MeyerK; Göttingen: Vandenhoeck & Ruprecht, 1977) 164.

[17]Dans la LXX, λαγχάνω n'apparaît qu'en 1 Rois 14:47, Sag 8:19 et 3 Macc 6:1.

Luc. Les termes διακονία (Matthieu 0, Marc 0, Luc 1, Actes 8) et διακονέω (Matthieu 5, Marc 4, Luc 8, Actes 2) lui sont particulièrement familiers, et c'est comme un "service" qu'il présente l'activité apostolique (cf. Actes 6:4; 20:24; 21:19).

2.6. Les observations que nous venons de faire se tenaient au niveau de la rédaction de Luc. Notre dernière remarque concerne la rédaction des targums. Il convient de se demander, en effet, si ceux-ci témoignent d'une tradition réellement originale, fournissant des données qui n'auraient pas pu parvenir à Luc par un autre canal. Il semble clair que ces targums de Gen 44:18 ne font que reporter sur Dinah et sur Benjamin des expressions que la Bible employe fréquemment en parlant des Lévites. Ce sont ces derniers qui n'ont "ni part ni héritage avec" Israël dans la partage de la terre (cf. Nom 18:20-24; Deut 10:9; 12:12; 14:27,29; 18:1), suivant la formule que Actes 8:21 a reprise à la LXX[18]; ce sont les Lévites encore qui ne doivent pas être recensés (ou comptés) avec les fils d'Israël, puisqu'ils ne reçoivent pas de part parmi eux (Nom 26:62). En faut-il davantage pour expliquer le langage de *Pal. Tgs.* Gen 44:18, et pour montrer que le texte des Actes peut s'expliquer autrement que par les targums.

2.7. S'il est exact que les expressions empruntées à la Bible y concernaient avant tout le cas particulier des Lévites, il doit être clair que leur remploi n'évoque la situation des Lévites ni dans la déclaration que le targum prête au patriarche Juda, ni dans celles que les Actes attribuent à Pierre à propos de l'apôtre Judas ou à propos de Simon le Magicien (8:21). Il s'agit simplement de tournures bibliques, dont on néglige les attaches originelles pour ne retenir que leur frappe littéraire.

Un rapprochement de textes peut être extrêmement suggestif: c'est bien le cas pour celui qui nous a été proposé par Wilcox. Mais un contrôle s'impose, pour éviter de projeter sur le texte qui nous intéresse un éclairage étranger à sa perspective propre. Devant la nouvelle voie d'interprétation qui nous était proposée, plusieurs questions se sont posées à nous, nous invitant à considérer les textes de plus près. Nous sommes reconnaissant à Wilcox de nous avoir fourni l'occasion de ce nouvel examen, même si nous devons avouer que la piste sur laquelle il nous a mis ne nous a pas paru pouvoir nous conduire à des résultats sûrs concernant l'origine précise de la tradition sur Judas conservée

---

[18]Voir Haenchen, *Apostelgeschichte*, 294.

dans les Actes, ni sur la manière exacte dont la première communauté
chrétienne de langue araméenne a compris le rôle des Douze.

IS STREETER'S FUNDAMENTAL SOLUTION TO THE SYNOPTIC PROBLEM STILL VALID?

William R. Farmer

1. Preface

IN THE BOOK, *The Synoptic Problem*, published in 1964 and reprinted with necessary changes in 1976,[1] fifty-nine pages are devoted to an analysis and refutation of Streeter's arguments for the priority of Mark and the existence of 'Q'. The most substantial defense of Streeter in the face of that analysis has been made by Joseph Fitzmyer in a paper for the Pittsburgh Festival on the Gospels.[2]

Since the effect of Fitzmyer's paper has been to restore confidence in some respects in the viability of Streeter's fundamental solution to the Synoptic Problem, while in other respects confidence in Marcan priority and the existence of Q continues to erode, an analytical treatment of Fitzmyer's arguments would seem to be in order.

The analysis of Fitzmyer's Pittsburgh paper leads to the conclusion that Streeter's fundamental solution is not viable and that the classical arguments for the two-document hypothesis do not sustain critical confidence in either Marcan priority or the existence of Q.

2. Introduction

Fuller has listed Fitzmyer's paper for the Pittsburgh Festival as a "defense" of the two-document hypothesis, and in his survey of the response to the book *The Synoptic Problem* he characterizes Fitzmy-

---

[1]William R. Farmer, *The Synoptic Problem: A Critical Analysis* (New York: Macmillan; London: Collier-Macmillan, 1964; repr., Dillsboro, North Carolina: Western North Carolina Press, 1976) 118-77.

[2]Joseph A. Fitzmyer, "The Priority of Mark and the 'Q' Source in Luke," *Jesus and Man's Hope* (A Perspective Book 11/1; Pittsburgh: Pittsburgh Theological Seminary, 1970), 1:131-70.

er's article as providing "the most extensive and formidable critique."[3] Even during the course of the Festival itself, the programmatic character of Fitzmyer's contribution commanded special attention.

Fitzmyer's paper is a response to a request from the steering committee of the Pittsburgh Festival on the Gospels to prepare a survey of the present state of the question of Luke's dependence on Mark and Q. Before he began his survey, he listed three preliminary observations. First, the corporate effort of scholars has advanced the critical study of the gospels in spite of the fact that no "wholly satisfying solution" to the Synoptic Problem has been found. "Indeed, the literary Source Analysis of the Synoptic Gospels has long since yielded to other phases of Gospel study: to Form Criticism and to *Redactionsgeschichte*, to mention only the two most important phases."[4] "Sometimes the advances were made in one phase or another because of previous misdirected or even false steps, as we can recognize today when we view the process with hindsight. . . . On the other hand, if arguments used in the past seem to have been inadequate or weak, it does not necessarily mean that they are such today; presuppositions affecting them may have changed, or the arguments may have received further analysis, confirmation or support."[5]

The second observation was to the effect that the history of Synoptic research reveals that the Synoptic Problem is "practically insoluble." The reason for this is that "the data for its solution are scarcely adequate or available to us."[6]

In the third place Fitzmyer observed that "because the corporate critical study of the Synoptic Problem has resulted only in a theory or theories about its solution, there are at least two other criteria that have been operative."[7] These are "appeal" and "usefulness." Since both of these "criteria" are important in understanding the present state of the question, it is needful to comment on them in some detail.

---

[3]Reginald H. Fuller, "Review Article: The Synoptic Problem: After Yen Years," *PSTJ* 28 (1975) 63-68, esp. 64.

[4]Fitzmyer, "Priority of Mark," 131.

[5]Fitzmyer, "Priority of Mark," 132.

[6]Fitzmyer, "Priority of Mark," 132.

[7]Fitzmyer, "Priority of Mark," 133.

2.1. *Fitzmyer's Criterion of "Appeal"*

"The Two-Source Theory has certainly appealed to the majority of twentieth-century scholars. In saying this, I do not intend 'an appeal to authority,' as if the sentiment of the majority closed the issue. It is a simple statement of fact."[8] Fitzmyer does not explain what the "appeal" of the two-document hypothesis is. Although he makes clear that this is a criterion that involves "critical judgment," it is not clear exactly what he has in mind.

Following his statement that the Two-Source Theory has appealed to the "majority of twentieth-century scholars," he adds an extended footnote which begins: "This includes at present many Roman Catholic scholars."[9] Fitzmyer singles out as a significant contribution the work of de Solages, *A Greek Synopsis of the Gospels: A New Way of Solving the Synoptic Problem*,[10] and quotes the following from a review by K. Grayston and G. Herdan: "The outcome of this laborious study is that the two-document hypothesis is systematically established; and it is worthy of note that the book has an approving preface by Cardinal Tisserant, President of the Biblical Commission."[11] Thereafter, Fitzmyer makes several comments, with references to relevant literature, which illuminate the importance of the *volta face* that de Solages' work, so prefaced, represents in the history of the Biblical Commission and in the realm of Roman Catholic synoptic studies in this country.[12] In the course of his discussion, Fitzmyer permitted himself to make the following personal observation:

> I personally find it difficult today to rid myself of the impression that the Commission's earlier opposition to the Two-Source Theory was basically the reason why an older generation of Roman Catholic scholars sought for solutions to the Synoptic Problem that differed considerably from the Two-Source Theory. While there were some who espoused modifications of it that made it possible to live with the *responsum* (e.g., by insisting that Aramaic

---

[8]Fitzmyer, "Priority of Mark," 133.

[9]Fitzmyer, "Priority of Mark," 163 n. 7.

[10]Bruno de Solages, *A Greek Synopsis of the Gospels: A New Way of Solving the Synoptic Problem* (Leiden: E. J. Brill; Toulouse: Institut Catholique, 1959).

[11]K. Grayston and G. Herdan, review of de Solages, *Synopsis, NTS* 7 (1960/61) 97-98, esp. 98.

[12]The fact that Cardinal Tisserant was the president of the Biblical Commission could be understood as implying that the Commission's negative *responsum* of 26 June 1912 to the question about the two-source theory had become inoperative.

Matthew was at the basis of Q, or by adopting other modifications), . . . most
of the other attempts at a solution subconsciously at least proceeded from the
responsum.[13]

As examples of the works by Roman Catholic scholars, which he
thought were at least subconsciously influenced by the *responsum*,
Fitzmyer lists: Chapman, *Matthew, Mark and Luke*,[14] Butler, *The
Originality of St. Matthew*[15] and Vaganay, *Le Problème synoptique*.[16]

If Fitzmyer is correct in this matter (in what at best we can only take
to be a surmise on his part), this would be an example of what I would
term an "extra-scientific" or "nonscientific" factor which exercised a
deep underlying influence on the work of these scholars.[17] Since Fitzmyer is prepared to think that "an older generation of Roman Catholic
scholars" could have been influenced against the two-document
hypothesis at least "subconsciously" by pressure from the Biblical
Commission, he may be willing to consider the possibility that a
younger generation of Roman Catholic scholars may have reacted in
the opposite direction for reasons no more or less valid. Certainly the
two-document hypothesis has an "appeal" to the younger generation
of Roman Catholic scholars and no doubt that "appeal" involves
critical judgment. But does it involve *only* critical judgment? Does it
involve other factors as well? For example, does it involve the very
reasonable desire to participate in the international world of New
Testament scholarship, to have one's work taken seriously and not
dismissed as work influenced by "ecclesiastical directive"? Is it not
among Catholic scholars, a "badge of academic freedom"?

In this connection we have the benefit of some remarkably candid
comments by Reginald H. Fuller, made in his address to the Southwest
Regional meeting of the Society of Biblical Literature in March 1974.
In the autobiographical statement with which he prefaced his analysis

---

[13]Fitzmyer, "Priority of Mark," 164 n. 7.

[14]John Chapman, *Matthew, Mark and Luke: A Study in the Order and Interrela-
tion of the Synoptic Gospels*, edited, with an introduction and some additional matter
by John M. T. Barton (London: Longmans, Green, 1937).

[15]Basil Christopher Butler, *The Originality of St Matthew: A Critique of the
Two-Document Hypothesis* (Cambridge: Cambridge University, 1951).

[16]L. Vaganay, *Le Problème synoptique: Une hypothèse de travail* (Bibliothèque de
théologie 3/1; Paris: Desclée, 1954).

[17]See Farmer, *Problem*, 190.

of the present state of the Synoptic Problem, he spoke as follows: "Of course, I heard of B. C. Butler's *The Originality of St. Matthew* when it came out in 1951, but I didn't bother to read it. After all, what could you expect from a Roman Catholic and a convert from Anglicanism but a defense of the Augustinian hypothesis?" Pierson Parker's *The Gospel Before Mark*[18] made very little impression on Fuller since it seemed to be no more than a variant of similar proposals by Vaganay and Benoit, whose views "could be attributed to their commitment to the decisions of the Pontifical Biblical Commission." Fuller rejected any implication that Parker's conclusions were so motivated, but nevertheless Parker seemed to Fuller to be very much of a loner, "an eccentric in the field of non-Roman New Testament Studies." It must be emphasized that Fuller was speaking autobiographically, and not representing his present understanding of and attitude toward Roman Catholic gospel scholarship.[19] But his statements are no less revealing, for they make clear the pressure that is exerted upon every Roman Catholic scholar who aspires to have his work read and taken into account by the international community of New Testament scholarship. For let there be no mistake, the international world of New Testament scholarship is dominated by liberal Protestant scholarship, which, as Fuller's candid autobiographical remarks reveal, can be prejudiced against the work of even the most eminent Roman Catholic scholar, if ecclesiastical rivalry is involved.

2.2 FITZMYER'S CRITERION OF "USEFULNESS"

Fitzmyer's argument under this heading may be summarized as follows: The two-source theory has served as the springboard for both form-criticism and *Redaktionsgeschichte*. In principle neither of these methods of gospel study is tied to the two-source theory, but in fact the work of Dibelius and Bultmann is manifestly dependent on this theory as is the *Redaktionsgeschichte* of Marxsen, Conzelmann, Bornkamm, *et al.* Fitzmyer concludes that until scholars working on some other

---

[18]Pierson Parker, *The Gospel Before Mark* (Chicago: University of Chicago, 1953).

[19]Cf. Raymond Brown, Karl P. Donfried and John Reumann, ed., *Peter in the New Testament: A Collaborative Assessment by Protestant and Roman Catholic Scholars* (Minneapolis, Minnesota: Augsburg; New York: Paulist, 1973). However, even in this ecumenical study Marcan priority is assumed without question, which, in view of the state of international research, suggests that this was still as late as 1973 a precondition of some sort.

hypothesis produce results that rival the work of those who have presupposed the two-source theory, this argument of "usefulness" is a "valuable, but extrinsic, criterion for judging the worth of the hypothesis."[20]

Fitzmyer closes his preliminary remarks, however, by acknowledging that they do not touch the real issue. "But they have been made to clear the air on certain aspects of the problem before we confront the major task."[21]

3. An Analysis of Fitzmyer's Defense of the Two-Document Hypothesis

Fitzmyer's major task was to take account of criticisms that had been made against Streeter's fundamental solution to the Synoptic Problem: to acknowledge points where he thought those criticisms were valid, to rebut criticisms he thought invalid, and to point out difficulties in alternate solutions. Fitzmyer first took up Streeter's five arguments for the priority of Mark, then his arguments for the existence of Q.

3.1 FITZMYER'S TREATMENT OF STREETER'S FIVE REASONS FOR THE PRIORITY OF MARK

3.1.1. First of all, there is the fact that the bulk of Mark is found in Luke and in Matthew. Fitzmyer concedes that in itself this does not argue for the priority of Mark. For example, it would appear that it could be explained as well on both the Augustinian and the Griesbach hypotheses. Fitzmyer sets aside the Griesbach Hypothesis, however, after listing six objections against it.[22]

3.1.2. Within the triple tradition, Matthew and Luke never agree with one another against Mark in regard to the order of episodes. When Luke's order differs from that of Mark, Matthew's order is generally the same as Mark, and when Matthew's order differs from that of Mark, Luke's order is generally the same as Mark's. Stated abstractly, this argues only for the intermediary position of Mark. But when one concretely compares the order of Luke with Mark, and the

---

[20]Fitzmyer, "Priority of Mark," 134.

[21]Fitzmyer, "Priority of Mark," 134.

[22]Fitzmyer, "Priority of Mark," 134-35. These objections have been answered, cf. William R. Farmer, "Modern Developments of Griesbach's Hypothesis," *NTS* 23 (1977) 283-93.

order of Matthew with Mark, it is easier to explain the redactional choices made when one assumes that Matthew and Luke have independently modified Mark. Fitzmyer notes the names of scholars who have found this argument fallacious, credits Butler especially, but cites favorably Wood in rebutting Butler's Augustinian solution: "Why, having Matthew in his hands, Luke should follow Matthew's order only when it reappears in Mark is difficult to understand and explain. If Dom Butler's thesis were true, there should be numerous agreements in order between Matthew and Luke against Mark, and admittedly there are none or next to none."[23]

Fitzmyer then adds a remark on the so-called Lucan transpositions. "In at least five places Mark and Luke do not have the same order of episodes, where they might have. . . . In any case, a more plausible reason can be assigned for the transposition of the five episodes by Luke than for their transposition by Mark. This would again argue for the priority of Mark over Luke."[24] Here Fitzmyer reasons from within a critical tradition stemming from Karl Lachmann. For purposes of clarification it is necessary to consider Lachmann's views on the phenomena of order within the context of other major alternatives.

> The great merit of the Griesbach hypothesis was and remains that it offers a credible explanation for the phenomenon of order—lacking in the alternative accounts. In order to clarify what might otherwise be confusing it is important to bear in mind that there are actually three arguments from order that have played an important role in the history of synoptic criticism. The best known argument is associated with the name of Streeter and is based upon the observation that Matthew and Luke never agree against Mark in the order they give to pericopes. Streeter argued that this can best be explained if Matthew and Luke have independently copied Mark. Butler showed that this observation only indicates that Mark is in some sense a middle term between Matthew and Luke and that as an argument of Marcan priority it is inconclusive. I concur in this judgment.
>
> A second argument from order, much older, is associated with the name of Griesbach and is based on the observation that whenever the order of Mark is not the same as that of Matthew, it follows the order of Luke, i.e., that Mark has no independent chronology. Griesbach held that this is best explained if Mark is third and is dependent for his order on Matthew and Luke. I concur with this view and regard it as a weighty consideration in favour of Mark being third. Griesbach's point may be simply put this way: all

---

[23] Fitzmyer, "Priority of Mark," 137-38.

[24] Fitzmyer, "Priority of Mark," 138.

that is needed to understand the order of events in Mark is that given in Matthew and Luke. Mark's order shows no independence of Matthew and Luke (excepting the single case of his ordering of the cleansing of the temple). This seems explicable only by a conscious effort of Mark to follow the order of Matthew and Luke. Neither Matthew nor Luke could have achieved this alone. They would have had to conspire with one another or find some other way to contrive this chronological neutering of Mark, i.e., robbing his chronological independence. Mark on this view can only be third and must have known Matthew and Luke. There seems to be no other satisfactory solution. Such an extraordinary state of affairs is made possible when the author of one narrative document has followed and preserved much of the order of the events given in another. Only someone writing later who was attempting to combine the two narrative documents has the possibility of preserving what order the second preserved from the first and then, wherever the second departed from the first, following the order of either one or the other. It was the great merit of Griesbach that he was able to grasp and comprehend the interrelatedness of all three of the synoptic gospels in a single synthetic judgment. Schleiermacher, F. C. Baur, Strauss, Bleek, and De Wette all concur that it was Griesbach's demonstration that he could account for the order of Mark by the simple device of showing that Mark's order of events was explained by postulating that he was following either the order of Matthew or the order of Luke, that compelled their assent to the view that Mark was third. There was no possible way that these critics, acquainted with Griesbach's demonstration, could ever agree that Mark was the first evangelist. This hypothesis simply could not explain Mark's lack of an independent chronology. The way to belief in Marcan priority had to be prepared by appeal to the existence of an Ur-gospel which all three had independently copied. This led to a third argument from order.

The third argument from order is associated with the name Lachmann and is based on the observation that the disagreement in order is greatest when one considers the three synoptics together, and that when one considers Mark in relationship to Matthew on the one hand and then Mark in relationship to Luke on the other, the differences in order are not so great and can be explained. This indicated to Lachmann that the order of Mark was closest to the order of an Ur-gospel upon which all three were dependent. My objection to this argument is that it involves what seems to me to be a methodological oversimplification. It seems simple enough to explain what seems easy to explain. But in this case the relationship between all three, where the differences in order are more complex, remains unexplained. It is both the great advantage and at the same time the great demerit of the Ur-gospel hypothesis that it creates a situation where the mind can take refuge in the thought that if we had the Ur-gospel we would be able to explain what otherwise remains unexplained. The advantage of the Griesbach hypothesis is that it offers a credible explanation of the order of Mark in relationship to both Matthew and Luke taken together and without taking refuge in an appeal to the order of some hypothetical Ur-gospel. Of course, on the Griesbach hypothesis, to be fully convincing it must be demonstrated that it is possible to explain the order of Luke in relationship to Matthew. That has been most adequately accomplished to date in Bernard Orchard's *Matthew, Luke and Mark*, pp. 37-68.

The force of the argument from order for the Griesbach hypothesis cannot be fully appreciated when it is stated abstractly. But when it is considered in relation to a careful examination of the text of the gospels, as for example in Griesbach's original *Commentatio* of 1790, and with reference to the internal structure of given pericopes, as in Longstaff's dissertation, it becomes a persuasive argument, which is further strengthened by modern developments. The *Commentatio* volume of papers presented at the Griesbach Colloquium of 1976 includes an English translation of the eighteenth-century Latin text of Griesbach's *Commentatio*.

3.1.3. Fitzmyer's (Streeter's) third argument for the priority of Mark concerns the actual wording of passages in the triple tradition. This wording is frequently the same. Fitzmyer is impressed by that part of the argument that singles out the agreement of Matthew or Luke with Mark, when the other disagrees. "When it is so considered, I find it hard to see Mark as a mere connecting-link. And even less can I find a plausible reason for saying that Mark borrowed from Matthew or Luke."[26] But on the Griesbach Hypothesis this agreement is explained very well.

3.1.4. Fitzmyer's (Streeter's) fourth reason for espousing the priority of Mark is the more "primitive character" of its narrative. Fitzmyer reviews the work of Butler, Farmer, and Sanders under this heading. Butler explains the "primitive character" of Mark as due to the influence of Peter, who, as a preacher, used Mark as his *aide-mémoire*. Fitzmyer observes that, as such, Butler's idea of interposing a preacher between Matthew and Mark means "another stage in his solution of the Synoptic Problem," an oral source. "It is a hypothetical element that is really devoid of any control, and this is its deficiency."[27]

The criticisms of Streeter under this heading by Farmer, where it is shown that Streeter's argumentation is inconclusive or reversible, are generally accepted by Fitzmyer. But Farmer's dependence on the laws of form-criticism is criticized in the light of the findings in *The Tendencies of the Synoptic Tradition* by Sanders.[28]

---

[25]B. Orchard & J. R. W. Longstaff (eds.), *J. J. Griesbach* (Cambridge: University Press, 1978); see also W. R. Farmer (ed.), *New Synoptic Studies: The Cambridge Gospel Conference and Beyond* (Macon, Georgia: Mercer University Press, 1983).

[26]Fitzmyer, "Priority of Mark," 139.

[27]Fitzmyer, "Priority of Mark," 140.

[28]Fitzmyer, "Priority of Mark," 142. See E. P. Sanders, *The Tendencies of the Synoptic Tradition* (SNTSMS 9; Cambridge: Cambridge University, 1969).

3.1.5. Streeter's fifth point, having to do with the distribution of
Marcan and non-Marcan material in Matthew and Luke respectively,
is regarded by Fitzmyer as the weakest reason appealed to by Marcan
priorists. It is less an argument than a preliminary statement to explain
(a) omissions of Mark made by Matthew and Luke, and (b) the minor
agreements. Fitzmyer acknowledges most of Farmer's criticism of
Streeter under this heading, but notes some inadequate documentation
and correctly observes that the "web of minor but closely related
agreements" is difficult to see with the use of any existing synopticon.[29]

What is meant by this expression "web of agreements" may be seen
from the following example taken from Keech's *A Complete Table of
the Agreement of Matthew and Luke Against Mark in the Triple
Tradition.*[30]
(See Illustration on next page.)
Keech comments as follows:

> Verses 12 and 13 in Luke (vv. 2 and 3 in Matthew) contain a truly
> outstanding phenomenon of agreement. Beginning with λέγων, they proceed
> verbatim for eighteen consecutive words. Streeter (pp. 309f.) cites good
> textual evidence for the use of κύριε in Mark (which does not disturb the
> verbatim reading of Matthew and Luke), as well as less conclusive (but
> suggestive) evidence for the readings ἥψατο αὐτοῦ and εὐθέως. But Streeter,
> not crediting common omissions, does not thereby account for the total
> agreement of Matthew and Luke. Easton (pp. 63f.) notes all the above
> agreements except the omission of αὐτῷ from Mk. 1:40, with reason to
> believe that Luke has used another source in addition to Mark. Yet to
> maintain the independence of Matthew and Luke means that both independ-
> ently would have to omit αὐτῷ ὅτι, add κύριε, omit σπλαγχνισθείς, trans-
> pose αὐτοῦ, substitute λέγων for καὶ λέγει omit αὐτῷ and substitute εὐθέως
> for εὐθύς. Apart from coincidence which, in this case, I believe is fantastically
> improbable, literary dependence alone accounts for the identical readings of
> Matthew and Luke; for (because) eighteen consecutive words is verbal
> identity on the order of that associated with the Double Tradition.

Fitzmyer concedes that the minor agreements of Matthew and
Luke against Mark constitute a real problem; it is a "loophole in the
Two-Source Theory."[31] But this phenomenon, Fitzmyer concludes,

[29]Fitzmyer, "Priority of Mark," 145.

[30]I. M. Keech's study of the minor agreements is presently deposited in the Drew
University Library, Madison, New Jersey. See also Franz Neirynck, ed., *The Minor
Agreements of Matthew and Luke against Mark with a Cumulative List* (BETL 37;
Gembloux: Duculot; Leuven: Leuven University, 1974).

[31]Fitzmyer, "Priority of Mark," 144.

45. The Healing of a Leper

Matt 8:1-4	Mark 1:40-45	Luke 5:12-16
2 ...ἰδοὺ... λέγων κύριε, ἐάν θέλῃς, δύνασαί με καθαρί- σαι. 3καὶ ἐκτείνας τὴν χεῖρα ἥψατο αὐτοῦ λέγων· θέλω, καθαρίσθητι. καὶ εὐθέως...	40... λέγων αὐτῷ ὅτι ἐὰν θέλῃς δύνασαί με καθαρί- σαι. 41καὶ σπλαγχνισθεὶς ἐκτείνας τὴν χεῖρα αὐτοῦ ἥψατο καὶ λέγει αὐτῷ θέλω, καθαρίσθητι. 42καὶ εὐθὺς... 43 καὶ ἐμβριμησάμενος αὐτῷ εὐθὺς ἐξέβαλεν αὐτόν.	12 ...ἰδοὺ... λέγων κύριε, ἐάν θέλῃς, δύνασαί με καθαρί- σαι. 13 καὶ ἐκτείνας τὴν χεῖρα ἥψατο αὐτοῦ λέγων θέλω, καθαρίσθητι· καὶ εὐθέως...

scarcely weighs as evidence that completely counterbalances the other data pointing to Marcan priority.[32] But as we have seen, when analyzed, these preceding arguments remain as before Fitzmyer's attempt to defend Streeter, inconclusive at best and sometimes reversible.

Fitzmyer comments on the idea of Ur-Marcus and declines to reject it since it would offer an explanation among other things for Marcan passages omitted by both Matthew and Luke and for the minor agreements of Matthew and Luke against Mark. The possibility is mentioned that *Redaktionsgeschichte* "may allow for some of the differences that the hypothesis itself was seeking to handle."[33]

3.2 FITZMYER'S DEFENSE OF 'Q'

Fitzmyer observes that to establish the independent existence of Q is more difficult than to establish the priority of Mark. He acknowledges that arguments for Q presuppose "the incredibility" of Luke having used Matthew. So he begins by reviewing five reasons for denying Luke's use of Matthew.[34]

First there is the apparent reluctance of Luke to reproduce typically Matthean "additions" within the Triple Tradition. Immediately we note that this statement presupposes something that is still at issue, i.e., the priority of Mark. If Mark was not written until after Matthew and Luke, there are no "Matthean additions." That is a way of referring to the text of Matthew that is quite unjustified if one is concerned impartially to decide whether Luke used Matthew without presupposing any solution to the problem of their relationship to Mark.

The second difficulty is to explain "why Luke would want to break up Matthew's sermons, especially the Sermon on the Mount in order to incorporate a part of it in his Sermon on the Plain and scatter the rest of it in an unconnected and disjointed fashion in the loose context of the travel account."[35] This is not difficult to explain if one does not confuse the issue by intruding Mark into the picture. And, since on the Griesbach Hypothesis Mark was not in existence when Luke used Matthew, it is proper simply to ask at every point, what is Luke doing

---

[32]Fitzmyer, "Priority of Mark," 146.

[33]Fitzmyer, "Priority of Mark," 147.

[34]Fitzmyer, "Priority of Mark," 148-50.

[35]Fitzmyer, "Priority of Mark," 149.

with the text of Matthew. Addressing ourselves to Fitzmyer's specific questions we can say that Luke's access to other very important source material presented an editorial problem, which he solved very intelligently. He made an editorial decision to reduce the length of the Matthean discourses (1) by omitting some sayings, and (2) by redistributing others, placing most of them in what has come to be recognized as the great central section of his gospel. That he indeed was dependent on Matthew is indicated by the following considerations: (1) Luke knows all six of the Matthean discourses as is indicated by his use of the opening parts of each, and (2) the sequence of these episodes is very nearly the same in Luke as in Matthew. Sayings Luke took from Matthew's six discourses are found in Luke in the same general sequence they have in Matthew with the exception of those found in the central section. This offers striking support for the view that Luke composed his gospel with Matthew as one of his basic sources. He began by using Matthew as his basic source, moving forward in Matthew, taking up material from Matthew he wished to retain and working into his narrative material from his other sources where he thought it fit best. As he composed his gospel, however, he not only worked in material on the same or related themes from other sources, he sometimes skipped over material in Matthew in order to take up something in Matthew that fit the theme of the section he was then composing. Sometimes after having moved forward in the text of Matthew in this way and with the incorporation of this material having completed his composition on the theme at hand, he would continue his composition by incorporating into his text the literary unit immediately preceding. The literary effect of what Luke has done is to reduce the impact of the Matthean discourses both by reducing their content and by creating his own extended teaching section into which he incorporated most of the very valuable Jesus tradition that came to him from his special source material. All will agree that the central section of Luke's Gospel dominates his presentation of the teaching of Jesus. What has gone unnoticed is that in this section where Luke obviously is no longer using Matthew as his main source, he apparently found some other guide for his arrangement of material. Of course, he may be creating his arrangement entirely *de novo* as he proceeds. But the very different sequence given to material from Matthew suggests that whereas earlier he was working his special source material into a basically Matthean sequence, in the central section the opposite is taking place.

Of course, if Mark is working with Matthew and Luke and is seeking to reduce the discrepancies between these gospels by reducing sequential differences, then we immediately have a credible explanation for why he has omitted Luke's central section from his gospel. For in Luke's central section the sequential discrepancies between Luke and Matthew are at a maximum. Moreover, when viewed in this way, we can see that there was no way Mark could have reconstituted the Matthean discourses without creating sequential discrepancies between his gospel and that of Luke. Furthermore, much of what Luke had omitted from these Matthean discourses as unsuitable for gentile churches was no less unsuitable for the churches for which Mark was composing his gospel.

Fitzmyer's third reason for positing the independence of Matthew and Luke reads as follows: "Aside from 3:7-9, 17, and 4:2-13 Luke has never inserted the material of the Double Tradition into the same Marcan context as Matthew."[36] Once again we have a "reason" which presupposes the most important point at issue, i.e., Marcan priority. If Mark is not first, Matthew and Luke cannot rightly be said to be inserting material into any kind of "Marcan context." As we have seen from the description of Luke's compositional method, there is frequent disagreement between Matthew and Luke as to the sequence and context they give to many of Jesus' teachings. But all of these differences fall well within the reasonable limits of change in order and context that an author of a gospel may be presumed to have exercised if Luke was using Matthew. Here also the appeal to abandon abstract argumentation is apropos.

Fitzmyer's fourth reason reads: "Analysis of the Double Tradition material in Matthew and Luke shows that sometimes Matthew, sometimes Luke has preserved what can only be described as the more original setting of a given episode. This would seem to be scarcely the case if Luke were always dependent on Matthew within this tradition. It is, however, readily intelligible on the hypothesis that both of them have been following and editing a common source."[37]

Two points may be made by way of answer to this. First, if Luke

---

[36]Fitzmyer, "Priority of Mark," 149.

[37]Fitzmyer, "Priority of Mark," 150.

were dependent on Matthew within this tradition, he would still have the editorial freedom to create new settings for given episodes, and it would be very difficult to determine whether his setting or that of Matthew were the more original. Certainly in the Gospel of Matthew there is little concerted effort made to write history. The genre of Matthew is closer to that of popular biography or *encomia* than it is to history. In this genre no great importance is attached to giving the "more original setting" of an episode. What is important is the rhetorical effect in bringing out the character of the subject. The author is allowed great freedom in pursuing this goal.[38] But with Luke it is somewhat different. While his gospel still is closer to a *bios* or *encomium* genre than it is to history, Luke as the author of the two-volume work, Luke-Acts, as is indicated by his preface, and as is generally recognized, does seek to produce a gospel that will be somewhat more acceptable to those sensitive of the standards of Hellenistic historiography.[39] Under these circumstances, the impression of having given a particular episode its "more original setting" could sometimes occur.

The second point is this. If Luke had other source material besides Matthew, there is always the possibility that a given episode has retained its more original setting in this material. There certainly are sayings of Jesus which occur in different forms in Matthew and Luke, respectively, where Luke sometimes has the saying in its more original form. We may take the Parable of the Lost Sheep as a case in point. It can be argued that in Luke this parable has been given a more original setting in the context of Jesus' conflict with the Pharisees. But any number of cases of this kind could occur without leading to the conclusion that Matthew and Luke where independent. For the conclusion that Luke used Matthew is based upon the striking similarities between the two gospels, and does not in any way entail that Luke was bound to copy or follow Matthew at any given point, least of all when he had access to another source or sources which provided him alternate editorial or compositional choices. Under these circumstances one could expect that Luke would sometimes preserve an episode in its

---

[38]Cf. Philip Shuler, "The Synoptic Gospels and the Problem of Genre" (Ph.D. diss., McMaster University, Hamilton, Ontario, 1975).

[39]For example, he tends to eliminate doublets from his gospel, and when they are retained, we find that the second occurrence reflects his own effort at rewording.

more original setting.[40]

Fitzmyer's fifth reason is in the form of a question: "If Luke depends on Matthew, why has he almost constantly omitted Matthean material in episodes where there are Matthean, but no Marcan parallels, e.g., in the infancy and resurrection narratives?"[41] Luke has omitted the infancy and resurrection narratives from Matthew because he has access to infancy and resurrection narratives from other source material or because he prefers to create new ones, or both. What Mark has done with these narratives can best be determined by a concrete approach to the text of Mark in relation to Matthew and Luke. But wherever he has followed Luke as his guide for omitting material from Matthew, he has created a situation that can be perceived on the Marcan hypothesis as the conundrum Fitzmyer poses. There is, of course, a very major exception to what Fitzmyer describes even on his own terms of Marcan priority, e.g., the second feeding of the multitudes and *all* that comes between the two feeding stories in Matthew is omitted by Luke, but there are Marcan parallels. On the Griesbach Hypothesis, Mark here follows Matthew as his guide and chooses not to omit these narratives as did Luke.

Fitzmyer next took up the three main reasons for postulating the Greek written source Q.[42] The first is the number of critical texts in which Matthew and Luke agree almost with identical wording. This argues against an oral Q tradition, but it is certainly no reason to posit Q if Luke used Matthew.

The second reason is stated thusly: "It is scarcely coincidental that the material of the Double Tradition inserted into the First and Third Gospels in different contexts manifests a common general underlying sequence or order."[43] Fitzmyer correctly observes that this can hardly be due to oral tradition and it seems to argue for a written source. But by itself it does not argue for Q any more than for Luke's dependence on Matthew.

---

[40]Cf. William R. Farmer, "A Fresh Approach to Q," *Christianity, Judaism and Other Greco-Roman Cults: Studies for Morton Smith at Sixty*, Part 1: *New Testament*, ed. Jacob Neusner (SJLA 12/1; Leiden: E. J. Brill, 1975) 39-50. See this study also for a fuller statement of Luke's editorial procedure in using Matthew.

[41]Fitzmyer, "Priority of Mark," 150.

[42]Fitzmyer, "Priority of Mark," 150-53.

[43]Fitzmyer, "Priority of Mark," 151.

So the first two main reasons for postulating Q turn out to be reasons not to postulate an *oral* Q. If it could be shown that Luke and Matthew were independent, then there would be reasons to think that the common source they were copying was written in Greek. But if this independence is doubtful, then these two reasons do not argue any more for the Q hypothesis than for a direct literary relationship between Matthew and Luke.

Fitzmyer's third reason for postulating Q is found in the doublets of Luke and Matthew.

> By a "doublet" is meant here an account of the same event or saying occurring twice in either Luke or Matthew and related in such wise that they seem to be part of the Triple Tradition on the one hand and of the Double Tradition on the other—or to put it another way, that one belongs to a tradition parallel to Mark and one to a tradition not parallel to Mark. The conclusion drawn from this phenomenon is that Matthew and Luke have retained in their Gospels the double accounts of the same event or saying as they inherited them independently from Mark and Q.[44]

This conclusion rests upon the fact that in chapters 8 and 9 of Luke there are six passages which have doublets in Luke's central section. The bearing of this fact on the solution of the synoptic problem calls for a detailed approach to the texts of the three gospels. But once it is granted that Matthew has doublets, there is no reason why Luke could not have retained one member of each doublet (six in all) in following Matthew up to the beginning of his central section, and utilized the other member where appropriate in composing his central section. Mark, in omitting almost everything in Luke's central section, has created a situation where *on the assumption of Marcan priority* the passages concerned which are found in the central section, *without* Marcan parallels (but with verbal agreement with Matthew), are perceived to have been taken from one source, whereas the passages concerned which are found in Luke 8-9, *with* Marcan parallels, are perceived to have been taken from another. Once again we have a reason which is vitally affected by how one perceives the problem in the first place.

Fitzmyer then discusses some objections to the Q hypothesis and concedes that it has difficulties and inadequacies. But "until a more useful hypothesis is convincingly proposed—one that is freer of serious

---

[44]Fitzmyer, "Priority of Mark," 152-53.

objections to it than is Q," the Q source will continue to command the attention of students, "despite its difficulties."[45]

This ends Fitzmyer's defense of Q and of the Two-Source Hypothesis. There is a final paragraph devoted to the so-called "overlapping of 'Q' and Mark," which rounds out his presentation on Q but neither adds to nor detracts from his argument for the Two-Source Theory.

As this analysis of Fitzmyer's defense of the Two-Source Theory shows, his reasons for postulating Q presuppose the independence of Matthew and Luke or the priority of Mark. His reasons for presupposing the independence of Matthew and Luke presuppose the priority of Mark or are inconclusive or even reversible. And the reasons given for the priority of Mark were also inconclusive if not reversible, *so long as the Griesbach Hypothesis is considered as a viable hypothesis.* In fairness to Fitzmyer, it should be pointed out that in most of his presentation he gives reasons for what he presupposes. For example, before he dismisses any further consideration of the Griesbach Hypothesis, he stated serious objections to the Griesbach Hypothesis in the form of six questions. These questions, taken together with his discussion of the Griesbach Hypothesis in the closing section of his paper, make it clear that he had several reasons for not regarding the Griesbach Hypothesis as a viable hypothesis. These have been discussed by me in another place.[46]

---

[45]Fitzmyer, "Priority of Mark," 155.

[46]Farmer, "Developments," 283-93.

LUKAS 9:51-56—
EIN HEBRÄISCHES FRAGMENT

David Flusser

JUDÄA WAR DAMALS unter römischer Herrschaft, der Statthalter hieß Cumanus (48-52 nach Chr.). Die Galiläer pflegten, als sie zu ihren Festen nach der heiligen Stadt Jerusalem pilgerten, durch das Gebiet der Samariter zu ziehen. Da geschah es, daß bei einem Dorfe, das in der großen Ebene Samariens liegt, das damals Gema und heute Jenin heißt, aus der großen Zahl der Juden, die zum Feste hinaufzogen, ein Galiläer von den Samaritern getötet wurde.[1] Der Grund des Todes war ideologischer Haß, der von der Seite der Juden zur Rache und Mord geführt hat, dann zur römischen Intervention, und es gab wieder Tote; dann wurde die Sache in Rom zur hohen Politik und endlich wurde der römische Statthalter in die Verbannung geschickt und ein anderer, der berüchtigte Felix, hat in Judäa Karriere gemacht.

Es ist nicht schwer sich vorzustellen, warum der galiläische Pilger seinen Tod durch die Samariter gefunden hat, obzwar wir die näheren Umstände nicht kennen. Wahrscheinlich empfanden die Samariter den ständigen Durchzug jüdischer Pilger aus Galiläa nach Jerusalem gerade durch ihr Gebiet als eine Provokation, die ihre religiösen Gefühle treffen sollte. Siehe, da zieht eine große Zahl von Galiläern zu den unheiligen, prächtigen Tempel in Jerusalem, wo doch die wahre heilige Stätte der Berg Garizim ist! Und warum müssen diese Galiläer nach Jerusalem gerade nicht weit von dem wahrhaft heiligen Berg pilgern? Die Samariter haben sich also damals zusammengerottet; ob sie die galiläische Pilgerschar tätlich hindern wollten, oder nur drohend

---

[1] Josephus, *Ant.* 20.118; *Bell.* 2.232. Siehe auch Emil Schürer, *Geschichte des jüdischen Volkes im Zeitalter Jesu Christi*, 3 vols. (Leipzig: J. C. Hinrichs, 1898-1901 [vol. 1, 1901]), 1:569-70; Menahem Stern, "The Province of Judaea," *The Jewish People in the First Century: Historical Geography, Political History, Social, Cultural and Religious Life and Institutions*, 2 vols. (Compendia Rerum Iudaicarum ad Novum Testamentum; Assen: Van Gorcum, 1974), 1:363-65. Wir folgen hier der glaubwürdigeren Darstellung des *Jüdischen Krieges*. Nach den *Altertümern* wurden im Tumult viele Galiläer getötet.

dabeistanden, wissen wir nicht. Jedenfalls können wir uns vorstellen, daß die Galiläer ihrerseits empört gewesen sind; vielleicht hat nicht einer von ihnen gewünscht, Gott möge auf die Samariter Feuer vom Himmel herunterkommen lassen. In dieser geladenen Atmosphäre kam es also zu einem Zusammenstoß—und ein Galiläer wurde dabei getötet. Die Zeit, wo die wahrhaftigen Anbeter den Vater im Geist und Wahrheit anbeten werden, läßt auf sich bis heute warten.

An die zwanzig Jahre vorher zog auf demselben Weg eine andere Pilgerschar galiläischer Männer und Frauen nach Jerusalem (Lukas 9,51-56), um dort am Passa im Tempel zu opfern und das Fest zu feiern. Jesus, der Führer dieser Pilgergruppe, schickte Boten in ein Dorf der Samariter, um für die Pilger eine Herberge zu suchen, aber die Samariter nahmen ihn nicht auf, weil er in der Richtung nach Jerusalem zog.[2] Ob die Samariter den Grund ihrer Ablehnung offen ausgesprochen haben, oder ob sie eine fadenscheinige Entschuldigung vorgeschützt haben, warum es für die Galiläer in ihrem Dorf keinen Platz gibt, wissen wir nicht. Den Galiläern war klar, daß man sie im Dorf der Samariter nicht empfangen wollte, weil sie nach Jerusalem pilgern. Zwei von den Pilgern empfanden die Beleidigung des Jerusalemer Tempels und der Juden durch die Samariter so scharf, daß sie sich an Jesus gewandt haben mit der Bitte, auf diese Menschen Feuer herunterkommen zu lassen,[3] doch Jesus schalt diese Hitzköpfe und sie zogen in ein anderes, jüdisches[4] Dorf.

---

[2]Auf die Ähnlichkeit des Zwischenfalls unter Cumanus und dem in Lukas 9,51-56 Erzählten verweisen sowohl Paul Billerbeck (Str-B, 1:557) als auch Henry St. John Thackeray (*Josephus: With an English Translation* [Cambridge, Massachusetts: Harvard University; London: William Heinemann, 1927], 2:415) und Alfred Plummer (*A Critical and Exegetical Commentary on the Gospel According to S. Luke*, 5th ed. [ICC; Edinburgh: T. & T. Clark, 1922] 263). Hugo Grotius (zu Lukas 9,53) hat die Weigerung der Samariter richtig verstanden.

[3]Dieser Wunsch der Zebedaiden kann sehr wohl historisch sein, da sie Jesu eine solche Macht, um das Wunder auszuführen, zutrauen konnten. Mir persönlich ist es allerdings schwierig anzunehmen, daß die zwei Jünger annehmen konnten, daß sie selbst solche übernatürliche Macht besitzen, Feuer vom Himmel herabzubeschwören, obzwar auch dies nicht unmöglich ist. Vielleicht haben die Brüder im ursprünglichen Bericht nur von Jesus verlangt, er selbst solle das Wunder vollbringen, und die Änderung wurde von dem griechischen Redaktor angebracht. Sicher ist jedenfalls, daß die Worte "willst du, daß wir sagen" griechisch und nicht hebräisch stylisiert sind.

[4]Warum würde es denn Jesus für nötig gefunden haben, nach der Weigerung des einen samaritanischen Dorfes ein anderes Dorf der Samariter anzufragen? Ob man ein

Im Evangelium ist der Grund der samaritanischen Weigerung klar ausgedrückt: sie nahmen ihn nicht auf, weil er in der Richtung nach Jerusalem zog. Die Reaktion der Samariter ist, wie wir gesehen haben, historisch verständlich und darum ist an der Historizität des Zwischenfalles nicht zu zweifeln. Wie steht es aber mit der Überlieferung der Geschichte selbst? Wir werden uns hier nicht mit der Stellung des Fragments in Lukas und mit seiner Funktion befassen; es ist nicht von Lukas erfunden, sondern er hat es aus einer schriftlichen Vorlage abgeschrieben, und wenigstens die Verse 51-53 waren in dieser Vorlage wörtlich aus dem hebräischen ins griechische übersetzt.

Wir haben gesehen: der ganze Abschnitt handelt von der Pilgerfahrt Jesu und seiner Jünger nach Jerusalem. Doch die Geschichte beginnt bei Lukas (9,51) so: "Es geschah aber, als sich die Tage seiner Himmelfahrt vollendet haben, da richtete er sein Angesicht nach Jerusalem, um dorthin zu reisen". Das griechische Wort für Himmelfahrt, das sonst nie in dem Neuen Testament oder in der griechischen Bibel vorkommt, entspricht dem lateinischen *assumptio*. Es bedeutet hier "Himmelfahrt" und nicht einfach "Tod", obzwar es sprachlich möglich wäre.[5] Es war Professor Bo Reicke, der richtig vermutet hat, daß hinter dem griechischen Wort für Himmelfahrt ein hebräisches Wort für die Pilgerfahrt nach Jerusalem steckt.[6] Das gesuchte hebräische Wort ist zweifellos עליה. Das Wort kommt in der hebräischen Bibel nicht vor[7]; es ist nachbiblisch und bedeutet unter anderem die Pilgerfahrt nach Jerusalem,[8] und daß dasselbe hebräische Wort gleichzeitig der

konkretes Politikum als eine "Beschreibung des Wirkens Jesu unter dem objektiv-christologischen Gesichtspunkt" (Hans Conzelmann, *Die Mitte der Zeit: Studien zur Theologie des Lukas*, 5th ed. [BHT 17; Tübingen: J. C. B. Mohr, 1964] 58) verstehen soll, ist mir fraglich.

[5]Siehe z.B. Walter Bauer, *Griechisch-deutsches Wörterbuch zu den Schriften des Neuen Testaments und der übrigen urchristlichen Literatur*, 5th ed. (Berlin: Alfred Töpelmann, 1958) 113.

[6]Bo Reicke, "Instruction and Discussion in the Travel Narrative," *TU* 73 (= *SE* 1; Berlin: Akademie, 1959) 211. Der Verfasser vermutet, daß das hebräische Wort מעלה sei, welches in den Überschriften von Psalmen 120-134 vorkommt.

[7]In 2 Chr 9,4 ist es eine innerhebräische Korruptel (vgl. 1 Kön 10,5), die nicht einmal in allen hebräischen Handschriften vorkommt.

[8]Siehe z.B. Sifre Num. 89 (H. S. Horovitz, ed. [Jerusalem: 1966] 90 unten) und Pas. 8ᵇ. Die Pilger ziehen bekanntlich nach Jerusalem hinauf sowohl in hebräisch als auch in griechisch, auch im Neuen Testament. Auch bei der Schilderung des Inzidents mit

einzige Äquivalent für das Wort "Himmelfahrt"ist, ist klar. Es hat also der griechische Übersetzer unseres Abschnittes das Wort עליה nicht richtig übersetzt: anstatt "Pilgerfahrt" schrieb er "Himmelfahrt". Der Abschnitt begann also ursprünglich: "Es geschah aber, als sich die Tage seiner Pilgerfahrt vollendet haben, da richtete er sein Angesicht nach Jerusalem, um dorthin zu reisen". Der Übersetzer, der die zwei Bedeutungen des hebräischen Wortes verwechselt hat, konnte kaum Lukas gewesen sein, denn Lukas hat nicht hebräisch verstanden. Wir werden noch den Übersetzer besser kennen lernen.

Man kann die Hebraismen noch in der Übersetzung erkennen, und sie wurden von den Forschern schon gesehen, so, unter anderem, die dreimalige Erwähnung des Antlitzes, über die wir noch sprechen werden. Es wurde auch schon erkannt, daß die Wendung "als sich die Tage vollendet haben" viele Parallelen in der hebräischen Bibel hat.[9] Soweit ich weiß, wurde nicht beachtet, daß die Wendung "und er sandte Boten vor seinem Angesicht"(Lukas 9,52) aus den Geschichten Jakobs im ersten Buch Mosis (Gen 32,4) übernommen wurde, und zwar, wie wir noch sehen werden, aus dem hebräischen Text und nicht aus der griechischen Übersetzung. Doch auch dies genügt noch nicht, um zu zeigen, daß unser Abschnitt nicht im biblischen Griechisch verfasst wurde, sondern daß sein Original hebräisch gewesen ist. Aber so ist es: die historische Schilderung im Lukas 9,51-53 ist wörtlich aus dem Hebräischen übersetzt[10]—das Gespräch (Lukas 9,54-55) dagegen ist entweder eine freiere Übersetzung oder es wurde vom Redaktor ein

---

den Samaritern im *Bell.* 2.232 spricht Josephus von den vielen Juden "die zum Fest hinaufzogen".

[9]Nur ein Beispiel hier: Jer 25,12. Dies ist auch die einzige Stelle in der griechischen Bibel, in der das griechische Wort συμπληροῦν vorkommt, das auch Lukas für das Zeitwort "vollenden"an unserer Stelle (9,51) benutzt. Dieses Kompositum kommt im Neuen Testament nur bei Lukas vor (Lukas 8,23; 9,51; Apg 2,1). Die letzte Stelle ist der unseren ähnlich.

[10]Nur das Wort "er"in Lukas 9,51 fehlte im hebräischen Original. Es kann sein, daß das Wort "er" in Lukas 9,51 von dem jüdischen Übersetzer oder Redaktor in den Vers eingefügt wurde, weil es in Lukas 17,11 steht, einem Vers, der über dieselbe geographische Situation spricht und ähnlich gebaut ist: "Und es geschah, als er nach Jerusalem ging, und er zog mitten durch Samaria und Galiläa hindurch". Vielleicht bildete in der Quelle Lukas 17,11-19 die Fortsetzung von Lukas 9,51-56. Das wäre hübsch, denn der dankbare Samariter in Lukas 17,15-19 steht im Gegensatz zu den widerspenstigen Samaritern im Lukas 9,51-56.

wenig umstilisiert.[11] Dies kann am besten durch eine Rückübersetzung gezeigt werden:

(51) ויהי במלאות ימי עליתו, וישם פניו ללכת לירושלים,

(52) וישלח מלאכים לפניו, וילכו ויבאו בכפר השמרונים כדי להכין

לו. (53) ולא קבלו אותו כי פניו אל ירושלם.

Die Rekonstruktion des hebräischen Textes ist so gesichert, daß wir wagen dürfen, sie ins Deutsche wörtlich zu übersetzen:

(51) Und es war, als die Tage seiner Pilgerfahrt sich vollendeten, setzte er sein Angesicht, um nach Jerusalem zu gehen, (52) und er sandte Boten vor seinem Angesicht, und sie gingen und kamen in ein Dorf der Samariter, um ihm vorzubereiten (53). Und sie nahmen ihn nicht auf, weil sein Angesicht nach Jerusalem (gerichtet war).

Daß man auch im Zeitalter Jesu hebräische historische Prosa im biblischen Stil schreiben konnte, ist sicher nicht erstaunlich. Auch wenn wir von dem bewußt archaischen und gekünstelten biblischen Stil der Schriften der Sekte vom Toten Meer absehen, gibt es doch den hebräischen Teil des Buches Daniel aus der Zeit des Antiochos Epiphanes, und die Geschichte von dem Zwist zwischen Alexander Jannäus und den Pharisäern, die im Babylonischen Talmud (*Sota* 66) erzählt wird, stammt aus einer geschriebenen hebräischen Quelle, die im biblischen Stil verfasst wurde. Warum soll also nicht ein Teil der hebräischen Berichte über Jesus stilistisch in der alttestamentlichen Tradition gestanden haben? Daß es dem so war, beweist endgültig unser Fragment, dessen hebräische Vorlage im ganzen nicht neuhebräisch, sondern nach der alttestamentlichen Art geschrieben wurde.

In dem sehr kurzen Text kommt, sowohl in hebräisch, als auch in der griechisch erhaltenen Übersetzung dreimal das Wort "Antlitz" vor. In allen drei Fällen handelt es sich um Hebraismen, die der griechische Übersetzer bewahrt hat. Bei dem ersten (Lukas 9,51) und dritten (Lukas 9,53) handelt es sich eigentlich um dieselbe Sache: als Jesus seine Pilgerfahrt angetreten hat, "setzte er sein Angesicht, um nach Jerusalem zu gehen", das heißt, er hat sich entschlossen, nach Jerusalem zu pilgern und begann in dieser Richtung zu wandern; die Samariter nahmen ihn nicht auf, "weil sein Angesicht nach Jerusalem"

---

[11]Der abschliessende Vers (Lukas 9,56) kann, aber muß nicht eine wörtliche Übersetzung aus dem Hebräischen sein. Er konnte genau so in hebräisch als auch in griechisch verfasst worden sein.

gerichtet war, das heißt, weil er in der Richtung nach Jerusalem zog. In diesen beiden Fällen fiel es dem Übersetzer schwer, frei zu übersetzen, ohne die Prägnanz der hebräischen Wendung aufzugeben—aber war in diesen beiden Fällen die Sucht nach der außerordentlichen Treue, der wirkliche Grund dafür, daß er das Idiom wörtlich übersetzt hat? Sonst pflegen ja die griechischen Übersetzer in den synoptischen Evangelien nicht in der Art Bubers oder Akylas zu übersetzen. Wahrscheinlich war also dem Übersetzer das Wort "Antlitz" aus irgendeinem Grunde inhaltlich wichtig, und wurde auf das Wort aufmerksam, weil es in seinem kurzen Text *dreimal* vorkommt. Als Beweis für die Richtigkeit dieser Annahme kann das zweite, noch nicht erwähnte Vorkommen des Wortes "Antlitz" in unserem Texte dienen (Lukas 9,52): "Und er sandte Boten vor seinem Angesicht". Wie wir gesehen haben, sind diese Worte aus Gen 32,4 übernommen, und dort, wie auch in dem neuen Kontext in Lukas, hat das Wort "Angesicht" nicht dieselbe prägnante Bedeutung von Ausrichtung wie in den zwei anderen Fällen bei Lukas. Hier will der Text einfach sagen, er habe Boten "vor sich her" gesandt—und so, ohne das Wort "Antlitz" zu wahren, übersetzt er auch das griechische Alte Testament im Gen 32,4. Doch nicht so der neutestamentliche Übersetzer: dieser wollte auch hier, wie in den beiden anderen Fällen, das Wort "Antlitz" auch in griechisch nicht missen. Er war also von dem dreifachen "Antlitz" in seinem hebräischen Text beeindruckt und hat vermutet, daß das so oft wiederholte Wort irgendwie gewichtig sei. Er hielt also den ganzen Abschnitt wegen seines vermutlichen religiösen Gehalts für so bedeutend, daß er die Sätze streng wörtlich aus dem hebräischen ins griechische übersetzt hat. Das ist für uns ein Glücksfall: so konnten wir lernen, daß in diesem Fall das Original im biblischen hebräisch verfasst wurde. Wir haben auch gesehen, daß der griechische Übersetzer aus Versehen das hebräische Wort עליה anstatt "Pilgerfahrt" mit "Himmelfahrt" übersetzt hat. Wurde er zu diesem Fehler verleitet, weil er hinter dem dreifachen "Antlitz" eine christologische Lehre vermutet hat, zu der die Himmelfahrt Christi besser paßt? Wenn wir Recht haben, dann stimmt auch für unseren Text, was wir einmal früher[12] behauptet haben: "Die Tradenten und die Evangelisten wachen gewöhnlich nur für einen Augenblick auf, und fast immer ist es der falsche Augenblick".

[12]David Flusser, *Die konsequente Philologie und die Worte Jesu, Almanach* (Hamburg: Friedrich Wittig, 1963) 26.

Welcher Art war die Christologie, die nach der Vermutung des griechischen Übersetzers hinter unserem Abschnitt stecken sollte? Wir können darüber mehr wissen, wenn wir die griechische Übersetzung des dritten "Antlitzes", in Lukas 9,53, näher betrachten. Ursprünglich, in hebräisch hieß es: "weil sein Antlitz nach Jerusalem (gerichtet war)". Doch unser Übersetzer sagt: "weil sein Antlitz war gehend nach Jerusalem". Diese Wendung schien schon in alter Zeit schwer verständlich zu sein, und darum wurde in einigen lateinischen Handschriften, denen dann die Vulgata folgt, verbessert. Dort liest man: "weil sein Antlitz eines nach Jerusalem gehenden war"—und so lesen wir auch schon in einem griechischen Papyrus (p⁴⁵) aus dem dritten Jahrhundert.

Wie kam aber der griechische Übersetzer zu der Vorstellung, daß damals das Antlitz Jesu nach Jerusalem "gehend war"? Schon mit Grotius gibt es manche Interpreten, welche meinen, daß diese seltsame Wendung ein Hebraismus ist, und zwar auf Grund von 2 Sam 17,11. Dort sagt Husai zu Absalom: "Dein Antlitz muß mit ins Treffen gehen". Das ist höchst wahrscheinlich eine Floskel der Hofsprache, die nur hier erhalten ist—sie ist auch sonst nicht im alten Orient belegt. Anders ausgedrückt sagte Husai zu Absalom: "Deine Herrlichkeit muß mit ins Treffen gehen". Aus der hebräischen Sicht ist es also völlig unmöglich anzunehmen, daß die einmal vorkommende hebräische Höflichkeitsformel entweder das hebräische Original von Lukas 9,53, oder den griechischen Übersetzer des Verses beeinflußt hat.

Es gibt aber einen anderen alttestamentlichen Abschnitt, den man bei der Untersuchung von Lukas 9,53 vergessen hat, nämlich Exod 33,14-15. Dort, nach der Sünde des goldenen Kalbes, sagt Gott zu Moses: "Mein Antlitz wird (mit)gehen und ich will dich zur Ruhe bringen". Und Moses antwortet Gott: "Wenn nicht dein Antlitz (mit-) geht, so laß uns nicht von hier hinaufziehen". Der Ausdruck "Antlitz" Gottes bedeutet hier seine Herrlichkeit (hebräisch כבד; siehe Vers 18: δόξα). "Antlitz" bedeutet die Hypostase der Gottheit nicht nur in der hebräischen Bibel, sondern auch schon bei den Kanaanäern.[13] So heißt zum Beispiel die Göttin Tanit "das Antlitz des Baal" bei den Puniern. Die Göttin mit diesem Namen wurde in Palästina noch im

---

[13]Siehe David Flusser, "Paganism in Palestine," *The Jewish People in the First Century: Historical Geography, Political History, Social, Cultural and Religious Life and Institutions*, 2 vols. (Compendia Rerum Iudaicarum ad Novum Testamentum; Assen: Van Gorcum, 1976), 2:1075-76.

Zeitalter Jesu und später verehrt. Die schon erwähnte Höflichkeitsformel in 2 Sam 17,11 zeigt, daß man die hypostatische Bezeichnung von
der Gottheit in der Hofsprache auch auf einen Herrscher übertragen
konnte. Kurz gesagt: wenn der griechische Text von Lukas 9,53 sagt,
daß Jesu Antlitz "nach Jerusalem gehend war", so ist diese Wendung
nicht zufällig mit der Aussage in Exod 33,14-15 verwandt, wo davon
gesprochen wird, daß das Antlitz Gottes (mit)gehend wird. Anscheinend hat also das dreimalige Vorkommen des Ausdruckes "Antlitz"in
der hebräischen Vorlage von Lukas bei dem Übersetzer die Erinnerung
auf eine hypostatische Auffassung von dem Antlitz Christi hervorger-
ufen, die er schon früher gekannt hat, nach der das Antlitz Christi eng
mit der Idee von Gottes Doxa verbunden war. Darum hat er gesagt,
daß das Antlitz Jesu damals nach Jerusalem "gehend war".

Gibt es aber im Neuen Testament Spuren von solch einer urchristlichen Auffassung? Man findet sie im zweiten Korintherbrief des Paulus, wo sie vorausgesetzt ist. In unserem Abschnitt in Lukas wird
dreimal von dem Antlitz Jesu gesprochen, und im zweiten Korintherbrief kommt das Antlitz Christi zweimal vor (2 Kor 2,10; 4,6). Die
ganze zweite Stelle (2 Kor 4,3-6) ist von einer besonderen Wichtigkeit.
Paulus sagt:

> Wohl ist unser Evangelium verhüllt, aber verhüllt für die, die verloren sind,
> in denen der Gott dieser Welt den Sinn der Ungläubigen geblendet hat, damit
> nicht erstrahle[14] das Leuchten des Evangeliums der Herrlichkeit des Chris-
> tus, der da ist das Ebenbild Gottes. Denn nicht nur uns selbst verkünden wir,
> sondern Christus Jesus als Herrn, uns aber als eure Knechte um Jesus willen.
> Denn der Gott, der da sprach: Aus der Finsternis soll leuchten das Licht, ist
> es, der es in unseren Herzen hat leuchten lassen zum Erleuchten der Erkennt-
> nis der Herrlichkeit Gottes im Antlitz Christi.

Die Stelle ist schwer, hauptsächlich, weil da sicher Paulus vorpauli-
nisches Gedankengut bearbeitet; und es ist kaum möglich festzustellen,
was er aus sich hinzugefügt hat, und wo er dem überlieferten Material
neuen Sinn gegeben hat. Wenn er von "dem Erleuchten der Erkenntnis
der Herrlichkeit Gottes im Antlitz Christi" gesprochen hat, dachte er
sicher auch an das Antlitz Mosis, aus dem die Herrlichkeit Gottes
geleuchtet hat (Exod 34,29-35), da Paulus ja selbst gleich vorher (2 Kor
3,7-18) über die Sache gesprochen hat. Doch dadurch wird der Sinn
der Stelle noch nicht ganz erklärt. Die eben angeführten Worte sind

---

[14]Oder: damit sie nicht sehen.

nämlich zu 2 Kor 4,4 parallel: ". . . damit nicht bestrahle das Leuchten des Evangeliums der Herrlichkeit des Christus, der da ist das Ebenbild Gottes". Die Wendung "das Leuchten des Evangeliums der Herrlichkeit des Christus" entspricht dem "Erleuchten der Erkenntnis der Herrlichkeit Gottes". Die Erkenntnis und das Evangelium sind also eigentlich gleichbedeutend und der Zusammenhang zwischen dem Erleuchten und der Erkenntnis ist nicht nur vorpaulinisch, sondern sogar aus dem Judentum übernommen. Man leitet es aus dem Wortlaut des Priestersegens (Num 6,24-26) ab: "Leuchte Er sein Antlitz dir zu und begnade dich" (V 25). Diese Worte werden im essenischen *Sektenkanon* (2,3) so paraphrasiert: "Er erleuchte dein Herz mit dem Verstande des Lebens und begnade dich mit der ewigen Erkenntnis". Auch in dem rabbinischen Midrasch *Sifre* wird dieser Vers des Priestersegens mit dem Licht der Weisung und mit der Erkenntnis und dem Wissen verbunden.[15]

Paulus spricht in 2 Kor 4,6 vom Erleuchten des Herzens,[16] welches zur Erkenntnis der Herrlichkeit Gottes führt; auch der essenische Text spricht von dem Erleuchten des Herzens und von der Erkenntnis. Der essenische Text beruht auf dem biblischen Priestersegen, in dem von dem Leuchten des Antlitzes Gottes gesprochen wird. Das Antlitz Gottes hat bei Paulus einerseits eine Parallele in der Herrlichkeit Gottes, aber andererseits spricht ja Paulus auch ausdrücklich von dem Antlitz Christi. Wir haben gesehen, daß im zweiten Korintherbrief 2 Kor 4,4 dem 2 Kor 4,6 entspricht. Von Christus sagt Paulus, er sei das Ebenbild Gottes. Hing einmal das Antlitz Christi im Vers 6 mit dem "Ebenbild Gottes" im Vers 4 irgendwie zusammen? Wir können hier den möglichen Zusammenhang nur andeuten.[17] In Col 1,15 wird gesagt, Christus sei das Ebenbild des unsichtbaren Gottes. Wichtiger

---

[15]H. S. Horovitz, ed., Sifre Num., 44 unten. Siehe auch Ps 119,29 und die vierte Benediktion in dem Achtzehngebet Siehe auch Moshe Weinfeld, Tarbiz (1975-1976), 45:21 Anm. 40 (hebräisch).

[16]Vgl. Eph 1,17-18: "auf daß Gott . . . euch gebe einen Geist der Weisheit und Offenbarung durch seine Erkenntnis, erleuchtet die Augen eueres Herzens".

[17]Rudolf Bultmann, *Theologie des Neuen Testaments*, 3rd ed. (Neue Theologische Grundrisse; Tübingen: J. C. B. Mohr, 1958) 134-35. Siehe auch Jakob Jervell, *Imago Dei: Gen 1,26f. im Spätjudentum, in der Gnosis und in den paulinischen Briefen* (FRLANT 76; Göttingen: Vandenhoeck & Ruprecht, 1960) 45, 168 (über das "Antlitz").

für unsere Betrachtung ist, daß nach Heb 1,3 Christus der "Abglanz Seiner Herrlichkeit und Abdruck Seines Wesens" ist. Das griechische Wort "Abglanz" ist aus demselben Stamm gebildet, wie das "Erstrahlen" in 2 Kor 4,4 und die Herrlichkeit kommt ja in unserem Abschnitt im 2 Korintherbrief vor. In Bezug auf Heb 1,3 wird oft angeführt, daß die griechische Schrift *Weisheit Salomos* (7,26) von der Weisheit sagt, sie sei "ein Abglanz des ewigen Lichtes und unbefleckter Spiegel des Wirkens Gottes und ein Ebenbild Seiner Güte". Es scheint also, daß unsere Stellen mit der jüdischen hypostatischen Spekulation zusammenhängen. Aus Heb 1,3 und der Parallele in der *Weisheit Salomos* könnte man folgern, daß die Herrlichkeit Christi ein Abglanz der Herrlichkeit Gottes ist, aber es kann sein, daß man auch gemeint hat, die Herrlichkeit Christi sei einfach die Herrlichkeit Gottes. Wir haben gesehen, daß im 2 Korintherbrief einerseits von dem "Evangelium der Herrlichkeit des Christus, der da ist das Ebenbild Gottes" gesprochen wird, und andererseits von dem "Erleuchten der Erkenntnis der Herrlichkeit Gottes im Antlitz Christi". Vielleicht darf man auch annehmen, daß nach den Spekulationen, die unserer Stelle zugrunde liegen, das "Antlitz Christi" ein Ausdruck für die Herrlichkeit des Christus war. Wir konnten ja feststellen, daß der Ausdruck "Antlitz" schon im Alten Testament—und sogar noch früher—mit der Hypostase der Gottheit identisch war. Und wenn wir jetzt zu unserem Ausgangspunkt, Lukas 9,51-55, zurückkehren, haben wir eigentlich den Beweis für unsere Vermutung geliefert. Die dreimalige Erwähnung des Antlitzes in Bezug auf Jesus in seiner hebräischen Vorlage war für den griechischen Übersetzer wichtig, und was er darunter verstanden hat, verrät er, wenn er sagt, das Antlitz Christi "war gehend" nach Jerusalem. Er spielt da auf Exod 33,14-15 an, wo von dem Gehen des Antlitzes Gottes gesprochen wurde.

Das Schönste, was ich über das Antlitz Christi gefunden habe, sind die Worte Bengels[18]: "Qui Filium videt, Patrem videt, *in facie* Christi. Filius Patrem exacte repraesentat ac refert. [Die gloria Filii ist eben darin groß, daß die Gloria Patris an ihm und durch ihn erscheint] ... *in facie Jesu Christi*, qui est Patris unigenitus et imago, et *manifestatus*

---

[18]Johann Albrecht Bengel, *Gnomon Novi Testamenti in quo ex nativa verborum vi simplicitas, profunditas, concinnitas, salubritas sensuum coelestium indicatur* (Stuttgart: J. F. Steinkopf, 1891) 698-99.

est in carne cum gloria sua ". Dies sagte Bengel in Bezug auf den zweiten Korintherbrief. In diesem Sinn wird das Wort "Antlitz" schon bei den griechischen Kirchenvätern benutzt.[19] Schon Klemens von Alexandrin (*Paed*. 1.7 [*PG* 8.320]) sagt, das Antlitz Gottes sei der Logos, durch das Gott beleuchtet und erkannt wird.[20] Und Origenes (Ps 20,7), auf Heb 1,3 Bezug nehmend, spricht vom "Antlitze Gottes, dem Abdruck Seines Wesens". Handelt es sich in der griechischen patristischen Literatur nur um eine hellsichtige Interpretation, oder um eine Überlieferung seit den urchristlichen Zeiten, die hinter den Worten des zweiten Korintherbriefs sichtbar wird? Wir nehmen an, daß der Ausdruck "Antlitz Christi" in der Bedeutung der Herrlichkeit Christi schon dem Übersetzer Lukas 9,51-56 bekannt war. Da Lukas selbst anscheinend nicht hebräisch verstanden hat, ist es klar, daß der hypostatische Ausdruck "Antlitz Christi" schon vor Lukas in den urchristlichen Gemeinden heimisch war.

Wenn wir dazu noch annehmen, daß der Übersetzer nicht nur das dreimal wiederholte Wort "Antlitz" in seiner Vorlage hypostatisch verstanden hat, sondern auch daß er es schon war, der das hebräische Wort für Pilgerfahrt als Himmelfahrt mißverstanden hat, dann hat er den theologisch-christologischen Gehalt seiner hebräischen Vorlage annähernd so verstanden: schon vor seiner Himmelfahrt, als Jesus seinen Weg nach Jerusalem begonnen hat, richtete er sein Antlitz nach Jerusalem und sein Antlitz, seine Herrlichkeit, ging ihm voran. Dürfen wir noch weiteres vermuten? Vielleicht kann uns das apokryphe *Petrusevangelium*, aus dem zweiten Jahrhundert, weiter helfen. Dort heiß es vom Tode Jesu: "Und der Herr schrie auf und rief: 'Meine

---

[19]Siehe G. W. H. Lampe, ed., *A Patristic Greek Lexicon* (Oxford: Clarendon, 1972) 1186. Photius (*Bibliothèque*, 3 vols., ed. René Henry [Collection byzantine; Paris: Les Belles Lettres, 1959-1962], 2:80) führt das folgende Zitat aus den verlorenen *Hypotyposeis* des Klemens von Alexandrien an: "Auch der Sohn wird Logos genannt, gleichnamig mit dem väterlichen Logos, aber dies ist nicht der, welcher Fleisch geworden ist, und auch nicht der väterliche Logos, sondern eine Kraft Gottes, eine Art Emanation seines Logos, die Geist (nus) geworden, die Herzen der Menschen durchdringt". Wenn diese Worte—wie auch das andere, was Photius in den *Hypotyposen* des Klemens von Alexandrien gelesen hat—nicht eine häretische Verfälschung ist, dann kann man vielleicht das Zitat im Lichte der alten griechischen Patristik verstehen: der Sohn ist als Logos eine Kraft, die eine Emanation des göttlichen Logos ist.

[20]Siehe auch das Zitat in der vorigen Anmerkung.

Kraft, O Kraft,[21] du hast mich verlassen!' Und indem er dies sagte, wurde er aufgenommen" (5,19). Das griechische ἀνελήμφθη 'er wurde aufgenommen' ist dasselbe Wort, wie das Hauptwort ἀναλήμψις 'Himmelfahrt' in Lukas 9,51. Nach dem *Petrusevangelium* verließ also Jesus seine Dynamis, seine Kraft, schon vor seinem Hinscheiden. Es wird der Bischof Serapion von Antiochien (um 200) Recht gehabt haben, wenn er einen Zusammenhang zwischen dem *Petrusevangelium* und dem Doketismus gesehen hat (Eusebius, *Hist. eccl.* 6.12.4-6). Allerdings, streng genommen, ist die Anschauung, daß der göttliche Teil, seine 'Herrlichkeit', Christus schon vor seinem Tode verlassen hat, nicht rein häretisch. Die Idee konnte gehegt worden sein, um die Möglichkeit auszuscheiden, das Göttliche in Christus sei mit ihm auf dem Kreuze gestorben. Schwebte eine ähnliche Auffassung unserem Übersetzer vor, als er den hebräischen Abschnitt gelesen hat? Vielleicht meinte er so: auf dem Wege zur Passion wandte Jesus sein Antlitz nach Jerusalem und als sich die Tage seiner Erhebung erfüllt hatten, ging ihm das Antlitz Christi vor. Die Göttlichkeit Christi, seine Herrlichkeit, begann sich im Hinblick auf den Kreuzestod von dem Menschen Jesus loszulösen. Die Vorstellungen des Übersetzers lassen sich nicht klar erkennen, weil er sich besonders streng an das hebräische Original gehalten hat; er meinte in ihm seine Ideen erkannt zu haben und wollte sie nicht in den Text hineinbringen. Eigentlich konnten wir auf die Spur seiner Christologie nur darum kommen, weil er ein einziges, erklärendes Wort hinzugefügt hat: im Vers 53 hat er gesagt, daß Jesus' Antlitz nach Jerusalem 'gehend war'. Aus seiner Sicht heraus konnte dann der Übersetzer das hebräische Wort für Pilgerfahrt als 'Himmelfahrt' fruchtbar mißverstehen.

Wenn wir mit unseren Vermutungen Recht haben, dann hat sich die Christologie des Übersetzers aus dem Zusammenwirken von zwei Ausgangspunkten gebildet. Bevor er an den hebräischen Text gegangen ist, hat der Übersetzer eine bestimmte Christologie gekannt und angenommen. Er hat den Ausdruck 'Antlitz Christi' hypostatisch als die Herrlichkeit Christi verstanden und hat eine ähnliche Vorstellung

---

[21]Der hebräische oder aramäische Ruf Jesu wird hier also nur auf Griechisch gebracht. Das ursprüngliche "Eli Eli" heißt hier "Meine Kraft, O Kraft"; es wird also das Wort gedeutet, als wäre im aramäischen Original הילי הילי (meine Kraft, meine Kraft) geschrieben. So wäre es auch auf Syrisch. Und man hat vermutet, das *Petrusevangelium* wäre im syrischen Raum verfasst (Mitteilung von Sh. Pines).

von dem Verlassen der Kraft Christi vor seinem Hinscheiden wie das *Petrusevangelium* gehabt. Der zweite Ausgangspunkt war seine hebräische Vorlage, mit der dreimaligen Erwähnung des Antlitzes Christi. Aus dem Wortlaut dieser Vorlage hat er gefolgert, die Herrlichkeit Christi habe sich von Jesus schon früher begonnen loszulösen. Der Übersetzer ließ sich also von seiner Vorlage belehren und dachte, er wäre auf der Spur eines wichtigen Geheimnisses, dessen Tiefe er natürlich nicht ganz erfassen vermochte—weil es in Wahrheit nicht existiert hat.[22]

Der Abschnitt in Lukas ist zwar ein Einzelfall, aber die Ergebnisse unserer Betrachtungen können zu breiteren Fragestellungen führen. Gewöhnlich nimmt man heute an, daß die synoptischen Evangelien im Ganzen und ihre Perikopen im einzelnen in ihrem Wortlaut umgeformt worden sind, um eine bestimmte theologische Botschaft auszudrücken. Doch unser Fall lehrt, daß *wenn* eine ausgeprägte Ideologie im Spiele ist, die Übersetzung sich gerade außergewöhnlich streng an das überlieferte Original halten kann, und zwar deshalb, weil man nicht die theologische Anschauung in den Text hereintragen will, sondern man meint, sie aus dem Text herauslesen zu können. Man darf sogar annehmen, daß der historische und geographische Rahmen der einzelnen Episoden in den synoptischen Evangelien darum so große Unterschiede in den verschiedenen Evangelien aufweist, weil im allgemeinen den Redaktoren und Evangelisten an einem genauen Wortlaut nicht viel gelegen ist. Das kann auch sonst in den Evangelien oft der Grund für die freie Bearbeitung gewesen sein, und nicht das Interesse der Schreiber, ihre persönliche religiöse Meinung in die Text einzuschmuggeln. Es ist ja auch sonst bei Schriftwerken allgemein üblich, daß man dort die Vorlage paraphrasiert, wo sie einem nicht sehr wichtig erscheint, und daß man dagegen mehr auf den Wortlauf der Vorlage aufpasst, wo sie etwas für den Bearbeiter Bedeutendes aussagt. Und die Redaktoren und die Verfasser der synoptischen Evangelien waren nicht theologische Pamphletisten, sondern fromme Christen, "und darum durften sie nicht an dem anvertrauten Gut ungerecht handeln, denn sie mussten den Zorn des Himmels fürchten".[23]

---

[22]Es ist nicht unsere Aufgabe, Erwägungen anzustellen, wie weit der "Fund" des Übersetzers unseres Abschnittes die Natur des ganzen lukanischen Reiseberichtes beeinflußt hat.

[23]Siehe Flusser, *Philologie*, 249.

Doch wer auch nicht bereit sein wird, diesen allgemeinen Betrachtungen zu folgen, um sie dann durch eigene Arbeit zu überprüfen, wird
jedenfalls gewahr werden, daß während gewöhnlich der historische
und geographische Rahmen stark bearbeitet vorliegt, der Rahmen der
Erzählung von der Weigerung der Samariter in Lukas 9,51-53 so streng
wörtlich aus dem hebräischen übersetzt wurde, daß man den hebräischen Wortlaut genau rekonstruieren kann. Das geschah darum, weil
der griechische Übersetzer irrtümlicherweise gemeint hat, die Worte
beinhalten eine wichtige Information, die er seinen Lesern nicht voren-
thalten wollte. Deshalb konnten wir lernen, daß die Einleitung zu der
Geschichte des Samariterdorfes ursprünglich im biblischen Hebräisch
geschrieben war. Vielleicht gilt dasselbe auch für die ursprüglich
hebräische Form wenigstens von einigen der übrigen Rahmen.[24]

Noch zwei weitere Lehren können wir aus unserer Untersuchung
gewinnen. Die erste haben wir schon behandelt: wenigstens in unserem
Fall hat der Übersetzer seinen Text nicht nach seinen Anschauungen
wesentlich umgestaltet, sondern er wollte seine Auffassung aus dem
Text herauslesen (und darum hat er wörtlich übersetzt). Die zweite
Lehre betrifft die Geistesgeschichte des Urchristentums. Es ist eigentlich sicher, daß der griechische Übersetzer des Abschnittes das 'Antlitz
Christi' hypostatisch verstanden hat, als das Göttliche in Jesus, als
seine Herrlichkeit. Vielleicht hat er gemeint, die göttliche Kraft habe
Jesus vor seinem Tode verlassen, und lernte irrtümlicherweise—wegen
dem dreimaligen Antlitz aus seiner hebräischen Vorlage—daß schon
mit dem Anfang seiner letzten Reise, im Hinblick auf die bevorste-
hende Passion, als sich die Tage seiner Himmelfahrt vollendet haben,
sich die Herrlichkeit Christi von dem Menschen Jesus loszulösen
begonnen hat. Die theologischen Prämissen, von denen der griechische
Übersetzer ausgeht, verraten eine reflektierte, entwickelte und fort-
geschrittene Christologie des Übersetzers. Solche Christologie war
also schon vor Lukas vorhanden, denn der Übersetzer war nicht Lukas
selbst, der nicht hebräisch verstanden hat. Das wäre an sich nicht so

---

[24]Vielleicht müßte man die Frage nach dem Wesen der Rahmen neu fragen. Wenn
es stimmt, daß gerade die Rahmen, als für den Gehalt nicht wesentlich wichtig, von den
griechischen Bearbeitern frei behandelt worden sind, dann ist ihre Verschiedenheit in
den einzelnen synoptischen Evangelien nicht ein Beweis für ihre späte Entstehung, und
also könnten die Rahmen in ursprünglicher Form ein wesentlicher Bestandteil der
alten Berichte gewesen sein.

überraschend, da schon Paulus eine entwickelte Christologie vertritt. Sonderbar ist es, daß der Verfasser ein hebräisch sprechender Jude gewesen ist, der griechisch schreiben konnte. Welchen Ursprungs war also der Übersetzer und was war sein 'Sitz im Leben? War er ein palästinensischer Jude, oder ein hellenistischer Jude, der hebräisch beherrscht hat? Ist seine Christologie palästinensisch oder hellenistisch? Und darf man immer zwischen der 'palästinensischen' und 'hellenistischen' Christologie so streng unterscheiden?

DIE EINHEIT DER KIRCHE
NACH DEM NEUEN TESTAMENT

Gerhard Friedrich

"IN DER MODERNEN Christenheit besteht dieselbe Spannung wie hier zwischen Judenchristen und Heidenchristen. . . . Die Einheit der Kirche besteht nicht darin, daß alle Unterschiede zwischen geschichtlich bedingten Richtungen um jeden Preis ausgeglichen werden müssen. . . . Diese vollkommene Einheit liegt aber hauptsächlich in der Zukunft".[1] Diese Thesen von Professor Bo Reicke sollen im folgenden näher erläutert werden.

1

Die Einheit der Kirche beruht nach den Zeugnissen des Neuen Testaments nicht auf menschlichen Aktivitäten. Sie besteht nicht in dem Zusammenschluß einzelner Menschen, die sich durch denselben Glauben miteinander verbunden fühlen, sondern sie ist durch den Heilsplan Gottes und das Wirken Jesu allem menschlichen Tun vorgegeben. Der eine Gott (1 Kor 8,6), der über alle herrscht (Eph 4,6), will die eine Kirche.

Im Epheserbrief, dem zentralen Schreiben über die eine Kirche aus Juden und Heiden, wird in der großen Eingangseulogie der Blick auf die Erwählung der Christen durch Gott und auf die Vorherbestimmung zur Sohnschaft durch Christus gerichtet (Eph 1,4-5). Die Erwählung der Christen, ganz gleich, ob sie vorher Juden oder Heiden waren, geschah schon vor Grundlegung der Welt in Christus. In dem präexistenten Christus ist das Christsein der Christen bereits enthalten. Die Kirche ist nicht dadurch entstanden, daß einige Menschen sich nach dem Tode Jesu zusammenschlossen und den Verein Kirche gründeten. Sie ist nicht das Produkt einer geschichtlichen Entwicklung, sie ist vielmehr vorzeitlich in dem Liebeswillen Gottes begründet. Darum

---

[1]Bo Reicke, "Freiheit und Einheit nach dem Neuen Testament", *LR* 5 (1955/1956) 9-10.

muß die Einheit der Kirche nicht erst geschaffen werden, sondern sie ist von vornherein gegeben und sichergestellt. Was in Gottes Heilsplan von Ewigkeit her vorhanden und vor allen Äonen in Gott verborgen war (Eph 3,9), daß Heiden Miterben, Miteinverleibte und Mitteilhabende der Verheißungen sind (3,6), daß die Kirche als Leib Christi Juden und Heiden als Einheit umfaßt, das hat Gott nach seinem Ratschluß kundgetan und in Christus verwirklicht (Eph 1,9-11; 3,1-12). Durch den Kreuzestod hat Christus Juden und Heiden in einem einzigen Leib versöhnt (Eph 2,16). So realisiert das Kreuz die vorgegebene Einheit auf Erden. Darum ist die Einheit der Kirche vom Kreuzesgeschehen nicht ablösbar. Die Tat Jesu bestand nicht darin, daß er zwei disparate Teile lose miteinander verbunden hat, sondern er hat, wie es Eph 2,15 heißt, die zwei in ihm zu einem einzigen neuen Menschen geschaffen. Die Einheit braucht darum nicht durch irgendwelche Aktionen herbeigeführt zu werden, sondern sie ist im Heilswillen Gottes gegründet und durch das Heilswirken Jesu realisiert. Dementsprechend wird Eph 4,3 die Gemeinde auch nicht aufgefordert, die Einheit erst noch zu schaffen, sondern sie soll die durch das Pneuma gegebene Einheit bewahren. Sie soll ihren ganzen Eifer darauf richten, das ihr zuteil gewordene Geschenk nicht zu verlieren, sondern es zu behüten und zu bewachen.

Ganz ähnlich denkt das Johannesevangelium. Auch bei Johannes, dem das Einssein im hohenpriesterlichen Gebet so stark am Herzen liegt, entsteht die Einheit nicht durch menschliche Initiative, nicht durch theologische Diskussionen, synodale Beschlüsse und organisatorische Maßnahmen, sondern sie ist eine Wirklichkeit, die vor allen menschlichen Aktivitäten da ist; denn Christus hat sie durch sein Heilswirken geschaffen. Er ist der gute Hirt, der die Schafe auf zwei ganz verschiedenen Ställen zusammenführt, so daß die trennenden Unterschiede hinfallen und eine Herde unter einem Hirten entsteht (Joh 10,16). Juden und Heiden sind unter dem einen Hirten Jesus Christus zusammengeschlossen. Diese Einheit ist nicht eine soziologische Größe; sie besteht nicht in einer breiten Gesinnungsgemeinschaft aller Beteiligten. Überhaupt ist sie mit irgendwelchen Formen sonstiger menschlicher Zusammenschlüsse nicht zu vergleichen, sondern sie ist eine Gemeinschaft eigener Art; denn sie kommt aus einer Gemeinschaft, die außerhalb der Welt liegt, aber nicht transzendent bleibt, sondern durch die apostolische Tradition der Verkündigung vermittelt wird. Der Verfasser des 1. Johannesbriefes schreibt: "Was wir gesehen und gehört haben, das tun wir euch kund, damit ihr Gemeinschaft mit uns habt, und unsere ist zugleich die mit dem Vater und mit seinem Sohne Jesus Christus" (1 Joh 1,3). Die Gemeinschaft der Christen untereinander gründet in der Gemeinschaft der Jünger mit dem Vater und dem Sohn. Im Johannesevangelium ist die göttliche Einheit Urbild und Vorbild der kirchlichen Einheit: "Sie sollen eins sein, wie du, Vater, in mir bist und ich in dir" (Joh 17,21). Das "Wie" hat vergleichende wie begründende Bedeutung.[2] Wie Gott in Jesus Christus und Jesus in Gott ist, so daß Jesus keine Sonderinteressen verfolgt, sondern mit Gott ganz eins ist, so sollen Christen nicht ihren individualistischen religiösen Besonderheiten anhängen, sondern alle egoistischen Bestrebungen ablegen und für den andern da sein. Weil die Einheit der Christen das Abbild des göttlichen Urbildes ist, hat sie ihren Grund nicht im menschlichen Willen, sondern in Gott selbst. Die kirchliche Einheit gleicht also nicht nur der göttlichen, sondern sie beruht auf ihr. Das Einssein der Christen ist gleichbedeutend mit dem In-uns-Sein der Christen in der göttlichen Einheit: "Wie du, Vater, in mir bist und ich in dir, so sollen auch sie in uns sein" (Joh 17,21). Die Einheit der Kirche besteht darin, daß die Jünger in die Einheit von Vater und Sohn hineingenommen sind. Darum wird im Johannesevangelium genau so wie im Epheserbrief die Gemeinde gar nicht aufgerufen, die Einheit zu realisieren. Sie wird auch nicht ermahnt, sie zu erhalten, sondern die Einheit wird von der bewahrenden Liebe Gottes erbeten: "Heiliger Vater, bewahre sie in deinem Namen, die du mir gegeben hast, damit sie eins seien wie wir" (Joh 17,11). Wie im Epheserbrief so ist auch im Johannesevangelium die Einheit nicht nur eine überweltliche und überzeitliche, sondern sie ist real auf Erden durch den Tod Jesu gewirkt. Nach Joh 11,49-52 prophezeit Kaiphas als amtierender Hoherpriester, Jesus sterbe, damit er die in der Welt verstreuten Kinder Gottes zur Einheit zusammenführe. Der Tod Jesu hat das Ziel der Einheit der Gemeinde. Das kommt auch Joh 10,16-17 zum Ausdruck, wenn Jesus nach den Worten von der einen Herde und dem einen Hirten sagt: "Deshalb liebt mich der Vater, weil ich mein

---

[2]Walter Bauer, *Griechisch-deutsches Wörterbuch zu den Schriften des Neuen Testaments und der übrigen urchristlichen Literatur*, 5th ed. (Berlin: Alfred Töpelmann, 1958) 773; Friedrich Blass, Albert Debrunner, and Friedrich Rehkopf, *Grammatik des neutestamentlichen Griechisch*, 14th ed. (Göttingen: Vandenhoeck & Ruprecht, 1976) §453,1-2.

Leben einsetze, um es wieder zu empfangen". Durch den Kreuzestod Jesu schafft Jesus die Einheit der Kirche auf Erden. Er ist die Voraussetzung und der Mittelpunkt der Gemeinschaft der Christen untereinander.

Paulus äußert sich über das überzeitliche Sein der kirchlichen Einheit nicht so ausführlich, wie es die Verfasser des Epheserbriefes und des Johannesevangeliums tun. Aber er setzt sie voraus, wenn er von der Kirche als dem Leib Christi spricht. Diese entsteht nicht durch den Zusammenschluß von Individuen zu einer Gemeinschaft, sondern das σῶμα Χριστοῦ ist schon da, und die Menschen werden in der Taufe in den Leib Christi versetzt (vgl. Röm 6,3; Gal 3,27).

2

Die von Gott gewollte, durch Christi Heilstat geschaffene Einheit ist von Anbeginn an gefährdet.[3] Das zeigt das Neue Testament auf Schritt und Tritt. So selbstverständlich die Einheit der Kirche ihrem Wesen gehört (Eph 4,4-6), so natürlich ist es, daß ihre Einheit nicht unangefochten bleiben kann, so lange die Glieder der Kirche zwar nicht von der Welt (Joh 17,14.16), aber doch in der Welt (Joh 17,11) und damit nicht frei von Gefährdungen (Joh 17,15) sind. Die Geschichte der Urchristenheit ist eine einzige Geschichte von Differenzen und Auseinandersetzungen zwischen einzelnen führenden Männern und ganzen Gruppen in den Gemeinden. Bereits zu Lebzeiten Jesu streiten sich die Jünger, wer der Größte von ihnen sei (Markus 9,34), und wer bei der göttlichen Machtergreifung zur Rechten und zur Linken des Herrschers sitzen darf (Markus 10,37). Die Streitigkeiten werden nach der Auferweckung Jesu nicht geringer. Wohin man auch blickt, von der von Gott gegebenen Einheit ist in den urchristlichen Gemeinden wenig zu sehen, obwohl man sich darum bemüht. Der Schreiber des Matthäusevangeliums sucht die Kluft zwischen den strengen, rabbinisch orthodoxen Judenchristen und den pneumatisch-universalistisch denkenden Judenchristen zu überbrücken. Dieser Versuch zeigt deutlich, daß in der Gemeinde, für die er schreibt,

---

[3]Heinrich Schlier, "Die Einheit der Kirche nach dem Neuen Testament", *Besinnung auf das Neue Testament: Exegetische Aufsätze und Vorträge II* (Freiburg: Herder, 1964) 176.

gegensätzliche Theologien vorliegen. Wenn das Johannesevangelium
so stark den Gedanken der einen Herde und des einen Hirten herausstellt, so hat dies ganz sicher innergemeindliche Gründe. Die Apostelgeschichte schildert zunächst das vorbildliche Zusammenleben der
urchristlichen Gemeinde, daß sie beständig in der Lehre der Apostel, in
der Gemeinschaft, im Brotbrechen und im Gebet bleiben (Apg 2,42).
Aber wie der Fortgang zeigt, entspricht diese Schilderung mehr einem
Idealbild als der Wirklichkeit. Bei dem Zusammenstoß der Hellenisten
mit den Hebräern (Apg 6,1-6) geht es nicht nur um Differenzen bei der
sozialen Betreuung der Gemeindeglieder, sondern um grundsätzlich
verschiedene theologische Anschauungen über die Einstellung zum
Kult und damit auch zur Heidenmission. Dieses wird bei dem Gespräch auf dem Apostelkonvent offensichtlich (Apg 15,1-29). In Rom
sind Streitigkeiten zwischen Heiden und Judenchristen und zwischen
Starken und Schwachen. In Korinth habe sich sogar drei bis vier
verschiedene Cliquen gebildet. Der Galaterbrief berichtet von dem
antiochenischen Zwischenfall mit der Auseinandersetzung zwischen
Petrus und Paulus (Gal 2,11-14). In unmißverständlicher Schärfe
wendet sich Paulus im Galaterbrief gegen die Judaisten, die ein anderes
Evangelium predigen. Diese meinten die Einheit des Gottesvolkes
dadurch wahren zu können, daß sie Heidenchristen zur Annahme des
Gesetzes aufriefen und sie so zu Gliedern des alten Gottesvolkes
machen wollten.[4] Der Verfasser des Epheserbriefes sieht sich durch die
Situation in den Gemeinden veranlaßt, so nachdrücklich auf die Einheit zwischen Juden- und Heidenchristen hinzuweisen. Das dritte
Kapitel des Philipperbriefes enthält ein Kampfschreiben des Apostels
Paulus gegen Irrlehrer in der Gemeinde, die ähnlicher Art sind wie die,
gegen die er sich im 2. Korintherbrief wendet.[5] In Thessalonich hat eine
falsche Einstellung zur Eschatologie Folgen für das Zusammenleben.
Erst recht kommen die Gefahren der Spaltung in den Pastoralbriefen
zur Sprache. Glieder der Gemeinde weichen von dem eigentlichen Ziel
der Verkündigung ab. Sie halten sich nicht an die gesunden Worte des
Herrn Jesus Christus und meinen, mit der Frömmigkeit Geschäfte
machen zu können (1 Tim 1,6-7; 6,3-5). Nach dem 2. Petrusbrief haben

[4]Lyder Brun, "Der kirchliche Einheitsgedanke im Urchristentum", *ZST* 14 (1937)
103.

[5]Gerhard Friedrich, *Der Brief an die Philipper* (NTD 8; Göttingen: Vandenhoeck
& Ruprecht, 1976) 131-35.

sich falsche Propheten und Lehrer in die Gemeinden eingeschlichen (2 Pet 2,1-3). Ebenso werden die Leser des Johannesbriefes vor falschen Propheten gewarnt (1 Joh 4,1). Die Sendschreiben der Apokalypse zeigen, von welchen Gefahren die Einheit der kleinasiatischen Gemeinden bedroht ist.

Die Anfechtung der Einheit ist nicht eine vorübergehende Zeiterscheinung. Das Neue Testament kennt die Gefahren und weiß von den immer stärker werdenden Bedrohungen (Markus 13,22; Apg 20,29-30; 1 Tim 4,1; 2 Tim 3,1-3; 2 Pet 2,1; 3,3; Jud 18). Wenn man sich dieses vor Augen hält, fragt man sich, ob man bei so viel Zwietracht und Auseinandersetzung überhaupt von der Einheit der Kirche im Neuen Testament sprechen kann. Da die zentrifugalen Kräfte sehr stark sind, wird immer wieder die Mahnung erhoben, eines Sinnes zu sein (Röm 12,16; 15,5; 2 Kor 13,11; Phil 1,27; 2,2-3; 4,2). Was ist das einigende Band, das alle in der Gemeinde Jesu Christi zusammenschließt?

3

Der Grund für die trotz der Gefährdungen unauflösbare Einheit der Kirche auf Erden ist die Person Jesu Christi, die Taufe auf den Namen Jesu Christi, die Gemeinschaft bei der Feier des Herrenmahles und das Dasein der Kirche als Leib Christi.

3.1 DIE PERSON JESU CHRISTI ALS GRUND DER EINHEIT

Für die Bedeutung Christi im Blick auf die Einheit der Gemeinde sind die Ausführungen des Apostels Paulus im 1. Korintherbrief die wichtigsten. In der Gemeinde herrscht Streit (1 Kor 3,3). Es haben sich Parteien gebildet, die die Einheit zu sprengen drohen. Aber die Gemeinde ist noch nicht so zerstritten, daß es bereits zu Trennungen gekommen ist. Wie begegnet Paulus den die Gemeinde zersetzenden Tendenzen? Ehe er auf die Differenzen zu sprechen kommt, weist er gleich zu Beginn des Briefes auf die Bedeutung Christi hin. Alle Glieder der Gemeinde sind dadurch miteinander verbunden, daß sie den Namen des Herrn Jesus Christus anrufen (1,2). Während Paulus in den andern Briefeingängen bei der Danksagung von dem Verhalten der Gemeinde spricht,[6] stellt er im 1. Korintherbrief in unüberhörbarer

---

[6]Vom Glauben der Christen (Röm 1,8); von ihrer Teilhabe am Evangelium (Phil 1,5), an der Liebe und dem Glauben (Phlm 5); vom tätigen Glauben, von der mühenden Liebe und der anhaltenden Hoffnung (1 Thess 1,3).

Weise die Bedeutung Christi heraus. Alles, was die Korinther sind, was sie haben und erwarten, kommt von Christus (1,4-9). Jeder Satz des einleitenden Abschnittes endet mit der Wendung "unser Herr Jesus Christus" (1,7.8.9). Dieser immer wiederkehrende christozentrische Akkord am Anfang des Briefes soll den Korinthern in das Herz dringen, damit sie nicht vergessen, worauf es beim Christsein der Christen ankommt.[7] Das ganze Leben der Gemeinde, ihr Denken und Handeln, ihr Lehren und Beten wurzelt in Jesus Christus, der sie vom verderbenden Gericht errettet hat (1,18), der ihnen zur Weisheit, Gerechtigkeit, Heiligung und Erlösung gemacht ist (1,30). Er ist das Fundament der Kirche, das Gott selbst gelegt hat. Ein anderes Fundament gibt es nicht. Aus der Gabe Christi und der Stellung zu ihm ist die Eintracht der Gemeinde erwachsen. Nicht eine starre Lehre, sondern das von ihm ausgehende Wort und der auf ihn gerichtete Glaube verbindet die Christen untereinander.[8] Weil Paulus die Bedrohung der Einheit vor Augen hat und er die Einheit der Gemeinde in Jesus Christus sieht, schließt er den 1. Korintherbrief mit dem Hinweis auf Jesus Christus, wie er ihn begonnen hatte. Nur der 1. Korintherbrief endet, was sonst in keinem paulinischen Schreiben der Fall ist, mit den Worten: "In Christus Jesus" (16,24). Er ist Grund und Ziel der Einheit der Kirche. Das soll jede Gemeinde bedenken, die eine Gemeinde Jesu Christi sein will, wenn sich Spannungen und Spaltungen bemerkbar machen.

Ähnlich wie im Korintherbrief argumentiert Paulus auch im Römerbrief. Auch in Rom ist die Einheit der Gemeinde ernstlich gefährdet, weil die Schwachen und die Starken sich nicht mehr in der Lage sehen, sich an einen Tisch zu setzen und gemeinsame Mahlzeiten abzuhalten. Die einen sehen gewisse Speisen als kultisch unrein an und enthalten sich ihrer. Andere haben keine Bedenken, alles zu essen (14,14-15.20). Paulus regelt die Angelegenheit nicht gesetzlich, indem er Normen für eine Disziplinarordnung erläßt, sondern er mahnt durch den Hinweis auf den Kyrios zur Eintracht und Einheit. Beide Gruppen, jede in ihrer Weise, sind mit Christus verbunden (14,4-6). Keiner hat das Recht, sich in das Verhältnis des andern zu seinem

---

[7]Gerhard Friedrich, "Christus, Einheit und Norm der Christen: Das Grundmotiv des 1. Korintherbriefs", *KD* 9 (1963) 235-58, bes. 238-42.

[8]Vgl. Adolf Schlatter, *Die Briefe an die Thessalonicher, Philipper, Timotheus und Titus* (Erläuterungen zum Neuen Testament 8; Stuttgart: Calwer, 1950) 108-10 (zu 1 Tim 1,3).

Herrn einzumischen. Beide sprechen bei Tisch das Dankgebet, so daß die Starken mit den Schwachen darin vereint sind (14,6). Es kommt nicht darauf an, daß man dieses tut und jenes unterläßt. Entscheidend ist, daß alles, was man tut oder unterläßt, im Herrn geschieht. Wenn die gemeinsame Grundlage und die gemeinsame Ausrichtung da sind, dann ist auch bei auseinandergehenden Meinungen über Speisen und andere Probleme, die aus der Umwelt, der Tradition und der Theologie entstehen, die Einheit der Gemeinde noch gegeben. Diese soll durch gegenseitiges Richten, durch Verachten und Verketzern nicht zerstört werden (14,13). Die Verbindung mit Christus schafft eine so tiefe Gemeinschaft, daß bestehende Unterschiede zweitrangig werden. Paulus ruft nicht zu mehr Toleranz auf. Er erstrebt auch nicht eine tote Uniformität des Denkens und Handelns, sondern man soll auf das Heil des andern bedacht sein und den nicht in das Verderben stoßen, für den Christus gestorben ist (14,15). Trotz verschiedener Anschauungen soll man mit einem Munde den Vater unsers Herrn Jesus Christus preisen (15,6). Bei einem solchen einmütigen, einträchtigen und einmündigen Lobpreis verblassen die trennenden Unterschiede.

In gleicher Weise ist Christus im Johannesevangelium das einigende Band. Es ist schon darauf hingewiesen, daß er der eine Hirte ist, der seine Herde um sich sammelt (Joh 10,16), und daß er sterben mußte, damit er die zerstreuten Kinder Gottes in eins zusammenbrächte (11,52). Weil Jesus diese Aufgabe der Einigung hat, ist auf die Eigenart der johanneischen Christologie zu achten. Im ersten Kapitel seines Evangeliums bietet Johannes einen Grundriß der traditionellen, urchristlichen Anschauung: Jesus ist der Prophet wie Mose (1,45), der König Israels (1,49), der Messias (1,41), der Christus (1,41), der Sohn Gottes (1,34.49), der Menschensohn (1,51). Johannes kennt alle diese Christustitel. Aber ihm genügt die Beherrschung der üblichen christologischen Dogmatik nicht. Joh 7,40 diskutiert das einfache Volk die Titel Prophet, Christus, Sohn Davids. Trotz anfänglicher Zuneigung wird Jesus schließlich doch verworfen, weil er nicht dem entspricht, was die Schrift über ihn sagt und die führenden Theologen von ihm wissen (7,45.51).[9] Die traditionelle Messiaserwartung und das starre Festhalten am Buchstaben der Schrift verhindern die Anerkennung

---

[9]Ulrich Luck, *Die kirchliche Einheit als Problem des Johannesevangeliums* (Wort und Dienst 10; Bethel: Verlagsbuchhandlung der Anstalt Bethel, 1969) 57-59.

Jesu als Heilsbringer. Für den Evangelisten genügt eine korrekte Beherrschung der herkömmlichen Christologie zur Erfassung der Person Jesu Christi. Eine denkerisch erworbene Vorstellung vom Heilsbringer schafft nicht die Einheit der Kirche, sondern kann den Zugang zu dem lebendigen Christus versperren.[10] Weil es Johannes nicht um den dogmatischen Christus der jüdischen Anschauung und der von dort übernommenen urchristlichen Tradition, sondern um den wirklichen, heilschaffenden Christus geht, darum gebraucht er ganz andere Worte und Bezeichnungen für Jesus, die alle die einzigartige soteriologische Bedeutung Jesu zum Ausdruck bringen. Das zeigen die "Ich bin"-Worte: Jesus is das Brot des Lebens (6:35); er ist das Licht der Welt (8,12); er ist der gute Hirte (10,11); er ist die Auferstehung und das Leben (11,25); er ist der Weg, die Wahrheit und das Leben (14,6). Nicht durch Akzeptieren der Tradition, sondern durch das soteriologische Wirken Jesu sind alle Glaubenden zu einer Einheit zusammengeschlossen. Johannes spricht nicht vom Leib Jesu wie Paulus. Er bringt denselben Gedanken in ähnlicher Weise durch das Bild vom Weinstock und den Reben zum Ausdruck (15,5).[11]

3.2 DIE TAUFE ALS GRUND DER EINHEIT

Ein konstituierendes Element der Einheit ist die Taufe. Eph 4,5 wird bei der Aufforderung, die Einheit des Geistes zu wahren, neben "ein Herr und ein Glaube" auch die eine Taufe genannt. Als Paulus sich gegen die Zerrissenheit der Gemeinde in Korinth wendet, fragt er sie bezeichnenderweise nach ihrer Taufe. Indem er sie auf ihr Getauftsein anspricht, will er die zerbrechende Einheit nicht neu konstituieren, sondern er erinnert sie an die durch die Taufe gegebene Einheit. Sie sind nicht auf den Namen des Paulus getauft (1 Kor 1,13), sondern auf den Namen Christi (Apg 2,38; 8,16; 10,48; 19,5). Oder wie Paulus es auch verkürzt sagen kann: auf Christus (Röm 6,3; Gal 3,27). Durch die Taufe auf den Namen Christi sind die Getauften Christus übereignet. Paulus kann von der Inkorporation in den Leib des Christus durch die

[10]Rudolf Bultmann, *Das Evangelium des Johannes*, 19th ed. (MeyerK; Göttingen: Vandenhoeck & Ruprecht, 1968) 224-25, 231.

[11]Eduard Schweizer, "Der Kirchenbegriff im Evangelium und den Briefen des Johannes", *Neotestamentica: Deutsche und englische Aufsätze 1951-1963* (Zürich: Zwingli, 1963) 254-71, bes. 260; Rudolf Schnackenburg, *Das Johannesevangelium*, Part 3: *Kommentar zu Kap. 13-21*, 3rd ed. (HTKNT 4/3; Freiburg: Herder, 1975) 240.

Taufe sprechen (1 Kor 12,13). In der Taufe werden die Getauften in das σῶμα Χριστοῦ versetzt, in einen Leib berufen (Col 3,15), so daß die vielen ein Leib sind (Röm 12,5). Oder wie es Gal 3,28 sagt: Sie sind ein einziger in Christus Jesus. Durch die Einfügung in Christus ist eine individualistische Sondergruppierung innerhalb der Kirche nicht möglich. Die Gegensätze, die vor der Taufe da waren, die religiöse Trennung zwischen Juden und Heiden, die oekonomisch-soziale Aufteilung in Sklaven und Freie, die verschiedenen Wertschätzungen von Mann und Frau sind beseitigt, allerdings nicht so, daß die Unterschiede überhaupt nicht mehr da sind, sondern so, daß sie nicht mehr scheidend wirken. In der "neuen Schöpfung" (Gal 6,15) wird der Wert der Unterschiede annulliert. Sie schrumpfen auf Null zusammen. Darum gibt es keine Herrschenden und keine Unterdrückten, keine Bevorzugten und keine Unterprivilegierten. Menschen verschiedener Rassen, verschiedener Bildung, verschiedenen sozialen Standes sind in Christus zu einer Einheit verschmolzen. Wenn man das beachtet, dann ist man nicht erstaunt, daß Paulus die sich vor Gericht streitenden Christen auf die Taufe verweist (1 Kor 6,11). Wer getauft ist, ist zur Einheit mit den Getauften berufen.

3.3 DAS ABENDMAHL ALS GRUND DER EINHEIT

Wie die Taufe, so ist auch das Abendmahl ein Sakrament der Einheit. Wenn eine Mahlzeit schon ganz allgemein Ausdruck der Gemeinschaft ist, so ist dieses in noch viel stärkerem Maße bei der Feier des Herrenmahls der Fall. Das macht Paulus den Korinthern deutlich, indem er die tradierten Worte umstellt. Er spricht nicht vom Brot und dem Kelch, wie es sonst üblich ist, sondern zuerst vom Kelch und dann ausführlich vom Brot, weil es ihm um die Einheit der Kirche geht, die er am Brotwort verdeutlicht (1 Kor 10,16). Der Leib Christi, der für die Menschen an das Kreuz geschlagen war und der als der im Herrenmahl gegenwärtige den Christen Anteil an sich selber gibt, macht die das Mahl Genießenden zum Leib der Gemeinde. Weil Christen beim Herrenmahl von dem einen Brot essen, das den für uns dahingegebenen, gegenwärtigen Christus repräsentiert, und sie dadurch des Christus teilhaftig werden, darum sind alle, die am Herrenmahl teilnehmen, nicht viele Leiber, sondern ein Leib, der Leib Christi. Wie das Brot aus vielen Körnern besteht, die Körner als solche aber nicht in Erscheinung treten, so sind die Christen mit Christus und untereinander als Einheit verbunden. Ein Sonderdasein ist unmöglich.

Die Gemeinschaft mit Christus schafft Gemeinschaft untereinander.[12] Zerreißt diese, dann ist auch die Gemeinschaft mit Christus nicht mehr intakt. Wer sich von der Gemeinde absondert und dadurch die Gemeinschaft stört, wie das in Korinth bei der Abendmahlsfeier geschah, macht sich bei der Teilnahme am Herrenmahl an Christus selbst schuldig (1 Kor 11,27). Differenzen in der Gemeinde sind Verstöße gegen Christus. Das Abendmahl aktualisiert und stärkt die durch die Taufe erwirkte Inkorporation in Christus. Bei der Feier des Herrenmahls tritt die Einheit der Kirche in Erscheinung.

3.4 "LEIB CHRISTI" ALS AUSDRUCK DER EINHEIT

Bei der Christusfrage wie auch bei der Taufe und beim Herrenmahl war auf das σῶμα Χριστοῦ hingewiesen. Um seine Bedeutung für die Einheit der Kirche herauszustellen, braucht zu dem dort Gesagten nur ganz wenig hinzugefügt zu werden. Es gibt im Neuen Testament keinen anderen Ausdruck, der so eindeutig die geordnete Einheit trotz der Vielgestaltigkeit und so anschaulich die unauflösbare Zuordnung zu Christus und der Glieder zueinander zum Ausdruck bringt wie die Wendung σῶμα Χριστοῦ. Die kirchliche Einheit beruht nicht auf einer gut funktionierenden Ordnung und Organisation, sondern sie besteht in der gliedhaften Zuordnung zueinander. Die Kirche gleicht nicht nur einem Leib mit verschiedenen Gliedern, sondern sie ist der Leib Christi. Darum teilt jeder, der die Gemeinde spaltet und sich von der konkreten Kirche als Sondergruppe absplittert, Jesus Christus selbst in Stücke (1 Kor 1,13). Wie Christus nicht zerstückelt werden darf, so darf auch seine Gemeinde, die sein Leib ist, nicht zerteilt werden.

3.5 DIE BEDEUTUNG DES AMTES FÜR DIE EINHEIT

Oft wird auf die Bedeutung des Amtes für die Einheit der Kirche hingewiesen.[13] Apg 20,28-31 wird den Bischöfen die Aufgabe zugesprochen, die Gemeinde vor dem Eindringen von "reißenden Wölfen" zu schützen und die Eintracht der Gemeinde aufrechtzuerhalten. In den Pastoralbriefen erhält Timotheus den Auftrag, über die Gemeinde

---

[12]Siehe Werner Elert, *Abendmahl und Kirchengemeinschaft in der alten Kirche hauptsächlich des Ostens* (Berlin: Lutherisches Verlagshaus, 1954).

[13]Heinrich Schlier, "Einheit der Kirche I. Im Verständnis der Schrift", *LTK*, 2nd ed. 3 (1959) 750-54; J. Auer, "Das 'Leib-Modell' und der 'Kirchenbegriff' der katholischen Kirche", *MTZ* 12 (1961) 24-31.

zu wachen und dafür zu sorgen, daß nicht falsche Lehren verbreitet werden (1 Tim 1,3). Dementsprechend soll Titus sektiererischen Judenchristen, die durch ihre Lehren ganze Familien durcheinanderbringen, den Mund stopfen (Titus 1,10-11). Jeder Bischof muß imstande sein, zu ermahnen und die Widersprechenden zu überführen (Titus 1,9). Von diesen Stellen abgesehen, spielt das institutionelle Amt des Bischofs für die Frage der Einheit der Kirche noch keine entscheidende Rolle. Weder im Römerbrief noch in den Korintherbriefen appelliert Paulus an die Amtsträger, daß sie bei den entstandenen Differenzen und Spaltungen sich um die Einheit der Gemeinden bemühen sollen.

Im Epheserbrief bildet der Abschnitt 4,1-16 den Abschluß der Mahnungen zur Einheit. Nachdem betont ist, die Einheit des Geistes durch das Band des Friedens zu wahren, und herausgestellt ist, worin die Einheit besteht: ein Leib, ein Geist, eine Hoffnung, ein Herr, ein Glaube, eine Taufe, ein Gott und Vater (4,3-6), kommt der Verfasser auf das Amt zu sprechen; und er fährt nicht fort: ein Amt, sondern er spricht von der Vielfalt der Gaben: "Jedem einzelnen von uns ist die Gnade in dem Maß der Gabe Christi verliehen" (v 7). Es scheint so, als ob der Verfasser fürchtet, die Vielfalt der Gaben könnte die Einheit der Kirche sprengen. Das darf unter keinen Umständen geschehen. Die hervorragenden Wortverkünder in der Gemeinde: Apostel, Propheten, Evangelisten, Hirten und Lehrer (v 11) sollen die Gemeindeglieder mit ihren Gnadengaben für den Dienst zurüsten, damit der Leib Christi erbaut wird (v 12), bis alle zur Einheit des Glaubens und der Erkenntnis des Gottesohnes gelangen (v 13). Die Vielfalt der Gaben darf nicht zu Konkurrenz und Chaos führen, vielmehr kommt es auf Klarheit und Liebe an (v 15). Jeder, der von Christus mit der Gnade beschenkt ist (v 7), soll nach dem Maß seines Vermögens in Liebe der Erbauung des Leibes dienen (v 16).

Um die Bedeutung des Amtes herauszustellen, verweist man oft auf die Autorität des Apostels Paulus, der durch seine Arbeit die Einheit sichert und, wo sie zu zerbröckeln droht, sich um sie müht.[14] Das ist wohl richtig. Aber neben Paulus stehen andere führende Männer der urchristlichen Gemeinde—Petrus und Jakobus, Apollos und Barnabas. Ihre theologischen Anschauungen und ihre Arbeit sind weithin Ursachen für Differenzen in der Gemeinde. Nach Matt 16,17-18 ist

---

[14]Schlier, "Einheit der Kirche", 181-83.

Petrus der Fels der Kirche. Aber Paulus erkennt diesen Felsen nicht
an, wie der Zusammenstoß mit Petrus in Antiochien und seine
Polemik gegen Petrus zeigen. In Antiochien macht Paulus ihm den
schweren Vorwurf der Heuchelei (Gal 2, 13), und 1 Kor 3,11 stellt Paulus heraus: "Ein anderes Fundament kann niemand legen als das, was
gelegt ist".

Anders verhält es sich bei den Apostolischen Vätern. Für sie ist der
Amtsträger für die Einheit verantwortlich.[15] So mahnt Ignatius in
seinem Brief an Polykarp: "Sorge für die Einheit!" (Ign. *Pol.* 1,2).
Bischof und Presbyterium schaffen und garantieren die Einstimmig-
keit der Gemeinde: "Es geziemt euch, mit dem Sinn des Bischofs
übereinzustimmen, was ihr ja auch tut; denn euer Presbyterium, das
seinen Namen zu Recht trägt und Gottes würdig ist, ist mit dem
Bischof so verbunden, wie Saiten mit einer Zither. Deshalb ertönt in
eurer Eintracht und zusammenklingender Liebe das Lied Jesu Christi"
(Ign. *Eph.* 4,1). Es heißt dann weiter: "Wieviel mehr preise ich euch
glücklich, die ihr mit ihm (dem Bischof) so eng verbunden seid wie die
Kirche mit Jesus Christus und Jesus Christus mit dem Vater, auf daß
alles in Einheit zusammenklinge" (Ign. *Eph.* 5,1). Bei Ignatius hat die
kirchliche Institution eine große Bedeutung für die Einheit. Der
Bischof mit dem Presbyterium ist Garant und sichtbares Zeichen für
rechte Gemeinschaft.

4

Einheit schließt eine Mannigfaltigkeit des Lebens und Lehrens in
der Kirche nicht aus. Das zu erstrebende Ziel der Einheit besteht nicht
in der Beseitigung von Unterschieden. Zum Wesen der Kirche gehört
vielmehr die Vielfalt in der Einheit.[16] Die akzeptierten Verschieden-
heiten sind nicht Gegensätze zerstörender Art, sondern dienen zur
Förderung des Ganzen, wie Paulus dieses im Bild vom Leib und den
Gliedern anschaulich darstellt. Gott hat den Leib als Einheit
geschaffen (1 Kor 12,24), in dem es kein rücksichtsloses Machtausüben
und gnadenloses Unterdrücken durch Bevorzugte und darum auch

[15]Josef Blank, *Das Evangelium nach Johannes*, 3 vols. (Geistliche Schriftlesung.
Erläuterungen zum Neuen Testament für die geistliche Lesung 4/1-3; Düsseldorf:
Patmos, 1977), 2:279-83.

[16]Ethelbert Stauffer, s.v. "εἰς", *TWNT* 2 (1935) 438-39; Ernst Käsemann, *Jesu
letzter Wille nach Joh 17*, 3rd ed. (Tübingen: J. C. B. Mohr, 1971) 118.

keine erniedrigende Unterwerfung gibt, sondern jedes Glied sorgt für das andere und dient ihm nach seinen Anlagen und Befähigungen (1 Kor 12,25) und kommt ihm in Ehrerbietung zuvor.[17] Wenn man in herzlicher Bruderliebe einander zugetan ist und in Ehrerbietung dem andern zuvorkommt (Röm 12,10), sich in Liebe gegenseitig erträgt (Eph 4,2), nicht auf das Eigene bedacht ist, sondern den andern höher achtet als sich selbst (Phil 2,3), dann gibt es keine ernsthaften Differenzen, und auftretende Spannungen kann man ertragen. Das Pneuma, das mit Christus zu den konstituierenden Elementen der Einheit gehört, bewirkt die Vielfalt der Charismen, deren Mannigfaltigkeit zur Förderung der Einheit dient. Die Kirche als Leib Christi braucht den Organismus der vielen Gaben, damit die Gemeinde lebt. Weil es in der Kirche viele Aufgaben gibt und nicht jeder alles tun kann, darum sind die verschiedenen Gaben Gottes vorhanden. Diese können, wenn sie als Gaben Gottes erkannt werden, die Gemeinde nicht aufspalten.

Auch die Pluralität der Theologie braucht die Einheit der Kirche nicht in Frage zu stellen, wenn Christus die unantastbare Grundlage bleibt. Wichtig ist es, auf das Verhalten des Apostels Paulus bei den Gesprächen mit den Führern der Urgemeinde in Jerusalem zu achten. Ganz offensichtlich liegen verschiedene theologische Anschauungen vor. Trotzdem kommt man zur übereinkunft. Paulus akzeptiert die Gemeinde in Jerusalem, ja, er fühlt sich ihr gegenüber sogar verpflichtet, und Jerusalem wiederum erlaubt Paulus die Heidenmission mit ihren folgenschweren Auswirkungen für das Zusammenleben in den Gemeinden. Diese Stellungnahme ist ein bemerkenswertes Ereignis. In Jerusalem wird die Mannigfaltigkeit und Variationsbreite der Christusbotschaft kirchlich sanktioniert. Man bejaht ganz offiziell in voller Einmütigkeit die Verschiedenheit. Paulus darf unter Heiden das Evangelium in anderer Weise verkündigen, als es Petrus unter den Juden tut. Die verschiedenen Voraussetzungen der religiösen Herkunft und der Umwelt verlangen eine Verschiedenheit der Verkündigung von dem einen Gott, aus dem alles ist, und von dem einen Herrn, durch den alles ist (1 Kor 8,6).

Die Verkündigung der Urchristenheit ist weder formal an ein bestimmtes Schema gebunden noch inhaltlich streng normiert. Das Ver-

---

[17]Ragnar Bring, *Der Brief an die Galater* (Berlin: Lutherisches Verlagshaus, 1968) 164.

bindende und Einheitliche ist die Verkündigung von Jesus Christus als dem Retter der Menschen. Diese erfolgt nicht in einer festgelegten Uniformität. Das beweisen die vielen Bezeichnungen Jesu, die das Neue Testament verwendet, um die Heilsbedeutung Jesu auszudrücken. Das läßt sich auch an der Vielfalt der christologischen Formeln der Tradition nachweisen. Es gibt im Neuen Testament eine ganze Reihe von Zeugnissen, die den Tod Jesu, der in der paulinischen Theologie eine so überragende Stellung hat, überhaupt nicht erwähnen, sondern nur von der Auferweckung und der Erhöhung Jesu sprechen (Röm, 1,3; 10,9b; 1 Thess 1,9-10; 1 Tim 3,16; 2 Tim 2,8; Col 1,15-20 [in der ursprünglichen Form]; Heb 1,3). Als im Laufe der Entwicklung die Reflexion darüber einsetzte, warum Jesus so grausam sterben mußte, kam man zu der Erkenntnis, "daß Christus für uns gestorben ist nach den Schriften und daß er begraben und am dritten Tag auferweckt worden ist nach den Schriften und daß er dem Kephas erschien" (1 Kor 15,3-4). Nach den einleitenden Worten des Apostels Paulus ist in diesen Sätzen die Summe des Evangeliums enthalten, und Paulus betont, daß er die Tradition wörtlich wiedergibt. Röm 1,3 zitiert er ebenfalls eine übernommene Formel des Evangeliums, die aber anders lautet. Und er nimmt sich sogar die Freiheit heraus, in das festgefügte Schema das Wort "in Kraft" einzufügen, wodurch aus der adoptianisch klingenden Christologie eine Präexistenzchristologie wird. Paulus unterläßt es aber, an dieser Stelle etwas über das Sterben Jesu zu sagen, das für seine Theologie so wichtig ist. Wie solche und ähnliche Zusätze zu übernommenen Traditionen zeigen (Phil 2,8; Col 1,15-20), dokumentiert sich die theologische Einheit der Kirche nicht darin, daß man gewisse Glaubensaussagen wortgetreu repetiert. Man wagt es, geprägte Formeln umzugestalten.[18] Damit bringt man zum Ausdruck, daß das Bekenntnis zu Jesus Christus nicht in präziser Zitierung festgelegter Sätze besteht, und es nicht an einen dogmatisch festgelegten Wortlaut gebunden ist.

Auch in den einzelnen Evangelien wird die Botschaft Jesu verschieden wiedergegeben. Jeder Evangelist verkündet das eine Evangelium unter einem andern Aspekt. Wie bei den christologischen Formeln, so wagt man auch in den Evangelien überlieferte Worte

---

[18]Gerhard Friedrich, "Auf die Verkündigung der Versöhnung kommt es an", *Wissenschaft und Praxis in Kirche und Gesellschaft* 67 (1978) 16.

umzugestalten, wenn es der Sache Jesu dient. Es ist ein erstaunliches
Faktum, daß die Kirche die vier Evangelien nicht zu einer Einheit
harmonisiert, sondern sie trotz ihrer Verschiedenheit akzeptiert hat.
Obwohl das Diatessaron, wie seine große Verbreitung zeigt, bei vielen
Christen sehr beliebt war, hat die Kirche sich nicht für das Einheits-
evangelium entschieden. Sie hat die schematische Uniformität abge-
lehnt und die vier Evangelien in ihrer Mannigfaltigkeit und
Verschiedenheit kanonisiert.

5

Trotz der von der Urchristenheit bejahten Vielfalt der Lehrweisen
und der Lebensäußerungen der Kirche gibt es eine Grenze der Freiheit,
die unter keinen Umständen überschritten werden darf. Gal 1,6-9
wendet sich Paulus gegen alle, die ein anderes Evangelium verkündigen, als er es kundgetan hat. Er sagt ganz eindeutig, was für ihn
Evangelium ist. Das Evangelium hat einen bestimmten Inhalt.[19] Es ist
aber nicht als ein Lehrstück, nicht als eine Sammlung von Lehrsätzen
zu charakterisieren, sondern als der Ruf in die Gnade (Gal 1,6), wie
Paulus ihn bei der Missionspredigt ergehen ließ (Gal 1,8-9). Es ist das
Heilshandeln Gottes, das die Kraft hat, aus Sündern Gerechte, aus
Gottlosen Heilige zu machen (Röm 1,16; 1 Kor 15,2).[20] Paulus macht
den Galatern nicht den Vorwurf, daß sie eine falsche Lehre vertreten,
sondern daß sie sich von dem abwenden, der sie durch die Gnade Jesu
berufen hat (Gal 1,6). Bei der rechten Verkündigung des Evangeliums
kommt es nicht darauf an, daß eine tradierte Formel korrekt weiterge-
geben wird, sondern daß die soteriologische Kraft des Christusgesche-
hens laut wird. Wird die universale Bedeutung des Heilswirkens Jesu in
Frage gestellt, dann ist der Punkt erreicht, wo eine Gemeinschaft nicht
mehr aufrechtzuerhalten ist. In einem solchen Fall ist die gemeinsame
Basis zerstört und die Möglichkeit zu einem Kompromiß nicht mehr
gegeben. Die Anerkennung der Hoheit Jesu und die Bejahung seiner
Heilsbedeutung gehören zum unaufgebbaren Bestand christlicher
Gemeinschaft. "Wenn es eine Gerechtigkeit durch das Gesetz gibt, ist
Christus umsonst gestorben" (Gal 2,21). "Wenn ihr euch beschneiden
läßt, wird euch Christus nichts nützen" (Gal 5,2). "Ihr seid von Chris-

---

[19]Gerhard Friedrich, s.v. "εὐαγγέλιον", *TWNT* 2 (1935) 727-28.

[20]Friedrich, s.v. "εὐαγγέλιον", 728-29.

tus geschieden, wenn ihr durch das Gesetz gerecht werden wollt. Ihr seid aus der Gnade herausgefallen" (Gal 5,4). Das Anathema soll nicht nur diejenigen treffen, die ein anderes Evangelium verkündigen, sondern auch die, die den Herrn nicht lieb haben und Christen sein wollen (1 Kor 16,22). Immer geht es um Jesus Christus, um sein Heilswerk, um die Stellung zu ihm. Wer die soteriologische Bedeutung Jesu angreift und das *solus Christus* als alleinige Grundlage der Errettung antastet, hat sich von Christus getrennt.

Der Johannesbrief zieht klare Grenzen gegen alle, die leugnen, daß Jesus der Christus (1 Joh 2,22), der Sohn ist (1 Joh 4,15; 5,1.5.10), daß er ins Fleisch gekommen ist (1 Joh 4,2; 2 Joh 7). An Jesus Christus scheiden sich die Geister. Die Trennung von solchen, die Christus nicht voll anerkennen, soll eine absolute sein, so daß man ihnen Gruß und Gastfreundschaft verweigert (2 Joh 10). Neutralität und Toleranz ist ihnen gegenüber nicht möglich. "Es ist in keinem andern das Heil, es ist auch kein anderer Name unter dem Himmel für die Menschen gegeben, durch den wir gerettet werden" (Apg 4,12). Er ist der Weg, die Wahrheit und das Leben (Joh 14,6). Es gibt keinen anderen Ausweg aus dem Verderben, keinen anderen Zugang zu Gott, keine andere Möglichkeit der Errettung. "Wer nicht in mir bleibt, wird weggeworfen wie die Rebe und verdorrt, und man sammelt sie und wirft sie ins Feuer, und sie verbrennen" (Joh 15,6).

In den Pastoralbriefen und anderen späteren Briefen ist nicht mehr die falsche Einstellung zu Christus die Grenze der Einheit, sondern die Heterodidaskalia und das unmoralische Verhalten zwingen zur Trennung. Der Vorwurf, daß Glieder der Gemeinde eine andere Lehre vertreten, zeigt, daß die christliche Gemeinde nun eine feste Lehre mit gültigen Normen hat, an der man festhalten muß und an der man Abweichungen feststellen kann. Timotheus wird beauftragt, gewissen Leuten zu untersagen, falsche Lehren zu verbreiten und endlosen Fabeln von Geschlechterfolgen anzuhängen (1 Tim 1, 3-4). Es kommt auf die Erhaltung der in der Kirche überlieferten Lehre an (2 Tim 1,14; 2,2). Die *vox evangelii* von Jesus Christus ist zur "gesunden Lehre" erstarrt (1 Tim 6,3). An die Stelle des Glaubens ist die Frömmigkeit getreten. Die gesunde, tradierte Lehre ist klar formuliert, so daß sich Irrlehren feststellen und dogmatische Abgrenzungen gegen sie vollziehen lassen. Mit falscher Lehre ist aufs Engste ein falsches Verhalten verbunden. Man wirft den Irrlehrern, die Einheit der Gemeinde durch ihre Umtriebe zerstören (2 Tim 3,6), Zügellosigkeit (2 Pet

2,2.18), allgemeine Lasterhaftigkeit (2 Tim 3,2-6; Judas 4,12,18; 2 Pet 2,10.13), speziell Habgier (1 Tim 6,5.10; 2 Tim 3,2; Judas 11; 2 Pet 2,3.14) und Unzucht (Judas 7.15; 2 Pet 2,10.14), kurz gesagt, allgemeinen sittlichen Verfall vor. Es sind dieselben Verschuldungen, die sonst in den Lasterkatalogen als typisch heidnische Vergehen geschildert werden (Röm 1,24-32; 1 Kor 5,10; 6,9-10; 2 Kor 12,21; 1 Pet 4,3-4). Mit der gesunden Lehre ist ein solches Verhalten unvereinbar (1 Tim 1,10). Weil es mit solchen Leuten keine Gemeinschaft geben kann, muß man sich von ihnen distanzieren (1 Tim 4,7; 2 Tim 2,23; 3,5; Titus 3,10).

6

Die Einheit der an Christus Glaubenden ist nicht nur eine innerkirchliche Notwendigkeit. Sie hat eine universale, alle Menschen angehende Bedeutung. Seit der Urzeit, seitdem Menschen durch den Sündenfall aus der Gemeinschaft mit Gott im Paradies herausgefallen sind und seit Kain seinen Bruder erschlagen hat, geht ein Riß durch die Menschheit. Durch den Turmbau zu Babel und die darauf folgende Sprachverwirrung ist die Zerstreuung und Trennung der Völker eine totale geworden. Nach Gottes Willen soll das nicht so bleiben. Mit Christus und der Kirche hat die Beendigung der Verwirrung und Entfremdung begonnen. Wo Kirche ist, ist sie immer auf die Gesamtheit der Menschen gerichtet. Die von Gott abgefallene und in sich zerstrittene Menschheit ist in der Kirche im Gehorsam gegen Gott und in der Anbetung Christi vereinigt.[21] Am Pfingstfest hören die Parther, Meder und Elamiter, die Einwohner aus Mesopotamien, Judäa und Kappadocien, Pontus und Kleinasien, Phrygien und Pamphylien, aus Ägypten und dem Gebiet Libyens bei Kyrene, Juden aus Rom, Juden und Proselyten, Kreter und Araber jeder in seiner Muttersprache die Großtaten Gottes (Apg 2,8-11). In der Kirche macht es nichts mehr aus, ob man als Jude oder Grieche geboren und aufgewachsen ist. Alle sind zu Nachkommen Abrahams dem die Verheißungen Gottes gegeben wurden, geworden. Alle diskriminierenden und trennenden Unterschiede sind aufgehoben. In Christus findet die zersplitterte und sich bekämpfende Menschheit ihre verlorene Einheit wieder (Gal 3,28-29).

---

[21]Heinrich Schlier, "Die Kirche als das Geheimnis Christi: Nach dem Epheserbrief", *Die Zeit der Kirche: Exegetische Aufsätze und Vorträge*, 5th ed. (Freiburg: Herder, 1972) 300-1.

Diese Gedanken betont in besonders eindrucksvoller Weise der Epheserbrief. Die Kirche ist auf dem Weg, die Einheit der Schöpfung wiederherzustellen (Eph 3,6-11). Sie ist der Ort, an dem sich der Heilswille Gottes mit der Schöpfung verwirklicht. Sie ist die Antizipation der kommenden, endgültigen Einheit. In Christus sind Juden und Heiden zu einem einzigen Menschen erschaffen (Eph 2,15). In Christus sind nicht nur einige wenige miteinander verbunden, sondern das ganze Universum, das in den Himmeln und das auf der Erde, ist in ihm einheitlich zusammengefaßt (Eph 1,10). Er ist nicht nur der Herr der Kirche, sondern der der Welt. Als das Haupt des Alls stellt er die eingebüßte Ordnung und Einheit wieder her. Das ist in der Kirche, die die Alleinherrschaft Christi anerkennt, bereits geschehen. In ihrer Einheit verwirklicht sie die Neuordnung Gottes (Eph 1,21-23).[22] Die Kirche in ihrer Einheit hat somit Bedeutung und Verantwortung für die ganze Welt. Sie führt nicht ein nur wenige interessierendes Sonderdasein, sondern sie ist ein kosmischer Faktor. Sie ist die Fülle dessen, der alles in allem erfüllt (Eph 1,23). Weil sich in ihr der Wille Gottes bereits durchgesetzt hat, eröffnet sie der Welt die Möglichkeit, zu ihrem eigentlichen, von Gott gewollten Sein zu kommen. So ist die Kirche "der Raum der Hoffnung in der Welt".[23]

7

Die Gemeinde, von der geschenkten Einheit kommend, durch die Gefährdungen in der Welt wandernd, ist unterwegs zu der endgültigen, vollkommenen, vollendeten, gottgewollten Einheit (Joh 17,23). Diese vollendete Einheit ist noch nicht eine aufweisbare, anschaubare Tatsache. Da sie in ihrer Vollkommenheit nicht ein weltliches Phänomen ist, ist sie noch nicht konstatierbar. Die gegebene Einheit ist als vollkommene das ersehnte und erstrebte Ziel aller Glaubenden. Paulus spricht nicht wie Johannes *expressis verbis* von der eschatologischen Vollendung der Einheit. Aber theologisch ergibt sie sich aus der unauflösbaren Verbundenheit von Christus mit der Kirche. Christus ist der Präexistente, und darum ist die Kirche nicht nur eine historische Größe, sondern dem irdischen Geschehen vorgegeben. Christus ist der

---

[22]Joachim Gnilka, *Der Epheserbrief* (HTKNT 10/2; Freiburg: Herder, 1971) 80-81.

[23]Gnilka, *Epheserbrief*, 125, auch 99-111.

Menschgewordene, der am Kreuz sein Leben gelassen hat, und auf ihn gründet sich die Kirche. Christus ist der Präsente, und die Christen werden durch die Taufe in Christus versetzt und haben im Abendmahl Anteil an ihm. Wenn Christus und die Kirche in der Präexistenz wie in der Präsenz zusammengehören, so muß das auch für die Eschatologie gelten und für die Frage der Einheit Bedeutung haben. Die vollendete Einheit aller Glaubenden wird dann eintreten, wenn Christus in Macht und Herrlichkeit die zu ihm Gehörenden von den vier Winden versammeln und die in Christus Gestorbenen erwecken wird. Dann werden alle Verstorbenen in Christus zusammen mit den in Christus Lebenden mit ihm in einmütiger Vollendung verbunden sein (1 Thess 4,17).

A NOTE ON
LUKE 1:28 AND 38

Reginald H. Fuller

IN HIS *Christliche Glaubenslehre* Graß makes the following observation:[1]

> Ganz problematisch ist die Art, wie Barth die Ausschaltung des Mannes und die Rolle der Frau bei der Jungfrauengeburt zu begründen sucht. . . . Nun, das heißt einfach das reformatorische sola gratia in . . . die neutestamentliche Anschauung eintragen. Barth bewegt sich damit auf derselben Ebene wie die katholische Mariologie, welche jedoch gerade umgekehrt nicht die völlige Passivität, sondern den Synergismus von Gott and Mensch in die Jung-frauengeburt hineinliest und kühn erklärt, Gott habe seinen Entschluß, seinen Sohn Mensch werden zu lassen, von der Zustimmung der allerhei-ligsten Jungfrau Maria abhängig gemacht (unter Berufung auf das fiat von Lk 1,38).[1]

Though neither a Roman Catholic nor a Barthian, I rubbed my eyes when I read these words. It occurred to me that the view of Barth and that attributed by Graß to Roman Catholics is, as he seems partially to sense, a caricature, not indeed of what happened historically at the annunciation, for we cannot penetrate far behind the Lucan text,[2] but at least of the theology of Luke at this point. Since Professor Bo Reicke has, among his many other interests, paid much attention to Lucan theology, this seems a fitting occasion to discuss the Lucan presenta-tion of Mary in the story of the annunciation.

---

[1]Hans Graß, *Christliche Glaubenslehre*, 2 vols. (Theologische Wissenschaft 12; Stuttgart: Kohlhammer, 1973-1974), 1:121. This quotation occurs in a section entitled "Das Problem des Ursprungs Jesu" (117-29). While there is much useful material in this chapter, it is sad that in this ecumenical age, after more than ten years of dialogue with the Roman Catholic Church, such Reformation slogans should continue to be bandied about, with no attempt to reach an understanding of the other's position.

[2]Raymond E. Brown *The Birth of the Messiah: A Commentary on the Infancy Narratives* (Garden City, New York: Doubleday; London: Geoffrey Chapman, 1977), 247 is of the opinion that the annunciation pericope is a Lucan composition, though perhaps based upon traditions whose precise contours can no longer be reconstructed. Matthew's annunciation story (1:18-25) has sufficient material in common with the Lucan story that we may postulate a pre-Gospel tradition. It would have consisted of

Luke seems to balance carefully the γένοιτο of v 38 with the initial greeting of the angel Gabriel at v 28, κεχαριτωμένη. Let us begin with γένοιτο. The closest parallel to this use of γίνεσθαι in the optative in Luke-Acts is the occurrence of the same verb in the third person negative imperative in the Gethsemane pericope: πλὴν μὴ τὸ θέλημά μου ἀλλὰ τὸ σὸν γινέσθω (Luke 22:42). This is a prayer, seemingly modeled in Luke's Marcan source upon the third petition of the Lord's prayer, which Luke himself omits at 11:3, asking God to accomplish his will.[3] However, in both cases the person offering the prayer is intimately involved in the carrying out of that will; for the will of God determines the destiny of the person who offers the prayer. Thus the prayer involves not only a petition but an act of self-oblation, expressing a willingness to be used as the instrument in the carrying out of that will. Therefore we cannot speak of *völlige Passivität*. This surely is the disposition of all Christian prayer and particularly of prayer which is modeled upon the Lord's prayer, as all Christian prayer is meant to be. Are we then to call that synergism? Surely in doing so we are importing into a Greek text the theological debates of later Western Christianity. The early Fathers can speak without inhibition of Mary's offering herself in order that through her the will of God may be done. To quote one such Father, Eusebius says: πίναξ εἰμὶ γραφόμενος· ὃ βούλεται ὁ γραφεύς, γραφέτω. Here we see an uninhibited recognition that Mary performed a necessary role in carrying out the redemptive purpose of God.[4]

But Mary's γένοιτο is preceded in the annunciation story by the angel's κεχαριτωμένη. There has been much controversy over this

the following elements: (1) an annunciation to Mary or Joseph, (2) Mary's premarital pregnancy, and (3) the faith assertion of a virginal-pneumatic conception.

[3]The third petition of the Lord's prayer is absent from the earliest texts of Luke 11:3, and we assume that it is not original here. But the concept of such a prayer is sufficiently attested for Luke in the Gethsemane pericope. Alfred Plummer's commentary (*A Critical and Exegetical Commentary on the Gospel According to S. Luke*, 4th ed. [ICC; Edinburgh: T. & T. Clark, 1901]) still contains much that is valuable, though it treats the annunciation story as history rather than as a Lucan composition and evidence for Lucan theology, as we do here. Plummer denies that Mary's γένοιτο is a prayer and insists that it is exclusively an act of submission (26). But he does not note the parallel in the Gethsemane story.

[4]We avoid speaking here of "incarnation". The Christology expressed in the infancy narratives is in our opinion a dramatization of the "sending-of-the-Son" Christology; see Reginald H. Fuller, "New Testament Roots to the Theotokos," *Marian Studies* (1978) 46-64.

word. Protestants have generally preferred, at least in English, the translation "(highly) favored one," while Roman Catholics, following the Vulgate's *gratia plena*, have generally opted for "full of grace."

It is questionable, however, whether we should draw such a sharp distinction between these two translations. On the one hand, if we translate κεχαριτωμένη "favored one", the "favored" means that God has predestined, elected and called Mary for a specific role in salvation history. But predestination, election and call imply the giving also of the grace which is necessary to sustain that role. This combination of predestination, election and call with grace is a recurring pattern in the infancy narrative, even though the word *grace* is not actually used. Of John the Baptist, who was chosen for his role in salvation from the moment of his conception (Luke 1:14-17), Luke says that from his birth "the hand of the Lord was upon him" (1:66c; cf. Acts 11:21, where the "hand of the Lord" similarly empowers the apostolic preaching in the post-Easter community). That this prior empowerment by God is associated with the Baptist's election for his role from the womb is suggested by the καὶ γάρ (1:66c), with which this notice is joined to the preceding pericope of his birth and naming. Plummer aptly interprets these two Greek particles to mean " 'for besides all that,' *i.e.*, in addition to the marvels which attended his birth."[5] Later on in the same chapter Luke is at pains to tell his readers that the child "grew and became strong in spirit" (1:80). Thus he is prepared to assume his public role at the proper time.

Nor is the situation different with Jesus himself. He too according to Luke was predestined, elected and called to perform a unique and final role in salvation history from the moment of his conception (Luke 1:22-38). The evangelist might have said that from the moment of his conception Jesus was κεχαριτωμένος. As with the Baptist, his election from the womb was followed by the years of preparation for the role: "The child grew and became strong, filled with wisdom; and the favor (χάρις!) of God was upon him" (Luke 2:40). One is almost tempted to translate this, "The grace of God was upon him." But the second Lucan summary on the growth of Jesus causes us to hesitate, for there we read that "Jesus increased in wisdom and in stature and in favor (χάριτι) with God and man" (2:52).[6] Jesus might have received grace from God

---

[5]See Plummer, *Luke*, 38.

[6]Brown, *Birth*, 469.

but hardly from man. So we opt for the rendering "favor."[7]

Therefore, in the Lukan theology the pattern emerges that when God destines human beings for distinctive roles in salvation history, he calls them from the womb, an action which might aptly be described by the verb χαριτόω, and continues to show favor to them during their preparation to fulfill that role. Thus when Mary is addressed as κεχαριτωμένη, we would be interpreting that verb consistently with Luke's theology of salvation history if we see in it the implication that Mary too had been chosen from the womb to fulfill her particular role, and that she too underwent a period of preparation under the divine favor. Divine favor seems to imply divine grace.

Could we then translate κεχαριτωμένη "you who have received grace"? Is there some justification after all for the Vulgate's *gratia plena*? The verb χαριτόω occurs in only one other passage in the New Testament, in Eph 1:6: εἰς ἔπαινον δόξης τῆς χάριτος αὐτοῦ, ἧς ἐχαρίτωσεν ἡμᾶς ἐν τῷ ἠγαπημένῳ. Here χαριτόω means something a little more concrete than "to show favor";[8] it means to bestow a gift of grace (cf. RSV, "grace which he freely bestowed upon us"). But it probably has that concrete meaning in this context, because the word χάρις is actually present; and we ought not to use this occurrence to support the translation of κεχαριτωμένη in Luke 1:28 as "you upon whom grace has been bestowed." Otherwise the angel's greeting should have been worded χάριν κεχαριτωμένη or χάριτι κεχαριτωμένη. So we hesitate to accept Plummer's rendering "endued with grace"[9] or to adopt the Vulgate translation. But as the other passages in the infancy narratives indicate, Mary, as one whom God favored, was *ipso facto* a recipient of his grace. Grace then, in the angel's greeting to Mary, is implied rather than asserted.

If then grace is implied, it means that Mary's act of submission registered in her γένοιτο is a submission not produced by her own initiative, but as a response to the grace of God. She was able to say γένοιτο precisely because before she had been κεχαριτωμένη. Mary's submission was entirely an act of her own will; and to that extent it would be appropriate to say that she did something that was necessary

---

[7]Hans Conzelmann (s.v. "χάρις," *TDNT* 9 [1974] 392 n. 148, 393) argues that Luke 1:30 interprets 1:28 and that χαριτόω therefore means "to show grace."

[8]See Conzelmann, "χάρις," 397 n. 198.

[9]Plummer, *Luke*, 22; cf. Brown, *Birth*, 326-27.

if the Christ-event was to take place in salvation history. But at the same time, since she was κεχαριτωμένη, her act of submission, according to the Lucan theology, was made possible by the grace of God she had already received. Probably Luke would have expressed this as a paradox. Mary's response was one hundred percent affected by the grace of God, yet at the same time it was one hundred percent her own act of submission. In this way we can overcome the alternatives, either *sola fide/sola gratia* or synergism.

Of course it is up to Roman Catholic theologians and exegetes to decide whether Graß has presented their position fairly. But as an outsider I wonder whether he has. I have no desire to defend the Roman Catholic dogma of the Immaculate Conception. But if I were Roman Catholic, I would object to Graß' description of that position as a caricature. For it is precisely the Immaculate Conception, properly understood, which rules out any synergistic interpretation of Mary's *fiat*. For the dogma of the Immaculate Conception as defined by Pope Pius IX affirmed that Mary's exemption from original sin was effected as an advance result of Christ's redeeming work. The precise words of the definition are:

> The most blessed Virgin Mary, in the first instant of her conception, by a singular grace and privilege granted by almighty God, in view of the merits of Jesus Christ, the Saviour of the human race, was preserved free from all stain of original sin.[10]

Now this statement is open to several objections. First, it asserts the doctrine of original sin in a form which is not scriptural, and few theologians would want to defend it in that form today. Second, Scripture is completely silent about such an act of God taking place at Mary's conception, although in other instances conception in itself plays an important role in the biblical theology of salvation history as we have seen. Third, the only Lucan examples of the saving benefits of Christ being applied in advance as it were, are those instances where Luke relates how Jesus imparted the remission of sins in response to faith (5:20,24; 7:47-49). But at least one must give the dogma credit for taking seriously the perfect tense of κεχαριτωμένη. For Luke, Mary was what she was at the moment of the annunciation because of a prior

---

[10]William J. Doheny and Joseph P. Kelly, *Papal Documents on Mary* (Milwaukee: Bruce, 1954) 25.

act of God upon her. We have interpreted that act, after the analogy of what Luke says elsewhere in the infancy narratives, as an act of predestination, election and preparation in grace. The trouble with the Immaculate Conception as defined in the dogma is that it goes beyond the range of Lucan theology by defining God's prior action in a way which has no analogy elsewhere in Scripture, and in terms of a non-scriptural doctrine of inherited sin.

In the Anglican tradition, specifically in the *Book of Common Prayer* of 1662 and its descendants in Scotland, Canada, and South Africa, December 8 is marked as the Feast of the Conception, not the Immaculate Conception, of the Blessed Virgin Mary. It has sometimes been thought that this Anglican provision really implies a doctrine of the Immaculate Conception on the ground that there would be no reason for celebrating otherwise.[11] Strangely enough, no one seems to have offered a rationale for celebrating Mary's conception as such. It is hoped that this discussion of these Lucan texts may pave the way for a scriptural understanding of the conception of the Blessed Virgin Mary.

I offer these thoughts to Professor Bo Reicke as a study of an aspect of the *"anawim* piety"[12] which the Lucan theology, especially in the infancy narratives, as also in the opening chapters of Acts, expresses. Professor Reicke has made notable contributions to our understanding of that theology.[13]

---

[11]See Gregory Dix, *The Shape of the Liturgy* (Westminster: Dacre, 1945) 377, 433, 585.

[12]The term is Brown's (see *Birth*, 350-55, 466-68), but it admirably expresses what has been a special concern of Professor Reicke. The "meek ones" or "poor ones" translates *anawim* (עניים).

[13]See among other works his *Diakonie, Festfreude und Zelos, in Verbindung mit der altchristlichen Agapenfeier* (UUÅ 5; Uppsala: Lundequistska; Wiesbaden: Otto Harrassowitz, 1951) esp. chap. 2. It is arguable that the traditions underlying both the Lucan birth stories and those of the primitive church of Jerusalem in the early chapters of Acts come from the same *anawim* circles. See the hints in Brown's discussion of the *anawim* (*Birth*, 350-55, 466-68).

THE MATTHAEAN VERSION
OF THE LORD'S PRAYER (MATT 6:9b-13):
SOME OBSERVATIONS

Birger Gerhardsson

DURING THE SPRING of 1950 Anton Fridrichsen held his next to the last
series of lectures as professor at Uppsala University. The subject was
the Lord's Prayer. I am certain that my old friend Bo Reicke
remembers those fascinating lectures as well as I do and therefore has a
special interest in the exegetical problems associated with this text. In
the pages which follow I will make some observations about the
Matthaean version of the Lord's Prayer, interpreted as a part of the
first gospel.

1. The Context

The place which the Lord's Prayer (Matt 6:9b-13) occupies in its
context is not without significance for the exposition of the prayer in
Matthew. To begin with, the section 6:7-15 has been inserted into an
older context structured in a remarkably strict fashion, though it is
difficult to decide at precisely which stage of a presumably drawn out
redactional process the insertion received its present place. As I have
attempted to demonstrate elsewhere,[1] Matt 6:1-6, 16-21 is a connected
composition made up of:

A. An introductory, summarizing statement (kĕlāl כלל; v 1);
B. Three examples (specifications, pĕrāṭŏt פרטות) following the
same pattern almost verbatim:
    (1) on alms (vv 2-4),

---

[1]Birger Gerhardsson, "Geistiger Opferdienst nach Matth 6,1-6.16-21," *Neues
Testament und Geschichte: Historisches Geschehen und Deutung im Neuen Testa-
ment. Oscar Cullmann zum 70. Geburtstag*, ed. Heinrich Baltensweiler and Bo Reicke
(Zürich: Theologischer Verlag; Tübingen: J. C. B. Mohr, 1972) 69-77, esp. 70-71.

(2) on prayer (vv 5-6),

(3) on fasting (vv 16-18);

C. Concluding admonition in metaphorical language (vv 19-21).

It is *possible* that the conclusion (C) is secondary in relation to the rest of the composition, though I am inclined to doubt this.

If we examine the section which I have here omitted (vv 7-15), we find that it consists of:

A. Introductory admonition (vv 7-9a);

B. The Lord's Prayer (vv 9b-13);

C. A comment on the prayer for forgiveness in v 12 (vv 14-15).

That we are dealing with an interpolation is evident. Four observations lead to this conclusion: (1) With regard to form, this section (vv 7-15) departs from the rigid pattern of the base composition (vv 1-6,16-21); the first two of the symmetrical examples are here separated from the third in an insensible, disturbing manner; (2) Whereas the base composition warns against hypocrisy and exhorts that righteousness be practised in secret, the interpolation (vv 7-15) warns against verbosity (vv 7-9) and a failure to forgive (vv 14-15); nor does the prayer itself (vv 9b-13) seem to be primarily conceived as an individual's prayer in his private room; (3) "The hypocrites", i.e. the Pharisees and scribes, are mentioned as a contrasting background in the base composition, "the heathen" in the interpolation; (4) In the base composition, prayer is classed as a "righteous deed" (v 1), i.e. a *geistiger Opferdienst*, which will receive its "recompense" and "reward" from God (ἀποδιδόναι, vv 4,6,18, corresponding with μισθός, vv 1,2,5,16). In the interpolation, on the other hand, prayer is petition—prayer for "what we need" (v 8)— which is "heard" by God (εἰσακούσθαι, v 7).

For these reasons it seems beyond dispute that the immediate context for the Lord's Prayer in the gospel of Matthew can be limited to vv 7-9a, 14-15.

For the interpretation of the prayer this is significant in the following ways. The immediate context of the Lord's Prayer in Matthew's version emphasizes that this prayer, which, according to him, comes from Jesus, is in the first place presented as a succinct prayer to that heavenly Father who already knows what his children need (v 8) and as a contrast to the babbling prolixity of heathen prayers (βατταλογεῖν, πολυλογία, v 7). Further, a particular weight is given to the petition for forgiveness—only those who themselves forgive will be forgiven by God (vv 14-15; cf. 18:21-35).

When the section vv 7-15 was attached to the base composition (vv 1-6, 16-21), the Lord's Prayer was formally subordinated to the main . theme governing this composition, viz. that our good deeds are not to be performed ostentatiously before men but as discreetly as possible. It is, however, worth pointing out that no *formulation* in the inserted section suggests that the primary thought of the base composition has been deliberately worked into the interpolated part. We can only observe that a short, didactic section on prayer (vv 7-15) has been loosely attached to one element of the base composition, namely, that which treated proper prayer (vv 5-6).

Thematic connections with vv 7-15 can also be found in what remains of chap. 6, specifically, in the composition in vv 24-34.

2. The Structure of the Prayer

The Matthaean version of the Lord's Prayer has a clear, artistic structure:

A. Invocation (v 9b);
B. "Thou-petitions" (vv 9c-10);
C. "We-petitions" (vv 11-13).

There are three "we-petitions," each quite independent of the others with regard to content; their independence is reflected as well by their form and the conspicuous connective καί. The third "we-petition" has both a negative and a positive element: "Lead us not into . . . but deliver us from " (μή. . . ἀλλά).

By way of contrast, the "thou-petitions" are distinguished from each other neither by form nor by content. Formally, we observe that they are attached to each other without καί (asyndeton) and that they are formulated with perfect symmetry—they are all in the third person and have the same number of words, same parts of speech, same word order, and the same rhythm (if we disregard the addition at the end of the petition regarding the divine will). As far as content is concerned, it is obvious that we are dealing with three aspects of the same subject: God's final redemptive act. It is surely more appropriate to understand the "thou-petitions" as one prayer in a three-part *parallelismus membrorum* than as three separate petitions.

With most exegetes, I regard the shorter Lukan form of the Lord's Prayer (Luke 11:2b-4) as more original, with regard to the extent of the prayer, than the Matthaean.[2] On the other hand, Matthew seems throughout to have better preserved the wording of the prayer than Luke in the parts which they have in common. With any degree of probability we can attribute only three additions to the Matthaean tradition (at the close of the invocation, at the close of the "thou-petitions" and at the close of the "we-petitions").[3] The result is the fine poetic form of the Matthaean version: two strophes, each with five *stichoi*.[4] As is his custom, "Matthew" has reworked the structure of a text which he has taken over into a stricter, more artistic form. Still, the basic structure of the two versions is the same.

3. The "Thou-Petitions"

The first section of the petitions in the Lord's Prayer can be characterized with the help of a well-known rabbinic formulation. However, before such characterization we should indicate how the petitions regarding the name of God, his reign and his will are to be understood. Since the prayer has been the subject of exceptionally penetrating analyses and debates,[5] a summary treatment should suffice.

It is clear enough that the "thou-petitions" of the Lord's Prayer speak of what *God* is to do, in spite of the fact that the imperatives are in the third person: ἁγιασθήτω, ἐλθέτω, γενηθήτω. It is clear as well

---

[2]For a different view (that the Matthaean version is more original), see Jean Carmignac, *Recherches sur le "Notre Père"* (Paris: Letouzey & Ané, 1969) 18-28.

[3]Joachim Jeremias, *The Lord's Prayer* (FBBS 8; Philadelphia: Fortress, 1964) 10-15 (= Jeremias, *Abba: Studien zur neutestamentlichen Theologie und Zeitgeschichte* [Göttingen: Vandenhoeck & Ruprecht, 1966] 157-60).

[4]See Carmignac (*Recherches*, 383-86), although he regards the Matthaean version as primary.

[5]Carmignac (*Recherches*) provides a detailed survey of the debate over the most important questions regarding the interpretation of the Lord's Prayer, as well as an unusually extensive bibliography (469-553).

that all three refer to the final, eschatological act of redemption. The imperatives are in the aorist tense, and the simple fact that in naive petitions for God's resolute intervention the aorist is the natural tense (witnessed e.g. by the Psalms [LXX]) has been too little observed in recent debate. Still, even if we allow this consideration its full weight, the conclusion is unavoidable that these three petitions speak of God's *final* intervention.

A suitable starting point is the petition in which this is most apparent: the prayer that God's reign may come. Such a petition in the aorist tense can scarcely refer to anything other than the final establishment of God's reign "in power" (cf. Mark 9:1). The Old Testament complex of motifs by which God "arises," "comes," "becomes king," etc. has here received that eschatological focus which we recognize from other texts in the gospels and Jewish documents from approximately the same period.[6] The meaning is not that a "Kingdom" is to be transferred to this earth, but that the living God is to assume power in a decisive way.

This petition is enclosed by the petitions regarding God's name and will. The perfect formal symmetry and the connection by asyndeton make it natural to understand these petitions as parallel to the one for God's reign. Quite rightly, interpreters have pointed to the Old Testament motif that God "sanctifies himself" by appearing in glory and demonstrating that he is God: in mighty works of redemption (delivering, gathering, feeding, etc.) or judgment (punishing, crushing, burning up, etc.). This motif is specially prominent in the prophetic predictions of Ezekiel: God will "sanctify himself" by redeeming and judging. And, in one of these texts (Ezek 36:23), "sanctify my name" is parallel to the usual "sanctify myself." With this background, it is natural to interpret the prayer regarding the divine name as parallel to the petition for the divine reign: God is to sanctify his name by saving and judging, thus demonstrating once and for all that he is God.[7] The

---

[6]This is especially clear when one observes how *Tg. Jonathan* renders such texts as Isa 24:23; 31:4-5; 40:9; 52:7 and Mic 4:7. This point is well brought out in Pierre Bonnard, Jacques Dupont, Raymond François Refoulé, *Notre père qui es aux cieux, la prière oecuménique* (Cahiers de la traduction oecuménique de la Bible 3; Paris: Éditions du Cerf, les Bergers et les mages, 1968) 85-89.

[7]Lev 10:1-3; Num 20:13; Ezek 20:41; 28:22,25; 36:23; 38:16,23; 39:27; Sir 33:4. Anton Fridrichsen ("Helliget vorde dit navn!," *DTT* 8 [1917] 1-16) argues this point

contexts in Ezekiel make clear that this is not conceived as an isolated show of strength forcing divine sovereignty on men in an authoritarian fashion; rather, that which takes place includes at the same time an inner transformation of God's people: their hearts are to be exchanged, their breasts filled with the spirit of God (esp. Ezek 36:22-32).[8]

The petition regarding the will of God is also parallel in form and in the aorist tense. God's final intervention—the realization of the divine purpose, the plan of salvation (τὸ θέλημα, הרצון)—appears to be the reference here as well. The parallelism with the previous petitions is made clearer by the addition "as in heaven, so also on earth." Without this addition, the petition is capable of a more varied usage (cf. Matt 26:42; Acts 21:14).

From the time of the early church (Origen) many interpreters have maintained that the words "as in heaven, so also on earth" are to be connected not only to the petition on the realization of the divine will, but also to the two earlier petitions.[9] The addition would thus be at the same time a conclusion to the final element and a conclusion to the whole first section of the prayer, a general rounding off of this section.[10] It is tempting to believe that the sophisticated "Matthew" conceived the matter so. True, the connection between the final words and the wording in the petition on God's reign is somewhat forced, but this in itself is not very important—the text of the first two petitions was already fixed, and the evangelist did not tamper with it. Still, even if Matthew intended the text in this way, it could hardly have been so understood in practical use. The simple fact is that this sense is difficult to convey when the prayer is recited.[11]

If it is true that the three elements of the first section of the Lord's Prayer are to be understood as petitions for God's intervention, why is this not stated in a straightforward manner, like the prayers in the "we-petitions" which follow? It is certainly conceivable that the matter

---

convincingly on the basis of analyses in his work *Hagios-Qadoš: Ein Beitrag zu den Vorun-tersuchungen zur christlichen Begriffsgeschichte* (Videnskapsselskapets, Oslo, Skrifter II; Hist.-Filos. Klasse, 1916, no. 3; Kristiania: Jacob Dybwad, 1916).

[8]This is rightly stressed in Bonnard, Dupont, Refoulé, *Notre père*, 82-85, 93-96.

[9]Carmignac, *Recherches*, 110-17.

[10]Cf. e.g., how Matt 5:17-48 ("antitheses") ends with a statement (v 48) which summarizes both the final section (vv 43-48) and the whole composition (vv 17-48).

[11]I thank Harald Riesenfeld for a stimulating correspondence on this point.

could have been expressed: ἁγίασον τὸ ὄνομά σου, [12] ἀνάστησον τὴν βασιλείαν σου, ποίησον τὸ θέλημά σου.[13] The answer is well known. At stake here are God's own central concerns; at such times, a religious discretion was felt to be necessary. One must not adopt the role of God's counsellor! A reverential circumlocution was employed when such requests were to be made known before God. This is certainly the primary explanation. But a secondary consideration seems justified as well. If the requests regarding the name of God, his reign and his will had been expressed with active imperatives, the formulations might have invited an authoritarian interpretation of God's intervention. It would have appeared as though God alone was to act. With the circumlocutory third person imperatives it is easier to combine the fact that God's mighty works in sanctifying his name, establishing his reign, and realizing his final redemptive purposes demand a suitable human response: with open hearts men in turn are to sanctify God's name in cult and other service, to be loyal supporters of God's sovereignty, and to conform to his plans and will. The form of the "thou-petitions" is thus an appropriate one.

Still, if these three petitions are so similar in effect, are not two of them superfluous? Has not the principle of avoiding verbosity (vv 7-8) been forgotten in the Matthaean expansion of the Lord's Prayer? The objection is not, I think, entirely unjustified. The third element—that concerning the divine will—adds little to what has been said in the previous two (cf. Luke 11:2). It is not the case, however, that the three elements are completely synonymous. Primitive Christianity had vivid pictures of heavenly things and the events of the end times. Three different aspects of the eschatological chain of events were thus actualized when one spoke of the sanctifying of God's name, the coming of his reign, and the realization of his will. The three elements complement each other. And, in any case, every comparison with other prayers shows that the "thou-petitions" of the Lord's Prayer are strikingly concise.

---

[12]Cf. the partly synonymous phrase δόξασόν σου τὸ ὄνομα (John 12:28). Note how "to make holy" and "to glorify" are parallel with each other in e.g. Lev 10:3.

[13]Even the rabbis, who in such cases preferred to express themselves with reverential circumlocutions, could at times express the matter directly in prayer: "Carry out (do, עשה) your will in heaven" (Eliezer ben Hyrcanus, *t. Ber.* 3.11 (Zuck. 7), *b. Ber.* 29b).

How is one to characterize in summary form the "thou-petitions" of the Lord's Prayer? I suspect that the scribe Matthew would reply that one must first of all *take the yoke of the reign of heaven upon oneself.*" Before the followers of Jesus pray for their most pressing personal needs they are to open their minds to the great perspective, to express their uncompromised solidarity with God and his cause by *praying* for the final sanctifying of the divine name, the coming of the reign of heaven on earth and the definitive realization of the divine purposes.

I might add parenthetically that I do not believe that the Jewish Christians of the Matthaean tradition ended their practice of reciting *Shema‘* evening and morning at a specially early period.[14] But when they did so, the Lord's Prayer—which probably had replaced Tephillah from the very beginning—was able to take over the role which Shema‘ had previously played. This was possible because the prayer which came from Jesus, particularly in its Matthaean form, so clearly placed the one who prayed under "the yoke of the reign of heaven." Moreover, πολυλογία was avoided by this concentration on a single basic text of prayer.

4. The "We-Petitions"

In this century many interpreters have been inclined to interpret the Lord's Prayer in its entirety—including the "we-petitions"—in a final, eschatological sense, as "a prayer for the Kingdom."[15] The various elements in the prayer invite such an interpretation in varying degrees. It is tempting to understand the petition for bread as a request to partake already today in the Heavenly banquet (cf. "sit at table with

---

[14]I do not share Jeremias's conviction (*Abba*, 78-80) that from the variation with which Deut 6:4-5 is cited in the New Testament one can draw the conclusion that, after the fall of the Temple, Shema‘ was no longer recited in the Greek-speaking part of the church.

[15]Krister Stendahl, "Matthew," *Peake's Commentary on the Bible* (London: Thomas Nelson and Sons, 1962) 779: "Thus the prayer in its Matthaean form is a prayer for the Kingdom, an expanded *Maranatha.*" Cf. Raymond E. Brown, "The Pater Noster as an Eschatological Prayer," *New Testament Essays* (Impact Books; Milwaukee: Bruce; London/Dublin: Geoffrey Chapman, 1965) 217-53; Bent Wenzel Noack, *Om Fadervor* (København: Gad, 1969). For recent literature, see Anton Vögtle, "Der 'eschatologische' Bezug der Wir-bitten des Vaterunsers," *Jesus und Paulus. Festschrift für Werner Georg Kümmel zum 70. Geburtstag,* ed. E. Earle Ellis and Erich Gräßer, 2nd ed. (Göttingen: Vandenhoeck & Ruprecht, 1978) 344-62.

Abraham, Isaac, and Jacob," Matt 8:11; "eat bread in the Kingdom of God," Luke 14:15). It is also tempting to take the prayer for forgiveness as a request to be acquitted at the judgment and the concluding double prayer to be spared and delivered as a request to escape the great tribulation which immediately precedes the judgment.

But even if the eschatological perspective is apparent in the Lord's Prayer, the prayer in its entirety is not conceived as a "prayer for the Kingdom." As far as the "we-petitions" are concerned—petitions which explicitly speak of "us"—the immediate context provides a sound reminder that the Lord's Prayer is formulated for people living on earth with elementary needs which must be mentioned before God. The "we-petitions" are concerned with "what we need" (cf. v 8), and that here and now (cf. "today" in the prayer for bread). It seems most natural to understand the "we-petitions" as prayers for simple human needs which the people of God have always had but which, in the eschatological situation, have certainly become more acute.[16]

Even when the reign of God has drawn nigh, the people of God need daily food. It is particularly appropriate that one pray for nourishment, simply and straightforwardly, in the classical biblical assurance that the heavenly Father gives "bread" to his people.[17] I do not intend to discuss here the well-known alternatives concerning the understanding of ἄρτος ἐπιούσιος.[18] Still, it at least seems to be clear that the petition refers to food needed in order to live, earthly bread, though of course it is seen as a divine gift and a blessing from heaven.

The prayer for forgiveness can hardly refer to acquittal at the last judgment. God's people need forgiveness today as well. Significantly, the duty to forgive is an obligation which applies now (cf. Matt 5:23-26; 18:21-35). The connection which is drawn between forgiveness and

---

[16]This must have been particularly true of the original circle of disciples surrounding Jesus, living "from hand to mouth," but even in the Matthaean church it must have been impossible to escape these elementary needs. Heinz Schürmann (*Das Gebet des Herrn aus der Verkündigung Jesu*, 3rd ed. [Freiburg im Breisgau: Herder, 1965]) gives attention in a convincing way even to the question what the Lord's Prayer meant when it was first prayed by the circle of disciples surrounding the earthly Jesus.

[17]See Ernst Lohmeyer, *Das Vater-unser*, 3rd ed. (Zürich: Zwingli, 1952) 92-110.

[18]Carmignac, *Recherches*, 118-221. Research does not seem to have made much progress in this question since Anton Fridrichsen wrote his instructive survey of interpretations half a century ago ("ΑΡΤΟΣ ΕΠΙΟΥΣΙΟΣ" [SO 2; Oslo: Some & Co., 1924] 31-41; [SO 9; 1930] 62-68).

healing (cf. esp. Matt 9:1-8) makes it not at all unlikely that the petition for forgiveness has a reference beyond that which the wording itself immediately suggests. It is presumably a prayer for the congregation's—and the individual's—spiritual and physical *health*. The prayer for forgiveness refers certainly not only to the soul's, but also to the body's well-being.

The petition that one not be led into temptation cannot be a request that one not be enticed to sin. Nowhere in the Bible do we find the thought that God "tempts" in the sense "entices to sin." On the other hand, it is a classical view in scripture that God "tempts" in the sense "puts to the test" (or permits Satan to do so) and that such a trial can even result in man's fall (cf. Israel in the wilderness).[19] In the Lord's Prayer, the people of God request that they may be spared from tempting of this kind which can thus lead to apostasy and the loss of one's share in the coming reign of God. For, even if the spirit is willing, human flesh is weak (cf. Matt 26:41). The primary—though scarcely the exclusive—reference is certainly to "tribulation and persecution for the sake of the Word" (cf. Matt 13:21; the Lukan parallel has πειρασ-μός, 8:13). We have, in the Gethsemane narrative, an illuminating example of what is meant by "being led into temptation" or "coming into temptation," i.e. into a situation where one, because of the weakness of the flesh, can stumble and fall away (Matt 26:31-56).[20] The word πειρασμός in the Lord's Prayer is without an article. This indicates that we do not have here a direct reference to "the great tribulation" (cf. Matthew 24), conceived as a single, eschatological event. Trials in a more general sense are certainly meant, though of course these are thought to be especially severe in the last days which have already begun. God's people cannot avoid "the great tribulation" as such; it may be "shortened" (Matt 24:22), but it must be undergone and endured. Perhaps one might say that God's people according to the Lord's Prayer are to pray that they may escape trials too great to be borne within the framework of the eschatological sufferings (cf. 1 Cor 10:13).

---

[19]See Birger Gerhardsson, *The Testing of God's Son (Matt 4:1-11 & Par): An Analysis of an Early Christian Midrash* (ConB, New Testament Series 2/1; Lund: C. W. K. Gleerup, 1966) esp. 25-35.

[20]I do not find Carmignac's interpretation of this prayer (*Recherches*, 236-304) convincing.

The final double petition is not in fact a prayer that one may pass through and endure testing, but that one may be spared such testing. One desires that one not be *led into* temptation (μὴ εἰσενέγκῃς. . .εἰς) but be *saved from* the evil one/what is evil (notice ῥῦσαι . . . ἀπό, not ἐκ). [21] The latter phrase adds of course little to the former, though it may have a somewhat broader sphere of reference.[22] The familiar question whether τοῦ πονηροῦ is to be understood as masculine or neuter is difficult to answer with any degree of probability;[23] the choice is, however, of little significance. If the word is masculine, it clearly refers to "the Evil One" in his capacity as "tester" (ὁ πειράζων, with the same shade of meaning as in Matt 4:3). If neuter, the word refers to the evil lot—primarily tribulations and persecutions—with which Satan tests the people of God in order to cause them to fall.

5. The Invocation

That the brief invocation "Father" (πάτερ) found in the Lukan version of the Lord's Prayer (Luke 11:2) must be considered original is, I think, inescapable.[24] "Our Father in heaven" seems to be an expansion which took place within the Matthaean tradition; a liturgical formula already in use in the synagogue has been taken over. The phrase "the heavenly Father"—in slightly varying forms—is characteristic of the Matthaean tradition, occurring twenty times in Matthew. By way of contrast, there are no exact parallels in Luke (cf., however,

---

[21]See especially Frederic Henry Chase, *The Lord's Prayer in the Early Church* (TextsS 1/3; Cambridge: At the University Press, 1891; repr. Nendeln, Liechtenstein: Kraus, 1967) 71-167. To me, however, Chase seems to weaken the distinction between ἀπό and ἐκ more than the examples cited allow.

[22]Noack, *Om Fadervor*, 96-111.

[23]See Gustaf Dalman, *Die Worte Jesu: mit Berücksichtigung des nachkanonischen jüdischen Schrifttums und der aramäischen Sprache*, Band 1: *Einleitung und wichtige Begriffe*, 2nd ed. with Appendix, A: Das Vaterunser, B: Nachträge und Berichtigungen (Leipzig: J. C. Hinrichs'sche Buchhandlung, 1930; repr. Darmstadt: Wissenschaftliche Buchgesellschaft, 1965), 1:347-60.

[24]For the view that the Matthaean form is original, see Witold Marchel, *Abba, Père: La prière du Christ et des chrétiens; étude exégétique sur les origines et la signification de l'invocation à la divinité comme père, avant et dans le Nouveau Testament*, new edition (AnBib 19A; Rome: Pontifical Biblical Institute, 1971) 179-97 and Carmignac, *Recherches*, 74-77.

11:13), and only one in Mark (11:25)[25]—and the reading there is disputed.[26]

Even if the Matthaean invocation is more ceremonious than the Lukan, it too is an intimate way of addressing God. In Christian exegesis of our times, it is not uncommon that the personal character of the invocation is one-sidedly stressed, suggesting a contrast with the same invocation in Jewish prayers. But this is not correct. In Jewish texts as well "the heavenly Father" strikes a warm, intimate note. Nor is it justified to draw a clear distinction between the invocation of the Lord's Prayer and the usual Jewish "Our Father, our King"(אבינו מלכנו), though such a distinction has also been suggested. Even in the Lord's Prayer God is approached with reverence. He is not only Father, but King and God as well—immediately after the invocation the petition is voiced that his divine name will be sanctified, that his heavenly reign will be established and that his royal will will be realized on earth. Thus, in the Lord's Prayer as well, God is "our Father, our King."[27]

Those who pray in this way will enjoy the status of "sons of the heavenly Father" (cf. 5:45), "sons of the reign [of Heaven]" (cf. 13:38). They turn to the heavenly Father with naive, straightforward requests that he give them food and forgiveness, that he spare and deliver them. These prayers build on the unexpressed conviction that God indeed has power, dominion, and glory, so that it is meaningful to come to him with requests.[28]

6. Some Characteristics of the Lord's Prayer

The petitions of the Lord's Prayer are pure requests. The one who prays is no modern man "come of age," who thinks he needs only divine encouragement and support for what he does. Nor do we even find petitions of the type, "Help us to be this or that, or to do this or that!" The Lord's Prayer presupposes an absolute dependence on God and contains only requests that God will act. The duties of the people

---

[25]Jeremias, *Abba*, 33-35.

[26]Krister Stendahl, "Prayer and Forgiveness," *SEÅ* 22 (1957/58) 75-88, esp. 76-77.

[27]Cf. Jesus' invocation in Matt 11:25: "Father, Lord of the heaven and of the earth."

[28]Since the concluding doxology (Matt 6:13c) is a secondary addition, I shall not discuss it.

3

of God—to do God's will and represent his cause in the world—are not taken up in the prayer. This is a pure prayer with no place for indirect teaching or exhortation. At a single point—the addition to the prayer for forgiveness (v 12b)—the boundary between God's action and our responsibilities might be thought to be blurred. This addition, however, is not really didactic in character but has the form of a declaration about what we already have done. First with the commentary which follows the prayer (vv 14-15) are the didactic implications drawn.

The "we" who pray are the "sons of the heavenly Father," "the sons of the reign (of heaven)"; but no delimitation is expressed. No formulation invites a nationalistic or narrow group-egoistic perspective. It is, however, interesting to note that the Lord's Prayer contains no concrete petition for fellowmen in need. There are "thou-petitions" and "we-petitions," but no "they-petitions." Care for one's fellowman seems to be absorbed in the great three-part request for the dawning of God's reign. One prays, not that patches may be sown on the worn-out clothing of this world, but that God may make all things new.

It has at times been said that the Lord's Prayer is structured according to the principle given in the logion "Seek first God's reign and his righteousness, and all these other things will be given you as well" (6:33). This is not the case. True, the structure of the Lord's Prayer corresponds perfectly with the first part of the logion: God's reign and righteousness are indeed the primary concern. But the second part of the prayer does not correspond with the second part of the logion. In the latter, "all these other things" refer primarily to food, drink and clothing (cf. vv 25-32); care for such things is pushed into the background. The thought seems to be that the heavenly Father will see to it in his own way that the needs of the children he loves on earth are met. On the other hand, in the Lord's Prayer certain elementary needs are singled out and explicitly taken up in direct prayer: food and forgiveness, sparing and deliverance. Hence the logion in 6:33 and the Lord's Prayer in 6:9b-13 do not follow exactly the same pattern.

What, then, can be said about these needs which are regarded as so basic that they are included in the brief, daily prayer? We note, first, that none of the petitions concern earthly favors which must be received at the expense of other men; there is no request that "we" might receive power among men, or external possessions, i.e. such things as come under the label *mammona'* (ממונא). This accords with the sometimes negative, sometimes disinterested attitude towards earthly power and property which the Jesus-tradition expresses. Instead the whole first part of the prayer speaks of God's power and glory. As far as the "we-petitions" are concerned, concentration is fixed on the man within the clothes, if the expression may be permitted, on the one who, with body and soul but not with external goods, may enter the Kingdom of God. This concentration also is typical of the Jesus-tradition. The concluding double petition expresses the watch-fulness on which the Jesus-tradition so often insists. Those who pray request that they may be spared the testing they may not be able to bear, that they may be able to stand "on that day" and enter the Kingdom: preserve us in body and soul and save us from a trial so severe that it might cause us to fall! These are the personal needs with which, according to Matthew, the people of God are to concern themselves in their daily prayer, at the same time as they serve their heavenly Father and await the dawning of his reign.

RECHTFERTIGUNG DES EINZELNEN— RECHTFERTIGUNG DER WELT: NEUTESTAMENTLICHE ERWÄGUNGEN

Erich Gräßer

1.

CHRISTLICHES VERSTÄNDIS läßt Gott definiert sein als τὸν δικαιοῦντα τὸν ἀσεβῆ (Röm 4,5).[1] Mit diesem Prädikat ist das unterscheidend Christliche des neutestamentlichen Gottesverständnisses gegenüber allen anderen möglichen Gottesverständnissen festgehalten. Es ist unstreitig, daß dieser so prädizierte Gott den Menschen rechtfertigt gemäß dem theologisch-anthropologischen Fundamentalsatz: ὁ θεὸς ἀληθής, πᾶς δὲ ἄνθρωπος ψεύστης (Röm 3,4). Demnach erscheint der je einzelne Mensch vor Gottes Augen nie anders denn als "Lügner". Und der je einzelne Mensch ist es, der im Urteil Gottes als der gerechtfertigte Gottlose vor ihm leben darf—in der *communio sanctorum*, von der er sich nicht trennen kann, wie wir noch sehen werden. Das Sündersein und das Gottlossein sind dabei mit keiner moralischen Kategorie angemessen zu umschreiben. *Gottlos* "ist das Prädikat dessen, der es radikal mit seinem Schöpfer zu tun bekommt und erfährt, daß er in der Gnade neu geschaffen werden muß. Er hat nichts, worauf er sich berufen könnte, und will nichts vorweisen, was Gottes Schöpfertat beeinträchtigen würde. Er ist der Mensch ohne Ruhm bei Gott".[2]

Dieses Rechtfertigungshandeln am Gottlosen, das nicht einen Grenzfall, sondern die Wahrheit des christlichen Glaubens schlechthin

---

[1]Vgl. Ernst Käsemann, *An die Römer* (HNT 8a; Tübingen: J. C. B. Mohr, 1973) 104: "Man hat zu beachten, daß die Formel liturgischen Gottesprädikationen nachgebildet ist und folglich das göttliche Handeln grundsätzlich charakterisiert".

[2]Käsemann, *An die Römer*, 104-5.

meint,[3] bedeutet eine eminente Individualisierung des einzelnen vor Gott. Nach Metz kann sie "als Grundpointe der neutestamentlichen Botschaft" betrachtet werden.[4] Ihre Legitimität ist unstreitig, und zwar wegen des ihr zugrundeliegenden Verständnisses vom Menschen als Sünder und vom Heil als Empfang der Gnade. Beides ist auf ein ἐγώ bezogen. Und in der Tat kann die in diesem Verständnis erschlossene Bedeutung des individuellen Lebens nur aufgehoben werden um den Preis der Sache selber, das ist das Verständnis des Menschen als des gerechtfertigten Sünders.[5] Das ist unstrittig.

Strittig ist allein, ob und wie der einzelne theologisch legitim den Kollektiven gegenüberzustellen ist. Geführt wird dieser Streit besonders in der Diskussion um die politische Theologie. Ihr gilt es als ausgemacht, daß vor allem durch den existential-analytischen Ansatz Bultmanns die Parole der bürgerlichen Welt des neunzehnten Jahrhunderts, wonach Religion Privatsache ist (also Trennung von Religion und Politik), neu in der Theologie aufgelegt worden sei.[6] Die Stimmungslage in dieser Hinsicht gibt Metz für alle so wieder:

> Es ist bekannt, daß die Evangelien keine Biographie Jesu im geläufigen Sinne bieten wollen. Die Nachrichten über Jesus gehören nicht in die Gattung der biographischen Privataussagen, sondern in die Gattung der öffentlichen Proklamation. Die exegetischen Arbeiten der sogenannten 'Formgeschichte' haben die Evangelien selbst als vielschichtigen Verkündigungstext erwiesen. Ich sehe nun ein gewisses Verhängnis darin, daß diese Einsichten und Entdeckungen der Formgeschichte sofort mit den Kategorien des theologischen Existentialismus und Personalismus ausgelegt wurden. Dadurch wurde nämlich das Verständnis der Verkündigung von vornherein privatisiert und gewissermaßen existentiell intimisiert. Das Wort der Verkündigung wurde verstanden als reines Anredewort, als Wort der personalen Selbstmitteilung Gottes, nicht aber als Wort einer gesellschaftsbezogenen Verheißung. Die Hermeneutik der existentialen Interpretation des Neuen Testaments bewegt

---

[3]Adolf Schlatter, *Gottes Gerechtigkeit: ein Kommentar zum Römerbrief*, 4th ed. (Stuttgart: Calwer, 1965) 162; Käsemann, *An die Römer*, 104.

[4]Johann Baptist Metz, *Zur Theologie der Welt* (Mainz: Matthias-Grünewald; München: Chr. Kaiser, 1968) 102.

[5]Dorothee Sölle, *Politische Theologie: Auseinandersetzung mit Rudolf Bultmann* (Stuttgart: Kreuz, 1971) 57.

[6]Jürgen Moltmann, *Perspektiven der Theologie: Gesammelte Aufsätze* (München: Chr. Kaiser, 1968) 132-35; vgl. auch Sölle, *Theologie*, 56. Zur Discussion vgl. Günter Klein, "Rudolf Bultmann—Ein Lehrer der Kirche: Zum 90. Geburtstag des Marburger Theologen", *Deutsches Pfarrerblatt* 74 (1974) 614-19; Erich Gräßer, "Jesus und das Heil Gottes: Bemerkungen zur sogenannten 'Individualisierung des Heils' ", in *Jesus Christus in Historie und Theologie: Neutestamentliche Festschrift für Hans Conzelmann zum 60. Geburtstag*, ed. Georg Strecker (Tübingen: J. C. B. Mohr, 1975) 167-84.

sich im Zirkel des privaten Ich-Du-Verhältnisses. Hier scheint deshalb eine kritische Entprivatisierung des Verständnisses der Grundlagen unserer Theologie vonnöten. *Diese Entprivatisierung ist die primäre theologiekritische Aufgabe der politischen Theologie.* Sie scheint mir in einem gewissen Sinne ebenso wichtig zu sein wie das Programm der Entmythologisierung.[7]

Wie weit und in welchem Sinne ist diese Aufgabe notwendig? Ist die Alternative "Gnade für die Welt"—"Gnade für die einzelnen" überhaupt eine dem theologischen Sachverhalt angemessene Alternative?[8] Kann das Heil Gottes für die Welt—mit Wilckens gesprochen: die "Heilstat der Gerechtigkeit Gottes als Heilskraft seiner Liebe", die bewirkt, "daß *alle* frei sind von *aller* Realität des Bösen, sofern sie nur dieser Liebe Gottes vollauf vertrauen"[9]—kann sie grundsätzlich anders als personalistisch beschrieben, verstanden und zur Geltung gebracht werden? Personalistisch heißt: als Relation Gott-Einzelner. Daß das diese Relation begründende Heilstun Gottes einen unverkennbaren universalistischen Zug hat (die Sünde der gesamten Menschheit wird im Tode Christi als Sühnetat seiner Liebe aufgehoben), ist ebenso unstreitig wie das andere, daß das darin gegründete neue Existenzverständnis einen eminenten Weltbezug hat. Aber *beides* ist nur zu begreifen und zu bekennen aus der Erkenntnis heraus, daß Christus *mich* geliebt und sich für *mich* hingegeben hat,[10] also in existentieller Betroffenheit als *Glaubender.* Die *hier* ansetzende existential analytische Hermeneutik, die Theologie als Anthropologie darstellt, deckt also den "Weltbezug" des Evangeliums von Gottes Handeln nicht *zu*, sondern *auf*, indem sie die überindividuellen Determinanten von Sünde und Heil allererst freilegt (Röm 5,12-21 in der Auslegung von Bultmann).[11]

Noch einmal also: In Frage steht die Grund-Struktur des Heilstuns Gottes. Wie stellt sie sich nach dem Zeugnis des Neuen Testaments dar?

---

[7]Metz, *Theologie*, 101.

[8]Cf. Gerhard Gloege, *Gnade für die Welt: Kritik und Krise des Luthertums* (Göttingen: Vandenhoeck & Ruprecht, 1964).

[9]Ulrich Wilckens, "Christologie und Anthropologie im Zusammenhang der paulinischen Rechtfertigungslehre", *ZNW* 67 (1976) 64-82, hier 80.

[10]Wilckens, "Christologie und Anthropologie", 76.

[11]Rudolf Bultmann, "Adam und Christus nach Römer 5", *Exegetica: Aufsätze zur Erforschung des Neuen Testaments* (Tübingen: J. C. B. Mohr, 1967) 424-44.

2

2.1. ÜBERNAHME DES GESCHICHTSBILDES DER APOKALYPTIK

Was den Befund im Neuen Testament anbetrifft, so ist der wichtigste Indikator für das hier gänzlich individualistisch strukturierte Heil die Übernahme des Geschichtsbildes der Apokalyptik. Und zwar gilt das sowohl hinsichtlich der Übernahme als solcher als auch vor allem hinsichtlich der an der Apokalyptik vorgenommenen Modifikationen bei Jesus und Paulus.

Die *Übernahme als solche*, die jetzt nicht begründet werden muß, ist für unseren Zusammenhang darum so wichtig, weil sie anzeigt, daß man das Geschichtsbild nicht von der Geschichte Israels genommen hat, wie sie das Alte Testament erzählt.[12] Damit entfallen das nationale und völkische Motiv. Positiv gewendet: Die vergangene Geschichte ist die Geschichte der Menschheit, die als ganze durch die Sünde bestimmt ist und aus der jeder einzelne nur so gerettet wird, daß er radikale Umkehr leistet. Die Gerichtspredigt des Täufers z.B. zerschlägt die Sicherheit jener, die sich im Verband der Erwählten für das Heil versiegelt wähnen (Lukas 3,8). Kollektive zählen nichts in der Apokalyptik. Was sie vor allem einprägt, ist der Entscheidungscharakter der gegenwärtigen Endzeit.[13] Ihr gegenüber ist der einzelne gefordert—endgültig! Die Gerechten werden leben. Im Blick auf diesen Äon hegen sie schrankenlosen Pessimismus; im Blick auf den kommenden haben sie große Hoffnungen. Mit diesem umfassenden geschichtlichen Dualismus, der dem einzelnen Menschen die Entscheidung zwischen beiden Äonen ermöglicht und abfordert, wie überhaupt mit dem für die Apokalyptik charakteristischen "Geschichtsverlust" hängt es zusammen, daß keine politischen Programme und keine gesellschaftsbezogene Verkündigung entwickelt werden.[14] Es ist am Tage, daß sich diese Linie bis ins Neue Testament hinein fortsetzt, ebenso die gegenüber dem Alten Testament vollzogene universalistische und individualistische Wende zugleich: Israels Geschichte ist

---

[12]Vgl. Rudolf Bultmann, *Geschichte und Eschatologie*, 2nd ed. (Tübingen: J. C. B. Mohr, 1964) 47.

[13]Vgl. Walter Schmithals, *Die Apokalyptik: Einführung und Deutung* (Sammlung Vandenhoeck; Göttingen: Vandenhoeck & Ruprecht, 1973) 31.

[14]Schmithals, *Apokalyptik*, 34.

ein ausgezeichneter Teil der *Weltgeschichte*, nicht die eigentliche Geschichte.[15]

Diesem universalistischen Denken, das nicht mehr primär am Geschick eines Volkes Interesse zeigt, entspricht die in der Apokalyptik zu beobachtende Individualisierung. Wenn die Welt ihr Ziel erreicht, findet der einzelne Mensch zu diesem Ziel. Nicht Heil und Unheil von Völkern, sondern Heil und Unheil der Menschheit als einer Summe von Einzelmenschen bewegt den Apokalyptiker. Das Endgeschick der Welt interessiert ihn im Blick auf das Endgeschick des Einzelnen; Gericht und Gnade treffen nicht Gemeinschaften, sondern jeweils den individuellen Menschen, ihn in die 'massa perditionis' oder in die Schar der auserwählten Gerechten versetzend. Nicht Israel und die Völker, sondern Fromme und Gottlose stehen einander gegenüber. In allem Geschehen sind die einzelnen Menschen unterwegs, sei es auf dem breiten Wege des Todes, sei es auf dem schmalen Pfad des Lebens. Über jeden einzelnen Menschen werden im Himmel Bücher geführt, die am Ziel der Zeit geöffnet werden. Auf einer Waage werden seine guten und seine bösen Werke gegeneinander abgewogen, und jeder einzelne empfängt sein Urteil, das Urteil des Lebens zum Leben oder des Todes zum Tode.[16]

Kurzum: Der einzelne wird mit geschichtlicher Verantwortung in der gegenwärtigen letzten Zeit belastet. *"Alles entscheidet sich jetzt, und an jedem einzelnen liegt es, wie diese Entscheidung ausfällt".*[17]

2.2. DIE MODIFIKATIONEN IM NEUEN TESTAMENT

Diese individualistische Grundtendenz verstärkt sich noch in den neutestamentlichen Modifikationen an der Apokalyptik, und zwar sowohl bei Jesus als auch bei Paulus und im übrigen Neuen Testament.

2.21. *Bei Jesus.* Die von Jesus angesagte Königsherrschaft Gottes "ist primär personal orientiert".[18] Sie hat gerade in ihrer unverwechselbaren Eigenart eine eminent individuierende Tendenz. Man darf als das unterscheidend Jesuanische der Basileia-Predigt die Verknüpfung von Gegenwart und Zukunft in der Person Jesu selbst benennen. Markus 1,15, die sachlich zutreffende Zusammenfassung der Reichspredigt Jesu, zeigt, daß das weltbildlich unausgeglichene Nebeneinander von Gegenwart und Zukunft des Reiches als sachliche Einheit im Verhalten Jesu verstehbar wird, welches als ganzes das Herrwerden Gottes als Heil manifestiert:

---

[15]Schmithals, *Apokalyptik*, 14.
[16]Schmithals, *Apokalyptik*, 14.
[17]Schmithals, *Apokalyptik*, 29.
[18]Leonhard Goppelt, *Theologie des Neuen Testaments*, Teil 1: *Jesu Wirken in seiner theologischen Bedeutung* (Göttingen: Vandenhoeck & Ruprecht, 1975), 96.

Heil (euch) Armen, denn euch gehört die Gottesherrschaft!
Heil (euch), die ihr jetzt hungert, denn ihr werdet
  gesättigt werden!
Heil (euch), die ihr jetzt weint, denn ihr werdet euch
  freuen (Lukas 6,20-21).[19]

Die Gottesherrschaft bei Jesus hat kosmisch-dualistische Struktur: Gottesherrschaft bricht Satansherrschaft (Lukas 11,20-22; Matt 12,28-29; Markus 3,27). Dadurch wird das Jetzt zur Entscheidungszeit für den einzelnen qualifiziert: μετανοεῖτε!

Was verlangt wird, ist nicht *etwas* vom Menschen, sondern er, der Mensch als ganzer, wie der um der Gottesherrschaft willen erfolgende Ruf zur Nachfolge beweist (Lukas 9,61-62; Markus 10,17, 21; Matt 10,38 u.ö.). In die Nachfolge werden nicht Kolonnen berufen, nicht Gruppen und Gemeinschaften. "*Du* aber folge mir nach!" Die "charismatisch-eschatologische Eigenart des Rufes Jesu in die Nachfolge",[20] die keinerlei Widerstände oder Einwände duldet, hat Hengel genauer untersucht mit dem Ergebnis: "Jesu Ruf ergeht im Blick auf die anbrechende Gottesherrschaft, und er stellt den einzelnen Gerufenen—unter bedingungslosem Bruch mit allen Bindungen—hinein in die Lebens- und Schicksalsgemeinschaft mit ihm selbst und damit zugleich in den Dienst für die Sache der Basileia".[21] Berufung und Sendung bilden eine unlösbare Einheit, wie neben anderen Worten besonders das Logion aus der Q-Überlieferung belegt: "Die Ernte ist groß, die Arbeiter sind wenige. Bittet nun den Herrn der Ernte, daß er Arbeiter in seine Ernte sende" (Matt 9,37-38; Lukas 10,2). Auch die Unbedingtheit des Rufes ist evident: "Laß die Toten ihre Toten begraben! Du aber gehe hin und proklamiere die Gottesherrschaft" (Lukas 9,60). Der Radikalismus ist nur verständlich vor dem Hintergrund einer hochgespannten eschatologischen Naherwartung. Weil die nahe Gottesherrschaft den ganzen Menschen beansprucht, muß er ganz frei sein. Auf diesem Hintergrund bekommt dann auch die in Lukas 9,57-58 geforderte Leidensbereitschaft ihren Sinn. Leiden sind unausweichlich, wo die Endzeit in den Wehen liegt.

---

[19]Vgl. Hans Conzelmann, "Reich Gottes: I. Im Judentum und NT", *RGG*, 3rd ed. (Tübingen: J. C. B. Mohr, 1961), 5:915.

[20]Martin Hengel, *Nachfolge und Charisma: Eine exegetisch-religionsgeschichtliche Studie zu Mt 8:21f. und Jesu Ruf in die Nachfolge* (BZNW 34; Berlin: Alfred Töpelmann, 1968) 41.

[21]Hengel, *Nachfolge*, 98.

Geschickt für das Gottesreich ist dann aber nur, wer frei ist von sich selbst. Wer jetzt noch sein Leben gewinnen will, der wird es verlieren. Wer es aber um der Gottesherrschaft willen verliert, der wird es gewinnen.[22] In jedem Falle geht es um eine radikale Entscheidung: entweder ist der Mensch dem Willen Gottes gehorsam und dadurch Teilhaber am Reich Gottes, oder er ist ungehorsam und damit Beförderer der satanischen Herrschaft. Jesu Kritik am Gesetz, am Kult und an den religiösen Observanzen hat den einen Sinn, jedem einzelnen Menschen zu zeigen, was Gott ganz persönlich von ihm will. "Ganz konkret zugreifend, fern aller Kasuistik und Gesetzlichkeit, unkonventionell und treffsicher ruft Jesus den Einzelnen zum *Gehorsam gegen Gott* auf, der das ganze Leben umfassen soll".[23] Ebenso pointiert individualistisch ist die Heilszusage formuliert: "*Dein* Glaube ist groß; *dir* geschehe, wie *du* willst" (Matt 15,28; vgl. Markus 5,34; Matt 9,22 u.ö.).

Wie sehr Jesus auf den "beanspruchten Hörer" und nicht auf den "distanzierten Betrachter" zielt, zeigt vor allem auch die Form seiner Gleichnisse. Beim Gleichnis vom Schatz im Acker und von der Perle (Matt 13,44-46) hat die Forschung verschiedene Pointen benannt: "verzichtende Entsagung"[24]; Jüngerschaft als "Preisgabe des ganzen Lebens und Seins"[25]; der Mensch steht vor dem großen Entweder/Oder[26]; ganzer Einsatz ist gefordert[27]; der Finder braucht sich nicht mehr zu entscheiden. "Die Entscheidung ist schon gefallen. Der Fund hat sie dem Finder abgenommen".[28] In jedem Falle aber ist deutlich: Wer es mit dem Gottesreich zu tun bekommt, erfährt die große Überraschung, die große Freude seines Lebens.[29] Solche "Glückspilze" können viele sein! Die Überraschung aber ist die des je einzelnen.

[22]Erich Gräßer, "Nachfolge und Anfechtung bei den Synoptikern", *Angefochtene Nachfolge: Beiträge zur Theologischen Woche 1972* (Bethel Heft 11; Bethel bei Bielefeld: 1973) 44-57, hier 53.
[23]Hans Küng, *Christ sein* (München: R. Piper, 1974) 235.
[24]Adolf Schlatter, *Der Evangelist Matthäus: sein Sprache, sein Ziel, seine Selbstständigkeit. Ein Kommentar zum ersten Evangelium*, 3rd ed. (Stuttgart: Calwer, 1948) 446.
[25]Julius Schniewind, *Das Evangelium nach Matthäus* (NTD 1; Göttingen: Vandenhoeck & Ruprecht, 1968) 172.
[26]Rudolf Bultmann, "Jesus und Paulus", *Exegetica*, 219-20.
[27]Eta Linnemann, *Gleichnisse Jesu: Einführung und Auslegung*, 6th ed. (Göttingen: Vandenhoeck & Ruprecht, 1975) 103-11, bes. 107.
[28]Eberhard Jüngel, *Paulus und Jesus*, 3rd ed. (Tübingen: J. C. B. Mohr, 1967) 143.
[29]Georg Eichholz, *Gleichnisse der Evangelien* (Neukirchener Verlag, 1971) 115.

Ähnlich die Gleichnisse vom Verlorenen (Matt 18,12-14; Lukas 15,1-7; Lukas 15,8-10, 11-32): Der Vergleichspunkt ist das Wiederfinden, das überschwengliche Freude auslöst. Jesu Verhalten bewahrheitet die Botschaft dieser Gleichnisse.

> Es verschlägt den Atem, wie Jesus, dieser Zimmermann aus Nazareth, Gott in Anspruch nimmt als den, der durch den Menschen betroffen ist in Verlieren und Finden. Wie er ihn in Anspruch nimmt für den gottlosen Menschen: nicht für den Menschen im allgemeinen, der "nun einmal Sünder" ist, sondern für ganz bestimmte Menschen mit solcher Sünde, auf die man mit Fingern zeigen kann, die diese Menschen "ummöglich" macht.[30]

In dieselbe Situation verweist uns das Gleichnis von den Arbeitern im Weinberg (Matt 20,1-16). Jesus demonstriert: die dem einzelnen widerfahrende Güte, Gottes Güte, kann man nicht mißbilligen.[31] Das Gleichnis vom großen Abendmahl (Matt 22,1-14; Lukas 14,15-24) lehrt, für jeden hängt die ganze Zukunft daran, daß er sich *jetzt* zu dem Feste Gottes einladen läßt.[32] Das Gleichnis vom viererlei Acker (Markus 4,1-9, 14-20) sagt: "Wo das 'Wort', das Evangelium von Jesus Christus, gehört und angenommen wird", da ist "das Leben eines Menschen zu dem geworden . . . , was es sein sollte", da bringt es Frucht.[33]

Die Reihe ließe sich mühelos fortsetzen. Überall, wo die Gottesherrschaft als Gleichnis zur Sprache kommt, liegt die Pointe darin, daß der Angeredete *jetzt* mit ihr konfrontiert ist und darin sein Heil erfährt. Damit ist die apokalyptische Wann-Frage grundsätzlich zugespitzt. Aufgliederung der Welt- und Völkergeschichte in Zeitperioden, geschichtliche Durchblicke, Staffelung der Eschata bis zum Telos entfallen. Die Umkehr jedes einzelnen ist unaufschiebbar. Kriterium des zukünftigen Gerichtes ist das gegenwärtige *Verhalten gegenüber* Jesus (Lukas 12,8-9; Matt 10,32-33; vgl. Matt 25,31-46). Und zwar ist der einzelne aufgerufen, für sich zu entscheiden, nicht eine prädestinierte oder determinierte Gruppe oder völkische Gemeinschaft.

2.22. *Für* Jesus offenbart sich Gott nicht mehr in der Volksgeschichte.

---

[30]Linnemann, *Gleichnisse*, 79.
[31]Linnemann, *Gleichnisse*, 87-94, bes. 92.
[32]Linnemann, *Gleichnisse*, 94-103, bes. 96-98.
[33]Linnemann, *Gleichnisse*, 120-25, hier 125.

In der Mitte von Israels Glauben, der die Mitte des Alten Testaments ist, steht der Satz: "Jahwe der Gott Israels, und Israel das Volk Jahves". Und zwar durchaus in der einst von Wellhausen vorgenommenen Zuspitzung: "Die Gottheit hat es nicht mit dem einzelnen Menschen und nicht mit der Welt zu tun, sondern mit einem bestimmten durch das Blut zusammengehaltenen Kreise, mit dem Volk Israel".[34]

Bei dem, was wir die Mitte des Neuen Testaments nennen, der sich dem Sünder gnädig zuwendende Gott, finden wir dies in sein glattes Gegenteil verkehrt: Jesus sagt nicht mehr JHWH, er sage *Abba!* Und dieser Vater hat es insofern mit der Welt zu tun, als er es mit jedem einzelnen Menschen als Sünder zu tun hat. Jesus hat Israels Erwählung selbstverständlich nicht bestritten. Ein Wort wie Matt 19,28; Lukas 22,30 und die Missionsanweisung an die Zwölf, sich auf das jüdische Volk zu beschränken (Matt 10,5-6; vgl. auch Matt 15,24), zeigen, daß er den Tatbestand als solchen nicht antastete. Aber schon die in Matt 19,28 vorgenommene Umkehrung—nicht die Heiden, sondern die Juden sollen gerichtet werden—zeigt die Richtung des neuen Denkens: der einzelne ist durch die Zugehörigkeit zum auserwählten Volk nicht gesichert, sondern gefordert. Wer des Vaters Willen tut, der ist ihm Bruder und Schwester (Markus 3,35). Damit sind *alle* zu Kindern Gottes gerufen. Die Zugehörigkeit zum jüdischen Volk begründet keinen Anspruch. Wer zu den "Gesegneten des Vaters" gehört, denen die Gottesherrschaft von Anbeginn der Welt bereitet ist, zeigt erst der Gerichtstag (Matt 25,31-46). Und einziges Kriterium wird sein, wie sie sich zu Jesu geringsten Brüdern (Matt 25,40) und zu Jesu Wort (Markus 8,38) verhalten haben.

Es hängt mit dem Übernehmen des apokalyptischen Geschichtsdenkens bei Jesus zusammen, daß er sich nicht primär dem religiösen Volksverband, sondern den Sündern zugewiesen weiß. In seine von allen völkisch-nationalen Elementen freie Eschatologie paßt darum auch die Stiftung einer organisierten eschatologischen Gemeinschaft, wie sie in Qumran vorgenommen worden war (vgl. CD 6,19), nicht

---

[34]Julius Wellhausen, "Israelitisch-jüdische Religion", *Die Kultur der Gegenwart* (Berlin/Leipzig: B. G. Teubner, 1905), 1/4:9 (= Julius Wellhausen, *Grundrisse zum Alten Testament* [TB 27; München: Chr. Kaiser, 1965] 74); vgl. dazu Rudolf Smend, *Die Mitte des Alten Testaments* (Theologische Studien 101; Zürich: EVZ, 1970) 56. Das folgende ist z.T. in Anlehnung an meinen Anm. 6 genannten Aufsatz formuliert.

hinein. "Jesus sammelt das Gottesvolk ausschließlich durch seinen Ruf und erwartet die sichtbare Sammlung beim Anbruch des Reiches. Er verweigert das, was in der Sekte von Qumran das konstituierende Element ist: die Erwählten als Gruppe auszusondern und sichtbar darzustellen".[35]

2.23. *Jesus entfaltet das Heil Gottes ohne Rückgriff auf den alttestamentlichen Bundesgedanken.* Das ist um so auffallender, als das Bundesverständnis in seiner Jer 31,31-34 vorliegenden Präformation durchaus integrierender Bestandteil seiner Verkündigung hätte werden können, weil auch bei Jeremia bereits deutliche individualisierende Tendenzen zu verspüren sind. Gottes Gesetz ist ins Herz geschrieben und jeder einzelne kann erkennen, wer Gott ist und was er von ihm fordert. Aber Jesus greift den Begriff "Bund" nicht auf. Er findet sich in der synoptischen Tradition überhaupt nur einmal in Jesu Munde (Markus 14,24; Matt 26,28; Lukas 22,20). Diese einzige Stelle, das Kelchwort der Abendmahlsparadosis also, ist jedoch umstritten, der ursprüngliche Wortlaut nicht mehr herzustellen. Auf keinen Fall läßt sich von dieser einzelnen Stelle her die Annahme rechtfertigen, für Jesus habe die Bundestheologie eine zentrale Bedeutung gehabt.

Diese Bedeutung kommt dem *Reich Gottes* zu. Und mit diesem Begriff wählt Jesus eine dem Bundesbegriff völlig inkongruente Vorstellung. Als Grund vermute ich den folgenden: Der "Bund" bleibt immer unter dem Obergedanken "Gesetz", das auf ständige Interpretation angelegt ist. Dagegen Basileia fällt für Jesus unter den Oberbegriff "Evangelium". Das Gesetz ist durch Jesus "erfüllt", insofern er es als an sich selbst klar herausstellt und es so der *interpretatio continua* entnimmt. "Damit ist freilich eine Individualisierung und Punktualisierung im Verhältnis des Menschen zum Gesetz eingeführt, die mit der nur auf Kollektive passenden heilsgeschichtlichen Terminologie nicht zu greifen ist".[36]

Auch die spätere Urgemeinde hat nicht auf Jer 31,31-34 zurückgegriffen, um das Heilstun Jesu zu charakterisieren. Sie hat dazu Jesaia 61 herangezogen, dessen Grundmotive wir dann in der messianischen Verkündigung und in den Makarismen der Bergpredigt wiederfinden. Der dem Bundesgedanken noch anhaftende Aspekt der Partnerschaft

---

[35]Hans Conzelmann, "Eschatologie: IV. Im Urchristentum", *RGG*, 3rd ed. (Tübingen: J. C. B. Mohr, 1958), 2:668.
[36]Hans Conzelmann, "Fragen an Gerhard von Rad", *EvT* 24 (1964) 113-25, hier 122.

mit Gott, die den Menschen überfordern könnte, ist damit getilgt. Er, der Mensch, darf sich als begnadeter Sünder verstehen und annehmen. Und wieder ist damit die eminent individualistische und keineswegs kollektiv strukturierte Form des Heils evident.

Es darf also festgestellt werden: Mit Jesu Heilsbotschaft findet eine völlige Umgewichtung vom Kollektiv auf den einzelnen statt. Die individualisierende Tendenz ist überall mit Händen zu griefen. Die Präfiguration des alttestamentlich-jüdischen Gottesverhältnisses, konstituiert durch die Relation Jahwe/Volk, Bund, Kult, Tora, verliert ihre normierende Kraft. Jesus greift kritisch durch sie hindurch und hinter sie zurück bis zu der allgemein ausschlaggebenden Grundsituation und -relation "Gott-Einzelner", "Vater-Menschensohn (= Mensch)". "Wie das Reich Gottes durch die Menschwerdung des Gottessohnes erst möglich wurde, so kann die Menschwerdung des Menschen erst durch die Realisierung der Gottesherrschaft erfolgen".[37]

Was den Weltbezug des in so radikaler Vereinzelung vorkommenden Menschen vor Gott anbetrifft, so ist er von Jesus in keiner Weise weggeblendet, wohl aber in eine bezeichnende "Prioritätenfolge"[38] gebracht, nämlich Lukas 12,31: "Trachtet nach seiner (Gottes) Herrschaft, so wird euch solches alles (worum sich nämlich die Menschen durchschnittlicherweise zu sorgen pflegen) dreingegeben werden".[39] Daß solche Vereinzelung im Glauben den welt- und geschichtsweiten Horizont nicht einschränkt, sondern im Gegenteil allererst eröffnet und die Universalität des Heils damit begründet sein läßt, ist jetzt nur zu betonen und nicht weiter auszuführen.[40]

2.24. *Bei Paulus.* Daß Paulus die individualisierende Tendenz eher noch vertieft, haben wir bereits bei seinem Verständnis von der Rechtfertigung gesehen. Er steht auch damit in der Tradition apokalyptischen Geschichtsdenkens. Von hier aus wird noch einmal deutlich, wie stark Paulus die Vorstellung vom Heil am Individuum orientiert

[37]Gerhard Friedrich, *Utopie und Reich Gottes: zur Motivation politischen Verhaltens* (Kleine Vandenhoeck-Reihe 1403; Göttingen: Vandenhoeck & Ruprecht, 1974) 50.

[38]Günter Klein, " 'Reich Gottes' als biblischer Zentralbegriff", *EvT* 30 (1970) 642-70, hier 658.

[39]Günter Klein, " 'Reich Gottes' als biblischer Zentralbegriff", 658.

[40]Vgl. Günther Bornkamm, *Paulus*, 2nd ed. (Urban-Taschenbücher 119; Stuttgart: Kohlhammer, 1970) 155-56; vgl. auch Conzelmann, "Fragen", 125.

232 The New Testament Age

sein läßt. Mit Stuhlmacher gesagt: "Weil der Kampf des Christus um die Welt heute und hier in jedem einzelnen Menschen entschieden wird (vgl. Röm 8,2-11), widmet sich Paulus mit einem im Neuen Testament nur von Jesus vorgezeichneten Ernst dem Thema der Anthropologie und der Menschwerdung des Menschen".[41]

Das apokalyptische Erbe bei Paulus zeigt sich vor allem darin, daß seine *Geschichtsanschauung* ganz von der Eschatologie bestimmt ist. So wenig wie Jesus blickt auch Paulus auf die Geschichte Israels als auf die Volksgeschichte mit ihrem Auf und Ab des Gehorsams und Ungehorsams, der göttlichen Strafe und Vergebung zurück. Vielmehr ist die Geschichte, auf die er zurückblickt, die Geschichte der Menschheit als eine Geschichte der Sünde (Röm 5,12-21). Soweit ist Paulus Apokalyptiker. Aber durch die folgende Modifikation hört er auf, es zu sein: er modifiziert das apokalyptische Geschichtsbild entscheidend dadurch, daß er der Vergangenheit eine *Positivbedeutung* für die Zukunft beimißt, sofern sie die "sachgemäße Vorbereitung auf die Gnade Gottes" ist.[42] Denn die Gnade soll da mächtig werden, wo die Sünde wirksam geworden ist (Röm 5,15-17, 20-21; Gal 3,19-23). Das aber besagt mit Bultmann:

> Paulus hat das Geschichtsbild der Apokalyptik *von seiner Anthropologie her interpretiert*: Die Tatsache, daß der Mensch nur von der Gnade Gottes leben kann, daß Gnade als Gnade nur von dem Menschen empfangen wird, der vor Gott zunichte geworden ist, und daß die Sünde, in der der Mensch verloren ist, die Voraussetzung für den Empfang der Gnade ist, - diese Tatsache findet in dem eigentümlichen Geschichtsbild des Paulus ihren Ausdruck. Das zwischen Adam und Christus hereingekommene Gesetz soll die Sünde zu ihrem Vollmaß bringen, damit die Gnade mächtig werden kann (Röm 5,20f.). So hat die Sünde eine positive Bedeutung. Ein Symptom dafür, daß das Geschichtsbild von der Anthropologie her gewonnen ist, daß die Geschichte der Menschheit für Paulus eigentlich die Geschichte des Menschen ist, ist es, daß Paulus den Gang der Geschichte von Adam über Moses bis Christus in der Form des 'Ich' beschreiben kann (Röm 7,7-25a).[43]

Wie sehr Paulus die Vorstellung vom Heil überhaupt am Individuum orientiert sein läßt, zeigen zuletzt die apokalyptischen Zukunftsbilder, die er aufgreift, aber doch—wie Baumgarten durchgehend gezeigt hat[44]—anthropologisch ausrichtet. Baumgarten stellt fest:

---

[41]Peter Stuhlmacher, " 'Das Ende des Gesetzes': Über Ursprung und Ansatz der paulinischen Theologie", *ZTK* 67 (1970) 14-39, hier 37.

[42]Bultmann, *Geschichte und Eschatologie*, 47.

[43]Bultmann, *Geschichte und Eschatologie*, 47-48.

[44]Jörg Baumgarten, *Paulus und die Apokalyptik: Die Auslegung apokalyptischer*

Wo immer kosmologische Züge bei Paulus auftauchen, müssen sie der *Tradition* zugewiesen werden (Phil 3,20f; 1 Kor 15,28; Röm 8,19ff); an keiner Stelle kann ein kosmologisches *Interpretament* aufgewiesen werden. Paulus qualifiziert ferner kein zukünftiges Handeln Gottes als zukünftiges *Schöpfer*-Handeln an Natur oder Kosmos unter Absehung vom Menschen. Gottes zukünftiges Schöpferhandeln wird vielmehr auf die Auferweckung der Toten beschränkt. Daß Paulus nicht vom "zukünftigen Äon" spricht, kann nicht als Zufall, sondern muß als notwendig erkannt werden.[45]

Wenn Baumgarten sich trotzdem einer Verabsolutierung der individualisierenden Tendenz bei Paulus widersetzt, so um der "Mehrdimensionalität der Apokalyptik-Rezeption"[46] bei Paulus willen, die sich nicht auf ein Schema verrechnen läßt. Wichtig ist nun aber: In der Verschränkung von Eschatologie und Ekklesiologie setzt Paulus ein kräftiges Korrektiv gegen einen sich solipsistisch mißverstehenden Individualismus.[47] Aber das hebt den Gesamteindruck nicht auf, daß das Verständnis des Heils als Gerechtigkeit, Heil und Freude im Heiligen Geist (Röm 14,17) kräftig *anthropologisch* orientiert ist.

3

Nach allem Gesagten ist deutlich, daß die christliche Gemeinde—bei Jesus, bei Paulus, bei uns heute—nicht durch völkische oder gesellschaftliche Motive konstituiert wird, sondern durch das die einzelnen zur Gemeinde berufende Wort. Man sieht das auch daran, daß die Tradition im ganzen Neuen Testament in erster Linie eine solche der Lehre ist, in der gesagt wird, was der Inhalt des Glaubens ist.[48] Was Inhalt gesellschaftspolitischen Verhaltens sein soll, fehlt und taucht in den Haustafeln oder dem Philemonbrief ansatzweise auf. Wenn darum heute der "individualistischen Verengung" der Kampf angesagt wird,

Überlieferungen in den echten Paulusbriefen (WMANT 44; Neukirchen-Vluyn: Neukirchener, 1975).

[45]Baumgarten, *Apokalyptik*, 240-41. Er schreibt ferner: "Wenn der Apostel trotz traditioneller Nennung der οὐρανοί selbst lieber von einem οὐρανός spricht, wenn er das Motiv der ἀλλαγή (1 Kor 15,52) allein anthropologisch verwendet, wenn er den κόσμος-Begriff fast ausschließlich auf die "Menschenwelt" reduziert und das Motiv der καινὴ κτίσις pointiert und ausschließlich anthropologisch rezipiert, dann wird man mit guten Gründen von einer 'Entkosmologisierung traditioneller Aussagen' bei Paulus sprechen dürfen" (*Apokalyptik* 241).

[46]Baumgarten, *Apokalyptik*, 242.

[47]Baumgarten, *Apokalyptik*, 242-43.

[48]Bultmann, *Geschichte und Eschatologie*, 45.

234 The New Testament Age

so ist demgegenüber im Bewußtsein zu halten, "daß die theologischen Grundbegriffe Beziehungen zu Gott bezeichnen: Glaube, Liebe, Hoffnung, Gnade, Gerechtigkeit. Werden sie nicht streng als Beschreibung dieser Beziehung verstanden, entarten sie zu teils moralischen Postulaten, teils schwärmerischen Utopien. Aber Hoffnung, die nicht Hoffnung auf Gott ist, ist trostlos. Die Verdrängung des Reiches Gottes durch Träume von einem idealen Weltreich wird beide 'Welten' entschwinden lassen, auch die politische".[49] Diese Perspektive aber deckt die Alternative "Individualisierung oder Kollektivierung des Heils" als ein Scheinproblem auf. Sie wird aber zum theologischen Fundamentalproblem in dem Augenblick, wo die *sola-gratia*-Struktur der von Jesus angesagten Gottesherrschaft und der von Paulus explizierten Rechtfertigungslehre aufgegeben und politische Hermeneutik die Theologie zu einer neuen Spielart von natürlicher Theologie verkommen läßt.

Erst wenn das klar ist, kann die "soziale Verschränkung" des in radikaler Vereinzelung vorkommenden Glaubenden sachgemäß erörtert werden. Denn natürlich wäre es an der Wirklichkeit vorbeigedacht, wollte man Individualisierung oder Kollektivierung jeweils so verabsolutieren, daß sie sich gegenseitig in die Stellung eines bloßen Epiphänomens herabdrücken.[50] Richtiger ist von einer "*Wechselwirkung* als ihrem Grundverhältnis" zu reden, die Litt in Bezug auf das dadurch sich formende Lebensganze eine "Wesensgemeinschaft" nennt. Er meint damit "ein Gesamtgebilde, das das soziale wie das individuelle Moment in sich befaßt, dessen Leben sich also gleichsam in zwei Brennpunkten sammelt".[51]

Diese Spannung zwischen Individuum und Gemeinschaft ist nun aber auch für die Theologie charakteristisch. Baumgarten hat mit seiner "Verschränkung von Eschatologie und Ekklesiologie" uns bereits in diese Richtung gewiesen. Das glaubende Ich wird *qua* glaubendes Ich und *eo ipso* in die Gemeinschaft der Glaubenden eingewiesen. Insofern ist der *Vorgang* des Glaubens mit seinen Lebensäußerungen Hoffnung, Liebe, Gewißheit, Anfechtung weder ein exklusiv individueller Vorgang noch ein Kollektivereignis. Er setzt vielmehr das Individuum und die Gemeinde in eine ausgesprochen

---

[49]Hans Conzelmann, "Vorwort", *Theologie als Schriftauslegung: Aufsätze zum Neuen Testament* (BEvT 65; München: Chr. Kaiser, 1974).

[50]Theodor Litt, *Individuum und Gemeinschaft: Grundfragen der sozialen Theorie und Ethik* (Leipzig/Berlin: B. G. Teubner, 1919) 34.

[51]Litt, *Individuum*, 35.

fruchtbare Spannung zueinander.[52] Erst innerhalb der immer schon vorgegebenen "Wir-Gemeinschaft" gewinnt das Ich seine nun allerdings nicht hoch genug zu veranschlagende Bedeutung.[53]

In dieser Verschränkung von Ich und Gemeinschaft ist die radikale Vereinzelung des Glaubenden zugleich und in eins damit "eine *soziale Tatsache*".[54] Und insofern kann man sagen, daßdie Glaubensentscheidung als das eigentliche *principium individuationis* höchst dialektisch ein Kollektivbewußtsein nicht schafft, sondern *ist*. Die Ekklesiologie ist dasjenige, was die legitime Individualisierung des einzelnen *coram Deo* vor falscher Privatisierung bewahrt. Denn die allerintimste Umkehr (μετάνοια) ist ja Umkehr zu Gott dem Herrn "und also zum Eintritt in den Dienst seiner Sache auf Erden". "In Ganzheit sich bekehrend und erneuernd, tritt der Mensch über die Schwelle seiner privaten Existenz hinaus". "In Ganzheit sich bekehrend und erneuernd übernimmt der Mensch in und mit seiner persönlichen auch öffentliche Verantwortlichkeit". "Dann und nur dann ist des Menschen Umkehr seine Umkehr zu Gott, wenn er sich mit ihr als *sanctus* einfügt in die *communio sanctorum*".[55] So und nur so wird die Rechtfertigung des einzelnen zur Rechtfertigung der Welt. So und nur so bleiben die

---

[52]Eberhard Jüngel, "Anfechtung und Gewißheit des Glaubens. Auf der Suche nach der Sache der Kirche", *EvK* 9 (1976) 454-58, hier 456: "Wer 'Gott' sagt, kann gar nicht umhin, auch 'mein Gott' und also 'Ich' zu sagen. Ein Blick z.B. in den Psalter erübrigt sich, weil das jeder aus ureigenster Erfahrung weiß. Aber 'mein Gott' ist er als 'unser Vater'. So sehr jeweils ein Ich betroffen ist, wenn sich Anfechtung ereignet, so wenig bleibt die Betroffenheit doch auf das Ich beschränkt. Wir haben zwar ganz und gar keinen Grund, der heute üblichen Diskreditierung der Kategorie des einzelnen das Wort zu reden. Zumindest in der Theologie ist die Verächtlichmachung des Individuums unerträglich. In Sachen der Gewißheit gibt es keine Vertretung. Gewißheit läßt sich nicht delegieren, Gottesgewißheit schon gar nicht. 'Ich bin gewiß, daß . . .'—z.B. 'weder Tod noch Leben, weder Engel noch Fürstentümer noch Gewalten, weder Gegenwärtiges noch Zukünftiges, weder Hohes noch Tiefes noch keine andere Kreatur uns scheiden kann von der Liebe Gottes, die in Christus Jesus ist unserem Herrn' (Röm 8,38-39)". Und Jüngel fährt fort: "Doch die Gewißheit des einzelnen schließt inhaltlich die Gemeinschaft der Glaubenden ein ('Ich bin gewiß, daß uns nichts von Gottes Liebe trennen kann') und erwächst formal aus der Kommunikation mit dieser Gemeinschaft. Das Ich fängt niemals mit sich selber an, das Ich des Glaubenden schon gar nicht. Ist es doch ein immer schon angesprochenes Ich, das dann, wenn es Gottes gewiß ist, einstimmt in das Bekenntnis der Gemeinde, die wiederum Gott als unseren Vater anruft".

[53]Jüngel, "Anfechtung", 457.

[54]Jüngel, "Anfechtung", 457. Hervorhebung von mir.

[55]Karl Barth, *Die kirchliche Dogmatik*, vol. 4: *Die Lehre von der Versöhnung* (Zollikon-Zürich: Evangelischer Verlag, 1955), 4/2:639-40.

göttliche Gerechtigkeit und die menschliche Gerechtigkeit unver-
mischt beieinander. Nur theologischem Irrglauben gelingt es, daraus
eine falsche Alternative zu machen.

JUDE 5 TO 7

A. F. J. Klijn

IT IS A GREAT pleasure to write about a passage in the New Testament which has been dealt with more than once by him to whom this article is gratefully dedicated. Already a long time ago Professor Bo Reicke defended the opinion that the author of Jude wrote against "libertinists" who were notable for their Zealot activities.[1] It is obvious that the entire problem of the background of the antagonists cannot be explained from vv 5-7. They are only part of the evidence for their characterization. Our inquiry is limited to what we are able to conclude from this passage regarding the problem as a whole.

The three examples mentioned in Jude 5-7 deal with Israel's apostasy in the desert, the fall of the angels and the sin of Sodom and Gomorrah. The offenders have in common that they were all finally condemned (ἀπώλεσεν, v 5; εἰς κρίσιν . . . τετήρηκεν, v 6; δίκην ὑπέχουσαι, v 7).

The question which is of importance for our conception of the antagonists mentioned in this writing is what Israel, the angels and the inhabitants of Sodom and Gomorrah actually did. Commentaries agree that the second and the third examples show that they were sexual libertinists, since the fallen angels mixed with women and the inhabitants of the cities of Sodom and Gomorrah ἐκπορνεύσασαι καὶ ἀπελθοῦσαι ὀπίσω σαρκὸς ἑτέρας (v 7). Especially this latter remark

---

[1]Bo Reicke, *Diakonie, Festfreude und Zelos in Verbindung mit der altchristlichen Agapenfeier*, (UUÅ 1951, vol. 5; Uppsala: Lundequistska bokhandeln, 1951) 360. See already Hermann Werdermann, *Die Irrlehrer des Judas- und 2. Petrusbriefes* (BFCT 17/6; Gütersloh: C. Bertelsmann, 1913) 80: "Die Gegner sind 'Libertiner,' 'Gnostiker,' die aus dem Geistbesitz ihre Freiheit, ihr Selbstbewusstsein, ihre Unvergänglichkeit und Furchtlosigkeit ableiteten und ihr Leben ganz diesen Sätzen entsprechend führten."

would have been meant to show the sexual perversity of the Sodomites.[2]

It is, however, striking that the second example speaks about the fall of the angels but does not say a word about their intercourse with women. It would be strange to omit this detail if one wants to give an example of sexual aberration. It might be possible to solve this problem by pointing out that the words τὸν ὅμοιον τρόπον τούτοις (v 7)[3] show that the author tries to compare the two examples. And since the inhabitants of Sodom and Gomorrah are said to have committed fornication, it would seem natural to accept that fornication was also implied regarding the fall of the angels. However, in the following we shall show that the matter of fornication is in fact not the *tertium comparationis*. In addition we might add that even were that the case, the first example would still have to be dealt with separately, since certainly it says nothing about fornication.

---

[2]Johannes Schneider, *Die Briefe des Jakobus, Petrus, Judas und Johannes: Die Katholischen Briefe* (NTD 10; Göttingen: Vandenhoeck & Ruprecht, 1961) 128: "Mit diesen Engeln vergleicht der Verfasser die Irrlehrer, die hemmungslos ihrer Sinnenlust fröhnen. . . . Die Lockung bestand nur darin, mit andersartigem Fleisch in enge geschlechtliche Verbindung zu kommen" (cf. Wolfgang Schrage, "Der Judasbrief," *Die "Katholischen" Briefe: Die Briefe des Jakobus, Petrus, Johannes und Judas*[NTD 10; Göttingen: Vandenhoeck & Ruprecht, 1973] 224); J. N. D. Kelly, *A Commentary on the Epistles of Peter and of Jude* (HNTC; New York: Harper & Row; Black's New Testament Commentaries; London: A. & C. Black, 1969) 258-59: "An essential ingredient in the angels' wickedness . . . was (as later Judaism saw it: e.g. 1 En. xii.4) the unbridled sexual passion which motivated it. . . . Both had made their sin even more appalling by lusting after different flesh"; K. H. Schelkle, *Die Petrusbriefe. Der Judasbrief*, 3rd ed. (HTKNT 13/2; Freiburg: Herder, 1970) 155: "Auf die Häretiker bezogen, ist der Engelsturz wieder ein warnendes Beispiel dafür, welche Strafe die zu gewärtigen haben, die hohe Würde verraten; zugleich aber auch ein Beispiel der Strafe für Unzucht"; Jean Cantinat, *Les Épîtres de Saint Jacques et de Saint Jude* (SB; Paris: J. Galbalda, 1973) 306: "Quelle faute Jude prête-t-il aux villes incriminées? Une faute, avons-nous dit, du même genre que celle des mauvais anges du verset 6, consistant à vouloir 'connaître' (Gn 19,5: Yâda' au sens biblique) les deux visiteurs angéliques de Lot"; Tord Fornberg, *An Early Church in a Pluralistic Society: A Study of 2 Peter* (ConNT 9; Lund: Gleerup, 1977) 47: "The author here [sc., in Jude 5-7] states that both the angels in v. 6 and the inhabitants of the five cities on the Dead Sea indulged in unnatural lust. This must refer to the fact that the angels left their proper dwellings in order to fornicate with the daughters of men, just as the men of Sodom wished to violate the angels who visited Lot, Gen. 19:5. This observation leads naturally to v. 8, 'Yet in like manner these men . . . defile the flesh' (σάρκα μὲν μιαίνουσιν). Thus the author is emphasizing sexual immorality."

[3]We need not repeat that this applies to the angels and not to the cities of Sodom and Gomorrah. Cf. Schelkle, *Judasbrief*, 155-56.

These considerations warrant a fresh approach to the three examples. Before we go into each of them, we should note that the second and third ones are often met in Jewish and Christian literature as examples warning against particular sins. But although they seem to speak about fornication, they were used to show that God is able to save and to punish (Wis 10:1-10, esp. vv 4, 6; 2 Pet 2:5-6; 1 Clem 9:4),[4] that one is not supposed to show arrogancy (3 Macc 2:4-5; Sir 16:7-9), that one is not allowed to alter the order of nature (*T. Naph.* 3:4-5), and finally also to warn against fornication (*Jub.* 20:5).[5] This demonstrates that the examples did not serve one but several purposes.

The first example deals with Israel's apostasy in the desert mentioned in Num 13:25-14:38. Those who returned after the exploration of Canaan reported that the inhabitants were too strong for the Israelites. The people became afraid and wanted to go back to Egypt. This lack of faith meant that the Israelites had to stay another forty years in the desert, where "this wicked community" had to die (Num 14:35). In Jewish literature this event is not used as a deterrent,[6] but Paul used it in this way to warn against false security (1 Cor 10:1-13) and the author of Hebrews to strengthen steadfastness in times of temptation (3:7-

---

[4]See also Alexander Böhlig and Pahor Labib, eds., "Apocalypse of Adam," *Koptisch-Gnostische Apokalypsen aus Codex V von Nag Hammadi im Koptischen Museum zu Alt-Kairo*, Wissenschaftliche Zeitschrift der Martin-Luther-Universität, Halle-Wittenberg 1963, Sonderband, 69, 2-6; 70, 10-15; 75, 9-10; 75, 22-23; and Martin Krause, ed., "Die Paraphrase des Sêem," *Christentum am Roten Meer II*, ed. Franz Altheim and Ruth Stiehl (Berlin/New York: Walter de Gruyter, 1973) 25:9-13; 29:27-33.

[5]For studies regarding these examples, see August Strobel, *Untersuchungen zum eschatologischen Verzögerungsproblem: Auf Grund der spätjüdisch-urchristlichen Geschichte von Habakuk 2,2ff* (NovTSup 2; Leiden/Köln: E. J. Brill, 1961) 97 n.5; Arthur L. Moore, *The Parousia in the New Testament* (NovTSup 13; Leiden: E. J. Brill, 1966) 153-54; Jack P. Lewis, *A Study of the Interpretation of Noah and the Flood in Jewish and Christian Literature* (Leiden: E. J. Brill, 1968) 167-73; Dieter Lührmann, *Die Redaktion der Logienquelle* (WMANT 33; Neukirchen: Neukirchener Verlag, 1969) 75-83; Anton Vögtle, *Das Neue Testament und die Zukunft des Kosmos* (Kommentare und Beiträge zum Alten und Neuen Testament; Düsseldorf: Patmos, 1970) 133-36; J. Schlosser, "Les jours de Noé et de Lot: A propos de *Luc* XVII, 26-30," *RB* 80 (1973) 13-36; Wolfgang Harnisch, *Eschatologische Existenz: Ein exegetischer Beitrag zum Sachanliegen von 1. Thessalonicher 4,13-5,11* (FRLANT 110; Göttingen: Vandenhoeck & Ruprecht, 1973) 104.

[6]In Str-B 3:412-13, Wis 18:20-25 is quoted as a parallel of 1 Cor 10:10, but the contents are quite different.

4:13).[7] In spite of this different usage we see that in both cases we are dealing with the danger of apostasy within the Christian Church. The meaning of the example is specifically Christian. The Christian had to make a decision on which he is not supposed to renege.

Jude 5 speaks about the event in its own way. Although the text was handed down differently in the various manuscripts, we contend that the word ἅπαξ should not be put into the subordinate clause beginning with ὅτι.[8] It is, however, uncertain whether the word κύριος or ᾽Ιησοῦς is original.[9] In this verse the expression τὸ δεύτερον is striking. It is not necessary to the sentence structure, but, since it is present, we would expect a preceding expression like "to begin with." In the present sentence it has to be connected with ἀπώλεσεν and a suppressed "at the beginning" would have been related to σώσας. Apparently the author wants to say that "salvation" is something definite which cannot be connected with the expression "to begin with," since nothing is supposed to follow anymore. If God is obliged to have something follow, He comes to condemn. This corresponds to the words in the preceding verse which depict the readers as εἰδότας ἅπαξ πάντα. The Christians came to know about salvation "once for ever," since faith was handed down to them ἅπαξ.[10]

---

[7]See Otto Michel, *Der Brief an die Hebräer*, 12th ed. (MeyerK; Göttingen: Vandenhoeck & Ruprecht, 1966) 188 n. 2: "Darf man vielleicht annehmen, daß ein fester Predigtstoff sich dieses Themas bemächtigt hat und daß die beiden exegetischen Abschnitte doch verwandt sind? Man achte aber auch auf die Verschiedenheit der Zielsetzung. I Kor 10,1-13 wendet sich gegen eine falsche Sicherheit und Freiheit innerhalb der Gemeinden. Hebr 3,7-4,13 dagegen will die Gewissheit in der Anfechtung stärken."

[8]See Allen Wikgren, "Some Problems in Jude 5," *Studies in the History and Text of the New Testament in honor of Kenneth Willis Clark*, ed. Boyd L. Daniels and M. Jack Suggs (SD 29; Salt Lake City: University of Utah, 1967) 147-52. It is to be regretted that the Greek New Testament of U. B. S.[3] and Nestle-Aland[26] altered the text of Jude 5.

[9]Matthew Black ("Critical and Exegetical Notes on Three New Testament Texts Hebrews xi.11, Jude 5, James 1.27," *Apophoreta: Festschrift für Ernst Haenchen zu seinem siebzigsten Geburtstag*, ed. Walther Eltester and F. H. Kettler [BZNW 30; Berlin: Alfred Töpelmann, 1964] 45) renders: "that the Lord who once delivered the People from Egypt, next time destroyed the unbelievers"; but cf. Bruce M. Metzger, *A Textual Commentary on the Greek New Testament: A Companion Volume to the United Bible Societies' Greek New Testament*, 3rd ed. (London/New York: United Bible Societies, 1971) 726: "Critical principles seem to require the adoption of ᾽Ιησοῦς, which admittedly is the best attested reading among Greek and versional witnesses."

[10]Cf. Schelkle, *Judasbrief*, 154 n. 1: "δεύτερον wird nicht etwa zu σώσας bzw. τούς

The second example starts from the assumption that the "sons of God" mentioned in Gen 6:2 have to be seen as angels. This idea is not only present in the LXX but is also common in contemporary literature, both Jewish and Christian.[11] We need not repeat that this verse reflects the influence of the Apocalypse of Enoch. In *1 Enoch* 6:1-2 it is said that the angels descended to earth and in 10:4-6 that the Most High commanded Raphael to bind Azazel's hands and feet and to throw him into darkness, so that he be kept for the fire on the day of the great judgment. It is, however, important to notice what the author of Jude omits and emphasizes. Nothing is said about intercourse with women, but there is mention of their leaving their ἀρχήν and οἰκητήριον. In Jude 6 it is emphasized that the angels had fixed positions in heaven. Here we notice the influence of astrological terminology on the description of angels. It is evident that the author was attracted by this astrological aspect of angelology.[12] It was this influence which made angelology a kind of heavenly science showing a fixed pattern.[13] The

---

μὴ πιστεύσαντας . . . , sondern zu ἀπώλεσεν gehören. Das πρῶτον, das dem δεύτερον voraufgeht, ist nicht explicit ausgesprochen. Es wird zu ergänzen sein: Das erstemal, da Gottes Hilfe notwendig war, hat Gott sie gerettet. Das zweitemal aber hat er die ewig Ungläubigen dem Untergang überlassen."

[11]To give but a few examples: Gen 6:2 (LXX); *Jub.* 5:1; *T. Reuben* 5:6; *T. Naph.* 3:4-5; *2 Apoc. Bar.* 56:12-14; Josephus, *Ant.* 1.73; Philo, *gigant.* 6; CD 2:17-19; *Pirqe R. El.* 22 (Gerald Friedlander, ed., *Midrash: Pirkè de Rabbi Eliezer [The Chapters of Rabbi Eliezer the Great] according to the text of the manuscript belonging to Abraham Epstein of Vienna* [First ed. London, 1916; repr. Hermon Press, New York, 1970] 160); Papias frg. 4; Athenagoras, *Leg.* 24.5; Justin, *Dial.* 79; *2 Apol.* 5.3; Irenaeus, *adv. haer.* 4.36.4; *Epid.* 10; 18; *Clem. Hom.* 8.12-14; *Recog.* 4.26; Tertullian, *de virg. vel.* 7.2; *de cultu fem.* 1.2.1; 2.10.3; *Apol.* 22.3; Clem. Alex. *paed.* 3.14.2; Cyprian, *de habitu virg.* 14; Lactantius, *instit.* 2.4; Bardesanes, *lib. leg. reg.* 9 (François Nau, ed., *Patrologia syriaca* [Paris: Firmin Didot, 1907], 2: cols. 546-49).

[12]See Bo Reicke, *The Disobedient Spirits and Christian Baptism: A Study of 1 Pet. iii.19 and its Context* (ASNU 13; Kφbenhavn: Ejnar Munksgaard, 1946) 84; cf. 1 Enoch 21:6; 88:1; Job 38:7 (MT, LXX, Peshitto); 11QtgJob 30:3-5; *2 Apoc. Bar.* 51:10; *Pirqe R. El.* 22 (Friedlander, ed., *Pirkê âe Rabbi Eliezer*, 161).

[13]The words ἀρχή and οἰκητήριον are astrological terms. Hippolytus (*ref.* 9.16.2) mentions the Elkesaites who say of particular stars: φυλάσσεσθε ἀπὸ τῆς ἐξουσίας τῶν ἡμερῶν ἀρχῆς αὐτῶν. In A. Martini and D. Bassi, eds., *Catalogus codicum astrologorum Graecorum* (Bruxelles: Lamertin, 1901), 3:25, a treatise bears the name Ἀρχὴ τῶν ιβ' Ζωδίων; Nemesius, *de nat. hom.* 38 (*PG* 40.760): οἱ δὲ Στωϊκοί φασιν, ἀποκαθισταμένους τοὺς πλάνητας εἰς τὸ αὐτὸ σημεῖον, κατά τε μῆκος καὶ πλάτος, ἔνθα τὴν ἀρχὴν ἕκαστος ἦν; D. Bassi et al., eds., "Excerpta ex Codice 11 (Mutin. 85)," *Catalogus codicum astrologorum Graecorum* (Bruxelles: Lamertin, 1903), 4:99:

angels, like the stars, have their allotted places, and they cannot abandon them without being punished.[14]

The third example (v 7) is connected with the preceding one by the words τὸν ὅμοιον τρόπον τούτοις. The cities of Sodom and Gomorrah apparently acted in the same way as the angels. Since nothing in connection with the angels is said about sexual aberrations, it is necessary to examine this sentence carefully.

The choice of the words σαρκὸς ἑτέρας is striking. It is commonly explained that, while the angels interfered with human beings, the Sodomites, on the contrary, tried to lay hands upon angels. It is credible that the angels visiting Sodom were supposed to be clothed in human flesh,[15] but it remains remarkable that the author is not more explicit. We have already noted with regard to the angels that nothing is said about their intercourse with women.

A closer examination of the sentence shows that the author writes ἐκπορνεύσασαι καὶ ἀπελθοῦσαι ὀπίσω σαρκὸς ἑτέρας. It has already been said by others that these words do not explicitly speak about a sexual action. The word ἐκπορνεύσασαι followed by ὀπίσω is used to convey that one has left God and followed idols. This idea is especially brought out by the author's addition of the word ἀπελθοῦσαι.[16]

Ἰστέον ὅτι οἱ Ἕλληνες τὰς ἑπτὰ ἡμέρας τῶν ἑπτὰ πλανήτων ἔφησαν εἶναι οἴκους, ἐν αἷς καὶ πολεύουσι.

[14]In early Christian literature it is often said that the angels left their τάξις; cf. Justin, 2 Apol. 5.3: οἱ δ'ἄγγελοι, παραβάντες τήνδε τὴν τάξιν; Papias, frg. 4; Aristides 4.2; Irenaeus, Epid. 10; Clem. Recog. 4.26: angeli quidem relicto proprii ordinis cursu hominum favere vitiis coeperunt et libindini eorum quodammodo indignum praeberi ministerium; and Bardesanes, lib. leg. reg. 9 (Nau, ed., Patrologia syriaca, 2:548-49): Intelligimus enim etiam Angelos si propriam libertatem non haberent, non potuisse se coniugere cum hominum filiabus et non peccavisse et non cedidisse a locis suis (ܠܐ ܗܘܘ ܡܢ ܕܘܟܝܬܗܘܢ).

[15]See T. Reuben 5:6; Philo, gigant. 12.

[16]Josephus, Ant. 1.194: οἱ Σοδομῖται . . . ἀσεβεῖς, ὡς μηκέτι μεμνῆσθαι τῶν παρ' αὐτοῦ γενομένων ὠφελειῶν. Friedrich Spitta, Der Zweite Brief des Petrus und der Brief des Judas. Eine geschichtliche Untersuchung (Halle: Buchhandlung des Waisenhauses, 1885) 329: "Gegen die erste Auffassung spricht, dass wenn LXX זנה nicht durch das einfache πορνεύειν, sondern durch ἐκπορνεύειν wiedergiebt, meistens daran sich eine präpositionale Näherbestimmung, mit ἀπό oder ὀπίσω, schliesst, welche das πορνεύειν als Verlassen eines ehedem innegehalten Standorts charakterisiert"; and Spitta, Judas, 333: "Hurerei im allgemeinen aber ist es nicht, was Judas veranlasst, die Sodomiter mit den Engeln zu vergleichen, sondern die besondere Art, dass sie ihr hurerisches Gelüste triebt, das eigene Haus und Geschlecht zu verlassen";

Therefore the author wants to show that the inhabitants of Sodom and Gomorrah deviated from a particular way of life. The sexual aberration in this case is subordinate. Thus the angels and the inhabitants of Sodom and Gomorrah can be compared because both abandoned a particular position. The corresponding words in the two sentences are ἀπολιπόντες in v 6 and ἀπελθοῦσαι in v 7. These again have to be compared to τὸ δεύτερον in v 5.

We may conclude that all three examples consonantly portray a particular group of people who left the status given to them in order to follow somebody or something else. This desertion can be to another way of life or to idols.[17]

In the wider context of vv 5 to 8, this means that the words εἰδότας ἅπαξ πάντα (v 5) represent the main motif. Not only the examples but also these words yielded many difficulties for both ancient copyists, as can be seen from the manuscripts, and modern commentators. It is evident that the author really wants to say that the Christians received all their knowledge once and for all. Here we recognize the same idea that is met in Paul's farewell speech to the elders in Ephesus, where he states that he disclosed to them the "whole" purpose of God (Acts 20:27; cf. Acts 20:20),[18] and other passages in the New Testament which speak about the command to "remain" in what was taught (2 Tim 3:14; Acts 14:22).[19]

---

cf. Bo Reicke, *The Epistles of James, Peter, and Jude: Introduction, Translation, and Notes* (AB; Garden City, New York: Doubleday, 1964) 199: "Jude ... is interested in the people who pass or are pulled from one group to the other, namely the apostates. ... Fornication may here, as often in the New Testament, refer to idolatry, while 'flesh' (as in I Pet i 24) denotes human society and its violent attempts at self-exaltation. Sodom and Gomorrah represent the leaders of apostasy, and the surrounding cities correspond to their followers." We do not entirely agree with Spitta and Reicke but their emphasis on "apostasy" is correct.

[17]See also Marinus de Jonge, *De nieuwtestamenticus als historicus en theoloog: Enige opmerkingen naar aanleiding van de brief van Judas* (Leiden: E. J. Brill, 1966) 38 n.36: "in beide gevallen werden de door God gestelde grenzen overtreden."

[18]Hans-Joachim Michel, *Die Abschiedsrede des Paulus und die Kirche, APG 20,17-38: Motivgeschichte und theologische Bedeutung* (SANT 35; München: Kösel, 1973) 81-83.

[19]Cf. Norbert Brox, *Falsche Verfasserangaben: Zur Erklärung der frühchristlichen Pseudepigraphie,* (SBS 79; Stuttgart: KBW, 1975) 119: "Es besteht in der Gewissheit, dass alles Relevante schon am Ursprung und in der Frühzeit der christlichen Predigt ... gesagt ist."

The New Testament Age

We are dealing with an aspect of anti-heretical preaching in the early Church which secluded itself from fresh revelations. In this way we are also able to connect Jude 5-7 with v 8. If one were to explain the examples mentioned above from the point of view of sexual aberration, one might possibly in support point to the words σάρκα μὲν μιαίνουσιν in v 8. However, the emphasis in this verse is laid upon the beginning, where the words οὗτοι ἐνυπνιαζόμενοι clearly refer to heretics. It is obvious that we are dealing with persons who are drawing on their own concoctions, adding these to well known Christian tradition.

However accurate this explanation may be, we must add that from Jude 5-7 nothing can be said about the exact nature of these heretics.[20] It is only after v 8 that the author goes into details. It is impossible to say more about this without a careful analysis of the text after v 7. The first part of this letter, vv 3-8, is a general introduction in which it is said that the contents of faith were handed down to the readers in the past once for all (v 3), and that this information is not to be replaced by additional revelations given by some dreamers.

---

[20]Douglas J. Rowston, "The Most Neglected Book in the New Testament," *NTS* 21 (1974/75): 555: "But putting a definite label on the heretics seems to be out of the question."

THE TESTIMONY OF JESUS
IS THE SPIRIT OF PROPHECY (REV 19:10)

G. W. H. Lampe

ANCIENT COMMENTATORS on the Apocalypse, who are in any case rather few in number, rarely attempt to explain that perplexing verse, Rev 19:10, which some modern exegetes have thought to be an interpolation. Those who do comment on it are sometimes concerned with anachronistic Christological difficulties arising from the apparent identification of the glorified Christ with the angel who is a fellowservant of the seer and his brethren (cf. Rev 22:9; 1:17). They say little about the problem of ascertaining the meaning in this context of "the testimony" or "witness" (μαρτυρία) of Jesus and "the Spirit of prophecy." The three Greek commentators of the first millennium do, however, offer some suggestions. The earliest, Oecumenius (sixth century), explains that the angel tells John that he is a fellow servant of all those who testify that Christ is God incarnate, and "all who testify to the lordship and deity of Christ are filled with the charisma of prophecy, and not I alone."[1]

Oecumenius clearly understands "the testimony of Jesus" to mean testimony about Jesus given by Christian believers, and "the Spirit of prophecy" to be the inspiration of their witness to him. In view of the emphatic rejection of this exegesis by many later writers in favor of the view that ἡ μαρτυρία ᾽Ιησοῦ should be interpreted subjectively as "witness borne by Jesus" and that prophecy is inspired because it repeats and confirms Jesus' own personal testimony, the confidence with which Oecumenius offers this brief exposition is noteworthy, even though he is obviously mistaken in supposing that the Apocalyptist

---

[1]Herman Charles Hoskier, *The Complete Commentary of Oecumenius on the Apocalypse*, (University of Michigan Studies 23; Ann Arbor MI: University of Michigan, 1928): 205.

was concerned with the witness of Christians to Christological orthodoxy.

Andrew of Caesarea is less confident. He presents two possible interpretations of ἡ μαρτυρία ᾿Ιησοῦ. One is given in the following paraphrase: " 'Do not worship me,' says the divine angel, 'because I am foretelling the things that are to come; for confession of Christ or witness to him (ἡ γάρ εἰς Χριστὸν ὁμολογία ἤγουν μαρτυρία) is that which provides the prophetic Spirit (αὕτη χορηγός ἐστι προφητικοῦ πνεύματος)'."[2] Andrew's alternative suggestion is that the genitive is subjective. The meaning then is that the purpose of prophecy is to confirm Christ's own witness and to testify to Christian faith through the saints. His later successor at Caesarea, Arethas (probably ninth century), repeats Andrew's former interpretation and adds that the prophetic charisma is bestowed as a reward for witness borne for Christ, being itself similar to that witness: "for prophecy was granted for the sake of my fellowservants, the martyrs."[3] Here, again, the testimony is witness *to* Jesus, and Arethas, despite the fact that he seems to regard the gift of prophecy as a reward for testifying rather than as the inspiration that enables a Christian to testify, shows a better appreciation of the nature of that witness. He realizes that in the Apocalypse prophetic witness is directly related not to the profession of credal orthodoxy, but to testimony given under persecution and so to martyrdom.

Among the rather more numerous Latin commentators Primasius (sixth century) is exceptional in taking notice of this passage. Like Oecumenius, Arethas, and Andrew in his former alternative, Primasius understands "the testimony of Jesus" to mean "witness borne to Jesus." This "witness," however, is not understood to have been by contemporary Christian prophets, as John certainly intended, but by the Spirit and the prophets in the scriptures, the witnesses signified by the presence of Moses and Elijah at the Transfiguration and explicitly referred to by Jesus in the saying recorded at Luke 24:44.[4] These ancient commentators, then, see no difficulty in translating ἡ μαρτυρία ᾿Ιησοῦ in this context as "the witness borne to Jesus," and, however

---

[2]Andrew of Caesarea, *Comm. in Apoc.* 19:10 (PG 106.400).

[3]Arethas of Caesarea, *Comm. in Apoc.* 19:10 (PG 106.740).

[4]Primasius of Hadrumetum, *Comm. in Apoc.* 19:10 (PL 68.910). Cf. Venerable Bede, *Explanatio Apoc.* 19 (PL 93.189).

fanciful may be their notions of the kind of testimony for which the prophetic gift is bestowed, in equating this witness with Spirit-inspired prophecy.

Modern exegetes, on the other hand, are more divided. In recent times many have favored the second interpretation offered by Andrew of Caesarea. They understand the text to mean that the Spirit of prophecy re-presents in the contemporary Church the witness borne by him who is the "faithful witness" of Rev 1:5. The witness of Jesus is identified by many with that "good confession" (καλὴ ὁμολογία) which, according to 1 Tim 6:13, he witnessed (μαρτυρήσαντος) before (ἐπί) Pontius Pilate. In the light of the very close connection so often and so strongly emphasized by New Testament writers between prophetic inspiration and witness to, or confession of (ὁμολογία), Jesus in circumstances of persecution such as are envisaged in the Apocalypse, and hence also between Spirit-inspired testimony and the nascent concept of Christian martyrdom, there may well be more merit than is often allowed in the exegesis of Rev 19:10 which interprets Ἰησοῦ as an objective genitive and identifies the operation of the Spirit of prophecy with the confession of Jesus made in times of persecution under pressure to deny him. Examination of this question also involves some consideration of 1 Tim 6:12-13. It ought properly to form part of a much wider study of the concept of "witness" in the New Testament as a whole. Much work, however, has been recently done on this subject,[5] and such a study in any case extends far beyond the scope of this present contribution.

Swete tried to combine the subjective and objective interpretations of ἡ μαρτυρία Ἰησοῦ : "While the original sense of ἡ μαρτυρία Ἰησοῦ [i.e. subjective as in Rev 1:2] is never wholly out of sight, the latter [i.e. objective] probably predominates here."[6] According to Swete, the

---

[5]For example, Otto Michel, "Zeuge und Zeugnis: Zur neutestamentlichen Traditionsgeschichte," *Neues Testament und Geschichte: Historisches Geschehen und Deutung im Neuen Testament*, ed. Heinrich Baltensweiler and Bo Reicke (Zürich: Theologischer Verlag; Tübingen: J. C. B. Mohr, 1972): 15-31; Ernst Günther, "Zeuge und Märtyrer," *ZNW* 47 (1956): 145-61; Norbert Brox, *Zeuge und Märtyrer: Untersuchungen zur frühchristlichen Zeugnis-Terminologie*, (SANT 5; München: Kösel, 1961); Allison A. Trites, *The New Testament Concept of Witness*, (SNTSMS 31; Cambridge: Cambridge University, 1977).

[6]H. B. Swete, *The Apocalypse of St John: The Greek Text with Introduction, Notes and Indices*, 3rd ed. (London: Macmillan, 1909; repr. Grand Rapids MI: Wm. B. Eerdmans, 1951): 249.

passage means that "the possession of the prophetic Spirit, which makes a true prophet, shews itself in a life of witness to Jesus which perpetuates His witness to the Father and to Himself."[7] Many other exegetes have come down more firmly on the side of the subjective sense. Beckwith comments laconically: "*The testimony of Jesus: i.e.* the truth revealed by Jesus. . . . The work of Jesus, *i.e.* of the Spirit of Jesus, in testifying is meant."[8] Similarly, Kiddle writes: "The prophet . . . proclaims the mind of Christ; for the testimony borne by Jesus is the breath of all prophecy."[9] This Pauline concept is evoked again by Preston and Hanson: "Jesus and his revelation of God, which Paul calls 'the mind of Christ,' is the content of the prophet's message as it is of what John has been told to write in his book."[10] For Kepler the testimony of Jesus means "the truth which Jesus' words and life reveal; God has divinely inspired Jesus with truth, as He also did prophets of former times, to become the instrument or the incarnation of His message to mankind."[11] Farrer links "the testimony of Jesus" with the description of Jesus as "the faithful witness" (Rev 1:5; 3:14), to which he detects an allusion in the verse which immediately follows this passage: the rider on the white horse is "called faithful and true." To "hold the witness of Jesus" means that Christians "stand by his testimony, and confirm his passion with their martyrdom (xii:11)."[12] The angel, then, is telling John that "it is not *my* testimony, but Christ's, that is the spirit of prophecy," and to worship Christ is not to direct worship away from God.[13]

[7]Swete, *Apocalypse*, 249.

[8]I. T. Beckwith, *The Apocalypse of John: Studies in Introduction with a Critical and Exegetical Commentary* (New York: Macmillan, 1919; repr. Grand Rapids MI: Baker, 1967) 729.

[9]Martin Kiddle, *The Revelation of St. John*, MNTC (New York: Harper; London: Hodder & Stoughton, 1940): 383.

[10]Ronald H. Preston and A. T. Hanson, *The Revelation of Saint John the Divine: Introduction and Commentary*, Torch Bible Commentaries (London: SCM, 1949): 120.

[11]Thomas S. Kepler, *The Book of Revelation: A Commentary for Laymen* (New York: Oxford University, 1957): 191.

[12]Austin Farrer, *The Revelation of St. John the Divine: Commentary on the English Text* (Oxford: Clarendon, 1964): 195.

[13]Farrer, *Revelation*, 195.

A very similar line to Farrer's is taken by Caird, who explains that "to hold the testimony of Jesus is to stand by the principle which governed his incarnate life, to confirm and publish the testimony of his crucifixion with the testimony of martyrdom. . . . It is unthinkable that John . . . should have committed himself to the view that the sole source of his inspiration was his own testimony to Jesus, that he was in fact self-inspired. The testimony of Jesus is the spirit that inspires the prophets. It is the word spoken by God and attested by Jesus that the Spirit takes and puts into the mouth of the Christian prophet."[14] Morris, while keeping both options open, also favors the subjective interpretation.[15] For Kraft this verse denotes the prophet's recognition that Jesus bestows his Spirit on him; it is the Spirit of Jesus who speaks.[16] Trites also is in no doubt that the testimony is that which was borne by Jesus, who is the "faithful witness" in his death and hence also "the firstborn from the dead" (1:5).[17]

None of these numerous attempts to explain ἡ μαρτυρία Ἰησοῦ on the basis of taking Ἰησοῦ as a subjective genitive seems, however, to give a satisfactory interpretation in this context, that is to say, in this part of the Apocalypse. The great vision has reached its climax, and the central theme of the vision is the struggle to the death, and beyond death, the stuggle between the spiritual powers represented by faithful witness to Jesus and, on the other side, by the worship of the Beast. In this lurid scene of persecution, agony, death, the destruction of "Babylon" and the triumphant marriage-feast of the Lamb, the pietistic and moralizing generalities offered by some of these commentators are strangely out of place. The angel is not talking, as Swete supposed, about a "life of witness to Jesus,"[18] but about the crisis of persecution—the choice between confessing Christ in the face of death or apostatiz-

---

[14]G. B. Caird, *A Commentary on the Revelation of St. John the Divine*, (HNTC, Black's New Testament Commentaries (New York: Harper; London: Adam & Charles Black, 1966): 238.

[15]Leon Morris, *The Revelation of St. John: An Introduction and Commentary*, The Tyndale New Testament Commentaries 20 (Grand Rapids MI: Wm. B. Eerdmans; London: Tyndale, 1969): 228.

[16]Heinrich Kraft, *Die Offenbarung des Johannes*, HNT 16a (Tübingen: J. C. B. Mohr, 1974): 245.

[17]Trites, *Witness*, 155-59, esp. 158.

[18]Swete, *Apocalypse*, 249.

ing. The angel is not speaking about a general "witness" of Jesus "to the Father and to Himself," but about Jesus as the prototype of faithful martyrs like Antipas at Pergamum (2:13). Nor is the angel making, as Kiddle would have it, a general observation that prophets proclaim the mind of Christ.[19] As the angel is speaking, the last battle is about to begin and the Beast and his false prophet are about to be cast alive into a lake of fire. It would scarcely be a time for him to offer the theological comment, however true in itself, that the Spirit communicates through prophets "the truth revealed by Jesus."

What, after all, *is* "the testimony borne by Jesus"? Most of the interpretations that have been offered of this are extremely vague, being along the lines of Kepler's "the truth which Jesus' words and life reveal,"[20] and to try to elucidate it by reference to the Pauline "mind of Christ" is only to misinterpret the latter phrase and so to render the former still more obscure. Farrer[21] and Caird[22] suggest a meaning for "Jesus's testimony" which is both less vague and more relevant to the context. According to them it is identical with "his passion"; it is "the testimony of his crucifixion." Yet if the witness of Jesus is his actual death, it might indeed be possible to say that his witness (i.e., the crucifixion) inspires Christian martyrs to die, but scarcely that it is the inspiration of *prophecy*. Martyrs and prophets, it is true, are very closely related, but martyrdom is not itself a form of prophecy. The "Spirit of prophecy" can only be the inspiration of prophetic utterance.

What utterance of Jesus, then, could this "testimony" be? If it is an inspiration for Christian prophets resisting the pressure to worship the Beast, it must be a testimony borne by Jesus in a similar situation of persecution, that is, at his trial. The Synoptic tradition contains an affirmative answer of Jesus to the high priest's question whether he is the Messiah: "I am, and you will see the Son of Man sitting at the right hand of the Power and coming with the clouds of heaven" (Mark 14:62, following the most probable reading). According to Matthew's version, Jesus replies with the ambiguous, "It is you who said this" (26:64). In the Lucan narrative Jesus' answer is also ambiguous: "If I tell you,

---

[19] Kiddle, *Revelation*, 383.

[20] Kepler, *Revelation*, 191.

[21] Farrer, *Revelation*, 195.

[22] Caird, *Revelation*, 238.

you will not believe; and if I ask, you will not answer" (22:68); and to a second question, "Are you then the Son of God?," his reply is: "You say that I am" (Luke 22:70). The question whether a man held the basic Christian belief that Jesus is the Christ, the Son of God, was one which certainly would have to be either affirmed or denied before persecutors; but it could not possibly be answered by repeating the words of Jesus. If they represent his "testimony," this could not become the inspiration of the prophet-confessors. Nor is the Synoptic record of the answer of Jesus to Pilate any less meagre: "You say (that I am king of the Jews)" (Mark 15:2; Matt 27:11; Luke 23:3). It is not any utterance, but rather the silence of Jesus before Pilate which is emphasized in the Synoptic Gospels.

A different tradition, however, may lie behind 1 Tim 6:13, which appears to mean that Jesus bore witness in the form of the good confession (ὁμολογία) before Pilate. Commentators have often sought to bring this passage into line with the early baptismal creeds, supposing that Timothy's own ὁμολογία, which is set in parallel with that of Jesus, to be his baptismal profession of faith. Pilate is, indeed, mentioned in summary expositions of the gospel (Acts 3:13; 4:27; 13:28) and in early credal formulas (Ign. *Magn.* 11:1; *Trall.* 9:1; *Smyrn.* 1:2; Justin, *1 Apol.* 13:3; 61:13). If this passage is to be reckoned among such references to Pilate as these, ἐπί would then mean "in the time of." Turner argues that a confession of Jesus before Pilate appears only in the Fourth Gospel which is unlikely to have been known to the author of 1 Timothy, and he interprets the ὁμολογία of Jesus as his actual death.[23] Turner is followed in this respect by Jeremias,[24] Kelly,[25] von Campenhausen,[26] and Dibelius.[27]

This interpretation was anticipated by Theodoret, who para-

---

[23]C. H. Turner, "1 Tim. vi 12, 13: ἐπί Ποντίου Πειλάτου," *JTS* 28 (1927): 270-73.

[24]Joachim Jeremias, *Die Briefe an Timotheus und Titus*, 4th ed., NTD 9 (Göttingen: Vandenhoeck & Ruprecht, 1968): 40.

[25]J. N. D. Kelly, *A Commentary on the Pastoral Epistles: I Timothy, II Timothy, Titus*, HNTC, Black's New Testament Commentaries (New York: Harper; London: Adam & Charles Black, 1963): 143-44.

[26]Hans von Campenhausen, *Die Idee des Martyriums in der alten Kirche*, 2nd ed. (Göttingen: Vandenhoeck & Ruprecht, 1964): 50-51.

[27]Martin Dibelius and Hans Conzelmann, *Die Pastoralbriefe*, 4th ed., HNT 13 (Tübingen: J. C. B. Mohr, 1966): 67-68.

phrases the text thus: καλὴν δὲ ὁμολογίαν τοῦ κυρίου, τὴν τῆς οἰκου-μένης κέκληκε σωτηρίαν· ὑπὲρ αὐτῆς γὰρ τὸ πάθος ὑπέμεινεν.[28] It is, however, most improbable. Μαρτυρεῖν, used absolutely, passes over from the sense of "to witness" to that of "to be a martyr" in the *Martyrdom of Polycarp* (1:1; 19:1; 21:1), Hegesippus (Eusebius, *Hist. eccl.* 2:23.18) and Irenaeus (*Adv. haer.* 3.3.4), and is perhaps beginning to approach this meaning in *1 Clem.* 5:3-7. However, there seems to be no parallel to the conjunction of μαρτυρεῖν in this latter sense with ὁμολογία. For ὁμολογία, though a technical term for a martyr's confession before his judges[29] and therefore very closely associated with the death which, as Justin said (*1 Apol.* 11:1),[30] was the appointed penalty for confessing, never actually means "martyrdom" in the sense of a martyr's *death.* Indeed, by the time of the persecution at Lyons and Vienne in 177 the distinction was beginning to be drawn between the μάρτυς whom Christ deemed worthy to be "taken up" in the course of his ὁμολογία, and who thus sealed it with his death, and the ὁμολογήτης who survived as a "confessor" but not as a "martyr" (Eusebius, *Hist. eccl.* 5.2.3).

It is unlikely, also, that in 1 Tim 6:13 ἐπί means "in the time of." Pilate is mentioned in the speeches of Acts and in early credal state-ments with different aims in view. In Acts 4:27 it is to prove the necessity of the death of the Messiah from Ps 2:2. In Acts 3:13; 13:28, it is to emphasize that the Roman authority exculpated Jesus. In Ignatius and later credal formulations reference to the death of Jesus "in the time of Pontius Pilate" is intended to anchor the gospel events in secular history. The present reference to Pilate seems to locate Jesus's "good confession." He witnessed it in Pilate's presence, like a Christian confessor before his judge; and the allusion must be either to the answer to Pilate recorded by the Synoptists[31] or to a tradition, perhaps lying behind the Fourth Gospel, of a more extended dialogue between

---

[28]Theodoret, *Interpret. Epist. I ad Tim.* 6:13 (PG 82.828).

[29]Cf. Justin, *1 Apol.* 4:6; Eusebius, *Hist. eccl.* 5.1.12 (*Epist. Lugd.*); Clem. Alex., *Strom.* 4.9.71-75.

[30]Cf. Origen, *Comm. in Joh.* 6:54: τῆς ὁμολογίας τῆς μέχρι θανάτου.

[31]So Guillaume Baldensperger, "Il a rendu témoignage devant Ponce Pilate," *RHPR* 2 (1922): 1-25, 95-117, and Hans Windisch, "Zur Christologie der Pastoral-briefe," *ZNW* 34 (1935): 219. Baldensperger ("Témoignage," 23) remarks that Jesus replied affirmatively to Pilate's question on his messiahship while otherwise remaining silent.

Jesus and Pilate. It is perhaps somewhat conceivable that the author of the Pastoral Epistles knew the Fourth Gospel itself and its account of how Jesus witnessed to the truth before Pilate.

In any case, it is difficult to see how this ὁμολογία of Jesus could be identified with the Spirit of prophecy which inspires confessors. For John Jesus is the μάρτυς ὁ πιστός, but the parallel with Antipas, Christ's faithful witness who was killed at Pergamum (Rev 2:13), suggests that μάρτυς should here be understood in the sense of "martyr," as it is in the Epistle of Lyons and Vienne (Eusebius, *Hist. eccl.* 5.2.3). In fact, μάρτυς—applied also to the martyr-prophets of Rev 11:3 and to the saints of Rev 17:6 slain by the persecuting power of "Babylon"—has already taken on the sense of "martyr" in the Apocalypse. Jesus is the archetypal martyr, but the prophetic Spirit is surely inspiring confessors to bear their testimony to him, not to repeat such testimony as he was believed to have uttered at his trial.

This objective sense also suits the usage of the expression μαρτυρία Ἰησοῦ elsewhere in the Apocalypse. John bore witness to the gospel ("the word of God") and to the Christian profession of belief about ("testimony to") Jesus (1:2), and for this, i.e. for his faithful testimony, he was exiled to Patmos (1:9). It was for the word of God and the testimony which they held that the martyrs were slaughtered (6:9). This is the μαρτυρία which the two prophets (11:7) completed before their death, and the "word of testimony" (i.e. confession of Christ before persecutors) by which the loyal martyrs overcame the Accuser (12:11). Faithful Christians keep God's commandments and maintain their witness to Jesus (12:17), and at Rev 20:4 we see the triumph of the souls of those who had been beheaded for testifying to Jesus and proclaiming the word or gospel of God. Ἔχειν μαρτυρίαν (6:9; 12:17; 19:10) appears to mean "to maintain" or "to hold fast to" the confessors' testimony; it is thus parallel to the idea of "keeping my word and not denying my name" (3:8). It is a quite different concept from that of the inward testimony (μαρτυρία) of God concerning his Son, which the believer, according to 1 John 5:9-10, possesses (ἔχει) in himself through the indwelling of the Spirit.

The objective interpretation of μαρτυρία Ἰησοῦ was favored by Charles,[32] who supposed, however, that Rev 19:9b-10 might be an

---

[32] R. H. Charles, *A Critical and Exegetical Commentary on the Revelation of St. John*, 2 vols., ICC (Edinburgh: T. & T. Clark, 1920) 2:130-31.

interpolation, partly because testimony to Jesus is here restricted to prophets, whereas at 22:9 the prophets of whom the angel is the fellow servant are all those who "keep the words of this book." But the distinction is unreal. "Those who maintain testimony to Jesus" and are inspired to do so by the Spirit of prophecy (19:10) are not a special "order" of prophets, but, ideally, include all Christian people. Lohmeyer seems to take the genitive case in the same sense, although he does not make this entirely clear. He makes an unnecessary distinction between the martyrs who *have* the testimony and, on the other hand, ordinary believers who "witness."[33] Glasson gives the sense of the passage as follows: "The alternative translation in the N.E.B. footnote gives the rendering. 'For testimony to Jesus is the spirit that inspires prophets'. The point seems to be that the angel and prophets like John were alike concerned with *testimony to Jesus*. They did not draw attention to themselves, and so any kind of honour or worship (such as John had offered to the angel) was inappropriate."[34] This is surely right, with the provision that these prophets are not the scriptural prophets, but the contemporary confessors, including John himself. As Féret expresses it, testimony is rendered by the Seer to Jesus under the inspiration of the Spirit of prophecy.[35]

John's phrase, μαρτυρία ̓Ιησοῦ, is thus a parallel expression to the μαρτύριον τοῦ κυρίου ἡμῶν of 2 Tim 1:8 and closely resembles both the Pauline use of μαρτύριον when it is virtually synonymous with εὐαγγέλιον (2 Thess 1:10; 1 Cor 1:6; 2:1 [if μυστήριον is not read here]) and with Polycarp's allusion to the μαρτύριον τοῦ σταυροῦ (Pol. *Phil.* 7:1). But John is speaking of testimony of a special kind—the witness of the martyr-confessor. The Synoptic tradition has much to say about this, for it carries Christ's promise of plenary inspiration. The prediction in the Synoptic apocalypse that Christ's followers will suffer persecution is accompanied by the promise that they need not be anxious beforehand about what they are to say in court, for "whatever will be given you in that hour, that you are to speak; for it is not you

---

[33]Ernst Lohmeyer, *Die Offenbarung des Johannes*, 2nd ed., HNT 16 (Tübingen: J. C. B. Mohr, 1953): 157.

[34]Thomas F. Glasson, *The Revelation of John*, The Cambridge Bible Commentary (Cambridge: Cambridge University, 1965): 107-108.

[35]Henricus Maria Féret, *L'Apocalypse de Saint Jean: vision chrétienne de l'histoire*, Témoignages chrétiens (Paris: Corrêa, 1946): 116.

who speak, but the Holy Spirit" (Mark 13:11), or, in Matthew's version, "but the Spirit of your Father that speaks in you" (10:20; cf. Luke 12:11-12). Luke has a second parallel to this: "I will give you a mouth and wisdom which all your opponents will not be able to withstand or refute" (21:15). Trial before governors and kings is the disciple's opportunity to testify: ἀποβήσεται ὑμῖν εἰς μαρτύριον, as Luke expresses it (21:13), or εἰς μαρτύριον αὐτοῖς καὶ τοῖς ἔθνεσιν, as Matthew has it (10:18). The faithful witness who acknowledges Jesus before men will himself be acknowledged before the heavenly court of God's angels (Luke 12:8) or "before my Father in heaven" (Matt 10:32). In these assurances there lies the root of the Christian concept of martyrdom and the source of its strength.

The obverse side of the promise of inspiration for loyal confession is warning against denial. Ομολογεῖν and ἀρνεῖσθαι are the alternative possibilities for the Christian in times of persecution (Matt 10:32-33; Luke 12:8-9), and such passages as Rev 2:13; 3:8 and *Herm. Sim.* 9.28.4 reveal the anxiety of the Church's leaders lest their followers should "deny"—hence the prominence of warnings against "being ashamed" of Christ and his words (Mark 8:38) or of the "testimony of the Lord" (2 Tim 1:8) and of warnings against "denying" him (Matt 10:33; Luke 12:9). To this context belongs as well the "saying" or hymn in 2 Tim 2:12: "if we endure we shall even reign with him; if we deny him, he too will deny us." Most impressive of all is Luke's identification of blasphemy against the Holy Spirit with denial of Christ. In the context into which Luke transfers the saying about this blasphemy it appears as the converse of confession; whereas the confessor will be taught by the Holy Spirit what to say at his trial, the apostate who rejects the inspiration of the Spirit commits the unforgiveable sin (Luke 12:10-12).

The witnessing Christian is thus an inspired prophet. It is for witness to the end of the earth that the Spirit is given at Pentecost (Acts 1:8). According to the Fourth Gospel, witness to Jesus is borne by the Spirit sent by Jesus from the Father to his disciples, the Spirit of the truth to which Jesus himself had testified, and the Spirit's witness is also that of the disciples themselves (John 15:26-27; 18:37; cf. 1 John 5:6). Indeed, persecuted disciples of Christ are the successors of the prophets of the Old Testament: "so persecuted they the prophets who were before you" (Matt 5:12; Luke 6:23). Stephen is presented in Acts 6-7 as the example of the prophetic witness for whom the promise of inspiration has been fulfilled. He is the ideal martyr-prophet, for testimony before persecutors naturally culminates in the death of the inspired witness.[36] The background of this Christian concept of the prophet-martyr is the tradition that prophets of the Old Testament had themselves been persecuted and put to death. This is deeply rooted in many parts of the New Testament: in the parable of the vineyard (Matt 21:34-36); in the woes on the Pharisees and Scribes whose ancestors slew the prophets whose tombs they now revere (Matt 23:29-36; Luke 11:47-51); in the lament of Jesus over Jerusalem (Matt 23:37; Luke 13:34); at the climax of Stephen's speech (Acts 7:52); in Paul's ferocious attack on the Jews in 1 Thess 2:15; in Heb 11:37, in Jas 5:10; and in the reenactment of the killing of Old Testament prophetic witnesses at Rev 11:3. This tradition was established in Judaism, as is evidenced by *Jub* 1:12, the *Martyrdom of Isaiah*, and numerous rabbinic allusions, and in the later *Vitae Prophetarum* all the prophets are also martyrs.

Throughout the New Testament the inspired witnesses to Christ are engaged in a struggle against the opposition of false prophets: Barjesus (Acts 13:6-12) who tries, as a prophet of recalcitrant Judaism, to prevent the conversion of a prominent Gentile; the prophetess at Thyatira (Rev 2:20); the false prophet who serves the Beast (Rev 16:13; 20:10) and, like the false prophets predicted in the Synoptic apocalypse (Mark 13:22; Matt 24:24), deludes the people with signs and wonders (Rev 19:20). The problem of distinguishing the true prophet from the false is as difficult in the Church as in the Old Testament. The criteria are "their fruits" and, above all, whether or not they testify to Christ; for this is the essential task of the Christian prophet, and this is what the Spirit inspires him to do. Thus, while a false prophet may curse Jesus, it is the mark of authentic inspiration to proclaim, "Jesus is Lord" (1 Cor 12:3). Only those prophetic spirits, that is, inspired prophets, who confess that Jesus is the Messiah who has come in flesh, are of God (1 John 4:1-3; 2 John 7).

There is more to be said than most commentators allow for Baldensperger's view that Timothy is represented at 1 Tim 6:12 as a confessor in a time of persecution.[37] It is a theory which goes back to

---

[36]At Acts 22:20 μάρτυς may conceivably already have the meaning of "martyr."
[37]Baldensperger, "Témoignage," 8.

Theodore of Mopsuestia: " 'confessus es', hoc est, 'passus es'."[38]
Timothy is said to have confessed (ὡμολόγησας) the good confession
(καλὴν ὁμολογίαν) before many witnesses. Many exegetes, among
them Turner,[39] Kelly,[40] von Campenhausen,[41] and Dibelius,[42] interpret
this as a reference to Timothy's baptismal profession of faith.
ὁμολογεῖν could certainly be appropriately used in that sense, as Rom
10:9-10 indicates, though in specifically religious contexts in the New
Testament it appears most often with reference to "confession" as
opposed to "denial" under persecution, and to the corresponding
acknowledgment by Christ of the confessors (Matt 10:32; Luke 12:8;
John 9:22; 12:42; Rev 3:5). Käsemann rightly rejects the baptismal
reference on the ground of the parallel between the "good confession"
of Timothy and the "good confession" of Christ, but he refers it to
Timothy's ordination,[43] which seems open to the same objection. This
parallel between Christ's confession before Pilate and Timothy's confession in the presence of many witnesses (recalling the Synoptic
testimony "before governors and kings" and "to the Gentiles") strongly
suggests that Timothy's confession was made in court. Whether this
was an actual historical event, or whether a picture of "Timothy" as an
ideal Church leader is being built up so as to include the presentation of
him as a faithful witness in persecution is not relevant to this discussion. In either case the imprisonment of Timothy implied in Heb 13:23
may well lie behind this passage.

A situation, then, in which Jewish and Gentile opponents of Christianity are trying to make its adherents deny that Jesus is the Messiah,
curse Christ, say that Caesar is Lord, and swear by the τύχη of Caesar
(*Mart. Pol.* 9:3; 8:2; 9:2), is the setting for the angel's assurance that it is

---

[38] H. B. Swete, *Theodori episcopi mopsuesteni In epistolas B. Pauli Commentarii.
The Latin version with the Greek fragments. With an introduction, notes and indices*, 2
vols. (Cambridge: Cambridge University, 1880-1882) 2:182-83.

[39] Turner, "1 Tim. vi 12, 13," 273.

[40] Kelly, *Pastoral Epistles*, 142.

[41] von Campenhausen, *Idee des Martyriums*, 51.

[42] Dibelius-Conzelmann, *Pastoralbriefe*, 67.

[43] Ernst Käsemann, "Das Formular einer neutestamentlichen Ordinationspar-
änese," *Neutestamentliche Studien für Rudolf Bultmann zu seinem siebzigsten
Geburtstag*, 2nd ed., ed. Walther Eltester, BZNW 21 (Berlin: Alfred Töpelmann,
1957): 261-68.

the prophetic Spirit which inspires every confession of Jesus, and, conversely that the form which inspired prophecy takes in this struggle is testimony to Jesus. This is the basis of the early Church's "pneumatology of martyrdom" which finds expression in the claim that the confessors at Lyons "had the Holy Spirit as their counsellor" as they waited in prison (Eusebius, *Hist. eccl.* 5.3.3), in Tertullian's "grieve not the Spirit who has entered prison with you" (*Ad mart.* 1.3), and in Cyprian's assertion that the confessor-bishop, although he ought not to surrender himself voluntarily, ought, when apprehended by the authorities, to speak, since God in us ("Deus in nobis positus") speaks in that hour (*Ep.* 81.2). Perhaps there is a difference of emphasis between this view of the martyr as Spirit-inspired, and therefore essentially a prophet-witness, and the "Christology of martyrdom" which developed side by side with it. According to the latter, it is Christ who suffers in the passion of the martyr (*Pass. Perp.* 15.6; *Mart. Carpi* 3:6; cf. Tert. *Pud.* 22.6). Christ's death is re-presented in each martyrdom.[44] Suffering and death for, with, and in Christ is then seen as the essence of martyrdom rather than Spirit-inspired, prophetic μαρτυρία 'Ιησοῦ.

---

[44] As the parallels drawn in the account of Stephen's death and, more extensively, in the *Martyrdom of Polycarp* (1:2; 6:2; 7:1; 8:1) suggest.

HAT DIE QUMRANLITERATUR
DAS NEUE TESTAMENT BEEINFLUßT?

Ragnar Leivestad

DIE ERSTE skandinavische Übersetzung von Qumran-Schriften ist das
Verdienst Professor Bo Reickes.[1] Es scheint am Platz, dem verdienten
Jubilar mit einem kleinen Beitrag über das Verhältnis zwischen den
neutestamentlichen Schriften und der Qumranliteratur zu huldigen.

In den vielen Arbeiten zum Thema Qumran und das Neue Testament bleibt die prinzipielle Frage, ob die neutestamentlichen Schrift-
steller Zugang zu den Qumranschriften hatten, meistens völlig
unberücksichtigt. Mit scharfem Blick und Sinn machen die Forscher
auf alle Ähnlichkeiten aufmerksam. Die Berührungen sind so zahl-
reich, daß die Versuchung, direkte Verbindungsstriche zu ziehen, sehr
nahe liegt. In Qumran meint man "the missing link" zwischen Judentum und Urchristentum gefunden zu haben. Wenn z. B. Black
behauptet, das Christentum stamme von einer essenischen Form des
Judentums,[2] stimmen ihm viele Forscher zu. Ob ein solcher Schlußbe-
rechtigt ist, sei vorläufig dahingestellt. Es besteht eine gewisse Tendenz
in Richtung von Pan-Essenismus, und aus früherer Erfahrung belehrt,
möchte ich etwas zurückhalten. Neue Entdeckungen können immer
nur einen Teil des großen Bildes ausfüllen. Dadurch wird auch die
Bilanz verrückt. Wir wissen plötzlich viel von einem kleinen Gebiet,
während größere Gebiete ebenso unbekannt bleiben wie vorher. In
heutiger Lage ist deutlich, daß wir schief unterrichtet sind. Wir besitzen ein großes Material über eine kleine Gruppe, eine Sekte, die im

---

[1]Bo Reicke, ed., *Handskrifterna från Qumran I-III* SymBU 14; Uppsala: Wret-
mans, 1952).

[2]Matthew Black, "The Dead Sea Scrolls and Christian Origins", *The Scrolls and
Christianity: Historical and Theological Significance*, ed. Matthew Black (Theological
Collections 11; London: SPCK, 1969) 97-106, bes. 99.

Neuen Testament unerwähnt ist. Das macht den Mangel an Information über Pharisäer, Sadduzäer, Zeloten u. a. Gruppierungen noch mehr fühlbar. Die Frage drängt sich auf: Wenn wir ebensoviel Material über die pharisäische Lehre und Organisation besässen, würden wir dann nicht ebenso viele und vielleicht noch genauere Übereinstimmungen entdecken? Was mich beunruhigt, ist die Frage, ob wir aus den Ähnlichkeiten zwischen Qumran-Schriften und dem Neuen Testament richtige Schlüsse ziehen. Können sie überhaupt einen essenischen *Ursprung* beweisen?

Es dürfte jedenfalls am Platz sein, die prinzipielle Frage zuerst zu stellen, ob ein direkter Einfluß der Qumran-Literatur auf das neutestamentliche Schrifttum überhaupt möglich oder wahrscheinlich gewesen ist. Ich bin der Meinung, daß wir genügend Gründe haben, diese Frage zu verneinen. Die Begründung ist zweifach: (1) daß die in Qumran verfaßten Schriften geheimgehalten werden sollten; (2) daß sie faktisch geheimgehalten wurden.

Es ist praktisch von der Beschreibung des Zutrittseides bei Josephus (*Bell.* 2.8.7 §141-42) auszugehen. Die Proselyten müssen u. a. schwören:

μήτε κρύψειν τι τοὺς αἱρετιστὰς μήθ᾿ ἑτέροις αὐτῶν τι μηνύσειν, κἂν μέχρι θανάτου τις βιάζηται. πρὸς τούτοις ὄμνυσιν μηδενὶ μὲν μεταδοῦναι τῶν δογμάτων ἑτέρως ἢ ὡς αὐτὸς μετέλαβεν, ἀφέξεσθαι δὲ λῃστείας καὶ συντηρήσειν ὁμοίως τά τε τῆς αἱρέσεως αὐτῶν βιβλία καὶ τὰ τῶν ἀγγέλων ὀνόματα. τοιούτοις μὲν ὅρκοις τοὺς προσιόντας ἐξασφαλίζονται.

Einige exegetische Fragen dürfen wir in diesem Zusammenhang liegen lassen. Uns ist wichtig, daß die Mitglieder der Gemeinde eine doppelte Verpflichtung übernehmen, nach innen nichts den Brüdern zu verhalten oder verbergen und alles was sie übernommen haben ungeändert zu überliefern, nach außen nichts davon zu verraten und die eigenen Bücher geheimzuhalten.

Es ist kein Wunder, daß wir keine Formel in Qumran gefunden haben, die wörtlich mit dem Bericht des Josephus übereinstimmt. Es gibt aber mehrere Sätze in der *Diziplinrolle*, die einen entsprechenden Sinn haben und die Existenz eines solchen Eidesformulars wahrscheinlich machen.

Nach 1QS 4,6 sollen die Gemeindeglieder "schweigen über die Wahrheit der Geheimnisse der Erkenntnis".[3]

---

[3]Wir geben die Übersetzung von Eduard Lohse (*Die Texte aus Qumran: Hebräisch und deutsch mit masoretischer Punktation, Übersetzung, Einführung und Anmer-*

In 1QS 8,11-12 wird verordnet, daß ein jeder, der während seines Studiums der heiligen Schriften etwas entdeckt, was dem Volke verborgen war, dies seinen Brüdern bekanntmachen muß "aus Furcht vor einem abtrünnigen Geist".[4] In der Hauptsache scheint der Sinn dieser Vorschrift ganz klar, nur die Begründung ist vielleicht mehrdeutig. Es dürfte ganz abwegig sein, an die bekannte rabbinische Regel, gewisse Abschnitte der heiligen Schrift nicht öffentlich vorzulesen, zu denken,[5] denn das entspricht dem Wortlaut sehr schlecht. Die Stelle redet von *Entdeckungen*, die ein Mitglied durch das persönliche *Studium* der Schriften macht. Was damit gemeint ist, wird unmittelbar einleuchtend, wenn wir an die in Qumran gefundenen Auslegungen von biblischen Schriften denken. Diese *pesarim* bestehen ja gerade von solchen "Entdeckungen" des vorher unbekannten und verborgenen Sinns der prophetischen Aussagen. Nach 1QpHab 7,4-5 wurden die Geheimnisse der Propheten dem Lehrer der Gerechtigkeit kundgetan, so wie sie früher nie erklärt worden waren. Die Begründung "aus Furcht vor einem abtrünnigen Geist" (מיראת רוח נסוגה) kann wohl sagen, daß wenn eine solche Entdeckung den Brüdern verschwiegen wird, die Gefahr entsteht, ein Mitglied könnte im stillen abwegige Anschauungen pflegen. Die Geister dürfen geprüft werden (1 Joh 4,1), und zwar durch die Überprüfung der Bruderschaft. Der Sinn mag auch der sein, daß eine Entdeckung, die nicht gleich *allen* Brüdern anvertraut wird, innere Spaltungen in der Gemeinde verursachen kann.[6]

1QS 9,16-17 redet wahrscheinlich von der Verschweigung der eigenen Lehre gegenüber Außenstehenden. Lohse übersetzt: "Und ferner: nicht zurechtzuweisen oder Auseinandersetzungen zu haben mit den Männern der Grube und den Rat des Gesetzes zu verbergen inmitten der Männer des Frevels".[7] Dies steht in einer Vorschrift für

---

kungen [München: Kösel, 1964] 13) wieder. Es macht in diesem Zusammenhang keinen Unterschied ob man etwas anders übersetzt, z.B. wie A. R. C. Leaney (*The Rule of Qumran and its Meaning: Introduction, translation and commentary* [The New Testament Library; Philadelphia: Westminster; London: SCM, 1966] 144): "concealing for the sake of truth the secrets of knowledge".

[4]Lohse, *Texte*, 31.

[5]So Leaney, *Rule*, 220.

[6]Es mag in diesem Zusammenhang bemerkenswert sein, daß die *pesarim* augenscheinlich nicht abgeschrieben wurden; es gibt immer nur ein einziges Exemplar. Das kommt wahrscheinlich daher, daß eine solche Auslegung nicht autorisierte *Lehre* war. Unantastbar und unveränderlich waren nur die heiligen Schriften, die den Kanon ausmachten, nicht ihre Interpretation.

[7]Lohse, *Texte*, 35.

hammaskil (המשכיל), der für den Unterricht der Gemeindeglieder verantwortlich war, "um sie mit Erkenntnis zu leiten und sie so Einsicht zu lehren in die Geheimnisse des Wunders und der Wahrheit inmitten der Männer der Gemeinschaft" (1QS 9,18-19). Leaney bringt hier einen sehr wohlangebrachten Hinweis auf Jes 8,16-18, eine Stelle, die als Schriftbegründung der Geheimlehre dienen konnte.[8] Diese Vorschrift mag wichtig sein, um die Tatsache zu erklären, daß die Evangelien niemals von Auseinandersetzungen mit essenischen Schriftgelehrten berichten. Solche Gespräche waren verboten, u. a. um die Gefahr dadurch Geheimlehren zu verraten im voraus abzuwehren.

Schließlich finden wir in 1QS 10,24-25 das Versprechen: "Im Rat der Einsicht will ich Erkenntnis verkünden, und mit weiser Klugheit will ich [sie] verwahren".[9]

Diese Hinweise beweisen eindeutig die Existenz einer strengen Arkandisziplin in der Qumrangemeinde. Es gab eine Geheimlehre und ein heimliches Schrifttum, und ein ungeheures Gewicht wurde auf die Geheimhaltung gelegt. Der beste Beweis, daß die Arkandisziplin rigorös durchgehalten wurde, ist die Tatsache, daß die in Qumran verfaßten Schriften vollständig unbekannt gewesen sind, bis sie durch eine zufällige Entdeckung ans Licht gebracht wurden. Früher wußten wir nur durch Josephus, daß es eine essenische Geheimliteratur gab; von ihrem Inhalt war uns nichts bekannt.

Um naheliegende Einwände abzuwehren, müssen wir nun genauer feststellen, was wir unter Qumranschriften verstehen, und dazu etwas über die schon früher bekannte Damaskusschrift bemerken. Wenn wir in diesem Zusammenhang über Qumranschriften, im strengen Sinn, reden, wird nicht alles schriftliches Material, was im Qumrangebiet gefunden ist, einbegriffen. Wir verstehen hierunter nur solche Schriften, welche in Qumran verfaßt und von der Gemeinde als authentische Lehre und richtige Schriftauslegung anerkannt und damit für Geheimhaltung bestimmt waren. Sehr viele Fragmente sind sicher nicht dieser Art. Nur wenige der untersuchten Höhlen haben gemeinschaftlichem Zweck gedient, als Bücherei, *Geniza* oder Notversteck. Nur in solchen Höhlen, die unter dem Schutz der Gemeinde standen, dürfen wir Aufbewahrung heimlicher Schriften voraussetzen.

---

[8]Leaney, *Rule*, 231.

[9]Lohse, *Texte*, 39.

Leider können wir nicht den Fundort als ein sicheres Kriterium benutzen. Davon abgesehen, daß der Fundort nicht immer bekannt ist, kann es gelegentlich schwer sein, den Charakter eines Verstecks zu bestimmen. Es ist auch nicht sicher, das alles Material, was in Verwahrung genommen wurde, heiliger oder geheimer Art gewesen wäre. Auch verdächtige Schriften können sich darunter befinden. Wir müssen den Fachleuten überlassen zu erläutern, welche Informationen aus Fundort und Aufbewahrungsweise ausgeleitet werden können. Da vieles Material noch nicht zugänglich ist, mag es schwierig sein, die natürlichste oder nützlichste Einteilung der Manuskripte aufzustellen. In unserem Zusammenhang möchte die folgende Aufstellung zweckgemäß sein:

(1) Heilige oder mindestens hochgeschätzte Schriften aus älterer Zeit, die fast kanonische Autorität besaßen;

(2) Schriften, die in Qumran verfaßt und von der Gemeinde anerkannt waren, Qumranschriften im strengen Sinn;

(3) Schriften, die im Laufe der Zeit von außen her aufgenommen wurden;

(4) Verdächtige Literatur, beschlaggenommene Schriften u. ä. m;

(5) Private und profane Dokumente.

Nur die zweite Abteilung enthält die besondere Geheimliteratur, Qumranschriften in strengstem Sinn. Eine ganz sichere Abgrenzung dieser Schriften ist kaum möglich. Es ist sehr wohl glaublich, daß einige ältere Schriften nur in Qumran erhalten worden sind, und es ist wahrscheinlich, daß Literatur, die ihren Ursprung in anderen essenischen Gemeinden hatte, in Qumran empfangen wurde. In Verbindung mit der Restauration nach Herodes dürfen wir mit einem gewissen Zufluß von außen her rechnen.

Aus der strengen Arkandisziplin, die grundsätzliche Bedeutung gehabt hat, dürfen wir aber gewisse Schlüsse von bedeutender Tragweite mit großer Wahrscheinlichkeit ziehen. Eine Gemeinde, die großes Gewicht auf die Geheimhaltung eigener Schriften legt, muß auch sehr restriktiv gegenüber fremder Literatur sein. Die Frontstellung gegen die Pharisäer macht z. B. undenkbar, daß Schriften pharisäischen Ursprungs Eingang finden konnten. Es ist für die Kanongeschichte sehr interessant, daß man in Qumran augenscheinlich fast genau denselben Schriften kanonische Autorität zuerkannt hat wie die Synode in Jamnia. Die Danielapokalypse wurde in beiden Kreisen gleich hoch geschätzt. Vor der Ausspaltung der Pharisäer gab

es auch eine chasidische Literatur, die sowohl unter den Essenern wie
in anderen frommen Kreisen tradiert wurde. Wir dürfen annehmen,
daß die meisten apokryphen Schriften, die uns früher bekannt waren,
aber nun auch in Qumran gefunden sind, ihren Ursprung vor der
Spaltung gehabt haben, das heißt wohl daß sie fast ausnahmslos älter
als die Qumrangemeinde sind. Dies ist ein Moment, das für die Datie-
rung gewisser Schriften miteinbezogen werden sollte. Das Jubiläerbuch z. B. dürfte aus diesem Grund nicht später als 150 v. Chr.
angesetzt werden. Es scheint auch ein notwendiger Schluß zu sein, daß
wir in der Zukunft nicht mehr irgendeine Schrift als essenisch beurteilen dürfen, wenn sie unter den Qumranfunden nicht nachweisbar ist
(jedenfalls nicht als eine Qumranschrift).

In diesem Zusammenhang müssen einige Worte über die *Damaskusschrift* gesagt werden, die bekanntlich 1869 in einer Geniza in Kairo
zusammen mit vielen karäischen Schriften gefunden wurde (in mittelalterlichen Abschriften), die aber in vielen Fragmenten aus verschiedenen Handschriften (mit bedeutenden Varianten) in den Höhlen 4,5,
und 6 gefunden ist. Auf die schwierigen Probleme, die aus dem Vergleich mit der *Disziplinrolle* entstehen, können wir nicht eingehen. Für
uns ist nur die Frage dringend, ob das Vorkommen einer der geheimen
Schriften in einer Synagoge für unsere These über die strenge Geheimhaltung dieser Literatur sich als verhängnisvoll erweist. Mehrere Er-
klärungen sind theoretisch denkbar. Die Qumranschrift setzt eine
Organisation voraus, die viele Lokalgemeinden umfaßt, was wohl eine
Verbreitung dieser Schrift in mehreren Gemeinden zufolge hatte. Ein
historischer Zusammenhang zwischen den Karäern und einer essenischen Gruppe wäre möglich. Nun sind wir aber darauf aufmerksam
gemacht worden, daß es gewisse mittelalterliche Quellen gibt, die eine
ganz sonderbare Erklärung nahe legen. Am wichtigsten ist ein Brief
vom Patriarchen Timotheus 1 an den Metropoliten Sergius in Elam,
wo er Auskünfte über einen sensationellen Fund von Schriften in einer
Höhle am Toten Meer erwünscht.[10] Das bedeutet wohl, daß auch vor
tausend Jahren mehrere geheime Schriften bei Qumran gefunden
wurden, worunter vielleicht gerade die Damaskusschrift, die dann in
einem sektiererischen Kreis von Juden mit besonderem Interesse stu-

---

[10]Vgl. Paul Kahle, "Die gegenwärtige Stand der Erforschung der in Palästina neu
gefundenen hebräischen Handschriften", *TLZ* 77 (1952) 401-12.

diert wurde.[11] Mag dies die richtige Lösung des Rätsels sein oder nicht, es ist jedenfalls unberechtigt wegen des Vorfindens der Damaskusschrift in einer mittelalterlichen *Geniza* die strenge Ausübung der Arkandisziplin in Qumran zu bezweifeln. Dasselbe muß man von den kleinen Fragmenten (eine Erweiterung des Psalters, die bestimmt nicht essenisch ist, und eine "Engelliturgie", deren Ursprung ungewiß ist), die sowohl auf Masada wie in Qumran entdeckt worden sind, sagen können. Da es Essener auf Masada gab, kann es nicht wundern, essenische Fragmente zu finden. Von den Qumranschriften im strengsten Sinn ist m. W. keine Spur gefunden.

Wie steht es aber mit den Informationen, die Josephus und Philo besitzen? Verraten sie nicht, daß die Geheimhaltung fiktiv gewesen ist? Dazu muß man sagen, daß vollständige Verheimlichung immer eine Fiktion ist. Man konnte die Lebensweise der Essener beobachten. Es wurden Proselyten geworben, was niemals ohne irgendeine Form von Propaganda geschehen kann. Josephus hatte sich in seiner frühen Jugend von einem Essener unterrichten lassen. Was er später von der essenischen "Schule" berichtet, enthält nur, was jeder Interessierte erfahren konnte, und beweist nicht, daß er zu geheimen Schriften Zugang hatte.[12] Nun können wir die Qumrangemeinde auch nicht völlig mit den Essenern identifizieren. Sie war eine Sondergruppe, die wahrscheinlich die geistliche Führerschaft der ganzen Bewegung innehatte, eine Elite, die nach strengeren Regeln und in größerer Isolation lebte. Es ist sogar möglich, daß die in Qumran verfaßte Literatur überhaupt nicht außerhalb Qumrans zugänglich war. Die Damaskusschrift dürfte, wenn sie aus Qumran stammte, eine Ausnahme sein.

Wenn wir schließen müssen, daß die Qumranschriften vollkommen geheimgehalten wurden, ist ein direkter literarischer Einfluß auf das Neue Testament ausgeschlossen.

---

[11]Wir haben nur Überreste der ursprünglichen Buchsammlung der Gemeinde gefunden. Archäologische Funde verraten, daß das Gebiet um 9 Jh. n. Chr. bewohnt war. Damals wurden wahrscheinlich mehrere Höhlen untersucht und viele Rollen entfernt. Die Karäer haben mehrere essenischen Schriften gekannt. Vgl. Paul Kahle, "The Karaites and the Manuscripts from the Cave", *VT* 3 (1953) 82-84.

[12]Die scharfsinnige Theorie von E. Kutsch ("Der Eid der Essener: Ein Beitrag zu dem Problem des Textes von Josephus bell. jud. 2,8,7 (§142)", *TLZ* 81 [1956] 495-98), das im oben zitierten Text aus Josephus *Bell.* 2.8.7 auffallende Verbot des Raubs beruhe auf einem Mißverständnis einer Formulierung in 1QS 8,17, reicht nicht zu, den Gegenteil zu beweisen.

Es erhebt sich dann die Frage, wie sich die vielen Ähnlichkeiten erklären lassen. Die nächstliegende und m. E. wichtigste Antwort ist, daß viele Motive und Ideen, die in den Qumranschriften belegt sind, nicht nur für die Essener, sondern für weitere Kreise von Frommen Gemeingut gewesen seien. Teilweise wird das vom Befund apokrypher Schriften in Qumran, die auch von anderen Gruppen geschätzt waren, bestätigt. Schriften wie *Jubiläerbuch, Testamente der 12. Patriarchen*,[13] die ältesten Teile des *1 Henoch* haben vieles mit den Qumranschriften gemeinsam, können aber nicht als essenisch, sondern nur als chasidisch charakterisiert werden. Historisch gesehen müssen wir ohne Zweifel die Essener als eine Verzweigung der chasidischen Bewegung betrachten. Es gab aber mehrere solche Verzweigungen, die meistens ihren Grund in den verschiedenen Haltungen gegenüber dem makkabäischen Aufstand und der Politik der Hasmonäer hatten. Die Essener haben sich als die echten Chasidim gerechnet und die Pharisäer, die eine andere, wahrscheinlich etwas spätere, Abspaltung von demselben Stamm ausmacht, als Abtrünnige beurteilt. Das heißt wahrscheinlich, daß Essener und Pharisäer ursprünglich nur über eine einzige Sache sich nicht einigen konnten.

Die Tendenz, die Qumrangemeinde als ein peripheres und merkwürdiges Phänomen im Judentum zu betrachten, beruht m. E. auf einem Mißverständnis. Wir haben unser Bild vom Spätjudentum viel zu stark vom Rabbinismus bestimmen lassen. Vielmehr dürfen wir den Essenismus als eine typische und in mancher Hinsicht repräsentative Schöpfung des Judentums beurteilen. Daß er mit der Zeit wegen der relativen Isolation Besonderheiten entwickelte, ist glaubhaft. Es ist aber wahrscheinlicher, daß die grundsätzlich konservativen Essener alte Gebräuche und Vorstellungen bewahrt haben, die sonst sicher veraltet und in Vergessenheit geraten wären. Man kann wohl behaupten, daß eine geschlossene Gemeinde, die sich von den Volksgenossen absondert, immer eigenartig oder besonderlich sei; jedoch mag

---

[13]Keine Fragmente aus dieser Schrift sind in Qumran gefunden worden, nur solche, die ähnlicher Art sind. Die Grundschrift läßt sich m.E. um 200 v. Chr. ansetzen. Schon Friedrich Schnapp (*Die Testamente der zwölf Patriarchen untersucht* [Halle: M. Niemeyer, 1884]) war der Meinung, die Grundschrift sei rein paränetisch (d.h. ohne Apokalyptik) gewesen. Ich habe seine These ausführlicher begründet (Ragnar Leivestad, "Tendensen i De tolv patriarkers testamenter", *NorTT* 55 [1954] 103-23). Vgl. Elias J. Bickerman, "The Date of the Testaments of the Twelve Patriarchs", *JBL* 69 (1950) 245-60.

das Entstehen solcher Sekten zeitgemäß und typisch sein. Es ist vielleicht nicht ganz irrelevant, daß ein jüdischer Tempel mit einem zadoqidischen Hohenpriester kurz zuvor in Leontopolis gegründet war.

Stegemann hat die These verteidigt, der Lehrer der Gerechtigkeit, der Organisator der Qumrangemeinde, sei der i.J. 153 v. Chr. durch Jonathan vertriebene, legitime Hohepriester in Jerusalem.[14] Ich finde diese These glaubwürdig und sehr verlockend, u.a. weil sie eine gute Erklärung des außerordentlichen Selbstbewußtseins des Dichters mehrerer stark persönlich gefärbten Dichtungen darbietet.[15] Dies Selbstbewußtsein ist nicht als profetisch zu bezeichnen, es ist vielmehr priesterlich.[16] Der treffende Titel ist gerade der richtige, der legitime und richtig lehrende, von Gott bevollmächtigte *Lehrer.* Wenn man sich die Lage so vorstellt, daß der aus Jerusalem geflüchtete Hohepriester, von einer Gruppe treuer zadoqidischer Priester gefolgt, unter chasidischen Kreisen, die sich schon vorher in Opposition gegenüber den Makkabäern befanden, Aufnahme gefunden habe, kann man sich leicht denken, daß er bald der geistliche Führer dieser Kreise wurde, und daß er eine Institution gründen konnte, die eine markant priesterliche Prägung hatte und *de facto* auch in mancher Hinsicht als ein Ersatz für den Tempel wirkte.

Ist dies der geschichtliche Hintergrund, dann kann es nicht wundern, das die Essener, die sich um Qumran sammelten, sich als den wahren Bund, den Rest Israels und die Wehr des Gesetzes ansahen. Dann wird es auch sinnlos, diese Gemeinde als ein peripheres Phänomen in der jüdischen Religionsgeschichte zu erachten. Wir können vielmehr vermuten, daß wichtige jerusalemitische, priesterliche Traditionen gerade in Qumran bewahrt seien. Daß ist gewiß der Fall in der einzigen, wesentlichen Frage, in der sich die Essener von den Pharisäern unterscheiden, nämlich im Kalender. In allen anderen Punkten scheint der Unterschied zwischen essenischer und pharisäischer Lehre

---

[14]Hartmut Stegemann, *Die Entstehung der Qumrangemeinde* (Dissertation Bonn: 1971).

[15]Vgl. die Analyse dieser Dichtungen bei Gert Jeremias, *Der Lehrer der Gerechtigkeit* [SUNT 2; Göttingen: Vandenhoeck & Ruprecht, 1963] 168-264.

[16]Vgl. Frank Moore Cross, *The Ancient Library of Qumran and Modern Biblical Studies* (Garden City, New York: Doubleday; London: G. Duckworth, 1958) 169; Ragnar Leivestad, "Das Dogma von der prophetenlosen Zeit", *NTS* 19 (1972/1973) 288-99, bes. 298.

unwesentlich. (Doch hat man in Qumran natürlich die mündliche Thora der Pharisäer grundsätzlich verworfen.) Es gibt zu denken, daß die nächsten Analogien zu klassischen Formulierungen der paulinische Rechtfertigungslehre gerade in der Ausdrucksweise des Gründers der Qumrangemeinde zu finden sind;[17] Paulus war ja ein Pharisäer und hat keine der Qumranschriften gekannt.

In 1QS 3,13-4,26 finden wir augenscheinlich eine summarische Darstellung hauptsächlicher Lehrpunkte der Gemeinde. Da gibt es keine Ketzereien, nur etwas zugespitzte Ausdrücke älterer Anschauungen, die auch anderswo im jüdischen Schrifttum zu belegen sind. Auch die messianischen Erwartungen, die in diesem Abschnitt unerwähnt sind, unterscheiden sich nicht. Tatsächlich haben wir in der Qumranliteratur reichliche Belege gerade für die in den Evangelien vorausgesetzten volkstümlichen messianischen Vorstellungen. Gerade hier wird "der Messias" als technische Bezeichnung des davidischen Sprosses angewandt.[18] Es ist eigentlich selbstverständlich, daß die eschatologische Hoffnung in einer Gemeinde, in der von Jerusalem ausgeschlossene Priester die Führung haben, die Wiederherstellung des legitimen Hohepriestertums noch stärker hervorheben als die Restauration des davidischen Königtums. Es ist aber kaum berechtigt, von einem priesterlichen Messias zu reden, denn der gesalbte Priester ist nicht in derselben Weise wie der (königliche) Messias eine individuelle Größe; er ist nur der zur Zeit des Messias amtierende Hohepriester.

Die Polemik der Essener richtet sich vornehmlich gegen die Pharisäer, ihre nächsten Verwandten. Das ist leicht verständlich, denn gerade von ihnen fühlten sie sich im Stich gelassen. Die Essener sind einfach eine Art Super-Pharisäer. Es mag nur überraschen, daß im Neuen Testament die Pharisäer ganz selbstverständlich als die strengste Partei im Judentum gilt (Apg 26,5; Phil 3,5), denn diese Ehre kommt unbedingt den Essenern zu, und nicht nur nach ihrer eigenen Beurteilung. Die große Hochachtung des moralischen Ernstes der Essener, die sowohl bei Philo wie bei Josephus ausgedrückt wird, ist sehr beachtenswert. Sie beweist, daß die Essener in den Augen vieler Juden ein

---

[17]Vgl. vor allem *Disziplinrolle* 11.

[18]In 1QSa 2:12 kommt (wahrscheinlich) המשיח vor; sonst wird vom Messias Israels gesprochen. Daß "der Gesalbte" eine technische Bezeichnung des erwarteten Heilands geworden war, verhinderte nicht, daß man auch untechnisch von mehreren gesalbten Personen sprechen konnte (z.B. CD 2,12).

religiös-ethisches Ideal repräsentiert haben. Gewiß machten sie oft einen komischen Eindruck, ungefähr wie die orthodoxen Juden heute, dennoch wurden sie mit Ehrfurcht betrachtet. Das vollständige Schweigen des Neuen Testaments ist schwer zu erklären. Man könnte jedoch vielleicht vermuten, daß der Täufer so etwas wie einen Ersatz bietet. Obwohl er nicht zu den organisierten Essenern gehörte, repräsentiert er doch den essenischen Frömmigkeitstypus in der idealsten Ausformung.

Nun bin ich jedoch nicht der Meinung, sämtliche Übereinstimmungen zwischen dem Neuen Testament und Qumran ließen sich dadurch erklären, daß die Essener allgemein verbreitete Ideale und Ideen repräsentierten. Ich hätte mich vielleicht mit dieser Erklärung genügen sollen, wenn der neutestamentliche Kanon ohne johanneische Schriften vorläge. Es scheint aber fast notwendig mit irgendeiner Verbindung zwischen Essenismus und dem johanneischen Kreis zu rechnen. Ist es allzu gewagt zu vermuten, "Johannes" vertrete den radikal bekehrten Essener so wie Paulus den radikal bekehrten Pharisäer? Der jüdische Krieg hatte gewiß katastrophale Folgen für Qumran und die ganze essenische Partei, konnte aber nicht allen Essenern ein Ende machen. Es ist nicht unglaublich, daß irgendeine essenische Gruppe zum Glauben an Jesus als Messias gelangt sei. Viele Forscher sind geneigt, den Verfasser des Hebräerbriefs als einen vormaligen Essener zu betrachten.[19] Das ist meiner Meinung nach wenig wahrscheinlich. Die sehr eigentümliche Ausdrucksweise der johanneischen Schriften deutet aber auf einen ganz besonderen Hintergrund. Daß die johanneische Form des Christentums aus einer essenischen Form des Judentums entstanden sei, möchte ich für wahrscheinlich ansehen. Wir müssen dann mit der Möglichkeit rechnen, einige neutestamentliche Verfasser haben vor ihrer Bekehrung eine gewisse Bekanntschaft mit essenischen Schriften gehabt (aber wohl kaum mit eigentlichen Qumranschriften).

Das Mißtrauen gegenüber der Möglichkeit der neutestamentlichen Verfasser, Qumranschriften lesen zu können, bedeutet nicht, daß das Studium der Qumranliteratur für die neutestamentliche Forschung an Gewicht verliere. Da ich vielmehr die Qumrangemeinde als ein typisches und charakteristisches Phänomen erachte, kommt den Qum-

---

[19]In erster Reihe Hans Kosmala (*Hebräer-Essener-Christen: Studien zur Vorgeschichte der frühchristlichen Verkündigung* [SPB 1; Leiden: E. J. Brill, 1959]).

ranschriften zentrale Bedeutung zu. 'Neben der pseudepigraphischen Literatur sind sie die wichtigste Quelle unseres Kenntnisses vom religiösen Leben und Denken der nächsten vorchristlichen Zeit.

SLAVE AND SON IN JOHN 8:31-36

Barnabas Lindars

RECENT TREATMENT of the parable of the slave and the son in John 8:35 exhibits the great change that has occurred in Johannine studies. Formerly this verse was felt to be an intruder in its context. The first part, asserting that the slave does not remain in the house forever, could be accepted as a comment on the preceding verse. Bernard complains that it alters the metaphor, which was concerned with slavery to sin.[1] He says that it "seems to be meant as a warning to the Jews, who are really slaves because of their sins, that they have no fixed tenure in the household of God."[2] The second part, that the son remains for ever, then has to be regarded as a way of reinforcing this point by introducing the contrasting status of the son in a household. But this is immediately followed in the next verse by ὁ υἱός used absolutely which cannot be taken as a continuation of the metaphor in v 35 because here the Jews are addressed directly in the second person. Hence it must mean "the Son" as a self-reference on the part of Jesus, who has the power to free the Jews on account of his relationship to the Father. Realising this, the reader is likely to revise his ideas about v 35b and assume that there also "the Son" is intended.[3] Verse 35b then hangs awkwardly as a christological statement unrelated to the flow of

---

[1]J. H. Bernard, *A Critical and Exegetical Commentary on the Gospel According to St. John*, 2 vols. (ICC 29; Edinburgh: T. & T. Clark, 1928), 2:307. But in v 34 τῆς ἁμαρτίας, omitted by D b syˢ and Clement of Alexandria, should be regarded as a gloss (so Rudolf Bultmann, *The Gospel of John: A Commentary* [Oxford: Basil Blackwell, 1971] 438 n. 1; C. H. Dodd, *The Interpretation of the Fourth Gospel* [Cambridge: Cambridge University, 1953] 177 n. 2).

[2]Bernard, *John*, 2:308.

[3]Moreover such an interpretation is supported by 12:34: ὁ Χριστὸς μένει εἰς τὸν αἰῶνα. Cf. also 6:27.

the argument. Bernard claims that this is the reason why it is omitted by several important manuscripts and by Clement of Alexandria.[4] He himself is inclined to dismiss the entire verse as a gloss.

More recent studies of the traditions behind the Fourth Gospel have rescued the verse from this banishment and given it a new status.[5] It is now seen to be a parable in its own right.[6] The articles with δοῦλος and υἱός are generic.[7] From this point of view the verse can stand alone as an item of previous tradition which John has incorporated into his argument. It will thus repay careful study for what it is in itself. At the same time its relationship to the actual context can be seen in a new light. It no longer appears as an illustration arising in a short paragraph about slavery and freedom, but it provides the point of departure for the paragraph and dictates its terms of reference.

(a) Once the parable of v 35 has been isolated, the question of its provenance naturally arises. Dodd held that it was derived from the tradition of the sayings of Jesus.[8] This may be disputed, but it is altogether probable that John introduced it into his argument in the belief that it was a genuine logion. Hence there is at least the possibility that the parable can be added to the meagre stock of sayings of Jesus which have been preserved outside the synoptic gospels.

(b) As an item of earlier tradition which John has taken over, the parable may be significant as one of the sources of the Johannine christology.[9] It can take its place alongside the parable of the appren-

---

[4]Bernard, *John*, 2:308. It is omitted by אּ W X Γ 0141; 33 124 *al*, but the omission is probably due to homoioteleuton. The omission in Clem. Alex., *Strom.* 2.5, on the other hand, appears to arise from simplification of the paragraph as a whole for the purpose of Clement's argument.

[5]The reassessment began with the work of Bent Noack, *Zur johanneischen Tradition: Beiträge zur Kritik an der literarkritischen Analyse des vierten Evangeliums* (Copenhagen: Rosenkilde, 1954), and culminated in that of C. H. Dodd, *Historical Tradition in the Fourth Gospel* (Cambridge: Cambridge University, 1963). Cf. also Barnabas Lindars, *Behind the Fourth Gospel* (Studies in creative criticism 3; London: SPCK, 1971) and Barnabas Lindars, "Traditions behind the Fourth Gospel," *L'Evangile de Jean: sources, rédaction, théologie*, ed. M. de Jonge (Gembloux: Duculot, 1977) 107-24.

[6]Dodd, *Historical Tradition*, 379-82.

[7]As is also the article with οἰκία. Cf. Bultmann, *John*, 440 n. 1.

[8]Dodd, *Historical Tradition*, 382, 331.

[9]Cf. J. A. T. Robinson, "The use of the Fourth Gospel for christology today," *Christ and Spirit in the New Testament: in honour of Charles Francis Digby Moule*, ed. Barnabas Lindars and Stephen S. Smalley (Cambridge: Cambridge University, 1973) 72.

ticed son (5:19)[10] as a logion on the meaning of sonship which John has taken from the teaching of Jesus and applied to the special relationship between Jesus and God. It may be objected that John has radically altered the meaning of these parables in order to press them into service for his christology. But a similar process can be observed within the synoptic tradition in Matt 11:25-27.[11] Moreover, it will be shown below that it is at least possible that the parable of the slave and the son in v 35 had already been interpreted in a christological sense before it was employed by John in its present context. Thus there may be a greater degree of continuity between John and Christian origins than is often supposed.

(c) The parable is the logical starting point of the short paragraph in which it stands (vv 31-36), and indeed of the whole argument which comes to its climax in the electrifying assertion of Jesus' preexistence in v 58. For reasons which will become clear later, John begins with the application of the parable in vv 31-34 before actually quoting the

---

[10]John 5:19-20a (αὐτὸς ποιεῖ) was recognized as a parable from pre-Johannine tradition independently by C. H. Dodd ("A Hidden Parable in the Fourth Gospel," *More New Testament Studies* [Grand Rapids, Michigan: William B. Eerdmans; Manchester: Manchester University, 1968] 30-40) and by Paul Gächter ("Zur Form von Joh 5,19-30," *Neutestamentliche Aufsätze: Festschrift für Professor Josef Schmid zum 70. Geburtstag*, ed. Joseph Blinzler, Otto Kuss, Franz Mussner [Regensburg: Friedrich Pustet, 1963] 65-68). I have accepted this in my commentary (*The Gospel of John* [The New Century Bible; London: Oliphants, 1972] 221), but I now think that v 20a belongs to John's exposition of the parable, which did not extend beyond v 19. This means that v 20a is to be regarded as a Johannine reformulation of the logion, adapted for a specific purpose. "The Father" now means God, as is clearly the case in v 21. It follows that "the Son" is also a definite person, though not necessarily identified with Jesus himself at this stage of the argument. He may, then, be regarded simply as God's offspring. When we add to this the Father's love (φιλεῖ, cf. 3:35; Gächter takes this as a sign of pre-Johannine tradition on the dubious supposition that John himself would have written ἀγαπᾷ), and the general reference to what the Father does (or makes), we are entitled to conclude that this half verse refers to the *creation*. Hence the relationship between the Father and the Son is drawn from the Wisdom tradition (cf. especially Prov 8:30). This reference back to the beginning paves the way for the eschatological reference of the second half of the verse, which is then specified in vv 21-22. As the functions there described are undeniably divine prerogatives, the Son is demonstrated to be the Father's delegate. Thus the conclusion is reached that the Son is the proper object of the honor which is normally held to belong to God alone (v 23a). The works of Jesus in his ministry both show continuity with the creation and anticipate the future resurrection and judgment. We shall see a similar combination of beginning and end in the argument of 8:31-58.

[11]Cf. Joachim Jeremias, *New Testament Theology*, vol. 1: *The Proclamation of Jesus* (New York: Charles Scribner's Sons; London: SCM, 1971), 1:56-61.

parable itself. In these opening verses the disciples who hold fast by (literally "remain in," μείνητε ἐν) the word of Jesus correspond with the son of the parable (v 31). Those who commit sin correspond with the slave (v 34). Thus, though the parable appears to be closely joined only to this latter verse about the slave, it does in fact summarize the whole of the preceding verses. But it deals with the son and the slave in reverse order, so that the son comes second. This allows John to introduce a fresh interpretation of the son in v 36. This time the son is Jesus himself, and the point is that he has the power to give freedom. This makes an inclusion with the opening verse, and the whole paragraph can thus be seen to have a chiastic structure:

```
a    those to whom freedom is given (31b,32)
ba   question on slavery and freedom (33)
b    those who are slaves (34)
ba'  parable of the slave and the son (35)
a'   the Son gives freedom (36)
```

This preliminary glance at the context is enough to show that the parable is the source of the leading ideas of vv 31-36, and that the whole purpose of these verses is to present Jesus as the giver of freedom, in contrast with the Jews, who have no power to do so. This is the basis of the argument which follows in the rest of the chapter. The metaphor of the slave, however, is dropped. In vv 37-47 the identity of the son in the parable is discussed in terms of paternity, and the contrast between Jesus and the Jews is worked out. It transpires that, whereas the Jews are spiritually sons of the devil, Jesus is the Son of God. Then vv 48-58 take up the thought that Jesus can confer freedom, though here expressed by the idea of immortality ("will never see death," v 51). The conclusion is drawn that, if he has such a capacity, Jesus must himself be preexistent (v 58).

The parable of the slave and the son thus has greater importance than has been commonly recognised. It is a logion on sonship which may perhaps go back to the teaching of Jesus himself. It forms part of the groundwork of the Father/Son christology in John. It also provides the starting point for his argument on the preexistence of Jesus.[12]

---

[12] *Pace* Bultmann (*John*, 327-28), John is not arguing for a timeless notion of eternity in opposition to the Jews' linear view of salvation, which would include a

These three points must now be considered in detail.

1. Rediscovering the Original Parable

Dodd supposed that the parable had survived in v 35 without any significant alteration on the part of John, and paraphrased it as follows: "A slave is not a permanent member of the household: a son is a permanent member."[13] He noted that the contrast between the status of a son and the status of a slave has several parallels in the synoptic tradition. For the status of a son he adduced Luke 15:31 and Matt 17:25-26, and he compared Matt 5:9,45; Luke 6:35; 20:36. He illustrated the insecurity of the position of a slave from Matt 18:25; 24:50-51; 25:30; Luke 12:46; 16:1-8.[14] It could thus be maintained that the parable would be at home in the teaching of Jesus.

The only difficulty was the obviously Johannine phrase μένει εἰς τὸν αἰῶνα. Dodd acknowledged that this phrase, with ὁ υἱός as subject, must have been intended by the evangelist himself as a christological statement in view of the use of the same phrase in 12:34.[15] But in fact it occurs outside John with a different subject in quotations from the LXX (2 Cor. 9:9; 1 Pet 1:25; cf. Heb 7:24), and of course εἰς τὸν αἰῶνα without μένειν is common. It is thus not impossible that the phrase here should go behind John.

But it still remains improbable, if the saying is attributed to Jesus. In the words of Jesus, εἰς τὸν αἰῶνα occurs with a negative particle as an expression for "never" on rare occasions (Mark 3:29; 11:14; Matt 21:19), but elsewhere αἰών always refers to the present or the coming age. Here, however, we have the one case in the whole of the New Testament where εἰς τὸν αἰῶνα following a negative does *not* mean

---

literal idea of preexistence. The point at issue is not the distinction between two world views, and it makes no difference to John's argument whether his words are understood in a temporal or a timeless sense. The real issue is whether the language of preexistence, involving a quasi-divine claim, can be properly applied to Jesus. This is why the Jews attempt to stone Jesus (v 59, cf. 5:18; 10:33).

[13]Dodd, *Historical Tradition*, 380-81. Thus Bernard (*John*, 2:307) comments: "The slave has no tenure." But it is hazardous to offer this as a translation of the Greek, as if μένει εἰς τὰ αἰῶνα were a normal and idiomatic expression for security of tenure or permanence of position in domestic service.

[14]Dodd, *Historical Tradition*, 381-82.

[15]Dodd, *Historical Tradition*, 380.

"never," but the negative applies to the whole of the following verbal expression. V 35a is in fact ambiguous, as it could be understood to mean "a slave never remains" (implying that slaves always have the misfortune of being turned out by their masters), and this is not the same thing as Dodd's interpretation in terms of status. It is only when we reach 35b that it becomes clear that μένει εἰς τὸν αἰῶνα is to be taken as a semantic unit. It thus appears probable that these words replace some other phrase in the underlying tradition.

If it is accepted that John has himself adapted the form of the parable, the conclusion follows that he has altered it in order to make it suitable for his christological application. This seems inescapable in the light of the connection between 35b and 12:34. In making this change John breaks the flow of the argument in vv 31-36, but at the same time he bends the parable into the argument of the discourse as a whole by subtle connections of vocabulary. Thus μένει has been anticipated by μείνητε in v 31, where it is the disciples who correspond with the son of the parable. And εἰς τὸν αἰῶνα occurs, with its normal meaning of "never" following a strong negative, in vv 51-52, where the whole expression "will never see (taste) death" is equivalent to "continues for ever" in the parable.

Within the rest of vv 31-36, however, the contrast is not between continuing and not continuing for ever, but between freedom and slavery. These ideas at once claim our attention, because they are extremely rare in John. "Slave" as a metaphor is used twice elsewhere in the Fourth Gospel, but then the contrast is with the master (13:16) and with friends (15:15). But ἐλεύθερος and its cognates never occur anywhere else in the gospel. Moreover, neither freedom nor slavery are necessary to the argument which follows in the rest of the discourse. As has already been pointed out, the slave is not mentioned any more. Instead of the contrast between slave and son, vv 37-47 are concerned with the contrast between sonship of the devil and sonship of God. Similarly, whereas in vv 31,36 Jesus confers freedom, in vv 51,52 where this point is taken up again, he conveys the capacity to escape death.

In the light of these facts it is fair to say that the idea of slavery would never have been brought into the discourse at all, if it had not been already present in the parable which John wished to use as his point of departure. But then the same can surely be said of the idea of freedom. Not only is the idea unnecessary for the following argument (for the concept of continuing for ever suits John's purpose better), but the very word ἐλεύθερος is not a normal item of John's vocabulary. This word also, therefore, is likely to come from the parable. It may thus be deduced that the pre-Johannine form of the parable had ἐλεύθερός ἐστιν in place of μένει εἰς τὸν αἰῶνα. The concept of freedom is then derived from the parable in exactly the same way as the concept of slavery. The parable may thus be tentatively reconstructed as follows: ὁ δοῦλος οὐκ ἐλεύθερός ἐστιν ἐν τῇ οἰκίᾳ· ὁ υἱὸς ἐλεύθερός ἐστιν.

If this reconstruction is approximately correct, the question arises why John altered the logion. This will be considered below. For the moment it may be useful to try to see the logion (which seems better described as a proverb than as a parable) in relation to the teaching of Jesus. The contrast between slave and son is unusual in the New Testament. Normally the contrast is either with the master or with a free man. Slave and free man occur together in 1 Cor 7:21-24; Gal 3:28; Eph 6:8; Col 3:11; Rev 6:15; 13:16; 19:18. The contrast between master and slave is more frequent, occurring in the *Haustafeln* (Eph 6:5-9; Col 3:22-4:1; 1 Tim 6:1-2; Titus 2:9-10; Phlm 16; 1 Pet 2:18), and quite often in the parables of Jesus.[16] But direct contrast between slave and son occurs only in Paul's celebrated argument in Gal 4:1-5:1.[17] It is often claimed that there is a connection between this passage and John 8:31-36, and this impression is enhanced by the fact that descent from Abraham figures in both. But the point at issue is quite different. Paul is concerned with liberation from bondage to the Law, whereby Christians gain the status of sons, and so the right of inheritance. The Law plays no part in John's argument, and descent from Abraham is applied only to the unbelieving Jews as a foil to an argument on descent

---

[16]Matt 10:24-25; 18:23-34; 20:27; 21:33-41; 24:45-50; 25:14-30; Mark 10:44; 13:34-36; Luke 12:36-38,41-47; 17:7-10; 19:13-27.

[17]Bernard (*John*, 2:308) cites Heb 3:5, but this is not a true parallel, because the contrast between Moses as a θεράπων and Jesus as a son is part of a larger typological comparison, in which Jesus is superior to Moses at each point. The point of the comparison is that both Moses and Jesus are "faithful" in their different situations. But Jesus, as son, is virtually the master (ἐπί) of the house. There is no direct contrast between slavery and sonship as such (θεράπων, only here in the New Testament, is derived from Num 12:7 [LXX], where it properly means "worshipper").

of another kind, as will be shown later. None of these issues are present in the logion itself.

There is, however, one item in the Jesus tradition which may have a bearing on our estimate of the logion. This is the story of the temple tax (Matt 17:24-27). Though the historical value of this story is hard to assess,[18] and it has clearly been subject to legendary embellishment, it is possible that the core of the pericope is a genuine saying of Jesus. In the story as it stands, Peter is asked whether his master pays the temple tax. Peter says yes, but subsequently Jesus makes it clear that he does so only as a concession to avoid scandal. He regards himself as exempt, on the analogy of kings' sons, who do not pay taxes as the subjects do: "Then the sons are free" (ἄρα γε ἐλεύθεροί εἰσιν οἱ υἱοί). The contrast is thus between sons and subjects, not between sons and slaves. But the words are very close to our reconstruction of the logion. Moreover there is a considerable similarity of meaning. If we may detach Matt 17:25-26 from the context of the temple tax, we have a general statement of the condition of those who rank as kings' sons. It is natural to refer this to the condition of those who have responded to the gospel, the people whom Jesus calls μακάριοι in the Beatitudes. They might well be referred to as "the sons of the kingdom," though this phrase is not actually used of the followers of Jesus in the gospels (but cf. Matt 5:45). Unlike subjects who have to pay taxes, they already enjoy "the glorious liberty of the children of God" (Rom 8:21).[19] So also, according to our logion, those who respond to Jesus' message have the freedom which belongs to sons but is not available for slaves. If this is

---

[18]The story presupposes that payment is still to be made to the temple funds, so that the tax has not yet been converted to the *fiscus Iudaicus.* Hence a date before A.D. 70 is required for the formation of the pericope (cf. Hugh W. Montefiore, "Jesus and the Temple Tax," *NTS* 11 [1964-1965] 60-71; J. D. M. Derrett, *The Law in the New Testament* [London: Darton, Longman, and Todd, 1970] 245-65). For an opposite view, cf. David Hill, *The Gospel of Matthew* (The New Century Bible; London: Oliphants, 1972) 270. If v 27 is excluded as an addition (warranting payment of the tax by Christians, and incorporating a folklore motif), then the question concerns only Jesus himself. It is also probable that Matthew has added Peter into the context, because the setting of the pericope corresponds with the redactional verse Mark 9:33 and includes reminiscences of its actual phrases (cf. G. D. Kilpatrick, *The Origins of the Gospel according to St. Matthew* [Oxford: At the Clarendon, 1946] 41-42).

[19]For the relation of Paul's cosmic eschatology to the teaching of Jesus see James D. G. Dunn, *Jesus and the Spirit: A Study of the Religious and Charismatic Experience of Jesus and the First Christians as Reflected in the New Testament* (Philadelphia: Westminster; London: SCM, 1975) 308-42.

correct, then the original parable behind John 8:35 belongs to Jesus' ethical teaching and may be compared to such developments of it as Rom 8:12-17, where the πνεῦμα δουλείας is contrasted with the πνεῦμα υἱοθεσίας.[20]

2. The Christological Application

John has taken over the parable from previous tradition for use in connection with a complex christological argument. He appears, however, to be aware of the ethical interpretation of it in connection with response to the message of Jesus, which may well have been its original meaning. This is suggested at the outset in v 31, where response to the word of Jesus is the condition of freedom.

On the other hand, the parable did not require alteration in order to be understood in a christological sense. This certainly seems to have been the case in the parallel passage in Matt 17:26.[21] For here the pericope of the temple tax makes a distinction between Jesus himself and Peter. The question is not whether both Jesus and Peter must pay the tax. It is taken for granted that Peter should pay. The question is whether Jesus is exempt. And the reason given is that he is in the position of a king's son. Naturally, Jesus, as the Son of God, does not expect to pay the tax for the house of God.

Similarly it is likely that the parable was remembered not only for its ethical meaning but also for its value in connection with christology. It is obvious that the singular υἱός with the generic article invites application to Jesus as the Son of God in suitable contexts. We cannot, of course, tell whether John received it as a christological saying or not, but clearly he has understood it as such. This applies to the parable in its original form. John's adaptation of the parable does not introduce the christological application, but uses it as the basis. For if μένει εἰς τὸν αἰῶνα replaces ἐλεύθερός ἐστιν, it concentrates attention on one

---

[20]The use of υἱοθεσία in Rom 8:15,23 strikingly illustrates the tension between the present and the future, which is characteristic alike of the teaching of Jesus and the teaching of Paul (Dunn, *Jesus and the Spirit*, 310). Jesus' personal experience of sonship was taken up into Christian spirituality through the *Abba* address to God (Rom 8:15) (cf. Jeremias, *Theology*, 1:56-68).

[21]H. Benedict Green, *The Gospel according to Matthew in the revised standard version: introduction and commentary* (The New Clarendon Bible: New Testament; Oxford: Oxford University, 1975) 158.

aspect of freedom, but it remains a static quality, a condition which attaches to a person on account of his sonship. But it is essential for John's argument that Jesus not only has this condition, but is able to confer it on others. This is expressed in v 36 in the vocabulary of the underlying logion (ἐὰν οὖν ὁ υἱός ὑμᾶς ἐλευθερώσῃ). It may be said that this capacity is a normal consequence of sonship. Any son is not only free in a house, but also has the capacity to free slaves. But, insofar as this is true at all, it is not because the son is free (or has a permanent place the household). The only person who can free a slave is the owner, and the son can only do so if he acts on his father's behalf. Thus, if it is claimed that the son can confer freedom, it is because of his sonship rather than his own freedom. The christological understanding of the logion, and also of John's adaptation of it, presupposes that he who has freedom can give freedom, and this is because it is Christ, and not any son, who is in mind.

It now becomes clear that the christological interpretation depends upon a certain ambiguity in the logion. Superficially the meaning is so obvious that it appears to be nothing more than a truism. But if it is found in a collection of logia with no more indication of context than the opening "Jesus said" (like so many of the logia in the Gospel of Thomas), it compels the reader to search for a deeper meaning. If the son is taken to mean any Christian, it refers to the freedom of the disciple in the kingdom of God. But if the son is Jesus himself, his freedom is a quality which he has for the sake of others, and so implies the capacity to give freedom. John has realised the potentiality of the text to suggest both these possibilities in his comment on the logion in v 36. The first half of the verse takes up the thought of Jesus' capacity to give freedom, the second half the freedom of all disciples. John sees a causal connection between these interpretations. Jesus is the Son of God, therefore he is free, and therefore he can give the freedom which belongs to God alone.

3. The Argument

It is now time to consider the question why John felt it necessary to alter the logion. The answer to this question will provide the clue to understanding the relationship between the parable and the argument of the discourse as a whole.

It has already been pointed out that freedom is not a normal word in John's theological vocabulary and occurs nowhere in the gospel outside these verses. John's usual concept for salvation is life, or eternal life. Thus John takes the parable to mean that Jesus, as the Son of God, has life in himself and also the power to give life (cf. 5:26). But this is not the purpose of his argument. His purpose must be deduced from the conclusion in v 58. It is to prove the preexistence of Jesus as the Son of God. Thus the capacity of Jesus to give life is only one step in the argument which leads to this conclusion. John wishes to say that the *experience* of eternal life as a result of belief in the teaching of Jesus proves that Jesus is the preexistent Son of God. This appeal to experience is apparent at the very beginning of the discourse, where Jesus addresses the disciples: "If you continue in my word, you are truly my disciples, and you will know the truth, and the truth will make you free" (vv 31-32). John returns to this point at vv 51-52, but first he has to draw attention to the consequence of accepting the truth of Jesus' words. The fact that Jesus speaks the truth proves that he has been sent by God (v 42). John makes it quite clear that he means not merely that Jesus has been commissioned by God as a prophet, but that he actually originates from God, who is the source of the truth which he conveys (vv 38,40,42). The argument thus presupposes an inevitable sequence of effects: God is the source of truth, and truth gives life. Jesus, however, is the mediator of God's truth. His words give life (v 51). But because such an effect can only be produced by one who has life in himself, it follows that Jesus—in contrast with all other men (v 53)—is not subject to the limitations of human life. He is eternal, and therefore he is preexistent.

This argument is accentuated throughout by being set over against its opposite. There is another equally inevitable sequence of effects. The Jews plot to put Jesus to death (vv 37,40). Such an intention can only proceed from falsehood, and the father of lies is the devil (v 44). Thus, though the Jews claim to be sons of Abraham (vv 33,37,39), their actions prove a different and far more sinister spiritual affiliation. In the construction of the argument the idea of affiliation to Abraham is used to build up suspense, so that the exposure of their real affiliation comes with all the more telling effect.

It is now clear that, though the starting point of the argument is the Christian experience of life through belief in Jesus, the cogency of the argument depends upon a dualistic understanding of spiritual relationships, comparable to the two spirits doctrine at Qumran. As John sees it, there can only be two alternatives. On the one side there is God, whose Son conveys the truth, which enables the hearer to avoid death. On the other side there is the devil, who conveys falsehood, and who "was a murderer from the beginning" (v 44). On each side there is an inevitable sequence of effects—divinity, truth, life, and devilry, lies, death. The connections between them are to John's mind so certain that he can argue from the Christian experience of life to the preexistence of Jesus as the Son of God.

In order to anchor the argument in the teaching of Jesus, John has selected the parable of v 35 from such logia as were available to him. The choice is not perfect, because the parable does not mention life and death. On the other hand, it has features which render it peculiarly apt for John's purpose. In the first place, the contrast between the slave and the son suits the dualism which is essential to his argument. In the second place, the fact that the interpretation of the parable easily oscillates between the christological meaning, in which Jesus is the giver of freedom, and the ethical meaning, in which the disciple has freedom through response to the message of the kingdom, suggests the sequence of effects which is worked out in the course of the argument.

The parable thus suits John's purpose, provided that he can translate the concept of freedom, which is a given feature of it, into his own terminology of eternal life. So he begins by setting out the main lines of the argument, but using the vocabulary of the parable.[22] It has already been shown that this applies to the whole of vv 31-36, with the exception of the parable itself. But here we must note another feature of John's technique. He frequently uses the "Amen" formula in relation to traditional logia (cf. 3:3,5; 5:19; 8:51; 13:16,20,21). Here the formula occurs at the beginning of v 34, although the logion does not appear until the next verse. This suggests that the three verses which follow the formula and contain the logion in the middle should be treated as a unit. It has already been pointed out that vv 31-36 form a chiasmus. The same is true of vv 34-36 within this frame:

---

[22]Consequently it is a complete misunderstanding of John's aim and method of composition to see in these verses reference to the Stoic ideas of the liberating effect of truth (Cicero, *Parad.* 5; Seneca, *Ep.* 78.2) or of enslavement to sin (Epictetus, 2.1.23).

Amen, amen I say to you,
a   every one who commits sin is a slave.
a' A slave does not continue in a house for ever;
b' a son continues for ever.
b   So if the Son makes you free, you will be free indeed.

The contrast, then, is between *a a'* and *b'b*. The Jews who are intent on sin (by seeking to kill Jesus, v 37) are spiritually slaves, and slavery is a condition which excludes eternal life. Sonship, on the other hand, is a condition which implies eternal life, so that, when the messianic Son gives freedom, it is the true freedom (i.e. eternal life). Thus the three verses unpack the meaning of the parable in such a way as to enunciate the basis of the following argument. The fact that John introduces an interpretative change into the parable itself is to be attributed to his overriding care to set out the main lines of the argument correctly.[23]

Nevertheless, John does not actually use the expression "have eternal life" as the substitute for "is free" in the parable. Nor does he use it later on. His preference for alternative expressions is dictated by the form of the argument. Eternal life can denote both continuance from the past and continuance into the future. In the parable μένει εἰς τὸν αἰῶνα implies the future. The phrase is capable of being understood strictly within the terms of reference of the parable (= is permanent), but it also prepares the way for the christological application which follows in v 36. It also recalls the μείνητε of v 31, as we have seen, referring to the condition of those who are capable of receiving eternal life. After v 36 the idea does not occur again until v 51. Here it is expressed in the long and emphatic phrase θάνατον οὐ μὴ θεωρήσῃ (οὐ μὴ γεύσηται θανάτου, v 52) εἰς τὸν αἰῶνα. The connection with the wording of the parable is clear. But the "Amen" formula again suggests that John is also indebted to another logion from the Jesus tradition.[24]

---

[23]This is not unparalleled in John. In 3:3,5 γεννηθῇ ἄνωθεν replaces στραφῆτε καὶ γένησθε ὡς τὰ παιδία in the parallel at Matt 18:3, in order to apply the logion to the issue discussed with Nicodemus. Matthew's version is independent of Mark 10:15 (which he omits) and nearer to the Aramaic original. Seeing that "turn and become" is a Semitism for "become again" (Jeremias, *Theology*, 1:155), it can be deduced that Matthew and John represent variant Greek versions of the same Aramaic. Thus John had before him γένηται ἄνωθεν ὡς παιδίον, but changed "become as a child" to "be born" and interpreted ἄνωθεν to mean "from above." It will be observed that it has to be presupposed that John was working from Greek versions of the traditional logia, rather than directly from the original Aramaic.

[24]Here again it must be assumed that John has adapted the logion for his purpose,

It seems at first sight that the reference is still to the future. But the introduction of the idea of death enables John to turn attention to the other side of eternity, continuance from the past. In the past men have always died, including Abraham, whom the Jews claim as their father in order to assert their freedom (v 33). But Jesus has a capacity greater than that of Abraham, which places him outside the limitations of a normal span of life which ends in death. By the same token his life from the beginning cannot be measured in terms of years (v 57). This is asserted finally in v 58, in words which seem to be explicable only from the Wisdom tradition (Sir 24:9).[25]

4. Conclusions

The parable of the slave and the son has been adapted from a logion which may have been spoken by Jesus as a vivid way of indicating the freedom of the sons of the kingdom of God. John has given it a christological interpretation and used it as the basis of an argument for the preexistence of Jesus as God's Son. This has importance both for understanding John's purpose and for determining his approach to christology.

However the purpose of the Fourth Gospel is defined,[26] the disputes with the Jews certainly reflect the debate between church and synagogue. From this point of view John's use of a logion as a basis of argument has an apologetic purpose. The discourse is aimed at proving that Jesus is the preexistent Son of God. It would be easy to object that this idea is an invention of the church with no foundation in the

without necessarily altering the meaning radically. The nearest synoptic equivalent is Mark 9:1, also an "Amen" saying, which includes the words οὐ μὴ γεύσωνται θανάτου. John's εἰς τὸν αἰῶνα is not *merely* the completion of the negative after οὐ μή, as the connection with the parable shows, and may well correspond with Mark's ἕως ἄν ἴδωσιν τὴν βασιλείαν τοῦ θεοῦ (hence the variant θεωρήσῃ in v 51). It is only at 3:3,5 that John has retained "the kingdom of God" from an underlying logion, but he then proceeds to interpret it in terms of his own concept of eternal life in the course of the argument (3:15-16,35-36).

[25]The statement is introduced by the "Amen" formula, but there is nothing comparable to it in the traditional logia. The nearest Wisdom parallel is Sir. 24:9, cf. Prov 8:22-25 and especially 8:27 (MT) where the pronoun אֲנִי corresponds with the idiomatic use of absolute ἐγώ εἰμι here (Bultmann [*John*, 327 n. 4] compares Ps 89:2 for the idiom). The influence of Isa 43:10, widely recognized as lying behind John 8:28, may also be suspected, though there the idiom is different.

[26]Cf. Robert Kysar, *The Fourth Evangelist and His Gospel: An examination of Contemporary Scholarship* (Minneapolis, Minnesota: Augsburg, 1975) 147-72.

teaching of Jesus himself. Consequently John makes use of an item from the sayings attributed to Jesus which appears to support his case. It has been argued above that it is not necessary to suppose that John was the first to understand the logion in a christological sense. It is even possible—though the point cannot be proved—that John genuinely believed that Jesus intended to make a christological statement when he spoke these words.

Though John has used the parable as the point of departure for his argument, it cannot be maintained that his argument is derived from it. This is obvious from the fact that he has found it necessary to adapt it for his purpose. He has not reached the conviction of Jesus' preexistence as a result of reflection on the logion.[27] But he has picked it out of such logia as he had at his disposal because it fitted the needs of his argument by its sharp dualism and its suggestion of a sequence of effects (sonship leading to freedom).

John's christology is part of his inheritance. There is room for difference of opinion concerning the sources of some of his ideas.[28] But he is not trying to introduce a new doctrine. He aims to support and deepen the tradition which he has received. As far as possible he uses traditional logia as the starting point of his arguments. There are two of these in the discourse which we have studied (vv 35 and 51-52). Both of them exhibit some degree of adaptation. But the changes which John makes are not intended to effect a radical alteration of their meaning, but to secure their relevance to the argument which they introduce.

The real basis of John's argument, however, is the Christian experience of life in Christ. It is precisely because the believers experience life in his name that Jesus, in John's view, can only be described as the preexistent Son of God. Jesus achieves what the Law (itself considered

---

[27]Christian belief in the preexistence of Jesus was reached early, not as a result of reflection on the sonship sayings (though these and the *Abba* address no doubt contributed to it), but as a kind of logical necessity arising from current presuppositions concerning divine mediation in the Jewish and Hellenistic world of the time (cf. Martin Hengel, *The Son of God: The Origin of Christology and the History of Jewish-Hellenistic Religion* [Philadelphia: Fortress; London: SCM, 1976]). Some of these presuppositions are mentioned briefly below. John's thought represents the fruit of thorough assimilation of these ideas.

[28]See the summary of recent trends in Kysar, *Fourth Evangelist*, 178-206.

to be preexistent in Jewish speculative thought) could not do.[29] The Law does not come into the argument of the present discourse, but there can be little doubt that this contrast is one reason why John is so insistent on the preexistence of Jesus. Another reason is that he thinks of Jesus as the Son of Man, designated from before the foundation of the world to be God's delegate, or agent, to carry out the eschatological functions of judgement and resurrection.[30] From this point of view the Christian experience is an anticipation of the coming age (5:24). Finally, John provides a metaphysical explanation of the preexistence of Jesus in the prologue, using the concept of the Logos, which is probably derived from Jewish Wisdom speculation.[31]

But the important thing for John is that men should accept Jesus as the Son of God and thereby have life. As he says at the outset of the discourse which we have considered, he wants his readers to continue in the word of Jesus, so that they may know the truth, and thereby may be free.

---

[29]The basic idea is already present in Sirach 24, where the preexistent Wisdom finds her ultimate expression in the Law. Severino Pancaro (*The Law in the Fourth Gospel: The Torah and the Gospel, Moses and Jesus, Judaism and Christianity according to John* [NovTSup 42; Leiden: E. J. Brill, 1975] 367-487) has shown that John's Christology entails not only "the transferral of symbols for the Law to Jesus" (esp. 452-87) but also "the metamorphosis of 'nomistic termini' " (esp. 367-451), whereby expressions used in connection with the Law are now applied to Jesus.

[30]Among the seven preexistent things recognized by the Tannaim were not only the Law but also the name of the Messiah. This is reflected in connection with the Messiah/Son of Man in *1 Enoch* 48:1-3. See Barnabas Lindars, "Re-enter the Apocalyptic Son of Man," *NTS* 22 (1975/76) 52-72, and Barnabas Lindars, "The Son of Man in the Johannine christology," *Christ and Spirit in the New Testament: in honour of Charles Francis Digby Moule*, ed. Barnabas Lindars and Stephen S. Smalley (Cambridge: Cambridge University, 1973) 43-60.

[31]Hengel, *Son of God*, 73. For a summary of the debate on this issue, see Kysar, *Fourth Evangelist*, 107-11.